"I Come Away Stronger"

How Small Groups Are Shaping American Religion

Edited by

Robert Wuthnow

WILLIAM B. EERDMANS PUBLISHING COMPANY
GRAND RAPIDS, MICHIGAN

00 99 98 97 96 95 94   7 6 5 4 3 2 1

Library of Congress Cataloging-in-Publication Data

"I come away stronger": how small groups are shaping American religion /
edited by Robert Wuthnow.
p.   cm.
Includes bibliographical references.
ISBN 0-8028-0737-2 (pbk.)
1. Church group work — Research. 2. Small groups. 3. United States —
Religious life and customs. I. Wuthnow, Robert.
BV652.2.I2   1994
253'.7 — dc20   94-34551
CIP

Contents

v

Acknowledgments

Support for the research presented in this volume was provided by a grant from the Lilly Endowment to the George H. Gallup International Institute in Princeton. We wish to thank Jeanne Knoerle and Craig Dykstra of the Lilly Endowment for their interest in the project and for their helpful advice and encouragement along the way. We also greatly appreciate the role played by the Gallup Institute in administering the project. The Institute is a nonprofit research organization that relies on extramural funding to conduct research on topics of current social importance. It was founded to honor Dr. George H. Gallup, Sr., the pioneer of modern opinion polling, and to carry on his interests in the areas of education, the environment, health, and religion. Special thanks go to George Gallup, Jr., chair of the Gallup Institute, for his support of this project and for his long-standing interest in religious research and his personal involvement in small groups. We appreciate the assistance of Corinne Kyle and Marie Swirsky of the Gallup Institute staff and of Institute board members Nicholas Van Dyck and Kenneth Briggs; we also wish to thank Curt Coffman and Dawn Balmforth of the Gallup organization for their role in conducting the survey.

Many more people than we can mention here provided valuable comments and suggestions, but we acknowledge our special debt to those who served on our advisory committee and who met periodically with various members of our research team: Roberta Hestenes of Eastern

College, Lawrence Hoffman of Hebrew Union College, Gareth Icenogle of the First Presbyterian Church of Bethlehem, James Louder of Princeton Theological Seminary, Edward Madara of the New Jersey Self-Help Clearinghouse, Sister Lorette Piper of the Duschesne Center, and Chavah Weisler of Lehigh University. Gray Wheeler assisted with the literature review and preliminary interviews. Timothy Dowd served as statistical analyst for the survey. Natalie Searl organized and supervised the transcribing of interviews. And Wendy Young served as Project Coordinator. Above all, we are indebted to the clergy, group leaders, and group members who opened their homes to us and who allowed us to ask questions about their spiritual lives.

Small Groups and Spirituality: Exploring the Connections

ROBERT WUTHNOW

Alcoholics Anonymous, Co-dependents Anonymous, Al-Anon, Adult Children of Alcoholics, Al-Ateen, Overeaters Anonymous, Parents without Partners, Debtors Anonymous, Compassionate Friends — these are just a few of the numerous self-help groups listed in local papers and community directories. Millions of Americans, it appears, are joining small groups.

Indeed, self-help groups of all kinds seem to be proliferating. High schools — and even some elementary schools — have been forming peer counseling groups, self-esteem groups, and drug awareness groups. Campus ministries have turned increasingly to small groups as mechanisms of community building in college and university settings. In the three decades since the Second Vatican Council, American Catholics have been encouraged to join small groups through Renew initiatives in their local parishes, through spiritual direction centers, and during weekend retreats. Protestant churches have been carving congregations into small "cells," "zip-code churches," and "neighborhood fellowships." Jewish families have also been banding together for *havurot*, or fellowship, both under synagogue sponsorship and in private homes.

In recent years, religious leaders have been paying increasing attention to small groups. Bible studies, prayer fellowships, house churches, and covenant groups are being touted as the wave of the future. They are the settings in which lonely people, yearning for community, can

1

find support and encouragement. Their members can care for each other, pray with one another, work together on community projects, and spark vitality in religious institutions.

Religious leaders are hoping, of course, that these groups will encourage their members to grow spiritually. Faith, it appears, is widespread in our society, but often shallow and ineffective. Small groups can be the means of deepening it. As people pray together, they can discover the power of prayer, drawing closer to God and witnessing answers to prayer in their personal lives. Studying Scripture together can promote biblical understanding and demonstrate how to apply sacred truths to personal needs. Group members can also hold each other accountable, encouraging greater consistency of faith and action. Some leaders envision small groups playing larger roles as well — for example, helping the needy in their communities, working for peace and justice, or mobilizing action on critical social issues.

The problem, however, is that virtually no systematic research has been conducted among the members of small groups. Thus, it has been impossible to say with any assurance whether or not these gatherings are nurturing spirituality. To be sure, countless anecdotes and personal testimonies can be found in the burgeoning literature on small groups, all suggesting that great things are in the making. But whether these are the exceptions or the rule has not been established.

The reasons for exercising caution are myriad. One is that most observers of American society still point out that we are fundamentally driven by self-interested individualism. It may be, therefore, that relatively few Americans are actually involved in small groups. They may be too concerned with themselves to join others in a collective search for the sacred. Or it may be that these groups are themselves fostering an individualistic, self-interested form of faith — for example, by focusing on personal needs at the expense of the corporate ministry of their churches. Another reason for caution is that the notoriously superficial spirituality observed in other contexts may be a feature of small groups as well. Small groups may be comforting their members, making them feel good about themselves, rather than challenging them to attain higher levels of spiritual maturity. Yet another reason for caution is that well-meaning religious leaders, caught up in the excitement of small groups and hoping to inspire others to join, can readily fall prey to hyperbole and special pleading. One can read, for example, that "Good things happen *whenever* people gather!" and yet not have to look far for more sinister outcomes of people gathering — stampedes, mob violence, lyn-chings, Ku Klux Klan rallies, gang rapes, military skirmishes. Even in the context of small groups, a more cautious appraisal would want to acknowledge the possibility that there will be hurt feelings and inter-personal conflicts, and that some groups will fly apart, while others will succumb to the pretensions of authoritarian leaders.

It may be that these caveats are unwarranted. Indeed, the evidence to be presented in this book suggests that small groups actually are contributing positively to the spirituality of many Americans. But if that is the case, there is all the more reason to understand what exactly is going on in these groups. What *kinds* of spirituality are they encouraging? And what are the *processes* by which they encourage it?

At present, scores of clergy, therapists, and lay leaders are offering their opinions about what makes small groups work effectively. Many acknowledge that they are writing from their own experience, restricting their generalizations to the particular kinds of groups with which they are most familiar. But others are much more willing to generalize. For example, one can read definitive statements asserting that small groups diminish in effectiveness with more than eight participants. Yet this is a generalization unsubstantiated by systematic research among those who participate in large groups. Or one can read that twelve-step groups (such as Alcoholics Anonymous) hold greater promise for the future than traditional Bible study groups, or that home fellowships are better than Sunday school classes. Different leaders have even broken into opposing schools of thought on the basis of what they think works best — some, for example, argue for structure and accountability, while others encourage spontaneity and informality. Leaders, of course, are often in a good position to know what works in their groups. But it is also helpful to know what members think, to hear them talk about groups, and to observe firsthand what actually happens.

The present volume seeks to fill this gap. It reports the results of a multiyear project involving a national study of small groups and field research conducted in a number of groups concerned with spiritual formation. It provides both an overview of the small-group movement nationally and an insider's look at what actually goes on in a number of groups. It reveals the diversity of small groups in various religious set-tings, but also suggests what they have in common in terms of basic components: how they function, how they are led, what they discuss, what they pray about, what keeps their members coming back, and how faith is nurtured in these contexts.

The project originated about five years ago in a series of conversations with clergy, lay leaders, and representatives of national religious organizations. Its roots, however, go back much further. From earliest childhood I have been a participant in small groups — church youth groups, Sunday school classes, campus ministries, couples groups, home fellowship groups, to name a few. I have also led groups, wondering whether or not they were effective, and participated in groups that sometimes worked and sometimes did not. At some point, I told myself, it would be interesting and useful to write something on this topic.

The opportunity to conduct a major research study was provided by a grant from the Lilly Endowment. The project, administered by the George H. Gallup International Institute in Princeton, combined both quantitative and qualitative research. During an initial planning phase, we held a consultation at the Gallup Institute to gain insights from an interfaith panel of clergy and academic scholars about the variety of small groups and to discuss issues that needed to be studied. We also conducted qualitative interviews with a number of clergy, did field observations in several small groups, surveyed the literature, and carried out a short national survey to test preliminary versions of questions.

The major part of the project consisted of a national survey and fourteen ethnographic studies of specific small groups. Through the survey (described in the essay in the appendix), we obtained information from a nationally representative sample of adults who were currently involved in small groups and from a comparable national sample of adults who were not members. The former answered questions about their own beliefs and backgrounds but also provided information on their groups. In this way, we were able to determine from a large number of groups (more than a thousand) what the most common kinds of groups are, what their typical activities include, how they are connected with churches or synagogues, and how they attempt to support their members and nurture their faith. From the nonmembers, we obtained some information on backgrounds and beliefs, as well as some evidence on why such people do not belong to small groups. The ethnographic component consisted of intensive participant-observation studies in selected groups. Over a period of at least six months (in several cases considerably longer), trained field researchers participated in a group, attended meetings, and interviewed participants.

The main results of the project are presented in two volumes. A companion volume entitled *Sharing the Journey* (Wuthnow 1994) provides an overview of the small-group movement and considers its implications for our understandings of ourselves and of the sacred, drawing mainly on the survey and using case material from individual interviews and small groups for illustrative purposes. The present volume summarizes some of the survey findings but focuses primarily on the results of the ethnographic studies. Each of the essays presents an in-depth account of a particular group, and a concluding chapter draws together observations about the role of small groups in spiritual formation.

We selected groups to represent some of the diversity that currently exists in American religion. We knew from the outset that we could not "sample" from a predefined universe of all existing groups, nor would our resources permit us to include even one representative of all the kinds of groups we knew about. We also knew from our preliminary survey that many small groups (perhaps as many as a third) provide caring and support but do not focus in any significant way on spirituality (e.g., civic groups and weight-loss groups). Thus, we opted to focus on groups that clearly had faith development as one of their aims and that, in virtually all cases, were formally associated with religious organizations. We also wanted to include groups from a wide range of confessional and theological traditions. The terms of our grant limited us to studying a dozen groups. However, through the cooperation of several graduate students who were interested in doing case studies as part of their training, we were able to increase this number to fourteen.

The groups we studied break down as follows (though there is some overlap among these categories): four are sponsored by old-line Protestant denominations, two are composed of Roman Catholics, three are associated with evangelical Protestant churches, two are charismatic fellowships, two are Jewish groups, and one is a twelve-step group. The groups also include several other dimensions of variation: one is part of a campus ministry, one is part of a large urban cathedral, two consist entirely of women, one is composed largely of older and retired people, several are quite small, one has grown rather large, one is a formal class, three are racially mixed, and several of the noncharismatic groups have also had charismatic influences. The groups are also geographically diverse, located in nine different states.

To ensure that comparable information was collected on all of the groups, we drew up at the start of the project a formal "protocol" listing the topics on which field researchers were to obtain data and a formal "interview guide" listing questions to be asked in in-depth interviews. Each field researcher contracted with the project director to make observations in his or her group for a period of no less than six months, to obtain information from the clergyperson or relevant person under whose auspices the group met, and to interview ten current or recent members of the group. (A majority of the interviews were transcribed.) Researchers selected their groups in consultation with the project director with the aim of representing certain kinds of groups.

In each of the case studies, our aim was to understand how the group functioned, what drew people to it, and how it contributed to the spiritual formation of its members. We did not assume that the groups were exemplary or that everything about them was positive. Accordingly, we tried to understand why the groups sometimes worked effectively, why there were sometimes problems and failures, and why some people dropped out while others stayed. We were interested in how the groups addressed questions of faith, but we recognized that groups might weaken as well as strengthen faith in particular cases.

"Spiritual formation" is a key term. We define it broadly as a deepening or maturing of an individual's faith. (We did not use the term "faith development" because of special connotations associated with this term in the literature.) We asked group leaders, clergy, and group members how they themselves defined spirituality and listened carefully as they discussed their faith in the groups and as they answered our questions about how the group had influenced their faith. We found that many individuals spoke of spiritual development or of spiritual journeys, but that others did not understand this language. We also explored a number of specific dimensions of spirituality to determine how these were dealt with in the various groups. For example, we asked about biblical knowledge and biblical narratives, about closeness to God, prayer, and forgiveness, about acceptance of self, and about service to others.

What small groups are like nationally and how their members understand spirituality can be gauged from the survey results presented in the appendix. Briefly, the survey shows that 40 percent of adult Americans are currently involved in some small group that meets regularly and provides support for its participants; 60 percent of these members belong to groups formally associated with a church or synagogue. Group members also report strong satisfaction with their groups, and most members say their participation has contributed positively to their spiritual formation. The essays that follow present the stories of particular groups, each of which follows its own trajectory and reflects the dynamics of its participants.

Answered Prayers:
The Rockhaven House Fellowship

DIANE WINSTON

Lynne catches herself; she had been drifting off. House fellowship has come at the end of a very long day, and it's easier to slip into the soft cushions of the plaid armchair than to focus on what the members of her small group are saying. Their words lap at her consciousness, but she's remembering the temper tantrum thrown by Sara, her four-year-old, and wondering why Benjamin, her two-year-old, refused to take an afternoon nap. Now they're with the baby-sitter, the baby-sitter whom Lynne is paying ten dollars so both she and her husband can be here tonight.

She thinks: For ten dollars, this should be better.

"Lord, I need your help," Lynne prays silently, her eyes closed. "Lead this conversation someplace tangible so I can connect. Help me be vulnerable."

Opening her eyes, Lynne concentrates on what the other women are saying. The larger group had divided into small groups by gender, and the five women sitting in Mary and Mike Hecht's den are discussing prayer, a conversation that has grown out of the week's lesson on Ephesians.[1] They raise questions about some of the more perplexing mysteries

---

1. Ephesians 1:16-19: "I have not stopped giving thanks for you, remembering you in my prayers. I keep asking that the God of our Lord Jesus Christ, the glorious Father, may give you the Spirit of wisdom and revelation, so that you may know

surrounding human petition of God: Who is it for? Can it effect change? Why are some prayers answered while others, like those of the Christian martyrs or the victims of the Holocaust, seem to be ignored? Mary Hecht says that she prays for healings and miracles but that none have occurred. Several others agree: prayers usually aren't answered — at least, not in the way we expect.

At this point Lynne wants to connect with the others, but her story may sound silly — still, she decides to try. She tells the others that when she realized she wanted to get married, she asked God for help. She had no role models for a good marriage. Her own parents had split up when she was a teenager. How would she know what to do? More important, where would she find a good man? God reassured her. He told her that she would get married, that it would be a good marriage, and that her husband would be Dennis Robbins, a man she had seen at church.

All this, Lynne and the others knew, had come to pass.

"Does God answer prayer and perform miracles?" Lynne asks, repeating the original question. "Yes. I believe he does."

Providing Support and Protection

These women belong to a house fellowship[2] that, for almost three years, has met on Thursday evenings at 7:30 in Mike and Mary Hecht's home in Highland Park, New Jersey. The Hechts, like most group members, belong to Rockhaven Church, a Southern Baptist congregation near New Brunswick. Rockhaven, unlike most Southern Baptist congregations, has

---

him better. I pray also that the eyes of your heart may be enlightened in order that you may know the hope to which he has called you, the riches of his glorious inheritance to the saints, and his incomparable great power for us who believe" (*Philippians/ Ephesians: Becoming a Caring Community,* Serendipity Group Bible Study [Littleton, Colo.: Serendipity House, 1988], p. 40).

2. House fellowships have been part of the Christian tradition since believers gathered in homes in first-century Palestine. More recently, nineteenth-century evangelicals, especially those in the Wesleyan and holiness movements, conducted house fellowships where Christians could share their faith in an intimate setting. The current movement, as it is evidenced within conservative churches, is more than two decades old. The goal of house fellowship is to provide a sense of community and accountability within a large church. It is also a way to extend church teaching beyond the Sunday service.

a charismatic flavor (see Ammerman 1990, 224-25). Bill Strickland, who pastored the 250-member church for almost two decades, fostered a contemporary, charismatic worship style that featured upbeat praise music, upraised hands, and spontaneous choruses of "Amen!" But for all his rhetorical enthusiasm for the "gifts of the Spirit," Strickland discouraged its more dramatic manifestations such as speaking in tongues and healings.

By the time I approached Strickland in the fall of 1991 for permission to study small groups in the church, he had announced his resignation. He and his wife had separated, and a reconciliation seemed unlikely. Strickland, along with the more conservative members of the church,[3] felt that it was inappropriate for a man in the midst of a divorce to head a church, but he was also eager for change. He planned to move to the Midwest and work in the family business. He hoped that his legacy would live on — in Rockhaven's vibrant style of worship, its pro-life ministries, and its house fellowships.

Strickland had started house fellowships in the late 1970s. His goal was to make the groups a place where church members could get to know each other on a deeper level and support each other in times of change and crisis.[4] When we met in his office, a large, sunny, surprisingly neat room across from the church sanctuary, he explained why he thought small groups were important:

> What I found is that people can listen to preaching for years and years, and have a nice little place in their brain where they can file that information and then walk out on a Sunday morning, and it doesn't have any impact at all on their life. When you sit down in a small group, it's harder to do that.

3. Divorce was among the issues dividing members of the church. The more fundamentalist members believed that a divorced man could not be a spiritual leader. A slightly less conservative group held that a man who was divorced before he became a Christian could hold a position of spiritual leadership. Most members of the house fellowship, taking a more moderate stance, felt a divorced Christian could be a spiritual leader provided he had a good reason for the divorce and had conducted himself correctly.

4. Strickland said his ideas about small groups were shaped by similar successful ministries at Church of the Rock in Rockwall, Texas; at Prestonwood Church in Dallas, Texas; at Willow Creek Church in Chicago, Illinois; and at Saddleback Valley Community Church in Mission Viejo, California. He also mentioned several books on the subject, which are included in the references at the end of the book.

If you can get to the point where you're asking people the real questions of life — What's going on in your marriage? What's going on with your children? What's happening in the workplace? — that has a way of bringing the truth of where people really are in their lives out into the open. And that, to me, is where you apply the gospel.

Strickland admitted that participation in the groups had been "a kind of up and down, success and failure story." No more than 30 to 40 percent of the church's membership had belonged to one of the groups at any point during the last twelve years. Moreover, membership and focus had varied in the 15 to 30 different groups that had been organized. Some concentrated on Bible study, others worked from Christian source books aimed at developing faith, and still others focused mainly on discussion. Most of these groups suffered from the discrepancies between people's expectations and their actual group experience; few groups actually made a difference in people's lives. Some groups did well, many others died out, and a few evolved into new configurations. Strickland said the biggest problem was not convincing people to join a group; rather, it was finding good leaders — skilled individuals who could help others to share openly, build community, and grow as Christians.

The group that Strickland suggested I study had started a year earlier when a larger house fellowship had divided in two. After careful assessment by Allen Scott, the group leader who worked as a research manager at a large chemical company, I was invited to a meeting.[5] I soon discovered that the group had a handful of members who had belonged to Rockhaven house fellowships for several years. An equal number had been active in this group since it started. Yet another dozen came and went, some remaining while others dropped out. On a typical night, about fourteen people attended, but group size could range from five to twenty-five participants. At most meetings, there were four or five married couples, two or three divorced people, one or two single people, and a handful of husbands and wives whose spouses had stayed home (ostensibly to take care of young children, although the Hechts'

5. Allen Scott, the group leader, wanted to make certain that I was not hostile to evangelical Christianity and that I was sympathetic to the group's philosophy and goals. After I had attended the group for several months, some members told me that Scott was more anxious than anyone else about allowing me to participate. The others, pleased that someone wanted to write about their house fellowship, encouraged him to invite me to attend.

daughters served as baby-sitters for the youngsters whom group members brought with them).

As I attended the weekly meetings, I saw the truth of Strickland's evaluation of why people joined house fellowship: most came because they wanted a Christian community where they could discuss their problems, deepen their faith life, and develop accountable relationships with like-minded believers. But I also found that the group provided a buffer against the "outside" world. At house fellowship, evangelical Christians could let down their hair. Here, they could admit that — despite their conversion experience — they were still not perfect. In fact, they were constantly wrestling with their weaknesses and wondering how best to express their faith in a seemingly indifferent and, at times, hostile secular world.

When confronted with setbacks and struggles, members asked what God was trying to teach them. And, if the problem persisted, they assumed that they had not yet learned the lesson. Members supported each other when they experienced these "lessons" — whether in the form of divorce, illness, or job loss. They also reminded each other that God had a plan for every life. The ability to share the suffering that accompanied "God's plan" made people more "real." Paradoxically, the more real you became as a human being, the closer you became to God.

Thus, Rockhaven house fellowship provided a language and a structure that bolstered an evangelical Christian ethos in a threateningly secular world. Members learned to live with hardships which occurred in that world by viewing their struggles as part of the divine plan. But that was not the only role that the group played in the lives of its members. After Strickland left, members of house fellowship also supported one another when confronted by the hostility of other interest groups in the church itself.

Strickland had held Rockhaven's disparate elements together — allowing traditional Southern Baptists, charismatics, and nondenominational evangelicals to feel at home. However, after he resigned, the differences between groups surfaced. Tension became acute as the church searched for a new pastor and members asked key questions of potential replacements: What stance did a candidate take on charismatic gifts? How did he feel about the role of women in the church? What did he mean when he described the Bible as the "word of God"?

The gap between members with more fundamentalist leanings and those who were charismatic widened — leaving those in the middle

11

feeling torn and vulnerable. Many members of the house fellowship fell into this category; even those who were not charismatic themselves tended to agree with the more tolerant views toward spiritual gifts and the role of women. House fellowship members did not all hold the same theological positions, but they had built up enough trust within the group that their differences were not divisive. For many, this level of trust, tolerance, love, and acceptance defined the essence of Christianity.

The divisions within the church reached a crisis point in the spring of 1993 when a ministerial candidate, brought in by the search committee, failed to receive a majority of votes from the church at large. Some members of the house fellowship — who had been vocal in their opposition to the candidate's fundamentalist positions — felt alienated from and even attacked by Rockhaven's more conservative members. Faced with the reality of doctrinal differences, house fellowship members were disappointed that their fellow Christians behaved uncharitably toward them. Several began to realize that house fellowship had replaced Rockhaven itself as their spiritual home and religious community.

In effect, house fellowship had evolved beyond the church to provide an alternate frame of reference. Members of house fellowship held a different view of Christianity and Christian community than did the more conservative members of the church. House fellowship was, thus, a double buffer — insulating members not only from the secular world's insensitivity toward evangelical Christianity but also from the fundamentalist congregants' hostility to more tolerant beliefs.

A Place to Be Nurtured

Members of the house fellowship reflected the demographics of Rockhaven's membership at large. There were a few African-Americans and some senior citizens, but most group participants were white, lower-middle and middle-class men and women in their thirties and forties. Many of the men were in helping professions, such as teaching and social work. Most of the women were full-time homemakers. Most of the men and women had completed high school; many had also attended college, and a few held graduate degrees.

These people looked like most anyone else at the local mall, Little League game, or school fair. Their clothes were comfortably conservative, not high-fashion chic. Men eschewed ties at Sunday services, and some women wore pants. Attire for house fellowship was even more casual: jeans in winter, shorts in summer. Like many baby boomers, those in house fellowship were seekers. Most were raised in churchgoing families (Episcopal, Roman Catholic, and independent Baptist),[6] and had had a personal experience of salvation that had led them to reject either the spiritual vagueness of old mainline congregations or the fundamentalist strictures of ultra-conservative congregations. They liked Rockhaven because it had an upbeat, praise-filled style of worship and a message that was evangelistic without being legalistic. That the church's range of ages and races was more diverse than that of many other congregations was another attractive feature.

House fellowship members were a self-selecting elite.[7] Although Strickland had actively encouraged participation in the fellowship groups — praising them at services and highlighting them in the church bulletin — people joined through personal contact.[8] Either they had friends who belonged, or someone invited them to attend. Almost as important as a personal invitation, however, was a positive experience with house fellowships at another church. Unfortunately, comparisons with previous groups made some visitors critical of the Rockhaven groups. Some wanted a heavier dose of theology; others wished there was more Bible study. Still others complained that no one paid attention to them.

6. Rockhaven belongs to the Southern Baptist Convention largely because Strickland was a Southern Baptist. Few members of house fellowship knew much about the denomination, and when Strickland left, the church briefly considered becoming independent. The deacons decided that Rockhaven should stay in the convention and remain accountable to the larger body. But in their search for a new minister, they did not make Southern Baptist affiliation a priority.

7. Members of house fellowship told me that some of Rockhaven's more fundamentalist members did not attend house fellowship groups and that they criticized the groups for trying to foist their positions on the rest of the church.

8. Rockhaven's descriptions of its programs included this explanation of house fellowship: "It's a place where you can find a relaxed, intimate gathering of friends. Meeting in homes throughout the area, House Fellowships are a place where we can belong, share our joys and sorrows, discuss our concerns and questions about our faith, discover God's purpose and plan for our lives. It's a 'family unit' where it is okay to be real, to laugh, to love, to celebrate, and to care for one another. If you are looking for a caring, spiritual fellowship, House Fellowship may be just what you are looking for. Led by a member of our lay pastoral ministry team, they are designed for growing Christians who are willing to meet together once a week to share around the Scriptures, to hold each other accountable, to call on one another when you are down, and to reach out to others."

Jim and Cheryl Saunders came to Rockhaven when they bought a house down the street. Their old church had vibrant fellowship groups, so they went to the Hechts with great anticipation. But Cheryl's expectations quickly faded, as she explains:

> I walked in with another couple and the man went off somewhere. The woman, with whom I had been talking, just left me standing in the middle of the hallway when she went off to talk to Mary. I was just left standing there. Nobody introduced me to Mary or Mike. And for the rest of the evening there was really no effort to try to get to know me.
>
> It was like they weren't all that glad I was there. It was a really lousy experience, and I almost didn't go back. I am not even sure why I went back. I think it was because I'm stubborn.

Another reason why the Saunders went back was Allen Scott, the group's leader. Scott embodied the kind of leadership that Strickland sought and rarely found. Affable yet conscientious, he was able to nurture individual sharing, community building, and spiritual growth. A father of three in his mid-forties, Scott had been raised in a nominally Roman Catholic home in the Southwest. His family had not been particularly close, although his mother, who became a Christian when he was in his early teens, had actively encouraged his conversion. Scott himself had become a Christian in his junior year of high school, and during college and graduate school he had been active either in a local church or in the Inter-Varsity Christian Fellowship.

Yet, despite these religious activities and an earlier commitment to scouting, Scott told me that he had never considered himself a "people person." As a young man, he had wondered how he would fare when he married. "*Loner* is not quite the right word, but I'm not a socially oriented person," he told me. Nevertheless, he had been involved in small groups at Rockhaven for several years because he wanted to know people "on a slightly deeper level." The earlier groups, he said, "were not really agents of change in people's lives":

> The chatting would be over some Scriptural passage or something, but it was essentially people in their own little fortifications talking about some objective idea out here on the table. It was "This is a nice verse" or "How does this verse feel?" but not really opening yourself up to one another in the sense of saying, "Here is where I really am."

14

Then, in the late 1980s, several men who were leaders in the church began experiencing severe personal crises. Strickland's marriage was faltering. One of the deacons confronted a long-standing addiction. Another had to face the previously suppressed resentment of his wife. These were not the kinds of problems that good Christian men were supposed to have. Yet, these men, many of whom were active in house fellowship groups, were beset by troubles. Suddenly, routine Bible study groups no longer were fulfilling. The change came first in the Sunday-morning group that Strickland led for the leaders of house fellowship. Scott, who was also coping with strains in his marriage at the time, recalled,

> The groups became a place where you didn't have to pretend you had everything together as a person. You could just come and say, "Here I am. This is the part of me that hurts. I need your help. I need to understand what God wants me to do in this case." And so we got to talking about the real issues that were really affecting us.
>
> There were some times I would come to that [Sunday-morning] group and just cry, saying, "Here's what happened this week and I'm really hurting." . . . And I think it was God using some painful experiences in my life which I couldn't solve. Because I have always been very successful, and here was the first time in my life I was not succeeding.

By this time, the Hechts' house fellowship had begun, and Scott was its leader. But the group's orientation was different from that of earlier groups which Scott had led. The goal now, said Scott, was "to build people in their Christian faith, but more broadly in their life — to provide healing and wholeness." Bible study was part of the process, but it entailed studying the Bible to see how it applied to people's daily lives. Scott gave an example:

> We went through the Book of Daniel looking at the issue of identity, and what's our identity in the midst of a non-Christian culture really, a pagan culture. And what does it mean to trust God in the midst of that? What does it mean to have an identity? What does it mean to succeed in the midst of a non-Christian culture? And, of course, the parallels between [the believers we read about and] what we're doing today and how we're succeeding and how we fit in and how we're different from the society around us.

15

Lynne Robbins, another member of the Thursday-night group, had been active in house fellowships almost longer than anyone else in Rockhaven. A member of the church for almost twenty years, she had started attending small groups in 1979, when they first started. For years the groups had focused on Bible study, but when Strickland's marital problems began, the groups started to change. "People wanted to think more about where they were in their lives," Robbins explained. "Also [Strickland] was on his way out, and we were feeling that we wanted to do some things, and this was the time to do it."

Robbins, who is in her mid-thirties, has two small children. She and her husband, a computer programmer, live in East Brunswick, down the street from her parents' old house. When she was growing up, her family attended a strict Wesleyan church. Women had to keep their heads covered, and they could not wear pants. But when the 1970s came, both Robbins and her family experienced some major changes. Her parents separated, and she took a job as a laboratory technician. She stopped going to church for a while, and when she went back, she was uncomfortable with what she perceived to be its narrow rules and regulations. Robbins prayed for an alternative. Soon after, a woman she barely knew invited her to a revival at Rockhaven. It was Strickland's first night at the church, too.

When Robbins first joined the Hechts' house fellowship, her husband went to the other fellowship group that met Wednesday nights in Franklin Park. His absence from the Hechts' group made it easier for Robbins to talk about some of the issues in their marriage. Moreover, the deepening of her faith through experiences she had in other Christian settings — including counseling groups, women's Bible study, and adult education — prepared her for the changes that she was experiencing through house fellowship:

> I was developing more of a picture of God. That is, if you have a really good friend, that can give you an idea of the relationship God wants to have with us. That's my idea of house fellowship. It's a broader picture of God. It gets him out of a box. It's more of a circle.
>
> For the first ten years I went to groups because I thought I was supposed to. But I wasn't happy, and I didn't relate to anyone. Now I go with a different vision. I don't think, What will God do tonight? Instead, I think, Who can I minister to? Who will minister to me? Relationships are more important to me than they used to be.

16

Observing Robbins over the course of the two years I attended the house fellowship, I could see the changes she described. In the early days she was very quiet, and when the group broke into smaller groups, she seemed reluctant to speak. But over time she became more confident, even volunteering to lead small-group discussions. She also served as an informal bridge-builder within the group. While Scott was the designated leader, Robbins was an informal leader — "ministering" privately to others during the week. She also started a writing group in the church and was instrumental in the women's Bible study.

One of Robbins' closest friends in the group was Mary Hecht, a woman who seemed her opposite in both personality and behavior. While Robbins was quiet and deliberate, Hecht was outgoing and impulsive. It was not surprising that Mary volunteered her home for house fellowship not long after she and Mike started attending Rockhaven.

Hecht — a mother of three in her mid-thirties — grew up in what she calls a *Leave It to Beaver*-type family in Youngstown, Ohio. Her father didn't go to church, but her mother insisted that Mary and her younger sister attend the local Methodist church with her. Hecht described the church as spiritually "dead"; the pastor talked more about world peace than the Bible. When her mother joined a charismatic prayer group, Hecht stopped going to church and immersed herself in music and cheerleading. At college, Hecht fell in with a group that took drugs and dabbled in the occult. But the seances she attended frightened her, and at her mother's urging she stopped her experimentations.

Several years later, when Hecht was teaching music to elementary school children, a friend asked her to join a Bible study group. But she didn't really get involved in a church until she and Mike were married. After both experienced conversion, they joined an independent church near their home, which was a disappointment to Mary:

> The church turned out really to be a cult. I was always on the outside looking in, and I spent many, many hours crying, just wanting a friend. Their teaching was that nobody outside the church really had any kind of truth, so I couldn't even communicate with anyone . . . They taught that you were in sin, and I really bought into that.
>
> I kept praying all the time, "Lord, help me to understand this." And one day, . . . I said [to a friend], "I know this sounds crazy, but I really believe God just told me to go out and look for another church, that I got his okay. . . ."

17

When the Hechts found Rockhaven, they were eager to be in a place where they could make real Christian friends. Mary joined a women's prayer group and pressed Strickland about joining a house fellowship. At first he put her off, but shortly thereafter he asked if the new group could meet at her house. From the start, Mary said, the group was characterized by "an acceptance of who you are, and even if you are struggling, it's okay":

> I think I've learned a lot about being myself and not putting on the holy little front that I used to put on a lot. I'm not so sure I learned all that in house fellowship, but house fellowship is the place where I've learned to act it out. I think I'm a different person now than when I started house fellowship. It's a place for learning how to live with other people during the times they're struggling with something and being able to love them even when you don't like what they're saying or doing.

Within the group, Mary Hecht was among the most open about her struggles. During the group's first year, she frequently discussed the stress she experienced in her relationship with her singing partner. A popular duet, the women performed at local schools, churches, and fairs. But Hecht was uncomfortable with her partner's overbearing manner and her insistence that they devote more time to their act. By the end of that year, Hecht had decided to quit. When that problem was solved, she began discussing family problems: relations with her mother were strained; she fought with a brother-in-law; her twin teenage daughters were rebellious.

Still, the worst blow fell in the fall of the group's third year, when her husband, a construction site manager, was laid off. Although her husband's subsequent job search lasted nearly a year, Mary rarely discussed her feelings about that with the group. In fact, both Mike and Mary expressed only optimism during this period, saying repeatedly that they trusted God had a plan.

A Typical Evening of Fellowship

For over a year, house fellowship began the same way. Members drifted into the Hechts' blue colonial house between 7:30 p.m. and 7:45 p.m., congregating in little groups in the Hechts' family room. Several chatted around the coffeepot, others talked near the fireplace, and still others spilled out onto the enclosed porch, seeking a little privacy. As 8 p.m. drew near, Allen Scott called the group together, encouraging everyone to get their coffee and take a seat in the circle of chairs and couches.

The room where the group gathered was a capacious, comfortably appointed den. In the front of the room was a brick wall with a built-in fireplace. There were poker and tongs on one side of the hearth and leather bellows on the other. Above the fireplace, red candles in fluted brass candelabras shared the mantelpiece with blue and green duck decoys. On either side of the mantelpiece, ceiling-high, built-in book-shelves were filled with a mix of popular thrillers and Christian titles (Robert Ludlum and Tom Clancy, Billy Graham and Hal Lindsey). A low, round coffee table of blond wood dominated the center of the room, and it was always decorated with seasonally appropriate items (in the fall, maize and apples; in the winter, poinsettias; and in the spring, a large straw basket containing a thriving rhododendron plant). The seasonal themes were echoed on the Parsons table behind one of the maroon leather couches. (The other couch, placed at a ninety-degree angle, rested against a white wall.) On the table, decorated with brass duck-head bookends, were treats appropriate to the time of year: a bowl of candy corn, a glass jar with red-and-silver-wrapped chocolate kisses, or a small basket of Easter eggs.

A few feet away, opposite the fireplace, was a wet bar — complete with sink and mini-refrigerator. (The Hechts did not use this space for an alcoholic bar.) Here, the coffeepot was set up with an after-dinner brew of French roast and chocolate hazelnut. For caffeine-watchers, Mary put out a sampling of herbal teas. On the counter behind the bar, Mary artfully arranged whatever desserts participants had brought that evening. The favored choices were various kinds of Entemann's pastries, although occasionally someone baked a cake or a pie. People walked in, checked out the desserts, and chose a seat.

Once everyone in the group settled down, Scott welcomed them. Then he announced an icebreaker, a little game or exercise intended to put people at ease. Sometimes the icebreaker was a simple scientific experiment that the group interpreted in a Christian fashion. Once, for example, Scott passed around two round balls that looked the same, but one bounced while the other thudded to the floor. The difference was in the quality of the materials. How did that relate to Christian spiritual development? At other times the activity was less pointedly instructional.

(One evening, members taped jigsaw puzzle pieces to their foreheads and tried to find who they were connected to.) At still other times the icebreaker gave members new insights into one another. (This was often accomplished with questions: "What animal is most like you?" "What movie best describes your spiritual journey?" "What would you like to change in your life?") Reactions to the games varied. Mary called them "corny, but fun." Cheryl Saunders deemed them "diddly-dink."

When the icebreaker ended, Scott asked the group if anyone had praise to offer or a prayer request. The aim was to share with everyone, although requests would not be prayed about until the large group broke into smaller groups. During this interlude, members often shared prayer requests from people outside the group ("My aunt was just diagnosed with liver cancer," or "My son's best friend is into Satanism").

The second phase of house fellowship began when Scott passed out a xeroxed section from the book by Robert McGee called *The Search for Significance* (1985). The book's front cover explained, "We can build our self-worth on our ability to please others, or on the love and for-giveness of Jesus Christ." In keeping with its thesis, the book had sections entitled "The Performance Trap," "Approval Addict," and "The Blame Game." Chapters illustrated problems with real-life anecdotes, and a workbook section engaged the problems from a biblical standpoint. (An example: "Read 1 Sam. 16:6-7 and Ps. 139:13-16. How does the truth of regeneration free you from the shame prompted by flaws in your physical appearance?"; McGee 1985, 345).

Next Scott split the large group into smaller groups of three to five, either by having members count off or by dividing them according to gender. Each group then headed to a different room to discuss the evening's chapter. They began with the workbook materials, but the discussions frequently segued into conversations that revolved around members' par-ticular concerns. For example, an all-male group might talk about the experience of feeling sexually attracted to someone other than one's wife. An all-female group might focus on problems with children or parents. A mixed group might delve into the problems of child custody (several divorced fathers were fighting for more access to their children) or work (a few members were looking for jobs, others were dissatisfied with what they did, and still others had problems with supervisors or those they supervised). As the meeting wound down, usually around 9:30 p.m., each group prayed aloud together — petitioning God, in Jesus' name, to remedy the problems that afflicted participants, their families, and their friends.

The Devil at Work?

By the early winter months of 1992, Allen Scott's marriage was falling apart. His wife had stopped attending house fellowship, and Scott regularly asked the group to pray for them. More candid than anyone else had been previously, Scott discussed the nature of their troubles as well as their experiences with a Christian therapist. His openness inspired others to speak more freely, but it also threatened to overwhelm the group. Sensing the potential problem and eager to devote more time to saving his marriage, Scott asked to step down as group leader. He also stated, echoing Strickland, that he didn't think someone in the middle of a marital crisis should head a Christian group. Many wondered aloud if Satan was afflicting their church with a plague of marital problems that embarrassed them and frustrated their efforts at outreach and revival.

The group agreed to Scott's request and asked two couples — the Hechts and the Daniels — to take over. However, since Mike Hecht and Sam Daniels were busy with work-related commitments, their wives frequently ran the meetings. Mary, uncomfortable in a leadership role, deferred to Sarah Daniels. Sarah, capable and efficient, was one of the few women in the group with a career. She was very direct in her manner, and she lacked Scott's easygoing style of leadership. She stopped doing icebreakers and replaced *Search for Significance* workshop questions with ones of her own. By early summer, attendance was down, and the group's very survival was in doubt.

Scott rarely attended meetings anymore, so when he showed up on a muggy evening in late June, he was surprised to find that only three other people were present. Sarah was away, and Mary, leading the group that night, decided to suspend the lesson in order to discuss what was going wrong with their house fellowship. She herself was unsure whether group members were uncomfortable with women leaders or just with Sarah and herself. The changes they had made were intended to help the group focus on Bible study and prayer. But instead of being more directed and worshipful, the meetings seemed joyless, and discussions were flat.

The problem seemed to be "both/and." When Scott was the leader, he undergirded group cohesiveness by meeting with members outside the Thursday get-togethers. Each month he had breakfast with a different member, and each week he telephoned several others to see how they were doing. His networking as well as his friendly style not only drew people in but also made them feel like a part of the group. According to Mary, however, she and Sarah didn't cultivate relationships outside the Thursday meetings. Mary did telephone members who didn't show up for house fellowship, but her calls seemed to evoke guilt rather than camaraderie.

Moreover, Scott and Hecht agreed that Rockhaven seemed to display an ambivalent attitude toward women leaders.[9] Women could not be ministers or deacons, but Strickland had placed women in leadership roles — as teachers, counselors, and group convenors (especially for women's Bible study and prayer circles). Nevertheless, he rarely supported them publicly. Scott said he believed that women had roles that were important but different from those played by men. In the Bible, for example, women could be judges but not priests. Scott suggested that Rockhaven needed to recognize the ministries that women performed in the church.[10]

A few weeks later, Sarah Daniels decided that the group should examine the nature and goal of Christian community. She began house fellowship that night by defining *koinonia,* the Greek word for community used in the New Testament: "The original Greek word means 'shared by all.' It means having communion together, being partners and distributing things equally among ourselves." Then, after asking participants to read aloud Scripture verses that mentioned koinonia, Sarah suggested that they talk about what they wanted for the group in light of what they had just heard from the Bible.

After a lengthy silence, members spoke up:

9. The issue of women's role in the church has been divisive for conservative Christians. Fundamentalists hold what they consider to be the Pauline position — requiring women to be silent in church and subordinate to their husbands. Evangelicals hold beliefs that cover a wider spectrum: some share the fundamentalist position, while others allow women to teach adult Sunday school classes and to speak from the pulpit. Historically, charismatics and Pentecostals have been the most open to women preachers, believing that the Spirit alights where it will. However, many Pentecostal and charismatic churches are no longer open to women's spiritual leadership. See Ammerman (1987), Rose (1991), and Ruether and McLaughlin (1979).

10. The acceptance of women's leadership in the group began to change perceptibly when Fay Blanton, a student at Princeton Seminary, joined in the fall of 1992. Although Fay had not decided whether she would seek ordination, her ministerial gifts were obvious, and she quickly became a leader in house fellowship. Many of the other women described Fay as someone who would force the church to confront women's gifts as ministers.

"It seems to me that the group is meeting needs, so if it's not broke, why fix it?" said Keith Perkins, a social worker who had recently gone through a painful divorce. "Dealing with *Search for Significance* has helped me think about how you fit your life in with God. Our sharing has been really helpful to me."

"I want to come away from here having been confronted with God's claims on my life and on the lives of my brothers and sisters," Allen Scott said. "I need to know the ways I can help carry their burdens."

"On Sunday, at the leadership meeting, we tossed around ideas about what to do next and got nowhere," Mary Hecht observed. "We talk things to death, but we don't get anywhere until we pray."

"Maybe on certain nights, instead of doing a lesson, we could focus on one person and pray for them," Keith Perkins said. "What God has been teaching me is that prayer is where we start. God is saying, 'When you get frustrated, come to me first.' He wants us to be in prayer."

"I feel alone in saying this," Sarah Daniels began, "but I have felt when I come away from this fellowship group [that] I am not sure if my fellowship with God has been enhanced. The focus is more horizontal than vertical, and I'm feeling frustrated. . . . The real focus of our fellowship should be God. Our aim should be for each of us to have a better relationship with God. I am not sure that's happening, and if it is happening, it is happening incidentally, because it doesn't seem like a purposeful part of this fellowship."

"I agree there is a risk we can get too horizontal," Mike Hecht said. "But it's a matter of adjusting the weights. We need a scriptural focus so this is not just a social club. But if all the weight is on Scripture, you have a Bible study that may have little or no application [to] the lives of members of house fellowship. I believe the emphasis has to be on application [to] our lives. If the vertical is lacking, maybe there's not enough emphasis on it. But we don't want to do just Bible study, either."

The discussion did not have a conclusive end, although most everyone agreed that the group needed to strike a balance between prayer, Bible study, and fellowship. But, by the fall, several changes had been made. The group had permanently stopped using *Search for Significance.* Sam and Sarah Daniels had started a new house fellowship that proved popular with college students from Rutgers University. Mary and Mike Hecht had asked to be relieved of their leadership roles, and Allen Scott had announced that he was ready to come back as leader if the group wanted him. He and his wife had separated, and although he hoped they would be reconciled, he wanted to move ahead with his life and reassume some of his religious responsibilities.

On a warm autumn night, with a large group in attendance, members discussed whether or not it was appropriate to accept Scott's offer. What kind of role model was a man with marital problems? Would his personal situation dissuade new people from joining house fellowship? Was the group opening itself to ridicule? Could this be the work of the devil undermining their efforts?

Some members said that if they were outsiders, they might not understand why a man in a broken marriage had a position of spiritual authority over others. Still, since they knew Scott and had watched him struggle with the problems in his marriage, they felt he could be a good leader. Scott's revelations about himself and his marriage had been painful, but he had been forthright with the group and was committed to seeking and doing God's will. In the end, the group consensus was that if Scott felt he was ready to come back, they would welcome him.

Telling Stories

As Allen Scott's experience demonstrates, the group made judgments about religious character based less on abstract standards of appropriate "Christian" behavior than on the subjective experiences related in their personal narratives. The explicit purpose of house fellowship — to grow as individual Christians and as a Christian community — was accomplished, ostensibly, through Bible study, fellowship, and prayer. Yet woven through these three were individual stories of child custody battles, broken marriages, unemployment, illness, and tragic accidents. Telling stories animated members' spiritual journeys and determined how they saw themselves, one another, and their relationship with God.

When I first began attending house fellowship, members spoke frequently about Skip Tepper. Every week, Scott asked if anyone had spoken to Skip, and whoever had talked with him related their conversation, detailing how Skip was doing and what kind of help he needed. Gradually, I pieced together the story: Skip was a young man with devastating problems who had recently been saved. Members of house fellowship were helping him take care of his children and find a job. Occasionally Skip backslid and went on a drug or alcohol binge. But group members bailed him out — housing him for short periods, taking in his children, helping him find an apartment — until he could take care of himself. Finally, during Strickland's next-to-last service, Skip was baptized at the church.

Several weeks later, when I asked Mary Hecht whose story stood out in her mind, she — like several others — spoke about Skip:

> This is one that God had set up, because mostly the group had 24 people, but this particular night, a really nice evening in the spring-time, we only had eight people. There was this new guy that came. We had seen him before at church and Mike told him, "If you are interested in coming to house fellowship, we would love to have you."
>
> We were sitting there doing a rather dry study. To the rest of us it was doctrinal stuff that we have had most of our Christian lives. But it meant so much to this guy. As we sat there, he came out and told us he was a drug addict, a sex addict, and an alcoholic. Then he went back over his life and said his mother had died not long ago, he had been married two years, and his wife had just left him with the kids.

Mary Hecht and others saw God's hand in Skip's story. God had brought Skip to Rockhaven, put Mike in his path, and steered him toward house fellowship. Skip's story — with its beginning, middle, and end — captivated group members whose own narratives frequently became mired in the middle. By recalling Skip's story, group members reinforced their conviction that, struggles notwithstanding, God had a plan for each person's life.

When members told their own stories, they tried to help each other see that plan — often by citing another account of struggle and triumph. In general, the stories that group members told were similar to those shared by close friends anywhere, except for one thing — these stories all had an explicitly religious dimension. Summaries of several stories make the point:

• At work, Sarah Daniels supervised a woman whose extreme con-
tentiousness was wearing her down. Since the woman was not a
Christian, Sarah was unsure how to help her. She asked the group
what it meant to behave like a Christian in this situation and

whether behaving like a Christian was an appropriate response in a business setting.

- Michelle Fletcher was a hostess in a restaurant whose owner, a wealthy Jewish businessman, was very abusive to his employees. She accepted his behavior because she believed that God had put her in that situation for a reason: to be a model Christian. The fact that she had survived his attacks longer than most employees further convinced her that God had a plan for her. Still, Michelle wanted to know if she should quietly accept her employer's abuse or witness more actively to him.
- Kevin Perkins' wife left him and made it difficult for him to see his son regularly. Kevin said she had even tried to align the boy's principal and guidance counselor against him. Before a custody negotiation with his ex-wife and their lawyers, Kevin asked house fellowship what he, the only Christian in the negotiating group, should do. How could he know God's will for this situation?

As these synopses illustrate, when group members related personal stories, they were seeking to reconcile their immediate dilemmas with divine intention. It is hard to find indications in these stories that group members had much of a sense of personal agency. Although they made decisions and took action, their goal was to understand how and why God led them there. When something untoward or unexpected occurred, group members rationalized it as part of God's plan. For example, one night several women said they had had a hard time deciding to work outside the home, but God had found them jobs because their husbands were out of work. Well-educated and well-qualified for their positions, these women needed to square their religious beliefs about women's roles (as mothers and homemakers) with their own professional competency.[11]

Members' stories, no matter how hopeless, were always well-received by the group.[12] After all, these personal narratives were the guts

11. For further discussion of religion and women's roles, see Ryan (1975), Welter (1966), and Ginsburg (1989).

12. Like most rules, this one, too, had exceptions. There were one or two people in house fellowship whose stories strained the group's ability to see God's hand at work. For example, one man was divorced and had lost his job. Initially the group stuck by him, encouraging his efforts to understand what God was doing in his life. But then he became involved in a self-defeating and dead-end relationship

of the meeting because they illustrated how God worked in individual lives. Group members rarely interpreted stories for each other; instead, they encouraged speakers to find their own answer — through prayer and Bible study. When the group prayed together, members petitioned God to help those who had shared a story. "Dear God, please help Kevin to know your will when he goes to the meeting with his ex-wife and their lawyers" or "Jesus, help Michelle find a way to bring her employer closer to you."

These narratives were also instrumental for group identity and cohesion: they reinforced the theological ties that bound members together. They provided a safe way for members to open up, become vulnerable, and build a caring community — all within an evangelical Christian context. For these Christians, that context included accountability. They checked up on each other with phone calls during the week or with conversation when they met at church: "Kevin, how did that meeting with the lawyers go?" or "Michelle, are things any better at work?" Sometimes, when a group member was particularly distressed, one or two others would meet with him or her to talk and pray.

Yet, this level of intimacy primarily characterized the stories told in the smaller groups; in the larger group, members revealed only so much. They tended to speak generally about work and family problems rather than discuss deeply revealing or potentially embarrassing struggles. For example, no one but Skip Tepper ever mentioned addiction problems. Allen Scott, who was among the most open of the members, chose to share his problems more intimately with several men from house fellowship. These men tried to keep each other accountable at a deeper level than that deemed appropriate for the larger group. Scott was ambivalent about whether the full group should be more pro-active:

> My feeling is that the group lets people be vulnerable to the level they want and lets them be accountable to their level of vulnerability. So people will say, "So how's it going?" But no one says, "You have to tell me how you are doing."

In John Wesley's small groups, people had to answer the questions "How have you sinned this week?" and "What have you done to get

---

with a woman who wasn't even a Christian. At this point, the man stopped coming to the group, claiming the relationship took all his time. When I asked some group members what had happened to him, they said he had made some ill-considered decisions. They did not indicate that God had anything to do with these decisions.

closer to God?" If those are the ground rules that a group sets, that's great. But you would need a more highly committed body than what we have now.

Prayer Time

While personal narratives strengthened the horizontal dimension of the group, prayer built up the vertical dimension. Prayer, along with fellowship and Bible study, was part of the group's tripartite base. Yet the actual practice of prayer in the group was continually under discussion. There was explicit contention about when prayer should occur; implicit in the disagreement was how it should occur.

During the first year I attended house fellowship, prayer took place at the end of the evening in the small study groups. Scott arranged the meeting this way because he felt people would be more forthcoming about their prayer requests if they were in a smaller group. Since there were no designated leaders for the small groups, one person in each — usually a longtime member — asked for prayer requests and then began praying. When he or she finished, others followed. Members not only prayed for each other but also repeated requests they had shared with the full group at the start of the meeting. Prayers tended to be very specific: "Lord, give me a clean X-ray when I go for a mammogram next week" or "God, help the search committee find a new pastor for the church."

In the early winter of 1993, during Scott's second stint as group leader, he suggested a new plan for house fellowship meetings. Scott and several others had attended a seminar led by Lyman Coleman, a specialist in Christian support groups, and they wanted to adopt Coleman's methods. Using text from the New International Version of the Bible, Coleman's Serendipity Group had produced eight group studies designed to build fellowship through reflection on the meaning of Scripture in participants' lives. Scott suggested that house fellowship start with the Serendipity's study of Philippians and Ephesians, subtitled "Building a Caring Community." Following Coleman's technique, house fellowship started with small groups studying a lesson; the groups then came together as a large group to pray. In addition, the small groups had designated leaders who facilitated discussion, reported that discussion to the large group, and helped lead prayer.

After several weeks of using the new format, members told Scott that they wanted to go back to the old one. Specifically, they wanted to start out as a large group, break into smaller groups, and pray there. Many said they were uncomfortable praying in the large group, although some felt there was more power when everyone prayed together.

In fact, several members told me that the most memorable house fellowship occurred in the spring of 1991, when almost the entire evening was spent in group prayer. Mary Hecht said that the week before that meeting, a woman in the group had reported that her daughter had Lyme disease. Subsequently a delegation from the church, including participants from house fellowship, went to her house and prayed for her child. Soon after that, the child was healed. When house fellowship met later that week, many were ready to praise God:

> That night, we all felt the Lord telling us just to pray. I always thought, "How can anyone pray for an hour and a half? Isn't that long and drawn out, Lord? I mean, what can you say?" But we just started praying and saw there were some people who needed healing.
>
> The whole evening was spent in prayer. We went from one to another, and there was a lot of love exchanged in prayer. I think everyone walked out feeling like they were ministered to individually by God. It was probably the most spiritual evening we ever had. I know that God is always here, but that night He ministered to each person, and it was great.

As this anecdote suggests, members were comfortable staying together if the group was no larger than eight or ten, which was the approximate size of the group that evening. Yet Mary Hecht's recollection also addressed a second issue concerning prayer: How and when should the group let go and move with the Spirit? The issue of control versus spontaneity was central in the church itself and reflected its uncertain attitude toward charismatic gifts.[13] Lynne Robbins suggested that Rockhaven mirrored the ambivalence of Bill Strickland, its longtime pastor:

> Bill had a charismatic experience in his home church. He believed there was more available spiritually than most Southern Baptists did. He thought God could talk to you and help you lead your life. In the

---

13. Members of the group told me that the more fundamentalist members of the church did not accept charismatic gifts at all.

early days, Bill was more willing to see what God was up to. We also had a number of people who went to CFO [Camp Farthest Out — a nondenominational Christian summer fellowship]. That drew people from a variety of backgrounds, especially charismatic, and the people who went influenced the church a lot.

We still have a number of these people, but they seem more reserved. There were instances when people spoke in tongues, but Bill did not encourage it. We say we're balanced. I think we sit on the fence.

Scott hoped to address this tension in house fellowship by leading several discussions on spiritual gifts during the fall of 1992 and the winter of 1993. He reasoned that if the house fellowship could work through the issue, perhaps the church could, too. Scott used Bible texts and teaching materials to illustrate the diversity of spiritual gifts and to help members identify their own. The gifts he cited went beyond the nine bestowed on believers during the Pentecost[14]: they included virtues such as teaching, hospitality, celibacy, and evangelism. Yet, after several months, members felt that they were still wrestling with the basic question: Is Rockhaven charismatic, and if so, how charismatic is it? That became clear during the discussion at one of the meetings:

"We did this study because we've been together long enough to know each other and, besides, we're one-sixth of the adults at church Sunday morning," said Allen Scott. "Dennis used the words 'feel safe.' We should all feel safe enough with each other to exercise our gifts here. And if there is something blocking the exercise of your gifts at this Thursday-night meeting, we should discuss it."

"But how does this plug back into the church?" asked Jared Day, one of the group's younger members and a graduate of a charismatic Bible college. "This opened up a forum for discussing our feelings, but we really haven't dealt with the basic issues: What about tongues? Are we charismatic or not?"

"I'd like to see miracles in the church and healings," Mary Hecht added. "I feel frustrated by this study. The disciples didn't stop to

14. In 1 Corinthians 12:8-11, these "charismata" (gifts of grace) are tongues, the interpretation of tongues, the word of wisdom, the word of knowledge, the gifts of healing, the working of miracles, faith, prophecy, and the discerning of spirits.

figure out what their gifts were. They just did what they had to do. I think we've got boxed in."

"If you have a gift, you are going to exercise it regardless of the situation around you," offered Kevin Perkins. "I remember times at church when people had a verse to share, they stood up and shared it. . . . With certain things, as long as they are appropriate for the corporate setting, you can't wait for someone to give you permission. If God says, 'Do it,' then you have to step out and do it."

"But it's easier to sit [it] out and wait, especially if you are speaking in unknown tongues in front of two hundred people," said Dennis Robbins, Lynne's husband, who was a deacon. "It would feel safer if someone got up and said, 'Now it's okay to use all your gifts.'"

"Last week there were only ten of us here, and I couldn't believe how good it was," said Mary Hecht. "God met us in this room. Kevin started to pray, and he prayed everything that was coming out of my mouth. Then we started singing and we didn't stop."

"What made that good was that the Spirit of God led it," said Jared Day. "In that kind of forum, there's no problem using your gifts. It becomes a natural thing. We still have to ask if the church is providing a forum for the Spirit to lead."

Dennis Robbins, who led the discussion that night, ended it before the issue could be resolved. In effect, there was no resolution. Members like Jared Day and Mary Hecht felt that the group had to be open to the power of the Spirit. Kevin Perkins and Allen Scott argued that the group already was open to it. Yet in the months that followed, no charismatic outbursts punctuated group meetings. Prayer continued to be a quiet, controlled event rather than a group celebration with singing and speaking in tongues.

The Rewards of Long-Term Membership

During the course of the two years I attended house fellowship, a core group of about ten members emerged. Others attended less frequently, citing child care, work responsibilities, and health problems as the reasons for their lack of consistency. A handful just dropped out. One man said

31

the trip to the Hechts' house was too far. One woman said she preferred women's Bible study. A married couple left the church.

Michelle Fletcher (the woman mentioned earlier who had problems with her boss at the restaurant where she was a hostess) began attending house fellowship a few months before I did. She had belonged to a church in Maryland that had a strong house fellowship program, and she was eager to base herself in a new group. When I interviewed her, Michelle was very enthusiastic about the Hechts' house fellowship, but she mentioned several significant differences when comparing it with her former experience.

For example, she told me that the Maryland group came together at the end of meetings to pray, that they had strong leadership, and that they never discussed church business at fellowship meetings. On the other hand, she pointed out that the Rockhaven group didn't pray as a body (this was before the experiment inspired by Lyman Coleman), that she didn't think the group leader was strong (this was during the period when Scott and his wife were deciding whether to separate), and that she disliked discussions that focused on Rockhaven itself (when Strickland left the church, Scott felt the house fellowships should provide leadership, so he devoted several meetings to discussing members' responsibilities as lay ministers).

After several months of active participation, Michelle stopped coming to house fellowship. Mary Hecht said that she invited her to come when they met in church, but Michelle still did not attend. After a while, she stopped coming to church altogether, and no one in the group knew what happened to her. Her experience was not unusual: long-term members of the group rarely pursued new members. Scott described the problem as a Catch-22:

> There's been no growth because of the deep friendships. It's a time of real instability in the church, since we have been without a pastor for almost eighteen months. For house fellowship, this has had to be a time for stability and for continuing ongoing relationships. People [who know each other] are busy ministering to each other.

For those who stayed with the group, the rewards were significant. House fellowship provided a network of friends who not only supported each other during crises but also played a major part in each other's social lives. Members met for breakfast, encouraged their children to play together, and gathered for dinner parties. Since most of them were very committed to the church, they saw each other not only at group meetings but also at Sunday services, at board meetings and committee meetings, and at picnics and fellowship activities.

Members of the house fellowship said that besides making friends, they also deepened their spiritual lives through participating in the group. "It sharpens my relationship with God," said Cheryl Saunders. "It's valuable to hear other people's spiritual struggles and to see how God is dealing with them in their lives." Mary Hecht made a similar comment: "The emphasis is on spiritual development. People in the group have been supportive. They remind me that God will pull me through, and, in the meantime, they are there to listen and understand."

Part of that understanding meant supporting one another in an explicitly evangelical context. Whether members were confronting problems at work, struggles at home, unforeseen illnesses, or the small indignities of daily life, they sought to respond in what they called a "Christian" manner. In the world around them — central New Jersey of the early 1990s — there was little support for a self-consciously evangelical Christian ethos. In fact, many believed that co-workers, neighbors, and colleagues would be surprised, if not discomfited, to hear talk about religious commitment spilling into everyday life. For example, when Lynne Daniels, who worked in an office, wanted to pray there, she wrote the words down in a journal, lest her colleagues think she was talking to herself or, even worse, praying. Lynne and the other group members were aware of the stereotypes of evangelicals: they were frequently ridiculed in the media as smarmy, self-righteous, and narrow-minded.[15]

For many, house fellowship provided one of the few contexts in

15. The group rarely discussed political or social issues, although it was evident to me, from their conversation and from the visits I made to the church, that Rockhaven and its membership were active in the pro-life movement. In April 1992, after the Rodney King verdict was announced, many in the house fellowship lamented the injustice of the decision and the riots that followed. Yet, they quickly added that God had a plan and that this was just another indication of the approaching end-times. Politics also came up after the 1992 presidential election. Members of the group were very distressed when Bill Clinton beat George Bush; they were particularly concerned about Clinton's pro-abortion stance. They prayed that God would change his heart and that God's plan in allowing this victory would become clear.

which they could just be themselves — admitting their struggles and learning from the trials others experienced. Allen Scott explained:

> We are trying to construct a comfortable Christian identity in the midst of a hostile world. There's tension there, which I guess is healthy, because we live in two worlds. Many of these people [at house fellowship] are saying, "There's a false picture of what it means to be a Christian, and this is a place where I can just be. I don't have to live a bifurcated life."

Yet refashioning their lives in order to feel more "whole" outside the group wrought changes that few expected. And grappling with their individual struggles made members more humble yet also more confident of their relationship with God. It increased the level of trust within the group, so that theological differences — whether over charismatic gifts, the role of women, or the issue of biblical inerrancy — were tolerated. Moreover, it gave members a new way to be Christians. Rather than accept the fundamentalists' notion that there are clear rights and wrongs, members of house fellowship saw situations nuanced by behavior, attitude, and authenticity. This development, however, put them at odds with Rockhaven's more conservative members, who considered the group's toleration of diversity to be misguided. Thus, house fellowship became a place where some members could find a medium between the secularism of the outside world and the fundamentalism of the church itself. In times of crisis, when some members felt particularly alienated from Rockhaven, the house fellowship became church.

Several long-term members made significant strides while in the group. Allen Scott, staunchly committed to his marriage vows, was still trying to work out his relationship with his wife. He assumed primary responsibility for their four children and started to cope with the kinds of problems — single parenthood, dysfunctional family histories, couples therapy — that he thought were outside the purview of conservative Christians. Yet, he said his struggles brought him closer to God and made him more sensitive to the complexities of faith.

Mary Hecht surprised even herself by remaining hopeful during Mike's unemployment. Moreover, she managed to resolve several long-standing problems of her own — an unpleasant professional partnership, difficult relationships with an insensitive mother and hostile children — all the while trusting that God would provide for Mike and her, too. She told me that house fellowship had helped by providing a buffer from the outside world while also demonstrating that she could share things with people who had different opinions and beliefs[16]:

> It is a place to express all those troubles that the world doesn't understand. For example, house fellowship understands the struggle with charismatics, and it understands the spiritual dimension of life.
>
> But I am more and more determined that my relationships don't have to be only with other Christians. I used to think anyone with whom I had a relationship had to be a Christian, but as time goes by I can see God in non-Christians, too. As a Christian, I believe that God wants us to love him through his Son, but I believe he loves us all.

Lynne Robbins did not face dramatic problems like her friends Mary Hecht and Allen Scott, but she did confront herself in new ways during the time I spent with the house fellowship. When I first noticed her, she appeared to be a shy woman who led a somewhat sheltered life. She had two young children, and she had never finished college. Yet, as the weeks went on, I was struck by the similarities between her attitudes and mine toward our families, our spiritual lives, and our self-perceptions. Listening carefully to Lynne, I became aware that she was facing a critical period in her life, and that the group was helping her deal with that:

> I have been trying to build the walls of a new house. I am trying to figure out my role as a woman in the church. Clearly, I have come to be much more myself because people in house fellowship value me.

16. Members of the group seemed to accept my explanation that I was a committed Jew, although several expressed the hope that I would allow God to reveal himself fully to me. Only once did a group member seriously challenge my adherence to Judaism, but his questioning was motivated as much by curiosity as by the desire to evangelize me. I occasionally felt uncomfortable in group discussions, especially when we were studying a New Testament text that seemed blatantly anti-Jewish to me. I had to remember that my purpose was not to explain why the passage was so vitriolic but rather to observe what the others made of it. One evening, during a discussion on justification which emphasized that Jesus had superseded the Jewish law, I felt particularly uneasy. Afterwards, one of the women in my small group told me that it was difficult for her to have that conversation in front of me. I was touched — and surprised — by her sensitivity.

35

House fellowship has helped me trust people. It's also helped me to trust myself and to become more of whomever God wants me to be.

In her search to be who God wanted her to be, Lynne realized how much of herself had been bound up in her fundamentalist church, her parents' expectations, and her dependence on her husband. Through the group and several other church-related venues, she began to untangle the knots that had restricted her emotional growth and spiritual development. Her journals were filled with pages seeking the real "I," with questions such as "How do we begin to recognize that which we have become, shaking off the facade of our perceptions of what is and entering the experience of what we are truly meant to be in the sight of God?"

The support that she received from friends in the group and in the church enabled Lynne to blossom. She began to broaden her commitments, making time for her writing and for groups that were important to her. She also became more empowered in her relationships, feeling that she could negotiate terms with the people she loved rather than just accept their terms. House fellowship had helped to answer some of her prayers:

> My whole concept of the real world is changing. I don't have a lot of contact with it. I have always seen a lot of the world from the way I have been taught. I had a belief, and I put it on a shelf: Here's my church; I'm a Christian; there's the world — but we don't relate.
>
> I don't feel that way anymore. People are people, [and] God loves them. I wanted the church to be a buffer for a lot of my life. Now I don't necessarily want to walk into painful situations, but I don't want to be buffered either. Seeing God work in people's lives is a strong desire of mine. . . . One thing I never looked at before is how much you can recognize of God in your brothers and sisters. I can see God much more clearly now because I can see Him in other people's lives.

Gracious Words: A Presbyterian Bible Study

J. BRADLEY WIGGER

"Each generation must struggle with the Bible in its turn, and come to terms with it."

Martin Buber in *On the Bible*

"In the part I was reading it says the Word was in the beginning, and that's right. I used to think water was first, but if you listen carefully you will hear that the words are underneath the water."

Norman Maclean's father in the book
A River Runs Through It

In the Sunday worship bulletin of the First Presbyterian Church of Rosemont, Delaware (near Wilmington), a very ordinary sort of announcement was made:

> A MORNING BIBLE CLASS on the life and teachings of Jesus in the Gospel of Luke, will be taught by the Rev. Mr. Stephens each Thursday morning, from 10:30 to 11:30, in the Adult Room. Bring a Bible and a friend: the only qualification for this class is a desire to

learn. A nursery for pre-school children is provided under the direction of Mrs. Henry Stephens.

That announcement appeared in January 1964. Although the stated goal of the class was to study the Gospel of Luke, the class went on to study other books of the Bible. Within a couple of years, with only a slight scheduling change (to Wednesday mornings from eleven to noon), the group became well established and was called the Women's Bible Study.

Eight years later, in 1972, the church hired a new pastor, the Reverend Jonathan Davis. He was thirty-nine years old, a born-and-bred Presbyterian, and this was his third congregation. He picked up where the former pastor left off, leading this class, which was attended by ten to fifteen women, every week during the school year.

Twenty years later, during the 1991-92 school year, I got to know this class and some of the people in it. Some things had changed. Now there was a range of fifteen to twenty-five people attending, and four or five of them were men (not counting myself or the leader). Although some people in the congregation still referred to the class as the Women's Bible Study, the senior pastor, Jon Davis, was always quick to correct them: "It's the Wednesday-morning study; there's men who go, too."

A few of the women who belonged to the group had been attending as long as Jon Davis had been there, maybe longer — the older ones weren't even sure. All were white; most if not all would be considered middle class, at least by current standards. All but two or three of the group were of retirement age. One woman who was in her late forties had a full-time job, but her mother was in the group. Another woman, who was about thirty, was married to the new associate pastor and was, in her words, "a stay-at-home mom." She came to class when baby-sitting was provided (a service no longer offered during the class), and then was quite grateful for the time-out from her three young children. Basically, the average age of the group had increased one year for every year it had existed. In other words, over the group's nearly thirty-year history, it had gone from being a women's Bible study that also functioned as a kind of "mothers' time-out" to a group of sixty and seventy year-olds who seemed simply to "want to learn the Bible better" and "enjoy the company." These were the people who were now in a position to meet at 11:00 on Wednesday mornings without requiring baby-sitting services. The group had been part of church life for so long that it was seldom even mentioned in the Sunday-morning bulletin.

The church itself, which was founded in 1708, is older than the country. It currently has about 800 members, with about twice as many women as men. Ninety-six percent of the members are white, and the church is situated in a town (contiguous with Wilmington) of 35,000 that is 78 percent white. The Wednesday-morning Bible study is but one of many educational opportunities provided by the church. There are two other adult Sunday School classes after the worship service. One is a Bible study (attended by five to ten people) that uses the "Uniform Lessons" curriculum.[1] Another is a "Contemporary Issues" class (with from 25 to 60 people attending, depending on the speaker and the topic), which, for example, may bring in a seminary professor for three weeks to discuss world religions, then a social worker for one week to discuss family dynamics. Offered also is an evening "Kerygma" course, which is an intensive Bible study designed to cover major sections of the Bible in one year. In addition, there are several short-term classes provided during the season of Lent. Although the senior pastor may lead a "Contemporary Issues" series or a class during Lent, he normally teaches the Wednesday-morning class only.

This is not an unusual profile of the educational ministry provided by a Presbyterian church of this size. Historically, Presbyterians, as well as others of Reformed heritage, have always tended to emphasize education and the Bible. In earlier times, the two were totally intertwined: when the First Presbyterian Church of Rosemont was founded, children learning to read did so with primers made up of Bible quotations and catechism questions. This is not to say that Presbyterians as a group are necessarily more biblically literate or more educated generally than those from other backgrounds. It is simply to say that both the Bible and education have been deeply valued in the history of Reformed churches, whether or not particular congregations or persons have embodied these values. This emphasis goes back to Calvin himself: "Now, in order that true religion may shine upon us, we ought to hold that it must take its beginning from heavenly doctrine and that no one can get even the slightest taste of right and sound doctrine unless he be a pupil of Scripture" (Calvin 1559, 1.4.2).

---

1. The "Uniform Lessons," which originated in the late nineteenth century, are biblical texts that have been organized to cover major portions of the Bible over a multiyear period. They are used internationally and function as a kind of "Sunday school lectionary."

The act of studying Scripture itself cannot be fully appreciated apart from its history as an ancient *practice*. The Reformation brought a renewed emphasis on the Bible as "the Word." Like Israel, Reformed Christians were "people of the text." And when combined with the doctrine of justification by faith, a theology of the Word allowed a de-emphasizing of the role of an institutional priesthood and an emphasizing of a "priesthood of all believers." As a priesthood, these believers — each believer — needed to study the sacred texts. The emphasis upon the Word, in this sense, had an individuating effect.

Reformers did not consider such study to be something new. To them it was a renewal of an old practice, traceable to ancient churches and, before that, to Israel. To use Calvin's words again,

> Finally, in order that truth might abide forever in the world with a continuing succession of teaching and survive through all ages, the same oracles he had given to the patriarchs it was his pleasure to have recorded, as it were, on public tablets. With this intent the law was published, and the prophets afterward added as its interpreters. (Calvin 1559, 1.4.2)

To become a pupil of Scripture, according to Calvin, is to participate in the abiding of truth through the ages, in the handing on of wisdom.

This is all to say that although thirty years is a long time for a Bible study to exist, the men and women of the Wednesday-morning class are participating in a much older practice, one older than Christianity itself. They are swimming in an ancient river.

Wednesday Morning

Although Bible study is an old practice, every particular study has its own character. What is the one at First Presbyterian of Rosemont like?

First of all, it begins a month or so following the beginning of the school year, after the dust settles. (This is a hectic time for churches too, because they're busy organizing their Sunday School programs.) The class meets in the "Adult Room" of the Education Building, which is situated across a busy street from the historic sanctuary and cemetery. The Adult Room also functions as the church library, and on Sunday mornings, before the larger, regular service, a small, informal service of worship is held here.

Most of the people attending the Bible study arrive five to ten minutes early. The custodian has prearranged about twenty chairs in a circle, since the group draws, on the average, about twenty persons in any given week. Most of them are regulars.

As people walk in, they are smiling and chatting. Someone comments on how chilly the room is and takes a peek through the glass encasing the thermostat. Someone else comments on the hint of cigarette smoke left over from an AA meeting held there. By 11:00 the room is buzzing with greetings and conversation. Besides talking about the latest weather forecast, people are finding out who is in the hospital (someone almost always is) and why, discussing other personal, community, or global news, and offering congratulations or sympathies. A close look reveals that on one side of the circle there are all women, and on the other side there is a mix of men and women. Three of the men who regularly attend are the husbands of women who had already been attending the class. Only one man, a retired college professor, attends without his wife.

At 11:00, Jon Davis walks in, sharply dressed in a suit and tie; his attire contrasts with the casual clothes and sweats sported by the group. "There he is." "Hi, Jon." Jon's eyes open wide as he smiles, almost surprised at the noise level being generated by this modest gathering. Someone pulls him aside and quietly passes on something that sobers the pastor's face; he nods as if he knows what must be done next. After that exchange, he sits down, says a few more "hi's," and chuckles a bit before he says, "Let's pray." (He chuckles because he knows that this little cue can quiet the whole room — and it does.) In his prayer, Jon thanks God for this communion of people and the opportunity to learn from Scripture. "Amen," says the group in unison.

A woman announces the birth of her ninth granddaughter, and the others congratulate her. Someone mentions last Sunday's sermon, which in turn initiates a discussion about a powerful moment that had taken place during the service — a woman had told a painful story about being a "preacher's kid." (Jon explains all this to me because he knows I wasn't there.) Jon admits to the group how close this woman's story is to his own family's story. (Everyone in the group knows that Jon's teenage daughter has had struggles with substance abuse. They know this because he has discussed the situation during worship services.) The conversation briefly turns to politics in the news, and then, as if remembering why they came, Jon puts on his glasses and opens his New English Bible. He says, understatedly, "We have some interesting texts this week." All the participants have brought their own Bibles (various translations) and open them; there is some general scurrying to find the first passage. "What's the chapter again?" "What book are we in?"

(Until the previous year, the group had always studied a particular book of the Bible. But over the twenty years that Jon had led the study, the group had covered all the New Testament books, some several times, and many of the major Old Testament ones. So, in 1990, Jon and the group decided to switch formats. Now they use ecumenical lectionary texts, which provide the basis for Sunday worship. The lectionary reading usually consists of an Old Testament text, a Psalm, a gospel text, and an Epistle lesson. Jon likes the new format because it encourages him to get his "homework" — the background study for the sermon — done by midweek. The class itself seems ambivalent about the format. Once someone suggested that perhaps the group should go back to the old format because following the lectionary led to "jumping all over the Bible" — whereas concentrating on one book of the Bible maintained the literary and historical integrity of the text. Jon asked group members if they were interested in this, but he really didn't encourage much discussion. He said that the associate pastor was thinking of getting just such a study going soon, in the evenings during Lent. But a number of group members did like the format because they felt that it gave them a greater connection to worship services. On the following Sunday, not only the sermon but also the liturgy, prayers, and music would be based on one or more of the texts they were studying. For these individuals, studying the texts ahead of time enhanced their participation in worship. In addition, it helped Jon to know what kinds of concerns and interests the texts evoked. Sometimes he would even mention the group's study of a passage in the sermon — to the group's delight. The lectionary format also made it easier for new members of the group to come at any point during the year, and for regular members not to "get behind" if they missed a week. For all these reasons, Jon was not motivated to change the format back to the book-by-book approach.)

Some people have read the passages ahead of time, perhaps as part of their daily devotions. Most have not. They have all been given a list of the upcoming lectionary passages with dates, but many have lost the list. At first, I myself read the passages ahead of time, but somewhere along the line I stopped, simply because it was one less thing to do, and there was no need to read them ahead of time.

Jon announces that the first passage is from the book of Nehemiah in the Old Testament. Before he reads the passage, he gives a brief rehearsal of the history of Israel, from the Exodus to its period of monarchy, to its division and fall, to its exile and restoration. In this way he provides historical context for the passage about to be read. In the midst of this rehearsal, Jon playfully catechizes: "Now who was Israel's first king?" Sheepishly someone answers, "David." "No," someone else corrects. "Wasn't it Solomon? — no, I mean Saul."

"Right," says Jon, while people squirm a bit. A ninety-year-old woman named Gertrude, sitting right next to Jon, declares loudly and slowly, "First there was Saul, then David, and then Solomon. Solomon was a rascal, and because of that God punished him, dividing the kingdom into ten tribes in the north, and that was called Israel; and two tribes in the south, and that was called Judah." She's about to go on, so Jon says, "Thank you, Gertrude."

Next Jon reads the passage from Nehemiah. It is the one in which the long-lost "law of Moses" has been rediscovered and read to the people of Israel. When the people hear the law, they grieve for their sins, but the priests tell them not to weep.

Jon suggests that this may be an anti-feminine passage; crying, he explains, might be perceived as unmasculine. No one in the group has much to say about this. There is a brief discussion about what precisely had been read to the Israelites, what this law was.

The group moves on to the Psalm. It is Psalm 19:

> The heavens are telling the glory of God. . . . The law of the Lord is perfect, reviving the soul. . . . Let the words of my mouth and the meditation of my heart be acceptable to you, O LORD, my rock and my redeemer.

"We have a law theme developing here," Jon comments. He asks if someone with a different translation would read the Psalm again, to see what differences in language there might be. After this other version has been read, a woman who sings in the choir mentions a Beethoven piece based on this psalm, and Jon helps her remember the title. (Jon is himself an accomplished pianist.) Someone else mentions — clearly struggling with — the words "the law is perfect," wondering how this is meaningful. A general discussion about "grace versus works" ensues. Jon emphasizes that God's law has to be understood in the larger context of

God's loving forgiveness. A well-known Reformation scholar had been leading the "Contemporary Issues" class the previous Sunday and had mentioned the Heidelberg Catechism. The same grace/law discussion apparently had taken place in that class as well. Jon recalls what the scholar had said, that the Heidelberg Catechism interprets the law as "guidelines for gratitude" for God's lovingkindness. One woman says, "I don't care. I still think you have to live the good life if you want to go to heaven." People squirm. "We're all sinners," Jon responds. "Would anyone in here claim they've lived perfect lives?" No one answers. The woman finally says, "Well, not *perfect.*" Jon comments, "Well, I think this is something we just disagree on, but I think it's up to God to decide who is saved." (This discussion occurred more than once in the months I attended the class.)

"The next passage is from Luke, chapter 4, beginning at verse 14," Jon says next. The class is relieved to move on. Jesus is reading from Isaiah in the synagogue of Nazareth, in effect proclaiming himself the Messiah:

> The Spirit of the Lord is upon me, because he has anointed me to bring good news to the poor. He has sent me to proclaim release to the captives and recovery of sight to the blind, to let the oppressed go free, to proclaim the year of the Lord's favor.

Jon observes how important the *person* of Jesus is to this passage. He says, "This is why we read the gospel — to know the person of Jesus. This is why we are here, why we do Bible study at all." He goes on to speak of what an "offense" this messianic claim had been to the synagogue and what an offense it still can be to be the "anointed one."

Bobby, the woman whose mother is also in the class, points out how crucial the *Spirit* is to this passage, and Jon nods in affirmation. She goes on to tell a story — which functions as a kind of testimonial — in which someone struggling with drugs asked the Holy Spirit to come into his life and subsequently found the power to go into recovery. "Of course," she warns, "there are still struggles."

Jon thanks her for the story and says, "You know, if you want to really see openness and honesty and vulnerability, sometime just go to one of the AA meetings and listen." (Jon made a semiregular practice of visiting the AA meetings held in the building.) There is a long pause.

"OK," Jon continues, "the last lesson is from Paul's first letter to the Corinthians. The church at Corinth had a lot of problems, a lot of fighting and bickering. Now let's see what Paul says to them. Chapter 12; I'll start with the first verse":

> Now concerning spiritual gifts . . . there are varieties of gifts, but the same Spirit; and there are varieties of services, but the same Lord. . . . To each is given the manifestation of the Spirit for the common good. . . .
>
> For just as the body is one and has many members, and all the members of the body, though many, are one body, so it is with Christ. For in the one Spirit we were all baptized into one body — Jews or Greeks, slaves or free — and we were all made to drink of one Spirit.

"What strikes you about this passage?" One of the men jumps in with, "We can't do it all by ourselves." The whole room nods and agrees. Jon adds, "You know, this also means that no one congregation or denomination can do it all. Perhaps God has seen fit to provide a nice diversity of believers." A short discussion ensues about the love of God empowering a kind of openness and hospitality to others — as opposed to rigid legalism and hostility. Someone brings up David Duke and his awful attitudes. Someone else brings up politics in the Middle East and wonders why Israel doesn't live by its own commands to be "open to the stranger." Another person responds, "Well, that's a tough situation."

One woman briefly tells a story in which a mother whose son was killed by a drunk driver actually forgave the driver. Another man adds, "Terry Anderson says he's forgiven his captors."

"That's amazing, isn't it?"

"Amazing grace."

"Yes."

"Uh-huh." Many have chimed in. After the brief excitement, the room turns quiet. "There *is* good in the world, after all," proclaims Bobby's mother. And there are a lot of smiles and nods. Sensing the end of the hour, the group seems to want the discussion to end on a positive note. Gertrude recites a cute poem, and Jon looks at his watch and says, "See you next time."

Within seconds, buzzing conversations resume, picking up where they had left off before the study hour.

Interpreting Texts, Interpreting Situations

The crucial place that sacred texts held in the life of this group as a group should be apparent. Some members made Bible study a daily personal practice; some read Scripture only in worship and in this group. Gertrude, for example, had read the entire Bible five times. Others had never read it all the way through, and knew only fragments of it. Nevertheless, they all viewed biblical authority as very significant. Although there would surely be debate concerning the precise nature of that authority, all would consider it very important to the Christian life.

But the importance or authority of Scripture was not a preoccupation of the group. There was little if any quoting from Scripture, or "The Bible says. . . ." Jon said to the group more than once, "I discovered long ago you can 'prove' about anything you want to prove in the Bible." Instead, what seemed important to the group was the act of interpretation itself. The texts generated stories, conversations, interpretations, and connections to life experiences. The group was a kind of living Midrash, an ongoing commentary upon these texts. The Word, it could be said, generated more words.

These new words, however, were more than "just talk"; they were expressions of existential struggles and deep searches for meaning, and rearticulations of ancient answers to life's questions. They were words that bespoke deep-seated values and convictions. They were words that had been and would continue to be interconnected with the words of Scripture.

The group had a basic pattern of interpretation: they took a text, used various means to try to understand it more fully, and then made connections to either their individual lives or their social lives (from personal history to global politics). Sometimes these connections simply illustrated a text; sometimes they questioned or challenged some aspect of the apparent message of a text — both analogies and dialectics were at work. In short, sacred texts were not the only thing being interpreted. Life itself was being interpreted in relation to the texts.

Edward Farley has identified this "interpretation of situations" as a key dimension of the life of faith itself. It is the core of "practical theology," he says. In a sense, he points out, all believers are "practical theologians":

> All human beings exist and act in situations and engage in interpretations of situations. This interpretive dimension of human existence

does not cease with faith and with life in the community of faith. On the contrary, faith and the world of faith shape the perspective, the "taken-for-granted stock of knowledge," the weighting of what is important, all of which affect the interpretation of situations. (Farley 1987, 11)

In most communities, this interpretation takes on direction and discipline and becomes intentional through educational efforts. In a community that prizes the Word and even identifies it with its Messiah — the eternal Logos — it should not be too surprising that words, discussion, the reading of texts, and interpretation through language in general should strongly characterize its way of passing on wisdom. This is different from how one engages and learns dance, or music, or the wisdom of a Japanese tea ceremony. At First Presbyterian of Rosemont, people pay particular attention to the Word through words, and to life through the Word.

The One and the Many

Having said this, it should be noted that the entire educational ministry of the Rosemont church, of which the Bible study group is a part, was but one dimension of its ecclesial existence, albeit a very important dimension. And virtually all the participants in the group I studied were involved in other aspects of the church and its work. These included worship (and music within that context), ministries of care (from mission sewing circles to AIDS dinners to fundraising for global concerns), and activities for "fellowship." During the time I attended this Bible study group, I sometimes couldn't follow the conversation because it assumed knowledge about events in the church or in the township that I didn't have. To paraphrase Paul, the study was one member of a body with many parts, one manifestation of the Spirit.

The group's use of lectionary texts illustrated this. Every Wednesday they studied texts that would be used in the following Sunday's worship — they would be prayed, sung, and proclaimed in addition to being read. All of that, at least in a tacit way, entered into what the group did on Wednesday, just as those who studied these texts entered the sanctuary doors on Sunday. If there was a mission cause being pursued and urged in worship, typically someone would quote texts from Scrip-

47

ture — ones that had been studied, sung, prayed, and proclaimed — to articulate rationales and motivations. That is, the community's sacred texts became mission language. And most of the participants in this Wednesday-morning group had, at one time or another, been actively involved in the church's mission work.

In other words, there is a kind of ecology of forms or practices that constitutes the church's life.[2] Each form — whether worship, prayer, song, learning, or the expression of care — has its own integrity and purpose and beauty, yet always assumes and exists in relation to the other forms. These practices compose the general life of the Rosemont church like the colors of a painting — playing off each other, mixing and blending, shading and highlighting. The Bible study is simply part of a larger color composition.

One of the effects of this interplay is that it takes a certain pressure off any one of the forms — whether it be worship, or prayer groups, or potluck suppers — to "do it all." The educational opportunities are just that — opportunities to learn. To use the language of this tradition, all these different practices are considered various "means of grace."

I mention this out of my own struggle to articulate the odd fact that although there was only a small amount of *explicit* support occurring in this Wednesday-morning group, I knew people had supported and would continue to support one another. If someone was struggling with something, there would be others from the group ready to help out, whatever the situation.[3] Support and community were not the focus of this group, but these were nonetheless visible in the "cracks" — particularly in the "buzzing" before and after the study proper. One woman, Naomi, who spoke only occasionally during the study hour, said that the group' had been a kind of therapy for her, "better than going to a psychiatrist." She had attended since 1968, longer than Jon Davis had been leading the group. "All through the years," she told me, "with five

---

2. I have been informed by a work by Maria Harris (1989), in which she helpfully identifies what she calls five basic "forms" that, working together, make up the church's life. They are (1) koinonia (community), (2) leiturgia (prayer and worship), (3) didache (teaching), (4) kerygma (proclamation), and (5) diakonia (service).

3. I learned this from my interviews and casual conversations with group members, and from my conversations with people involved in the church, but not from my participation in the group itself.

children there's always something going on, and it has continually been a support group for me." Her husband, a college professor, began attending a few years ago when he retired.

Of course, not everyone saw the group as Naomi did. I spoke with a forty-year-old woman named Helen who had attended the group the previous year but no longer went — yet her attendance had been rewarding. She had been raised a Roman Catholic and said she was never encouraged to read the Bible. She told me that she went to the group to learn how to read it, to take some of the unapproachability out of it. She went, and she learned. And now, although she no longer attends the group, she does read Scripture, at least occasionally, on her own. Unlike Naomi, she never saw the gathering as a "support group," but she did mention that all the women in the group were about her own mother's age, and that perhaps there was something "mothering" about it for her.

Bobby, whose own mother was in the group, was fairly dissatisfied with the group. There was not enough "spiritual heat" in the group, she said. Her own ideal of what a Bible study should be was based on a charismatic gathering she had once attended regularly: there had been singing and study, and then speaking in tongues and prayer. She saw herself as rather "addicted" to small groups (she was involved in several), and she could think of no particular reason that she was attending this one — except that her mother went. She described her family as "very dysfunctional," revolving around her father's alcoholism.

And then there was Tom. He was the only man (besides Jon and myself) who attended the group without his wife. He began going when he retired from teaching at a local college. He had a Ph.D. in history (focusing on Reformation history) and was eager to do more studying of the Bible itself. Because of what he was looking for, he found the group disappointing. He liked it when Jon provided critical information (e.g., literary or historical background) for the texts, but he found some of the discussions rather annoying, in a sense getting in the way of "good learning."

Although markedly different, the responses of Helen and Tom to the group show how it has remained true to the description printed in the bulletin in 1964: "The only qualification for this class is a desire to learn." In other words, this never was — and was never intended to be — a progressively structured study, with each week or year building upon the previous one. It was set up in such a way that new people could attend at any time. This was a strength for some, a weakness for others. It opened a whole new biblical world for Helen, but it was not thorough enough for Tom, who wanted to use his critical skills more fully.

"Openness"

Nearly all the members I interviewed named the pastor, Jon, as an important part of what made the study worth attending. Usually his "openness to different opinions" and his "knowledge of the Bible" were explicitly mentioned. Also, Jon had been intimately and intensely involved in these peoples' lives over the years in one way or another — through births and deaths, sicknesses, family and job troubles. He knew things about these people that perhaps few others, if any, knew. I can only imagine that it was an additional benefit of participating in the group to have a chance to be with Jon in a less intense, less difficult setting.

For the most part, Jon's theological liberalism seemed appreciated. The group wanted to be seen as "open" and not rigidly bound to a particular doctrine. Theologically speaking, many viewpoints were and would be welcomed, except if "openness" itself were not tolerated. Jon, who came from a rigidly conservative Presbyterian background, and the group in general did not want to be identified with any sort of "fundamentalism." They even took a certain pride in being open — that is, "not fundamentalist." (Ironically, this may be simply another kind of fundamentalism or at least a closed ideology; I'm not sure.)

When I asked people to relate a "memorable story" told in the group, nearly all those I interviewed brought up a story told by Gertrude, the ninety-year-old woman previously mentioned. (After one meeting, the class had a little birthday party for her.) Attending the group allowed her a rare chance to get out of her apartment during the week. (Someone from the group gave her a ride.) Because her hearing was poor, she always sat next to Jon. She was a kind of matriarch for the group. She told many stories, could quote whole Psalms, recited poems, and had a great, loud laugh. If Jon could be thought of as doing the play-by-play, Gertrude was doing the color.

The story she told that everyone seemed to remember was the one about the revival. When she was in the eighth grade, her class was taken to hear Billy Sunday. In the revival tent she was asked, "Do you want to hit the sawdust trail?" and she said, "No." Next she was asked, "Well, how would you like to shake hands with Billy Sunday?" She agreed to do that, but nothing more. She explained how difficult it was to get out of the packed tent: "The people stood. When you went out of your aisle, you couldn't get out of [the tent.] . . . They kept talking to you. . . . So I said, 'Let me out of here,' and I elbowed a man in the stomach. He gave way, and I got out. No, I didn't get to be one of his converts."

So we might say that part of the identity of this group was *not* being "conversionist" or "fundamentalist" or "charismatic" or "evangelical" as these were understood by the group. In fact, Gertrude had told her story in the context of a discussion of "being born again." And this emphasis played out against the larger history of Reformed Christianity *not* being Roman Catholic and Christianity itself *not* being Judaism. The group had a tendency to portray all these as legalistic or closed communities.

Spirituality

Increasingly, "spirituality" is taken to refer to an introspective, interior life, cultivated through particular prayer and meditative disciplines or events — whether through St. Ignatius or through glossolalia. One of the interview questions I asked was, "Can you talk to me some about your spirituality, your spiritual journey?" Repeatedly I was answered with blank stares, and I had to re-ask the question, using different words: "Tell me about your *faith journey*." "Spirituality" was not in the ordinary vocabulary of these group members, with the exception of the younger ones. When people spoke of their "faith journeys," they talked about going to church (worship), perhaps some of the different studies or groups they were involved in there, maybe a theological question they had struggled with at a particular point, a time of physical or emotional struggle (usually involving illness or death), and perhaps their daily devotions. Often their "faith journeys" were hardly distinguishable from what would be called "life journeys." Except for Bobby, Jon, and Sally (the young woman married to the associate pastor), few of the others talked of developing any sort of interior life besides that having to do with devotions and Bible study. This comes closer to what Calvinists traditionally have referred to as "piety." John Leith explains:

> The Reformed community has always been skeptical of religious exercises. Calvin knew that exercises easily become substitutes for

authentic piety. Furthermore, they lead to introspection and remoteness from life. For Calvin, the Christian life is lived amid the ordinary experience of life in the family and in the world. Therefore the exercises of Christian piety were very few and very simple. They were preeminently the worship of God on Sunday and the keeping of the Lord's Day holy, daily Bible reading, daily prayer, table blessings, and the stewardship of money and time. These are all routine activities of church members. Calvin and subsequent Reformed church people apparently believed they were sufficient. (Leith 1990, 130)

Leith goes on to claim that a church theology emphasizing the transcendence of God cannot draw devotional practices from mystics or from a general religiosity that minimizes the distinction between creator and creature. He sees current popular notions of "spirituality" as substitutes for authentic "piety" (Leith 1990, 131).

Whether or not all or even most Reformed theologians would agree with Leith, this description is a fair articulation of the situation of this particular group. Most of these assumptions are probably not even operating at any conscious level, but they do appear to be at work as a part of the group's taken-for-granted-world of what it means to them to be Christian.

Although the Reformed view of piety does not emphasize mysticism, in Reformed theology there is certainly an understanding of the "Spirit" at work, an understanding coming close to that of the passage from Corinthians cited above. In the Reformed view, there are many gifts, many services, many manifestations of the Spirit. Exercising these gifts and talents and undertaking these practices and tasks are ways of participating in the work of the Holy Spirit. The question is not so much whether a congregation "has the Spirit" but to what degree the church and its ministry exist "in the power of the Spirit." As Reformed theologian Jürgen Moltmann explains,

The New Testament knows no technical terms for what we call "the church's ministry." Paul talks about *charismata*, meaning the *energies* of the new life (I Cor. 12.6, 11), which is to say the powers of the Spirit.... They are the gifts of grace springing from the creative grace of God. (Moltmann 1977, 295)

The Rosemont church embraces this viewpoint: spirituality has to do with participation in the church's ministry, many members working as a body empowered by these charismata.

52

Even so, the Bible study group placed a different sort of emphasis upon "the Holy Spirit" as such, different from the emphasis in, say, the charismatic gathering Bobby once attended. Group members sometimes spoke of "following Jesus" or "our heavenly Father's love," but they didn't commonly speak of "participating in the Spirit's work" or say "The Spirit moved me to. . . ." Perhaps the language itself sounded too much like the language of an evangelical community. Perhaps the emphasis upon "Word" has come at the expense of "Spirit." Perhaps the potentially wild "energies" of the Spirit are threatening to a tradition that boasts of doing things "decently and in order." Perhaps it is a combination of all of these things and more; it is difficult to know. But it can at least be observed that in this group the Third Person of the Trinity is still the least spoken of (compared with "Father" and "Son") and, theologically, is probably the least understood.

The Last Meeting

In May the group held its last meeting for the year. It was like any other, with two major exceptions. The first was that Gertrude was not present. A few weeks before she had suffered a serious stroke and had been hospitalized. Subsequently her condition was often addressed in the "buzzing" before the group began its study. The day before the last meeting she had died. When Jon came in, he turned her chair around to acknowledge the presence of her absence. Little was said about this, or her, except concerning the details of the funeral arrangements being made.

On the one hand, this event revealed again the boundaries of the group's purpose. It was not, for example, a support group specifically designed to help people talk through their problems. It was still a Bible study. On the other hand, this event also clarified the importance of the entire life of the church — all its practices. It was clearly indicated that there was a whole different time and space and practice that would specifically address Gertrude's death and provide a communal opportunity to grieve.

The other exceptional thing that took place this day was a potluck luncheon at the end of the study hour. Cold cuts, raw vegetables, and ice cream provided this group's proleptic version of the eschatological feast. It was a casual affair, but one that allowed another glimpse of the community spirit at work beneath the study of words.

Drawing on creation texts, Jürgen Moltmann has noticed a certain complementarity at work between Word and Spirit. God speaks a word, and it is so. The Spirit (in Hebrew, "breath" or "wind") hovers over the face of the primordial waters. As Moltmann puts it,

> The word names, differentiates and appraises. But the breath is the same in all the words, and binds the words together. . . . The Word specifies and differentiates through its efficacy; the Spirit binds and creates symmetries, harmonies and concord through its presence. (Moltmann 1990, 289)

All this, says Moltmann, is "the song of creation" — with quickening breath and through form-giving word, the Creator sings out creation (Moltmann 1990, 289).

Who can say how old the practice of gathering with others and studying sacred words is? But, given the fact that it was so closely associated even with creation, with the very beginning, it must rest close to the heart of the community's very existence. No wonder, as Norman Maclean might put it, the people were listening carefully to the words underneath the water.

The Long Loneliness: Liberal Catholics and the Conservative Church

KATHLEEN M. JOYCE

Regina Mangan surprised even her closest friends when she announced that she would join a peace caravan headed for Washington to march against the Persian Gulf War. "Desert Shame, I called it," she said later as she explained what moved her, at the age of eighty, to brave the winter elements and join the peace march in January 1991. A widow with a long history of involvement in social and political causes, Regina is well known in her community as a devout Catholic of deep faith and spiritual strength. With her gray hair, quiet demeanor, and obvious devotion to her faith, Regina seems an unlikely church dissident. Yet her vocal criticism of both church and national leaders on issues of peace and social justice places her solidly with the activist left of the Catholic Church.[1]

1. The use of the term "activist left" requires some explanation. The Catholic left is not synonymous with the American political left, although the historically symbiotic relationship between American Catholics and the Democratic Party is still apparent. Liberal Catholics typically embrace a commitment to nonviolence that extends to wartime pacifism and disarmament advocacy as well as to opposition to capital punishment. They also tend to give more weight to human rights concerns than to geopolitical calculations when evaluating U.S. foreign policy, and to favor the involvement of both government and church agencies in programs to aid the hungry and the homeless. Liberal Catholics support efforts to promote the cause of equality for women and to further multicultural and interracial cooperation and

While Regina may be more liberal than most of her fellow American Catholics, she is not unique in combining dissent from church teachings with devotion to the church. In the decades since the Second Vatican Council (1962-1965), Regina's brand of devout dissent has become fairly common among American Catholics. Increasingly, lay Catholics have demanded the right to make their own moral choices, and have refused to view their differences with the church as adequate cause for separation from it.

Loyalty to the Church

Why do these Catholics remain so steadfast in their commitment to the church? Regina's experience suggests an answer. Like most American Catholics, Regina sees her Catholicism as part of her family inheritance. The Catholic Church is as much a part of her heritage as her Irish blood and the family lore she passes on to her grandchildren, and she would no more turn her back on her church than she would renounce that heritage. With its age-old traditions and timeless rituals, the church offers Catholics like Regina a way to link themselves with generations past and future.

It is the timelessness of such pillars of Catholicism as the sacramental system that accounts for their broad cross-cultural, intergenerational appeal. The "analogical imagination" of the faithful, to use the phrase of Catholic theologian David Tracy (Tracy 1981), is fed by the rich traditions of the church that have allowed Catholics of different times and places to interpret even the most universal of church rituals in a way that gives meaning to their individual experience. For the American church, this quality has been particularly important because American Catholics represent such a varied mix of ethnic and racial heritages.

---

understanding. There is no consensus on the issue of abortion rights, but those who oppose elective abortion do so because of their belief in the "seamless garment" ethic that connects the abortion issue to support for pacifism and disarmament and opposition to the death penalty.

Liberal Catholics are firm in their support of the individual's right to dissent from Catholic teachings, and are vocal in their insistence on more power for lay members of the church. They are likely to support the ordination of women to the priesthood and the right of priests to marry.

For polling data on American Catholics, see Gallup and Castelli (1987).

One product of the American church's heterogeneity was a tendency, in its early history, for Catholics to organize themselves on the basis of race and ethnicity. Nineteenth-century Catholics organized parishes according to each immigrant community's nation of origin, and twentieth-century Catholics who are African-American, Native American, and Hispanic have continued in this tradition of the immigrant church. Increasingly, American Catholics are extending this pattern of association to include groups distinct from the parish and formed on the basis of shared political views. This realignment of American religious loyalties into liberal and conservative camps has been the subject of extensive sociological analysis (Wuthnow 1988), and is by no means limited to the Catholic Church. Disaffected American Protestants have discovered that they can leave one denomination for another with political and social positions more consistent with their own, just as American Catholics have learned to switch parishes (Hoyt 1992) and turn to independent Catholic organizations in their efforts to find a community compatible with their own beliefs.

Pax Christi USA

Regina Mangan has belonged to one such Catholic organization, Pax Christi USA, for nearly a decade. Pax Christi, Latin for "peace of Christ," is part of an international network of Catholic peace groups with roots in post–World War II Europe. In the United States alone, Pax Christi has over 11,000 individual members and 300 local chapters. The organization devotes its efforts almost exclusively to education and activism concerning peace and human rights issues, a focus that makes it popular among liberal Catholics who find that their views on peace and justice are not shared by the church at large.

Throughout the 1980s, Pax Christi placed nuclear disarmament and international peace at the top of its list of social concerns. When the communist powers of Eastern Europe began to fall in 1989, and the potential for nuclear conflict between East and West appeared to diminish, many peace groups in the United States found support for their cause eroding as all but the most committed activists came to believe that the nuclear threat had passed. Some groups folded as interest in their cause waned, while others, such as Pax Christi, were forced to regroup.

The local chapter of Pax Christi to which Regina Mangan belongs, christened "St. Francis" by its members, has felt the effects of global political change. Throughout its ten-year history, much of its vitality has come from the participation of Catholics committed to nuclear disarmament. Indeed, it was through their involvement in a secular disarmament group that many of the original members of the St. Francis group came to know one another. When the urgency of the disarmament issue began to diminish, some of these members withdrew from active involvement in Pax Christi, saying that while they still believed in the importance of peace activism, the changing world situation gave them the opportunity to reorder their commitments, and Pax Christi no longer needed to be foremost among them. Other members whose attendance lapsed have quite the opposite opinion. For them, peace activism remains a chief concern, and they are frustrated that the St. Francis group now emphasizes discussion over direct action. Still others, however, have stayed with the group and worked to redefine its mission so that it embraces a broader understanding of peace and nonviolence in the post–Cold War world.

Group Meetings

The St. Francis group meets monthly at the Catholic campus-ministry center of Blydell College, a small liberal arts college in a suburban northeastern community. Since it was founded in 1982, St. Francis Pax Christi has had a core membership of about twelve members, well over half of whom have been women. Members currently range in age from forty-five to eighty, with at least a third over the age of seventy. Every member of the group is white, and virtually everyone is well educated and comfortably middle class. The group draws its membership from two different suburban communities, each of which is served by a large Roman Catholic parish. Most of the younger members belong to the same parish, St. Stephen's, and are active in the social justice ministry there. The older members have much looser parish ties because the church in their community is staunchly conservative, and they have long since detached themselves from it. Three members — two priests and a nun — have no formal parish ties, but instead are involved in a variety of ministries within the diocese.

By 1992, when the group was in its tenth year, nearly half of the core membership was made up of new members who had joined the group in 1988 and 1989. This infusion of new blood is partly responsible for the transformation of St. Francis Pax Christi into a discussion group bearing little resemblance to its more activist predecessor. St. Francis meetings initially were used to plan vigils, marches, and other protest activities, but the current membership prefers to limit its action to lobbying government officials through letters and phone campaigns. In addition to lobbying activities, the monthly hour-long meetings have included a time for prayer, the sharing of information on issues, and a talk by a visiting lecturer.[2] The national Pax Christi organization traditionally has focused on global concerns like the arms race and human rights abuses in Central America, and the St. Francis group shares this international perspective. The group directs most of its efforts toward countries with either a large Roman Catholic population threatened by war and poverty, or a Catholic minority facing government persecution. The group gives domestic issues far less attention, although the plight of immigrant communities in the U.S. is a problem of great concern to most members. The group has also made capital punishment, a measure that Pax Christi unanimously opposes, the subject of letter-writing campaigns and lobbying efforts. In general, however, members seem to be more comfortable acting and thinking globally.[3]

One consequence of this global focus is that it reinforces the group's natural tendency toward dispassionate discussion of the issues before it. Injustice in a distant land is less likely to generate the sort of emotional response that problems closer to home might, and, as a result, group

2. St. Francis Pax Christi meetings are held from September through June of every year. Members gathered at the June 1992 meeting to discuss plans for restructuring. With disarmament no longer its central and defining concern, the group was feeling pressure to move into a number of conflicting directions. The June meeting was set aside as a time for members to identify the issues that would be on the following year's agenda, and to discuss new ways to structure the meetings. In an attempt to balance the need for both group discussion and direct action, a new format was proposed and accepted. The following year, each hour-long meeting was to be divided into three parts: fifteen minutes for a prayer service, fifteen minutes for information sharing and discussion, and thirty (or more) minutes for letter writing on behalf of a particular cause.

3. This is evident when members are asked if they think domestic violence is an issue that Pax Christi needs to address. Everyone agrees that the group's concern for peacemaking should extend to working for peace in the home, but the group has made no move to put the issue on its agenda.

discussions have an impersonal quality. Finding common ground and keeping peace among the members are so important to the group that it tends to turn away from issues that might be controversial or cause dissension. Members are more likely to leave a meeting with their opinions confirmed rather than challenged, and, although this generates good feelings, it also prevents the group from moving to a deeper level in their relations with one another.

The lack of intimacy that marks group meetings contrasts sharply with the atmosphere that exists after the meetings end. The comfortable, softly-lit living room in which the meetings take place comes alive once the group adjourns and people linger to talk with each other and sample the refreshments the host provides. The warmth that members feel for one another is evident as they talk about sick parents, demanding jobs, grandchildren, and their own health and well-being. It is apparent at these gatherings that as important as the issues discussed are to the group, they are not the only reason for its members' devotion to it. The religious faith and political perspective that group members share create a strong personal bond that becomes more evident as they relax with one another and share individual concerns.

Most members are pleased with the way the group works together to keep separate the business and the social portions of the meetings. By working through the evening's agenda quickly, efficiently, and with few digressions, the group is often able to complete its business in just one hour. Members have come to expect this kind of focused efficiency, pointing to it as one of the features that keeps them faithful to the group even when their busy schedules provide them with justification to stay away.

The group's efficiency has its drawbacks, however. Often its habit of working quickly through the agenda affects the way the group approaches the prayer service, turning what should be an essential part of the group's time together into an item of business that is swiftly concluded. This concerns some people who feel that the group could do a better job of nurturing the spiritual lives of its members. Most members, it is true, are satisfied with the amount of time the group devotes to prayer. They say that the mere act of attending a St. Francis meeting gives them a spiritual boost, and they see no need to tamper with the group's routine. Others, however, think that the group needs to give greater emphasis to the religious beliefs that have shaped the group's political perspective. They feel that the prayer service too often fails to inspire or to challenge members, and they express a longing for more creative, and more daring, forms of spiritual expression.

The debate over the spiritual life of the group suggests one of the potential weaknesses of St. Francis Pax Christi. The group presents itself as a spiritual alternative to secular peace and justice groups, but it is in danger of allowing the political part of its mission to overtake the spiritual. This would be unfortunate, since most members agree that it was Pax Christi's reputation for uniting the spiritual and the political that initially attracted them to the group.

A Commitment to Peace

The experience of forty-nine-year-old Alice Brennan, one of the founders of the St. Francis group, illustrates how important the spiritual dimension of its work was to the group in its early years. Like so many of her fellow activists, Alice's commitment to nuclear disarmament grew out of her experience as a parent. "I was really very frightened by the arms race," she recalls. "I have four children, and I just did not know what their future would be [with the world] in such a volatile situation." Alice's concern about the proliferation of nuclear weapons first led her to involvement with the Coalition for Nuclear Disarmament, but she found that most coalition members were not interested in exploring with her the spiritual issues raised by the arms race. Since she was a lifelong Roman Catholic, it was natural for Alice to turn to Pax Christi to add this spiritual dimension to her work. Through Pax Christi, she was able to meet other Catholics who shared her concerns and who saw a concrete relationship between the work of the disarmament movement and Catholic social teachings. Soon after Alice joined St. Francis Pax Christi, the U.S. Conference of Catholic Bishops issued its pastoral letter on the nuclear threat. The Bishops' statement deepened Alice's commitment to Pax Christi and reinforced her belief that disarmament was a spiritual issue.[4]

Alice found, however, that she valued Pax Christi for more than just its peace witness. St. Francis Pax Christi connected her to a group

---

4. The Bishops' pastoral letter entitled *The Challenge of Peace: God's Promise and Our Response* was issued in 1983 to mixed reviews. Liberal Catholics hailed it for highlighting the moral implications of nuclear warfare, while conservatives were dismayed to see the Catholic hierarchy injecting itself into a foreign policy debate.

of people who felt, as she did, that the small-group experience deepened and invigorated their faith. The support that Alice received from the group in its early years was particularly valuable because she did not feel at home in her parish community. Although she had served her church as a Sunday School teacher and a parish board member, she was unhappy with the conservative pastoral leadership. Convinced that she did not need to suffer silently in an environment she found intolerable, Alice and a few friends began to hold their own worship service away from the parish. This group was dispersing as Alice's involvement in Pax Christi was increasing, and she found that the new group filled the void left by the old.

Alice entered the Pax Christi movement as a strong and independent lay leader, but her involvement in the St. Francis chapter provided a new and welcome outlet for her talents at a time when she was feeling limited by the ministries open to her in the parish. Since the 1970s, American Catholic parishes have expanded the role of the laity and provided people like Alice with new opportunities to serve the church. Still, religious associations like Pax Christi, which exist outside the parish structure, continue to empower laypeople in a way that the local church typically does not.[5]

Catholic Lay Movements

The strength and independence of Catholic groups like St. Francis Pax Christi are most often interpreted as a legacy of the Second Vatican

---

5. One of the most visible signs of the growth in lay ministries has been the use of eucharistic ministers in the Catholic mass. Eucharistic ministers are men and women who are trained and authorized to distribute the sacrament of the Eucharist to parishioners. They do not have the authority to consecrate the communion host, relying instead on a priest for this sacramental function.

The expanding role of the laity in the local parish during the 1970s and 1980s has often been interpreted as a measure of the success of Vatican II. It is true that the Council redefined the church as "the people of God" and loosened restrictions that had limited the power of the laity, thus opening the way for increased lay involvement, but it alone does not account for the changing face of the American Catholic parish. The significant drop in the number of women and men entering religious orders over the last twenty-five years has made it essential for parishes to involve more lay people in their ministry, and, as a consequence, even conservative parish priests have been forced to accept the new role of the laity.

Council. In truth, Vatican II's spirit of openness and renewal and its statement of a new ecclesiology did affect the church, but the impact of the Council on the lives of individual Catholics is easily overstated. It is quite possible, in fact, that the *aggiornamento* of Vatican II would not have taken root as firmly as it did in the United States if a tradition of lay leadership had not already been in place there.

Lay religious associations have long been a part of the American Catholic experience (MacEoin 1992). In the nineteenth century, American Catholic men formed fraternal associations modeled after the Protestant groups from which they were barred, while Catholic women joined devotional societies.[6] These groups, however, were actively encouraged and supported by the parish clergy. One of the earliest and certainly the most well known of the groups founded by and for the Catholic laity was Dorothy Day's Catholic Worker movement.[7] During the first two decades of the movement's existence, Day focused on serving the poor, but she was also a committed pacifist. When relations between East and West grew more frigid in the 1950s, Day began to devote more time to peace activism. As one of the most prominent lay Catholics of the twentieth century, Day exerted a tremendous amount of influence on successive generations of Catholics. Both Day and the Trappist monk Thomas Merton, whose popularity equaled or perhaps even surpassed hers, promoted an antimaterialist, self-denying form of spirituality that by the 1970s had become a common feature of liberal Catholicism. Together, Day and Merton affected the lives and, to some extent, shaped the thought of the two laypeople who founded Pax Christi USA, Eileen Egan and Gordon Zahn, in addition to inspiring many others to lives of Catholic activism.

6. The Knights of Columbus (for men) and the Altar and Rosary Society (for women) are the two groups most commonly found in American Catholic parishes.

7. Day, a former socialist and convert to Catholicism, had a radical vision of social justice and Christian responsibility. Born during the Great Depression, the Catholic Worker was both a lay apostolate, predicated on the conviction that union with Christ could be achieved only by suffering as he did, and a social service organization, dedicated to providing food and shelter to the poor. Day did not allow the Catholic Worker to become a charitable organization, dispersing its largess to the poor but always remaining apart from and above them. Suffering and self-abnegation were the core of her theology, and she hoped to demonstrate, through the Catholic Worker, that living in solidarity with the poor was the way of Christ.

For information on Dorothy Day and the Catholic Worker movement, see Piehl (1982) and Fisher (1989).

The members of the St. Francis Pax Christi group are somewhat more moderate in their social vision than were Day and Merton. The group is less concerned with advocating a specific lifestyle, such as discouraging materialism or supporting communal living, than with involving people in the global concerns that are its main focus. Members do share a sympathy for Latin American liberation theology, which itself echoes Day's emphasis on solidarity with the poor, but they are not ascetics. In its embrace of the lifestyle of the American middle class, the group suggests one way in which liberal Catholicism has accommodated itself to the culture of the 1980s and 1990s. The views of these Catholics may resemble those of the counterculture of the past, but their professions, homes, and habits of dress and recreation do little to distinguish them from other Americans of their social class.

Dissent from Church Teachings

While the St. Francis group members may be less radical than Dorothy Day in the lifestyle choices they have made, they are considerably more radical than she was in their insistence upon the right to dissent from church teachings. Day's social vision and theology made many Catholics uncomfortable, but she always remained obedient to the church hierarchy. This is not true of the St. Francis group. Its members are committed to remaining in the church, but they are not reluctant to express their disagreement with it. When a parish priest in their region organized a ceremony to welcome home troops who had served in the Persian Gulf War, the group sent a letter to him expressing their regret that he was offering implicit support for military actions they viewed as sinful. Some members of the group expressed uncertainty over the appropriateness of the letter, but only because they wondered if this isolated incident warranted protest. The members were not at all disturbed by the fact that they were criticizing the actions of a priest. In fact, it is not unusual for them to protest openly and directly the actions of their local bishop and parish priests. Several members of the St. Francis group also are involved on the national level with a Catholic advocacy organization known for its outspoken and controversial criticism of the church leadership. Ever firm in their convictions, they refuse to be silenced by the hierarchy's obvious displeasure with them.

The national Pax Christi organization has a much closer affiliation with the institutional church, but it too supports the right to faithful dissent. The national group was founded by laypeople and continues to maintain a high level of lay participation, but it also has sought the legitimacy and security that an episcopal connection provides. With a bishop as president, and a number of priests and women religious involved at the highest levels of Pax Christi, it is difficult for the national organization to remain completely independent of the church's authority structure. Still, it has publicly disagreed with church leaders, and it continues to view its role as a prophetic one despite its close ties to the institutional church.[8]

St. Francis Pax Christi has never sought ordained pastoral leadership or a parish affiliation. The professional clergy who participate in the group do so on an equal basis with other members. The group has no evangelical mission, and so does not actively work to convert people to the Catholic faith or to encourage membership in a particular parish. Official membership in Pax Christi USA requires payment of twenty dollars in annual dues, but the St. Francis chapter does nothing to encourage formal ties to the national organization. The group's open membership policy has never been tested, however, since only committed Catholics have been interested in participating, and most of these people have a prior history of affiliation with the national organization.[9]

Group Autonomy

Members of the St. Francis chapter clearly feel that the group is theirs to mold to their own needs. They maintain ties to the Pax Christi national

8. When the U.S. Bishops' Conference condoned the strategy of nuclear deterrence in 1988, Pax Christi USA responded with a statement of regret that the bishops "did not call nuclear deterrence by its true name — a sin situation, an evil from which we must extricate ourselves." "We are committed," the statement continued, "to initiating dialogue among ourselves, our bishops and our fellow Catholics in order to build a consensus on the immorality of nuclear deterrence" (Vanderhaar and McNeal 1992, 22).

9. Membership in the national organization does not necessarily indicate affiliation with a local chapter. Many people join Pax Christi because they value the group's publications and support its mission, but never become involved on the local level. Others participate in local chapters but don't take the additional step of becoming official members of the national group.

office and to other chapters in their region, but they chart their own course. Perhaps because individual members have so much responsibility for and control over the group, the level of commitment to it is quite high. Both Regina and Alice have stayed with the group even when personal crises and changing political realities presented them with legitimate reasons to limit their attendance. Just as they have refused to leave the Catholic Church despite their disagreements with it, they are committed to staying with St. Francis Pax Christi even if they do not always agree with the choices the group makes.

When asked, Regina, Alice, and other members of St. Francis Pax Christi agree that Vatican II had an effect on their lives as Catholics, but the Council is not an event that they refer to without prompting. Like so many Catholics who came of age before Vatican II, they acknowledge that the Council has affected them in somewhat contradictory ways. They credit Vatican II's liberalization of some rules and its call for the greater inclusion of laypeople in the ministry of the church with making them more hopeful and more committed to their faith, but they admit that it also changed the nature of their relationship to the church. They could no longer act as obedient children, pledging blind allegiance to the church fathers. The Council enabled them to mature as Catholics, and with maturity came a new willingness to evaluate more critically the teachings and practices of the church.[10]

Even so, it is quite possible that the experience of American Catholics would not have changed as significantly as it did if the drama of the Council had not been followed by the social tumult of the late 1960s, and by the promulgation in 1968 of the papal encyclical *Humanae Vitae*. The encyclical's condemnation of artificial birth control shocked American

---

10. The changes initiated by the Council were a shock to many Catholics who had believed that the teachings of the church were divinely inspired and not subject to human revision. Both the easing of the prohibition against eating meat on Friday and the introduction of the vernacular mass struck more deeply at the heart of Catholic culture than the Council fathers had foreseen. Lay Catholics, who were the intended beneficiaries of these changes, reacted as much with confusion and doubt as with gratitude. Many Catholics began to call into question the authority of a church that could so swiftly and so radically transform itself.

Mary Douglas explores the symbolic meaning of the Friday abstinence rule and the implications of its revocation in "The Bog Irish," in *Natural Symbols* (1982). New York *Times* columnist Anna Quindlen discusses the cultural consequences of Vatican II in an interview with Alexander Santora (Santora 1992).

Catholics, a vast number of whom had fully expected Pope Paul VI, in keeping with the spirit of Vatican II, to relax traditional teachings on this issue. The high hopes that Catholics had for the encyclical made their disappointment in the final version all the more serious, and caused many members to become even further alienated from the church (Seidler and Meyer 1989). The sense of alienation that *Humanae Vitae* generated among Catholics was intensified by the social currents dividing the nation at large. *Humanae Vitae* was issued at a time when protest against the Vietnam War was escalating, and a general challenge to established authority was becoming the hallmark of the American counterculture. Interviews with members of St. Francis Pax Christi indicate that this protest culture of the late 1960s, more than any other single factor, was responsible for the flowering of liberal Catholicism that Pax Christi represents.

Seeds of Catholic Activism

Most of the older members of the group agree that the foundation for the political and social activism that has been so much a part of their lives since the 1960s was laid for them early in life by their families. Both Regina and Patricia Gaughan, her seventy-two-year-old friend, credit their mothers with planting in them the seeds for a life of social activism. Regina recalls that, during the 1930s, her mother ran a soup kitchen on the family's back porch and cared for the impoverished black families in the neighborhood. Regina recognizes that the world she grew up in was a segregated one, and knows that her mother did not fully appreciate the injustice of segregation, but she still is able to value the work and witness of her mother for what it taught her about Christian responsibility.

Regina's mother was a devout Catholic, but one who did not allow her devotional obligations to distract her from the practical work she had to do. By contrast, Regina's grandmother was inflexible in her insistence that family members join her in kneeling for the evening rosary recitation. Regina respected her grandmother's unwavering devotion to church tradition, but she was much more comfortable with her mother's brand of religiosity, crediting it with nurturing both her faith and her social conscience. Throughout her adult life, Regina has consistently sought ways to integrate faith and social responsibility, and she believes, as her mother did, that her work on behalf of her community has been as much an act of devotion as her grandmother's recitation of the rosary was.

Patricia's parents were raised in Tennessee, and she remembers how the experience of being a Catholic in the South continued to haunt her mother even after she had resettled in Delaware. In her youth, Patricia's mother had felt the sting of the Ku Klux Klan's anti-Catholicism, and she had witnessed its torment of blacks and Jews. She made sure that her children understood how much the Klan's "absolutely mad hate and bias" had affected her, and how important it was to fight injustice and prejudice. Patricia's mother also taught her importance of other forms of community involvement and helped her to understand the connection between faith and social responsibility. Those early lessons have continued to shape the way Patricia lives out the precepts of her faith.

Eleanor Griffin's experience of growing up in the 1920s and 1930s was similar to that of her friends Regina and Patricia. Eleanor remembers her mother fondly, but it is her mother's irreverence, not her good works, that influenced Eleanor most. Her family was "very Catholic" and counted the parish priests among their close friends, but Eleanor's mother maintained a healthy skepticism regarding the church and its clergy. Eleanor inherited her mother's skepticism. Declaring that she "never has listened to a sermon in her life," Eleanor describes her religious journey as largely an intellectual one. She does not credit priests with nurturing her faith and shaping her theological beliefs, but instead points to years of self-study and public debate as the source of her religious understanding. A lifelong Catholic, Eleanor insists that she disagrees "with practically anything the church says." At the age of seventy-three, she is an energetic and forceful witness to Catholic intellectualism at its most vigorous and its most stubborn. "I don't leave things" is her firm response to questions about her decision to remain in the church.

Eleanor is not alone among St. Francis group members in expressing this sentiment. These Catholics know that their liberal beliefs make them a minority in their church, their community, and even their nation, but it does not disturb them. Like Eleanor, they cope with their minority status in part by seeking the company of like-minded Catholics at Pax Christi meetings.

Coming of Age as Catholics

Regina, Patricia, and Eleanor all had their first experience with being treated differently as members of a religious minority when they were

68

in college. The women attended Catholic schools throughout their child-hood and adolescence, but, unlike the vast majority of Catholic women of their time, they did not attend Catholic colleges. All three women had parents who appreciated the value of higher education for women and had the financial means to send their daughters to leading univer-sities. Eleanor was sent to Radcliffe, Patricia to Vassar, and Regina to Johns Hopkins, and each woman remembers the problems that came with being the rare Catholic in a decidedly Protestant environment. Ultimately, however, the experience had a positive effect on the women. They emerged from college with both a strong commitment to the Catholic Church and the analytical skills they needed to understand and evaluate their faith more objectively. At their respective institutions, the women were exposed to ideas and modes of thought that would not have been accessible to them in the insular world of Catholic higher education before World War II.

World War II was the defining experience of each woman's young adulthood, the event that forced her to confront the uncertainty and harshness of life. By the war's end, Patricia had lost three family members and several friends. She became a pacifist, and remains one today. The war left both Regina and Eleanor with deeply ambivalent feelings about military conflict, but they did not define themselves as pacifists until the Vietnam years.

Regina, Patricia, and Eleanor spent the two decades between the end of World War II and the escalation of American involvement in Southeast Asia occupied with family concerns. They all married, and their husbands all chose academic careers that placed the women in intellectual communities similar to the ones they had known as college students. As they supported their husbands' careers and raised children, the women found that their time for activism and group involvements was limited.

Regina and Patricia met during this period, and both became part of a Catholic women's group that met to discuss books and hear guest speakers. Dorothy Day once spoke to the group, as did Frank Sheed, a well-known Catholic writer and publisher. Patricia remembers that the friendship and community the group offered were more important to her than any other aspects of its meetings, and Regina agrees. In those years Regina was a regular reader of the *Catholic Worker* and the writings of Thomas Merton, but both she and Patricia agree that they were not the crusaders then that they have become in later life.

69

Eleanor did not know Patricia and Regina during this period, and her description of these years is quite different from theirs. What she remembers is not a small faith community but evenings of debate with Catholic scholars. Her husband's career brought people like Étienne Gilson and Jacques Maritain into her social orbit, and Eleanor made the most of her time with them. She enjoyed intellectual debate, and she became a skilled critic of the church. Eleanor was involved with the Catholic Worker house in her community during the 1950s and early 1960s, but the Vietnam War was the first political cause to gain her full attention.

The war spurred all three women to greater activism. They joined public demonstrations against U.S. policies, helped young people to struggle with the issues raised by the war, and supported antiwar political candidates. World War II had been the defining episode of their young adulthood, but the Vietnam War had an even more powerful impact on the women: it marked the beginning of the activist phase of their lives.

Children of the Cold War

Eleanor, Patricia, and Regina were able to become involved in the antiwar movement to a degree that some of their younger Catholic friends could not. At this juncture their children were grown and their husbands' careers secure, so they had the time and the freedom to direct their energies toward protest activities. For the generation that grew to maturity in the darkening shadow of the Cold War, however, the demands of family and career left little time for political protest during the Vietnam years. While women like Regina, Patricia, and Eleanor were reading the *Catholic Worker,* working among the poor, and demonstrating against the Vietnam War, young Catholic wives and mothers were busy with the day-to-day tasks of raising children and running a household. Eileen Reilly was a recent college graduate when she married in 1962. As campuses erupted in protest in 1968, she was at home caring for her two sons, an infant and a preschooler. Her husband, Frank, was busy in those years working to support the family by day and attending school at night. They didn't have time to attend peace marches, even if they had been inclined to do so.

Even though the Reillys' involvement in church and social causes was limited in their young adulthood, they were not untouched by the social climate around them. During the early years of their marriage, Frank was stationed with the Air Force in the South, and it was there that he and Eileen first confronted the full intensity of the civil rights struggle. Living amid racial segregation awakened Eileen's social conscience as no other issue had done before. She and Frank became "so converted by the whole civil rights struggle" that they insisted upon defying convention when they left the South to return to New York City. In the South they had come to appreciate the importance of interracial understanding, so when it was time for their older son to begin school, they chose to send him to an integrated public school rather than their all-white parish school. Their choice was not popular among their Irish-Catholic neighbors, and the Reillys had a difficult time finding their place in the parish community.

As a newlywed, Eileen had read articles about Vatican II in *Time* magazine, but it was some time before the Council had any measurable impact on her life. The adult education and community outreach ministries that she and Frank became involved with at their Bronx church were Vatican II innovations, but in general the parish clung to its old traditions. The Reillys' relationship to the church reflects the "people of God" ecclesiology of Vatican II, but their growth as Catholics is due less to the Council's populist message than it is to their own belief, born of years of personal experience with social upheaval, that respect for authority and tradition is not a value unto itself.

The Reillys, who now are in their early fifties, both were raised in traditional Catholic homes and attended parishes and Catholic schools that reinforced in them the traditional values of the immigrant church. Their current blend of independence from and devotion to the church would have seemed indefensible to them in their youth, when they believed devotion to the church meant obedience to its teachings. The Reillys' first show of independence was their decision to send their son to public school. They made an even bolder move years later when they joined Alice Brennan's small worshipping community. Like Alice, they were disenchanted with the parish leadership, and had come to believe that they had a right to find a worship experience that met their spiritual needs. When the Reillys joined St. Francis Pax Christi several years after Alice Brennan did, they were prompted less by the concern for disarmament that influenced her than by their desire for association with other liberal Catholics.

Searching for Community

Thomas Daley joined St. Francis Pax Christi soon after the Reillys, and for similar reasons. At seventy-two, Thomas is of the generation of Patricia, Regina, and Eleanor, and he, like them, has devoted an increasing amount of his time to activism as he has grown older. About ten years ago, he began to think about what he would do with his time once he retired from his job with the state government. He decided to train as a paralegal, and he has used his new skill to help other retired people with their legal problems. Today, he devotes a majority of his time to advocacy on behalf of the senior citizens in his state. Despite a long history of involvement in political and civic affairs and a lifelong affiliation with the Catholic Church, Thomas is a relative newcomer to the world of Catholic social activism. In fact, it was not until he joined St. Francis Pax Christi that he began to make explicit connections between his religious beliefs and his social commitments.

Thomas was raised in a strict, Irish-Catholic, working-class family in the Chelsea section of New York City. At home and at school, Thomas had "the fear of God and the fear of parents imbued" in him. Those fears were "a controlling factor" throughout his early life. He accepted all Catholic teachings without hesitation, but his devotion to the church was not heartfelt. Crediting Vatican II with allowing him to grow up as a Catholic, Thomas remembers that he began to think, "Who was the teacher, and who established the rules and regulations?" The impact of this realization on the practice of his faith was not immediate, however, and it was not until he joined St. Francis Pax Christi three years ago that Thomas had an affiliation with any Catholic organization outside of his parish. Today, he describes his relationship with God as very personal, and he no longer is certain that there is or needs to be an intermediary, such as a priest, between them. Involvement with the Pax Christi movement has awakened him to the problems facing the church today. He finds that he is more frustrated with the church than he was before he joined the group, but, like the others, Thomas will remain a Catholic.

With his political involvements, advocacy work, and family responsibilities, Thomas's life was already full when he joined St. Francis Pax Christi. Nevertheless, he went to his first meeting at the urging of friends who were involved in the national Pax Christi organization, and he was so impressed by the group that he added its meetings to his already busy schedule. The discussion at that first meeting focused on issues of concern to Thomas, but it was the group members, not the issues they debated, that affected him most. He had never realized that there were people in the church who so completely shared his interests and political perspective. In the three years that he has been a member of the group, Thomas has grown in unexpected ways. The prayer services at the monthly meetings have exposed him to a more personalized, expressive spirituality that is quite distinct from the rote prayers and reflexive rituals on which he was raised, and his prayer life has been enriched as a result. Perhaps more important, the group has helped him to establish a religious context for his political activism.

Activism and the Religious Life

St. Francis Pax Christi has had a much less dramatic impact on the spiritual lives of Sister Virginia Reese and Father Daniel McMahon. As members of religious orders, they do not have to go any farther than their own homes to find a Christian community, and as authorities on spiritual direction, they have devoted years to deepening and expanding the scope of their spiritual lives. Still, the St. Francis group offers them a community experience they don't find elsewhere in their lives: it offers them fellowship with laypeople who welcome them as friends, not as professional ministers.

Both Virginia and Daniel have more in common with the other members of St. Francis Pax Christi than their vocations might suggest. At fifty-two, Virginia is of the same generation as Eileen and Frank Reilly and Alice Brennan, but her life more closely parallels those of the older women in the group. Like them, she credits her mother with being an early and decisive religious influence. From her mother, Virginia learned how to make distinctions on issues of faith. "She taught me to see the difference between what was nonsense and what was essential," Virginia recalls. Her mother died when Virginia was thirteen, and the loss devastated her. Deprived of her mother's steadying influence, Virginia passed through adolescence feeling empty and unsure of herself. What peace she did find, she found in the church and, eventually, through a religious vocation. She entered the novitiate at the age of twenty.

Virginia is very direct when asked about her decision to join a religious order. "I wanted to be Thomas Mertina," she says with a laugh, referring to her desire to emulate the contemplative life of Thomas Merton. Virginia declared her vocation at a time when the church clearly elevated it as a higher calling, suggesting that the path to holiness was found only in the religious life. Virginia accepted the church's equation of holiness with a religious vocation, and strove to be a dedicated and devout nun. She does not regret becoming a nun, but she admits now that she had a very immature understanding of faith and the religious life.

Virginia's religious order changed dramatically in the years after Vatican II. The Council relaxed restrictions on the public ministries of women religious, opening up new opportunities for them. Again, however, it is important to emphasize that Vatican II is not solely responsible for the new directions in the lives of women religious. Virginia began her work in the inner city and as a prison chaplain at a time when the struggles of urban America were receiving unprecedented attention. Vatican II freed nuns like Virginia to engage in social justice ministries, but they probably would not have used their new freedom as they did if resolving the problems of the inner city had not been part of a broader national agenda for political and social issues.

Virginia joined Pax Christi after years of full-time social justice ministry. Although she continues to work part-time as a prison chaplain, she now spends the majority of her time leading retreats and giving individual spiritual direction. Because her career no longer directly engages her in work for peace and justice, she finds that involvement with Pax Christi helps to keep her focused on these issues.

Sixty-two-year-old Father Daniel McMahon values the St. Francis group for the same reasons Sister Virginia does. He too has spent his adult life as a member of a religious order, and so, like Virginia, he has less of a need for the spiritual community offered by St. Francis than the lay members of the group do. Daniel does find, however, that as his ministry has focused more on spiritual direction and less on direct social justice ministry, his appreciation of the St. Francis group has grown. Attending group meetings helps him to maintain an awareness of the centrality of the peace witness to the Christian message.

Daniel was a young boy when World War II erupted, and he sees its significance for his life more in retrospect than he did at the time. It was his experience as a missionary in Asia that most affected him. He served overseas in the 1960s, at a time when many of the countries he worked in were fighting to rid themselves of the final vestiges of colonialism, and his consciousness was stirred by the poverty and human rights

74

abuses he encountered there. During this period he also discovered the writings of Gandhi, and because of them he committed himself to a life of nonviolence.

When Daniel returned to the United States in 1970, he immediately became involved in the civil rights movement. Since then, peace and social justice causes have always been a part of his life, but they have become less central to his formal ministry. He is a popular retreat leader and guest preacher, but he spends the majority of his time working as a counselor and a spiritual director. Both he and Virginia are open about their differences with more conservative church leaders, but they do not allow their points of disagreement to alienate them from the church they continue to serve.

Conclusion

Virginia and Daniel differ from the rest of the active St. Francis members on a point that has little to do with their religious vocations. Both are anxious to maximize the time they devote to each of the many activities in their lives, and are easily frustrated by group discussions that lack a clear direction and meetings that do not set aside a time for direct action on issues. In their preference for action over discussion, they have more in common with past members of the group than they do with the current membership. Still, their commitment to the group remains firm.

That Virginia and Daniel continue to attend St. Francis meetings indicates that despite their frustration with the group, it still fills a need in their lives. Indeed, the need that Daniel and Virginia have for St. Francis Pax Christi is shared by the rest of the members and accounts for the strong bond that exists among this disparate group. Members come from different backgrounds and are at different life stages, but they still are able to find a great deal of common ground. Although some would argue that non-Catholics are welcome to join the group, it is clear that it is the shared experience of being liberal Catholics that binds the members together. St. Francis Pax Christi serves as a haven for the area's liberal Catholics, a retreat to which members turn to keep from becoming too embittered by the conservatism of the contemporary church. All share the same disappointment with the church and perceive the same need for groups like Pax Christi to pose a prophetic challenge to both the hierarchy and the Catholic faithful.

75

All also share the same loneliness, for it is lonely to stand on the margins of a community you love. Joining together as a community, members of St. Francis Pax Christi give each other the hope they need to continue their crusade in a church that does not seem to hear their voices. They stand as a collective witness to the church and to each other, demonstrating through their lives that the causes of peace and social justice will continue to be championed even if theirs is a lone cry in the wilderness.

Accountability and Fellowship in an Assemblies of God Cell Group

MATTHEW P. LAWSON

In the crystalline twilight of an autumn evening, I turn off a county road northeast of Philadelphia and into a suburban subdivision. The houses are finished in a variety of styles, but share a basic structure: three bedrooms and living space sit above a two-car garage, utility rooms, and a large family room. Near the end of the long, curving street is the Wilsons' house, and I park in front of it, behind three other cars. I cue up a blank tape and record the date and subject before tucking my tape recorder next to the Bible and note cards in my satchel. It is Sunday, October 13, 1991, at 6:27 p.m. This is my second meeting with the Wattstown-Belleview Home Fellowship Group, a local cell group of the Hamden Assembly of God Church, twenty miles away.

In this essay I will attempt to give the reader an account of the life of this small group and how the group contributes to the spiritual development of its members. I have organized my narrative around the events of a typical meeting, though I have fictionalized it to the extent that the personal events and crises of members that I include were not necessarily discussed on October thirteenth, but may have come up at any time in the group's annual cycle from October through June. I fill in details and context for these events not only from members' stories in meetings during this period, but also from private interviews with them that lasted three hours or more. Toward the end of the essay I discuss the pastor's perspective on how the group is supposed to foster

77

spiritual development, as well as historical and contextual factors that qualify its success. Throughout the essay I have fictionalized names and inconsequential personal characteristics to comply with assurances of confidentiality.

An Evening with My Group

Assembly

When I rang the doorbell, I was invited in by Marilyn Wilson, the group's soft-spoken, middle-aged hostess, who wore slacks and a plain blouse. As I came up the short flight of steps into the living room, I saw that several members of the group were seated, waiting for the meeting to begin. They greeted me warmly while I tried to remember their names and find a seat. Together the Wilsons' living room and dining room make a space of about twelve by thirty feet. In the living room a beige couch and two light-blue easy chairs are arranged on either side of a large picture window. The coffee table is polished brass and glass, and over the couch hangs a nail-and-string rendering of a sailing ship. When we had meetings, the chrome-and-glass dining room table was pushed to one side, and the dining room chairs were turned toward the living room to complete a circle of seats. I chose a seat a little off to the side, between the dining table and the couch, and retrieved the Bible, tape recorder, and note cards from my bag. I set up the recorder under my chair and turned it on. Several conversations, which had stopped when I first came in, had resumed. I listened to Ken Joraski, sitting on the couch to my right.

Ken, a "new Christian" and the youngest member of the group, is a gangly twenty-one-year-old with a shock of thick black hair. He talked about a world civilization course he was taking at the local community college while he bided his time before going to Wheaton College or Bob Jones University. He told of recently challenging his teacher's interpretation of Roman society, which he corrected based on his reading of the Bible. He said that after his comments, "the whole class turned against her."

Paul Christianson, a veteran high-school teacher, commented wryly, "Teachers love it when students turn on them."

"But she was really sweet about it," Ken responded. "She was really sweet. Now when I raise my hand she just says, 'You're right, you're right.'"

In my interview with Ken, he said that this group had been crucial to his spiritual development because he had been able to learn from "mature Christians" like the Christiansons and the Wilsons. Bob Wilson especially had been "like a father" to him, providing a model of patience, kindness, and understanding, which contrasted sharply with his own father's argumentative and authoritative manner. As the episode with the teacher indicated, Ken tended to be like his father, but he said that the group provided him with practical examples of how to be more loving and accepting, how to reach out to people rather than confront them. Paul Christianson's response — encouraging Ken to see the situation from the other's perspective — is one such example.

As conversation continued, I took attendance. The group's hosts, Bob and Marilyn Wilson, were there, of course, as well as their daughter Sylvia, a recent college graduate. Sylvia was talking to Jenny Wong, an Asian-American of her age. Paul and Carla Christianson, longtime friends of the Wilsons and, like them, former liberal Catholics, were sitting on the couch with Ken, also a former Catholic. David Cohen, an ex-Jew from Brooklyn, was there with his wife, Margarita, a Colombian immigrant who was an ex-Catholic. In terms of numbers, this was an average meeting (another couple came late, which made twelve, including me). The most people we ever had at a meeting was sixteen. At first I was struck by the high proportion of ex-Catholics in the group, but if conservative Protestant groups have been growing at the expense of other denominations, then they are likely to draw from the denominations prevalent in a particular area (Poloma 1989, 147; Ammerman 1987, 30). In the suburban northeast, that means Catholics.

During a lull in the conversation, Marilyn asked Carla Christianson how she had been. Carla responded emotionally: earlier in the week, Paul had been in an accident that had nearly totaled their van. This got the attention of the whole group, so Carla and Paul elaborated. In the accident, no one was hurt — "praise God." Since it was the other driver's fault, Carla and Paul would get some insurance money, but since the van had 225,000 miles on it, it might not be worth fixing. Perhaps, they said, this was a sign from the Lord that the van had seen its last days. They were now praying to see what the Lord wanted them to do. This practice, based on their belief that the Lord was involved in this rather minor decision, went beyond the relatively common conservative Protestant practice of praying for divine guidance in major life decisions (cf. Ammerman 1987, 57-58), and reflected their spiritual journey. A decade earlier, after leaving first the Catholic Church and then the Plymouth Brethren, the Christiansons had started their own house church—"I guess you could call it a home fellowship," Carla had said. They had bought the van and dedicated it to the Lord to use as he saw fit, and he had used it—as a church bus, as a moving van for other Christians, and as part of a "life train" (an interdenominational pro-life motorcade) only a few weeks before.

After the group had assessed details of the accident and offered condolences, Bob suggested that "maybe we should get started," and wondered about the whereabouts of John and Theresa Gaffney, the assistant group leaders who usually led the group's singing.

Worship

Bob Wilson had worn a suit to church that morning but was now dressed in slacks and a light sweater. His hair, graying at the temples, was neatly combed; his eyes were framed by permanent smile wrinkles. Leaning forward in his chair and bowing his head, Bob began the "worship" phase of the meeting with this prayer:

> Lord, again, we thank you for this day. We thank you for all that you provide to us, especially on this beautiful day, and we just ask now that you bless this meeting tonight and just open our hearts to understand the Word and share from the sermon that we heard today and share from the readings that we'll do tonight. Just continue to bless all those here. Bless all those who are not with us and just send the Holy Spirit into our group. We ask this in Jesus' name. Amen.

Bob's invocations usually followed this pattern, the style of which, he admitted, was a little formal, like the typed agenda he followed for each meeting. Bob was somewhat apologetic in our interview, saying that he was probably not the best leader for the group because two decades as a corporate executive had made him more businesslike than sensitive to the Spirit.

Bob was similarly businesslike when John Gaffney was not there to lead worship. On these nights he passed out photocopied song sheets which, he explained, he had used during the years he was involved in a nondenominational prison ministry. Later he told me that he had un-

80

dertaken this ministry after following Marilyn when she left the Catholic Church and went to a Bible-teaching Baptist church. He had continued the practice when they had moved on to another congregation in the area and then to the Hamden Assembly of God Church. In 1984, after Bob and Marilyn had been attending there for two years, the pastor asked them to lead their area's home fellowship group. When a new pastor was hired in 1986, he asked Bob to be on his board of stewards and Marilyn to help lead the women's ministry.

When we stood up to sing, we were visible to the now-dark neighborhood through the picture window of the living room. We limped through a few short choruses, interspersed with soft praises to God and perhaps a little glossolalia, though this was never easy to discern. As Bob had noted at the first meeting the week before, "We're Pentecostal, but we're not the emotional kind." Everybody was pleased when the Gaffneys came to the door, and people resumed their pre-worship talking and joking until the couple got settled.

The Gaffneys said they were tardy because their dinner with a member of the church singles' group had turned into a crisis control session. Later they would offer a prayer request for this person. In addition to helping lead the singles' group, John Gaffney, a former Presbyterian, sat on the board of deacons, helped lead worship at Sunday church services, and kept the church sound system working properly, contributing his professional expertise as an electrical engineer. Theresa Gaffney, a former Catholic, was just as busy at church: she ran the nursery, handled the overhead projector during worship services (showing song lyrics on transparencies), and contributed her professional expertise as a computer consultant by doing any troubleshooting needed for the church's computers. For home fellowship meetings, both of them dressed casually, often in jeans.

With the arrival of the Gaffneys, who took over for John, our singing became more confident. Some people even broke into harmony, and since we no longer needed the song sheets, we could clap. Between songs, the words of praise were also more enthusiastic. After we had sung a few more songs, Marilyn Wilson closed the worship segment with a quiet prayer:

> Thank you, Lord. Thank you, Jesus. Father, we just praise you and worship you. We just thank you, Lord, that we can gather together and just praise and worship you, Lord, and that we can look into your

Word and that you will just speak to us tonight, Lord, we thank you for that. We anticipate, Lord, the Word you have for us tonight. Thank you, Jesus.

Bob Wilson followed this with an "Amen" and "Thanks, John" (to John Gaffney) and sat down.

Praise Reports

Bob began the next segment by asking, "So, how's everybody doing? All these travelers coming home. We're going to have praise testimonies, if anybody would like to share anything." Marilyn clarified Bob's opening lines: "So, you know, [you can offer] basically any praise for anything the Lord has done this past week or any answers to prayer which you've had recently. How about you, Ken? Have you heard anything from those schools you applied to?"

Ken had been accepted at Wheaton, having applied in the spring, and was hoping to start there in January, but he was waiting to hear about financial aid. "Nope," he replied, "I haven't heard anything." The background to this exchange is a bit complicated. Ken had told me that he had dropped out of a state college because of the lax morality of the other students. When he had worked at a record store, he had discovered Christian rock, which led him to attend a concert at the Hamden Assembly of God Church. There he found fellow believers in strict morality who could back up their doctrine with Scripture, something he had not found in the Catholic church he had been raised in. (This scriptural backing gave Ken a moral high ground on which to stand when he argued with his father. Thus Ken's conversion had not radically challenged his family's confrontational interactive style, though, as I mentioned, Ken was trying to learn to follow Bob Wilson's example.) Once he realized that he was born again, Ken enrolled at Valley Forge Christian College, which was affiliated with Assemblies of God. There he wrote and directed an evangelizing show that was presented at local reform schools. His long-term goal was to get into Christian broadcasting, so he needed to transfer to another school because Valley Forge lacked a communications department.

After a moment of silence, Bob introduced and read a letter recently received from a man named Don Johnson, who had been active in the group in previous years and had assisted Bob in the prison ministry. Don had written to let the group know that his divorce was final, and to thank the group for its support and prayer during the three years he had struggled to keep his marriage together. Don had been married to an unbeliever, and his stories and crises had been almost weekly subjects of discussion and prayer in the group. Now, with his fervent prayers to preserve his marriage apparently unanswered, Don had cut back on extra church activities and contacts, though he was still attending services. In his letter he said that he had been ready to walk out on God, but that recent conversations with group members at church had restored his hope. When he had gone into the courtroom during his divorce proceedings, God had even given him a Scripture passage from Ecclesiastes (3:1-8) about this being a time to rebuild. (In my interviews, almost every member of the group cited Don's case as one in which the group had reached out to care for someone, and as an instance in which someone's personal story had entered into the life of the group.) Bob concluded his praise report on Don by saying that a lot of people saw Hamden Assembly of God as a very supportive congregation.

John Gaffney continued the theme of people ministering to each other with a story of two single men whose apartment was flooded during the week. The church secretary, looking for help, had called John at work. John was pleased by how people turned out to move the young men's furniture into a rented truck while the water was vacuumed up. "Then we went out for Chinese food," he concluded, "so we had a nice time."

"Food always enters [in]," Bob commented, causing general laughter. "That's the one thing that's consistent." He then went on to praise one of the men for his frequent volunteering at church, and said, "So it's nice that we can help him. Any other praise?"

Theresa Gaffney then volunteered that she had received a blessing that summer: landing a long-term consulting contract at a candy company. It was a great job, she said — and not just because of the bowls of candy everywhere. The people were so nice and the job so good that she didn't mind the two-hour commute. Marilyn seconded this praise report because she too now worked with wonderful people, and she pointed out to Theresa that it was "because we prayed for our jobs, remember, over the years? We all prayed, you, me, and [another member of the group]."

When Bob asked for other contributions, Carla Christianson gave praise that John hadn't been injured in the accident with the van. When no one else had anything to add, Bob said, "Well, all right, let's go to the lesson."

The Lesson

Bob continued: "[The Scripture for] today was James 4:4-17. What we'll do is we'll read it — the subject [of the sermon] was 'Playing God' — and then what I'll do is just ask for general comments about some of the things that you got out of it. However, the important thing for the meeting tonight is not so much to regurgitate, so to speak, what we heard today, but to take it the next step and see what the deeper meaning is, if you will, and then how are we going to *apply* it to our lives. So who can I get to read James 4:4-17?" When there's no response, he jokes, "The crowd roars." A woman named Sylvia then reads the passage from the New International Version.

When she finished, Bob said, "Just open it up to comment now. Does anybody hear something that they — maybe just the most important thing they heard, 'cause there's really a lot there in those three paragraphs. Is there anything that just jumped out at you all? [He is greeted by a few seconds of silence.] The thing that I wanted to mention was this thing about judging, which is one of the things that was mentioned [in the sermon] — how our nature is to judge others and judge ourselves." Bob then told a story of his own judging of another person while he was in the prison ministry. Once, when the participants in the ministry launched a crusade to drum up helpers, an older man expressed an interest, but Bob thought "they [the inmates] would just eat this guy up," and so he refrained from calling him for training sessions. But the man kept calling Bob, and Bob finally relented. Soon the man was going into the roughest tier of the prison for Bible studies, and at this point he had been in the ministry for about five years. "God says to me, 'Bob, you don't understand.' As the Bible says, God is always looking for the heart of the person, not the outward appearance or how sharp the person is. And each person has his own ability. So I learned a lot about being critical."

Marilyn said that she thought the sermon was timely, since the Clarence Thomas hearings for nomination to the Supreme Court were currently on TV. "It seemed like there was so much judgment going on. It bothered me. [I] worked in politics for the last seven years — and this was local politics, so I can just imagine what goes on on a large scale. [Marilyn's previous job was as assistant to the county commissioner.] It just shows you where the world's system has led us. It's like God is saying you can't even find a moral man. Every time someone comes up, someone can just slam into that person. Who would ever want to run for anything?"

Paul Christianson agreed with Marilyn about the judgments of the world, but added that Christians can be judgmental too. He pointed to his own personal experience. He had worked with a feeble eighty-year-old Jewish woman in a program for high school kids at risk of becoming delinquents. The kids and many faculty in the school had thought she should retire, but when Paul had watched her in action, he had seen how effective she was. After that he defended her.

Jenny Wong, a new member of the group who came to only a few meetings during the year, then raised a question which put the group into a teaching mode that I seldom saw again. Jenny asked to what extent Christians should judge "other nations or other people." She continued, "I am a believing Christian, but I just can't take a position on judging other nations of the world, judging another religion. I say, this is not my territory, this is God's territory. He made all human beings, and if another religion professes to believe in God, I refuse to judge that religion. I have always taken the position that I can't make a statement about who's going to heaven and who's going to hell, because I don't know."

Carla Christianson answered quickly. She said that her own struggle with this problem had been resolved when she learned that there are two Greek words in the Bible that get translated as "judge": one means to discern, and the other means to condemn. Quoting John 7:24 (from the King James Version), she interpreted this to mean that we are supposed to discern the unrighteousness of particular actions, "like someone committing adultery or cheating on their income tax," but not to judge the heart of the person. If we refuse to discern what is righteous, then ultimately "we can't tell evil from good." Whether or not someone was saved was up to God, but "we can righteously say that no man comes to the Father but by Jesus Christ."

"So when you say 'saved' and 'unsaved,'" Jenny continued, "aren't you passing judgment?"

"Yes, I tend to think that we are," Bob said, although he pointed out that we're not supposed to. "Whenever I start to get into that 'saved

85

versus unsaved,' the Lord now is speaking to me and saying, 'Stop looking at them and look at yourself.' Because when I look at myself, I see I'm a sinner. I know I'm a sinner because I don't have the ability not to do that, not to make those judgments. The only thing that matters is to grow close to God and listen to God, and he will tell you how to deal with that person: encourage them if they are a believer, and if they're not, we should share God's Word with them."

In this interchange, the group's methods of teaching and correction were clearly evident. Carla made a connection with Jenny by talking about her own struggle with the issue, then showed her authority as a teacher by quoting Scripture. (At Hamden Assembly of God, she teaches an AG-accredited "Berean" class on the Bible.) Bob made a similar move by saying that he tends to do the same thing as Jenny, then established his authority by saying that God tells him personally that this is sinful. When no one like Jenny was there to question or challenge other members (and before Jenny raised her question in this meeting), the typical contributions were similar, in essence seeming to say, "The sermon reminded me of a time the Lord convicted me of a need to change," or "That was a good point the pastor made; this is how I learned it on my own." Such contributions showed that the speaker was humble enough to be taught, but already knew the lesson. Seldom did group members say that the sermon was challenging them to apply the Gospel to new areas of their lives, or that they were vulnerable or struggling. Admittedly, most group members have been reading the Scriptures and listening to conservative Protestant sermons for a decade or more, but even Ken used this rhetorical tactic of admission and assertion of authority, and it was only the second year after his conversion.

After a few more contributions on the importance of sharing God's Word with saved and unsaved alike, John Gaffney raised the topic of criticism and gossip as modes of interaction in the workplace, which, he pointed out, were problems for him personally and for Christians in general. Other group members concurred, and collectively they worked out the difference between correction versus gossip and slander. One solution was not to interact with people when they were gossiping. Carla added that once we discern what is going on, we must listen for God to tell us how to respond.

Bob noted that this got to the last part of the reading, which was about making plans for the future. The Lord controls the outcomes of situations, he pointed out, so we should listen to what the Lord wants us to do, "and he may tell you to do nothing."

For Jenny, this raised the problem of how you would know what God wants you to do. Bob, Marilyn, Carla, and Theresa all made suggestions about how they discovered God's will — by spending a lot of time listening to God in prayer, by seeing patterns emerge from daily Scripture readings, by stepping out in faith after dedicating oneself and one's actions to God.

"But when you think you have been doing what God wanted you to do and it doesn't turn out the way you expected," Jenny asked, "doesn't that mean you weren't listening to God in the first place?" Almost in chorus, the group answered, "Not necessarily." Bob told the story of Saint Stephen, who probably didn't think his witnessing would result in his being stoned to death, but God had larger plans for him.

"Don't any of you have a problem with that?" Jenny asked, perplexed.

"Oh *yeah* I do," said John Gaffney, "but I just have to trust that God wants what's best for me in the end." Bob brought up the story of Don Johnson, saying that even though God had told him to work on his marriage, it had ended in divorce. Now God evidently had other plans in store for him.

After about forty minutes of discussion, Bob moved to the next point on his agenda. "Why don't we get into application now? The key thing is drawing near to God. So . . . if we could sum this up in terms of what are we going to do in the next week, now that we heard the sermon this morning. How are we going to draw closer to God? Any thoughts on that?"

Marilyn began, "My day is different when I start out praying. I leave my Bible by the coffeemaker." Carla suggested following Ephesians 4:29 and saying only things that were edifying for others. Jenny thought she should count to ten before speaking. Bob concluded with the suggestion of keeping a diary; that way, he pointed out, group members could document their actions in their praise reports to the group. "Accountability to other people is important. It gets back to relationships — both the relationship we have with God and relationships in the Body. We have to be in the right kind of relationships. We always have to ask ourselves if we are going through it with right relationships and with the right people. Anything else? . . . OK, why don't we go to prayer requests."

Prayer Requests

In this segment of the meeting, people offer subjects for intercessory prayer, which are then prayed over by the group. Because the focus is on intercessions, individuals seldom request prayers for themselves, though others may do so for them. If the person who needs prayer is present, he or she will then speak in more detail about the situation. Bob and Marilyn (and I) took notes on prayer requests.

On this night, Marilyn requested prayers for a couple from the congregation who had traveled to Nigeria to work as missionaries. The recent news was that, after two years of troubles, the Lord had called them out of this ministry. "We think about what other people's problems are, and ours get a lot smaller." John requested prayers for the conversion of his younger brother, and Carla for one of her students whom she knew to be an atheist. Jenny requested prayers for her uncle, who had recently begun dialysis treatments, which prompted Theresa to request prayers for her baby nephew, who needed medical treatments for a genetic blood defect. Bob asked for prayers for the "Singles' Option," a new singles' group for younger people that Sylvia was helping to organize. Sylvia then talked about the aims of the ministry, with input from John and Theresa. Bob asked for any other contributions. John then remembered the person he and Theresa had had dinner with, and requested prayers for her. At that point, Bob wrapped things up by suggesting that we pray to apply the teaching from the day's sermon, then said, "Let's go to the Lord in prayer" and read through the list of prayer requests for the evening.

With heads bowed, almost every group member offered a prayer based on a request that someone else had made. The prayers were conversational, and sometimes brought soft responses of "Yes, Lord." The contribution of Margarita Cohen, a surgical nurse, serves as an example:

> Father God, almighty God, merciful God, you are a great God, Father, and in Jesus' name I come to you to present Theresa's nephew. Father, you love children, and you healed us two thousand years ago on the cross of all of our sins and diseases, Father. Father, we ask you tonight to regulate that blood count and whatever is wrong in that organism in the nephew, in that child that you love, Father. And in Jesus' name I come to you, Father, to present him, Father, that he would be healed,

Father, and that he would be a testimony to you, Father, of your mercy, Father. In Jesus' name we ask this.

Prayer requests tended to be repeated over the course of several months, and what were taken to be answers to prayer were recycled back into meetings in praise reports. Thus, prayer requests amounted to on-going personal stories that evolved over the course of the year, making the group aware of the concerns of its members. A case in point: after the group had been praying for Theresa's nephew for several months, Theresa presented a praise report on a visit she and her husband, John, had made to the hospital. After they had prayed over the baby with his family present, his condition improved to the extent that he needed treatments much less frequently. John reported that Theresa's sister, the baby's mother, who was not born again, had remarked on the power of their prayer — a testimony of God's mercy. Don Johnson's marital strife was another example that had powerfully influenced the group. Other prayer requests became praise reports, especially prayers for conversions and for ministries at church.

During the course of the year, prayer requests fell into several categories. About 40 percent were prayers for health or healing, 18 percent for ministries at the church, 16 percent for job or financial difficulties, 13 percent for conversions, and 13 percent for other matters. In praise reports the figures were a little different. Successes in church ministries were most talked about (24 percent), followed by testimonies of evangelizing successes (e.g., forming a Bible study at work, or the conversion of a relative or friend, 22 percent). Blessings related to work and finances, healings, and other miscellaneous blessings each accounted for about 18 percent of praise reports over the year. These figures suggest the complementarity and continuity between prayer requests and praise reports, but they also show that the group's range of acceptable concerns is somewhat limited. Perhaps this is so because prayer requests are intercessory, or perhaps people do not want to come across as vulnerable or as still searching for answers. Whatever the reason, problems in personal relationships and personal spiritual or theological struggles are seldom brought up. As I noted above, Jenny's questions were out of the ordinary for the group, even though dealing with them seemed to generate excitement.

After checking to see that all the prayer requests on his list had been covered, Bob concluded the formal part of the meeting with this prayer:

Lord, as we close, I also ask your prayers for [a congregation member] who will be undergoing surgery next week. Put a peace on all of those who are on our sick list. We know that you can handle these situations with the individuals and families that are involved much better than we can, Lord. And we ask a special blessing on the food that we are about to receive and the fellowship we are about to partake [of]. We ask this in Jesus' name. Amen.

Fellowship

The final segment of the meeting would start about two hours after the meeting had begun and would last for an hour to an hour and a half—until 9:30 or 10:00 at night. Marilyn would disappear into the kitchen and bring out pastries, a pie, a cake, or cookies that she had made, as well as doughnuts or other store-bought items that others may have brought. The group would break into conversational clusters, with people sipping coffee or iced tea and making periodic raids on the goodies on the dining room table. Conversation was informal and covered the range of topics that might come up at a cocktail party, but also included more in-depth discussions of theological positions that came up in the meeting, or further details on situations brought up in prayer requests. In our interview, Ken said that this was the time when Marilyn had the chance to minister to people one-on-one. Indeed, I often spotted her in a corner of the dining room or in the kitchen, talking softly to one or two other people. As the evening wore on, people would slip away in twos and threes, sometimes continuing a private conversation in the driveway before parting for the week. The Gaffneys told me that they had had one such conversation during a time when they were experiencing financial difficulty. Another group member had led them to his car and given them two bags of groceries to help them through the week. The Gaffneys said they later helped another group member in this way.

Group Purpose in Perspective

From the perspective of the pastors of the Hamden Assembly of God Church, home fellowships help to solve two organizational problems:

they help provide adequate pastoral care to a large congregation, and they create unity in a geographically dispersed membership. When the congregation began its life in the 1940s, it met in its founder's living room. By the 1970s, the congregation had grown large enough to hire a full-time pastor and buy an empty Presbyterian church building in Hamden. Through both personal evangelism and a radio ministry, the congregation grew rapidly. Associate Pastor Frank Kelsey, who oversees the Home Fellowship Outreach and leads a group himself, told me that as the church "really started to grow bigger, there was a need to, in a sense, get smaller." The church's growth was not localized — only about 10 percent of the congregation resided in Hamden itself — so home fellowships were distributed geographically. The Home Fellowship Outreach was modeled on the early church, in which small groups met in members' houses and got together corporately in the temple court.

The church has all the groups follow a single program or format; this makes the groups uniform and reinforces their ties to the church. Originally the groups were somewhat independent Bible studies, but when one group left the church, a single study guide was adopted and leaders were more closely supervised by a pastor. Because groups had moved through the study guide at different rates, the current format of discussing the Sunday sermon had been instituted; this regulates "group speed."

Creating mutual "accountability" among group members is the chief means by which home fellowship groups are intended to solve the pastoral problems of congregational size and geographic dispersal. In the intimate setting of the group meeting, people interact with one another on an ongoing basis, which promotes honesty, trust, and compassion. In this setting, group leaders can provide counseling and spiritual guidance with a depth of knowledge of individuals' situations that the pastor of a large congregation is not likely to have. However, the head pastor, Vince Cavallo, explained to me that the relationship of accountability is not simply hierarchical. Ideally, group leaders also share with, are vulnerable to, and receive guidance from group members.

For Pastor Vince, the model church is a series of concatenated small groups, each fostering the spiritual growth of its members through mutual accountability. In my research, however, I noted an interesting phenomenon. Pastor Vince talked about being accountable in this way to his pastor friends at the district and national levels of the Assemblies of God, Pastor Frank talked about being accountable in the small group of the pastoral staff, and Bob Wilson talked about accountability in the small group of the board of stewards. Yet, although these congregational leaders talked about the personal value of being accountable in small groups, they seemed to experience this personal accountability more often when they were among peers than when they led a group. Perhaps filling the role of teacher and guide prevented them from giving up their authority and being accountable to the group.

Pastor Vince stressed another important pastoral function of home fellowship groups, that of "fleshing out" the ninety-minute Sunday sermons, which focus on how the Word of God could be applied in daily life. This is important because it specifies what people are supposed to be accountable *for*. "Fleshing out" or reaching a collective understanding of the sermon occurs when people share their reactions to it. Pastor Vince explained:

> The Bible is clear: God is a God of variety. Don't take this wrong, but your pathway in following Christ will be different from my pathway. . . . And that's not that it's a different Christ, but you're under different pressures than I am. And so we're reacting in different ways. Our working together balances us out and it helps us out. That's what the body of Christ is supposed to do. Because some person can get in [the group] and say, 'Well, I feel this, this, and this.' And if the group is strong enough it will balance out and bring [that person] back to the center perspective. That's what it's supposed to do, is restore the brother and give us a balance. Because you know what? My perspective is often different from other people's perspective, and when you see the whole picture you get a much better perspective. Usually God is glorified.

Perhaps as a result of the intensive training of leaders that Pastor Vince undertook after he arrived, the group I observed did seem to function the way he wanted it to. In the few cases in which people like Jenny raised questions or different perspectives, they seemed to learn from other people's contributions. For the most part, however, group members seemed to avoid rocking the boat; much of the discussion was one person after another adding a perspective that repeated the same basic point. People seemed to avoid making themselves vulnerable to criticism or correction by other group members by avoiding controversial topics and by not admitting the need for guidance in understanding or applying the Word of God.

Clearly, in the pastors' vision, small groups play a central role in Hamden Assembly of God, and there are a lot of them. There are specific groups for children, girls, boys, men, women (with nine special-interest subgroups), adolescents, young adults, single people, married people, single parents, Spanish-speaking people, and people suffering from "life-controlling problems." The board of stewards, the board of deacons, and the choir also function something like small groups. Although none of these other groups focus on the sermon, all of them deal to some extent with the pastoral needs of group members.

The ten local home fellowship groups thus compete with other groups for church members' attention. Several of the group members I interviewed attended home fellowships out of a feeling of obligation, since the importance of attendance was stressed by the pastoral staff. Sylvia Wilson, for instance, said she was involved in home fellowship primarily because her parents were hosts for a group, not so much because she got a lot out of it; the young adult group more often focused on issues she was dealing with. The Gaffneys recalled that when they had started to become active in the church, the previous pastor had told them that they could have better access to leadership positions in church ministries if they attended home fellowships. In the group I studied, most members participated actively in at least one other small group or church ministry.

Despite the competition for group members' allegiance, home fellowships seem to unify the diverse interests of the congregation to an extent. According to Pastor Frank, 30 to 35 percent of the congregation participated in home fellowships, with one small group for about every eleven of the 350 or so who attended Sunday worship (only about 200 are formal church members). Thus it seems that home fellowship groups like the one I studied are composed of the most committed congregation members. By geographically cross-cutting the special-interest groups in the congregation, home fellowships provide network nodes in which important information about church activities is shared. Sylvia mentioned that this was an important aspect of the group for her. In the meetings of her group, this information was given out through praise reports, in which church ministries were the most frequent subject, and in prayer requests, in which intercessions for church ministries were second only to health concerns.

As local network nodes, home fellowship groups may have a history that runs parallel to that of the congregation as a whole. Pastor Vince said that the experience in the local home fellowship "is not a part of the church, it *is* the church." In some cases, this might be true to a greater degree than a pastor would like. (I'm remembering the fellowship group that left the Hamden congregation.)

The group that I attended, the Wattstown-Belleview home fellowship group, had its formal beginning at the Hamden Assembly of God Church in 1986, when the previous pastor asked the Wilsons to lead the group. However, the Christiansons traced the group's beginnings back to 1973, when the Wilsons and the Christiansons began Bible study groups with friends in their Catholic parish, groups that functioned as local network nodes. The two groups, one for women hosted by Carla Christianson and one for couples hosted by the Wilsons, grew out of the couples' experience with Marriage Encounter, a movement to make marriages stronger by giving them a scriptural and spiritual foundation. When the Catholic priest who initially oversaw the Bible study groups turned his attention elsewhere, the Wilsons and the Christiansons asked for the guidance of two neighboring couples who were Bible-believing Protestants. These Protestants were gentle in their teaching, but eventually most members of the groups were born again. Some, including the Christiansons and the Wilsons, also came to see the Catholic Church as suffering from a variety of weaknesses, which led them to break from it. Both couples had been active in the parish, the women teaching CCD (Sunday school) classes, the men sitting on the parish council. In this instance, the experience of being in a small group without supervision led many people away from the larger congregation.

Both the Wilsons and the Christiansons (as well as Ken Joraski, mentioned earlier) had the same main criticism of the Catholic Church: that it lacked a unified dogma accessible to laypeople. According to the Christiansons, their pastor tried to convince them to stay by telling them, "You can believe in a lot of things and be Catholic." In response, they said, "*That's the problem* — that's pluralism. If you carry it that far, you don't believe. There's nothing solid then." While the Wilsons became Baptists, the Christiansons' "spiritual odyssey" led them through several small Christian congregations in the area. After having several traumatic experiences with authoritarianism and rigid conformity in these small congregations, the Christiansons were quite relieved to join the Hamden Assembly of God Church, where "Pastor Vince is not one who has the authority thing." They are also pleased that Pastor Vince accepts diversity, which was their policy for the short time that they ran their own house church.

In my interviews with the Christiansons, they talked about the home fellowship group as in some ways an outgrowth of their spiritual journey over two decades. Several people whom they had gotten to know in small congregations over the years had also switched to the Hamden church, including not only the Wilsons but also David and Margarita Cohen and others who had sometimes attended meetings at the Christiansons' house church. Marilyn Wilson and others in the group actively evangelized people at work and in other contexts, and some of these people ended up at the Hamden church and in the home fellowship. By evangelizing in their area, group members expanded the local network.

While leaders in the church like the Wilsons, the Christiansons, the Gaffneys, and Pastor Frank do not feel that home fellowships are very important for their own spiritual development, they are all committed to the small-group process. In the past, each one of them was profoundly influenced by participation in small groups. Now they believe that nurturing new Christians like Jenny Wong and Ken Joraski is one of the most important ways they can spend their time.

Conclusion

At this juncture I want to summarize the goals of the home fellowship program at the Hamden Assembly of God Church, assess the degree to which these goals are met by the Wattstown-Belleview group, and suggest one way in which the group might attain its goals more effectively.

From the pastor's perspective, the home fellowship groups are intended to relieve some of the burden of pastoral care in a large congregation. (As the congregation grows, the goal is to increase the number of groups to maintain intimacy.) The trust, honesty, and compassion that small-group intimacy engenders creates "accountability." Group members are accountable to each other for the ways in which they apply God's Word in their lives, which they learn to do by collectively "fleshing out" the Sunday sermon.

The Wattstown-Belleview home fellowship group fulfills the pastor's vision to a limited degree. Personal sharing and the fleshing out of the sermon are certainly apparent in the prayer requests, the praise reports, and the "lesson." But these activities do not seem to generate much excitement or commitment in group members. Excitement is generated, however, when someone exposes an area of pain or personal struggle and makes themselves vulnerable to the group but also gives the group an opportunity to help in a positive way. The support that the group could offer to Don Johnson in his marital struggles and the teaching and practical examples the group can offer to new converts give members a feeling of real accomplishment and a knowledge of their reason for existence. Without these experiences, group life can become a tedious rehashing of lessons everyone has heard before.

For an outsider to make suggestions for change is always fraught with danger, since the evolution of any given group involves a delicate balance of historical and contextual forces. To encourage group leaders' autonomy too much, for example, might lead to differences from the larger congregation, so some unity in the program the small groups follow is necessary. Within these constraints, however, it seems to me that the most important thing that leaders could do would be to encourage members to make themselves vulnerable to the group by bringing up real issues that they are currently struggling with, whether or not those issues are strictly spiritual. This might be done simply by encouraging members to make prayer requests for themselves rather than just intercessions for others. This would certainly require group leaders to lead by example and make *themselves* vulnerable, dropping the defenses of authority, experience, and deeper knowledge of Scripture, and accepting contributions from the many perspectives available in the group. If the leaders were to do this, they might find that the group would become more significant in their own lives. More importantly, it would make newer members of the group feel freer to express their vulnerabilities and feel as if their contributions were important, both of which would increase their commitment to and excitement about the group. As excitement and commitment increased, group members might encourage other members of the congregation to participate in the groups, thus not leaving that "task" to the pastors. Members might even feel good enough about the group process to invite newcomers who were not already members of the congregation. And having new members who were open about their spiritual questions and struggles would bring new rewards for more mature group members.

The Women's Bible Study:
A Thriving Evangelical Support Group

NATALIE SEARL

From September 1991 to June 1992, I was a participant/observer in the Women's Bible Study, a daytime Bible study group that meets in an evangelical church in the suburban Northeast.[1] According to Arlene

1. The church setting: In Springfield Township, halfway between Collegeville and the county seat, tracts of century-old farmland are rapidly falling victim to executive subdivisions, clusters of townhouses, and strip malls, while local planning boards fight to preserve the open green spaces that are disappearing. In the summer and fall you can still see farmers at work in their fields only minutes from your house; roadside farm stands offering local corn and fruit are not an unusual sight. Occasionally at a country crossroads, you'll come across the echo of an earlier time: a cluster of turn-of-the-century Victorian houses, a bandshell gazebo, a general store, a Dutch Reformed church with its high spire and white walls dominating the once-bustling village, its name having meaning only to the longtime locals.

Springfield Evangelical Church (SEC) rose twenty-six years ago in what was once farmland. The splinter group met in people's homes at first, then rented space at an elementary school, and eventually bought land and erected a little church in a former cornfield. They quickly outgrew the small building and purchased twelve acres across the street, where they are now. Susan, the cofounder of WBS, says, "You should have seen it thirteen years ago when we came. We just thought we were going out into the country. We couldn't believe there was a church out there. They gave us directions. We thought, 'Where are we going? This can't be a church out here on a farm!' But sure enough, it was out here." Their present facility is again too small, and they are undergoing a building expansion. Executive housing developments border two sides of the church; now the longest view from the church is

97

(I've changed group members' names), one of the group leaders, "Small groups should be the serving hands, empathizing hearts, listening ears, and encouraging words of Jesus" — and that is the motto of this group. By the time I concluded my study, the membership had swelled to twenty-five, and plans had been made to divide the group the following year. This decision capped ten years of the group's successful operation; to clone itself was the hallmark of achievement. Yet this group has flourished with no outside help, no secret formula, using no particular curriculum. The nature of the group itself and what it does that works so well is the subject of this essay. I discuss the group's genesis, composition, and functioning from my own viewpoint and from the viewpoints of its members. I also explain what kind of women choose this group and how it fills their needs.

When I first walked into the Women's Bible Study at Springfield Evangelical Church on a Wednesday morning last fall, I was struck by the unfolding scene. As the women drifted in, they picked out their name tags from a pile, got their coffee and snack, and then took a seat. They sat on folding chairs around a couple of big tables pushed together; women in their fifties sat side by side with young mothers. Several mothers nursed their babies (one of them had newborn twins). The table tops were crowded with infant seats, diaper bags, and well-worn Bibles

---

only across the parking lot, as bulldozers make way for a new development of $300,000 executive homes that will close off the church's last open boundary.

Growth in Women's Bible Study attendance parallels the church's growth. The lure of an easy commute attracts many families on their way up corporate ladders of companies such as AT & T, major pharmaceutical firms, and the financial institutions of New York City. The makeup of the church membership reflects a mix of service workers, technicians, middle managers, and vice presidents of brand-name companies. Several neighboring townships from which the church also draws its members are almost mirror images of Springfield Township, where proximity to rail lines and major highways extends the working reach of the breadwinners. On an average Sunday, about 400 of these white, middle-class suburbanites fill the pews. Only half of them are voting members of the congregation; however, a good number of the attenders vigorously participate in the various church programs.

The church's location makes it seem isolated from the world's problems. Susan observes that the church is removed from critical social problems. She describes the area as "almost separated from reality, ... [an] on-a-hill kind of thing. It's insulated from the world, from the homeless, from the alcoholics. It's not like anybody did that on purpose. Somebody sold a farm, developed it, sold the houses, and the people who could afford the houses aren't the homeless. You can't find homeless in there."

of all shapes and sizes—even some with gingham-and-lace covers. There was an air of camaraderie as the room filled and the women greeted each other and exchanged news. While waiting for the meeting to start, some women thumbed through back issues of *Today's Christian Woman* magazine brought in by one of the members. Soon the leader called for praise and petition items and wrote the responses in two columns on a big tablet; some mothers, who had to drop off their toddlers in the nursery, were just arriving. At this point the women settled in and quieted down, many of them balancing baby, coffee cup, Bible, and study guide. And so the Wednesday-morning women's Bible study began. The topics of discussion? How to be a good wife, and the attributes of God according to R. C. Sproul.

What makes this Bible study group distinct from any other gathering of women, whether it be a mothers' play group, a neighborhood coffee-klatsch, or a Methodist women's circle? Ruth, one of the leaders, explains: "The difference is the personal walk with Jesus that you're going to find in an evangelical church, which ours is, compared to a liberal group who corporately understands God and understands Jesus, and would pray the same way we do, but the difference is that personal walk that each of us has felt."[2]

The women in this group witness to each other and to the "new" Christians in the group by openly inviting Jesus into their everyday lives. For them, every prayer, every Bible passage discussed by using personal examples, and each act of caring become concrete evidence of God's presence. Certainly God and Christian values occupy front-row seats at their meeting table. Indeed, even a non-Christian like me was struck by the obvious presence of the Holy Spirit in the room, which seemed evoked by these women. Noticeably absent were the Bible-thumping and overt witnessing often associated with people such as fundamentalists. By giving examples of how God works in their own lives and how he answers prayers, and by striving to be good Christian women, wives, and mothers, these group members are in fact sharing their personal spiritual walks with each other. This sharing reinforces their mutual values and enables each woman to gain a sense of "ownership," not only of the group itself but of the spiritual process. Put simply, for these women, the group is the point of intersection between the business of their everyday lives and their spiritual journeys.

2. On the contemporary meanings of "evangelical," see Ellingsen (1988).

The group's purpose — "to have a place where the women of the church and the community can gather to develop a personal relationship with Jesus through fellowship, prayer and Bible study" — is not unusual. Indeed, many features of Women's Bible Study (WBS), such as the possibilities for fellowship and Scripture study, can be found in other Bible study groups and other women's groups. What makes this group distinctive is that the three components of Bible study, fellowship, and prayer are synthesized to help each woman develop her personal relationship with Jesus, which is the group's primary goal.[3]

But that's not all. These white, middle-class, suburban women choose a church Bible-study group because they are engaged in a struggle to keep their lives together in today's mobile society. They have been shunted around to new communities by their husbands. They stay at home all week with small children. They don't know many other people in the community very well. They are also dealing with important life events, such as learning how to be good wives and mothers. And some of them are coping with abusive childhood experiences. For all these reasons, the element of support is crucial. The group serves as a surrogate family, providing mentoring, friendship, caring, support, and accountability. It gives its members an opportunity to be needed and to fill each other's needs.

A Group Portrait

I got a clear sense of the group when I attended my first meeting. The women were warm, welcoming, and supportive of my project, and did not mind my tape recording the meetings. In fact, several women said that God had placed me there for a purpose. One, for example, told me, "We're really going to enjoy having you with us because it adds a dimension to the group, something besides just our own Bible study and just our own things. Here we're participating in something that's going to benefit people way out of our group that we'll never know about. . . . You just don't know who you're going to touch with something like this."

Between fifteen and twenty-eight women attend the meetings. The

3. In the decade since the group was founded, its leaders have consulted a number of books on small groups to clarify their purpose and methods; several they recommended were Hunt (1971), Jacobs and Spradlin (1974), Job (1972), McBride (1990), Peace (1985), Richards (1987), Richardson (1956), and Williams (1991).

group consists mostly of church members, and includes three mother-daughter pairs and two sisters, but is otherwise quite diverse, even in terms of religious backgrounds.[4] Because the group meets on a weekday morning, it does not attract working women; virtually all of the women are married mothers who elect to stay home. The group is completely self-run, which enhances the members' sense of ownership. Arlene is the main leader, and when she is gone every winter for three months, Ruth takes over. The group operates autonomously within the church; there is no pastoral supervision or accountability to the formal church organization, other than a requirement that the leaders have to be members of the church. The church lends its facilities and provides a supportive environment (meetings are publicized in the weekly bulletin), but the group receives no funding from the church budget. A collection is taken at each WBS meeting for the three babysitters the group hires. Members take turns providing refreshments.

The group meets from 9:30 to 11 a.m. every Wednesday, except during the summer. A potluck Christmas brunch closes the fall session, and another potluck brunch marks the final session in June. The "lesson" is covered in eight- to twelve-week segments, with the group choosing the study guides.[5] Arlene admits that they choose their own material, "and we like it that way because we feel that for someone who's not a part of the group to try and decide what we should study would not really be very good for us." Group members aren't required to study the lesson in advance, but the content of the lesson is meaty enough to provoke discussions of how Scripture applies to one's everyday life. Often the discussion will be so lively that the lesson won't be completed in a single meeting, so study of it will be carried over to the following week.

Because members want to have an uninterrupted hour and a half of Bible study and prayer, mothers take turns each week missing the meeting to watch the children. During the year I met with the group, attendance (and the number of children requiring babysitting) grew, so

4. In a survey of the faith backgrounds of 27 members, the breakdown by religious affiliation was as follows: 9 Catholic, 7 Lutheran Brethren, 3 Baptist, 2 Seventh Day Adventist, 1 Methodist, 1 Christian Missionary Alliance, 1 Lutheran, 1 UCC, 1 Presbyterian, and 1 Episcopalian.

5. During the time I attended the group, three study guides were used: *Homemaking: A Bible Study for Women at Home,* by Baukje Doornenbal and Tjitske Lemstra; *Walking What You're Talking: Principles from James,* by Harold Fickett; and *One Holy Passion: The Attributes of God,* by R. C. Sproul.

one of the group members took it upon herself to solve the logistical problem of hiring outside babysitters for the twenty to thirty infants and toddlers that would be in the nursery each week. The children now take up three primary rooms (they are divided into groups by age), one of which the group used to occupy. The group now meets in a partitioned-off corner of the church lobby.

The format of the meeting has remained basically the same for the last ten years. I'll let Lisa, one of the younger members, describe a typical meeting:

> Besides the fact that we all arrive late, all of us mothers shuttle our kids off into the nursery and hope and pray that the person that's coming there for nursery is there, so that we don't have to be the ones to take the kids on the spur of the moment. Right after we've torn the children off of our legs and left the nursery, we go in. Someone is in charge of having the coffee and munchies prepared and the tables and chairs set up. And Arlene is usually there — Arlene is the leader — with her book and her smile. We all just kind of mill in and find our seats and get our coffee and chitchat for a little bit past the time that we're supposed to start. Which is good — I enjoy that. Kind of like an unwinding . . . or like you stepped out of the hectic world, now let's sit down and study God's Word and be together.
>
> The Bible study begins with prayer. This is where we get a chance to pray for each other and see what news has happened. It's an opportunity to find out the needs of the women firsthand. And we can pray firsthand. After that, then we start our Bible study. That gets a lot of things going. Sometimes we only get one or two things done, and other times we go right through the lesson. But it brings out a lot. Women bring a lot of color to it in their experiences and stuff. It's neat that . . . even just one Bible verse could mean six different things, and everyone just throws into the batch their interpretation, and it's amazing that God's Word can come so alive. Because people are all talking about it. Then after that, at eleven o'clock on the nose we go rescue the babysitters, and clean up the nursery.

The Women of WBS

I observed two distinct subgroups among the members: two-thirds are "young mothers," between the ages of twenty-two and forty, with small children, and one-third are "older women," generally over the age of forty-five, with grown children. A strong bond of mentoring connects these two groups, both in and out of the meetings. As Ruth, one of the leaders, put it, "The younger mothers want the older ladies' input for leadership, for experiences that they've had in their life. They feel they can learn from the older ladies." The issue of mentoring was the deciding factor when the group split at the end of the year.

The easiest way to get a sense of what the members are like is to look at several representative women who attend regularly and review their backgrounds, needs, and interests. Arlene, Ruth, and Louise are three of the older women. Lisa, Roberta, and Amalia are among the young mothers.

Arlene, the leader for the last several years, is an attractive blonde in her late fifties. She met her husband in her church youth group. They have two grown children. They own a construction company and live in a subdivision they're building, which is about fifteen minutes away from the church. Arlene had a very religious upbringing in a Norwegian Lutheran church. "I grew up in a home where God was the proverbial guest," she says. "He was part of our family." She is related to several members of the congregation, either by blood or by marriage. Once very active in the church, she explains what happened a while back: "We weren't attending church on Sundays because my husband chose to travel on weekends, and I was losing contact with people, which upset me tremendously. I gave up most of the ministries that I was involved in, and my social contacts were cut off." She acknowledges that this was difficult for her: "Basically, I needed spiritual fellowship, and I needed emotional support from other women. Sometimes you just need some-body to talk to and share with. I found that if I didn't have the organi-zational-type thing, I wasn't getting [that support], because people just weren't prone to drop in and kind of get together, like they had been when we were younger. So I really felt a void." Her involvement with WBS has really helped her; at present, she considers the group her main ministry. "Because I'm not attending church regularly, this becomes my spiritual nourishment."

Ruth leads the group for three months every winter when Arlene is away. She and her husband are in their fifties and have two married children. They live in an established executive subdivision located about five minutes from the church. Ruth grew up on a farm. Her father's family had a strong Baptist affiliation, and she was raised Baptist. Her maternal grandparents were Dutch Reformed farmers who moved from Long Island to this state. Like Arlene and many other women in the group, she met her husband in a church youth group. For many years, she and her husband were active members of a Reformed church in Springfield Township, but they became increasingly discouraged with its "country club atmosphere." After Ruth completed a seven-year Bible Study Fellowship (BSF) course in Collegeville, she felt the need to continue her Bible studies, so she began attending the Women's Bible Study group. She says, "I realized that they were really teaching the Word over there — not afraid to talk about who Jesus was and how he affected our lives and what he died for." Soon after Ruth began attending the group, she and her husband changed their church affiliation as well. Her husband, a vice president of a national research and testing company, rose through church offices to become church president, and Ruth has also served in various church capacities. They both sing in the choir. Ruth and her husband are also part of a new small group at the church for "empty nesters."

Louise, a longtime church member and choir soloist, just joined WBS this year. She is in her sixties and has two grown children. She lives with her recently retired husband (whom she met at church) a few blocks from Ruth in a typical two-story colonial home. She is always meticulously dressed and coiffed. Louise attends many outside functions with other WBS members, including lectures by prominent Bible teachers. In her soft, southern accent, she tells about growing up in a very religious Seventh-Day Adventist home in Washington, D.C. Because she grew up with an alcoholic father, she empathizes with group members who struggle with similar experiences. Louise is always ready to mentor younger women in the group: "I thought it was time to get to know the younger girls who are now in the church, and as an older participant in the church, maybe I would have insight. I'm in the choir, and I don't really get to meet all the new people because I come in [on Sunday] and rush right back to choir." Louise's daughter joined WBS the year before she did. "I especially enjoy Bible study," Louise explains, "because it is something that my daughter and I can participate in together, now that she is an adult and a mother."

Most of the other older women in the group resemble Arlene, Ruth, and Louise in lifestyle. Although they come from different religious backgrounds and have been members of the congregation for various periods of time, they all find spiritual nourishment in WBS. They are mature mothers of grown children, but they find themselves drawn to the needs and interests of the young mothers in the group.

One of these young mothers is Lisa. In an informal survey, several of the younger women listed Lisa as one of their best friends, and many group members felt the loss of her presence very keenly when she and her husband and four young children moved away. They lived in a small townhouse. Lisa, thirty-one, was originally from the Midwest. She and her husband came to the community literally to build the church (her husband is a carpenter). Lisa comes from a dysfunctional background, which includes substance abuse, a broken home, and alcoholism. After hitting bottom, she found Jesus through friends and a nurturing family. Subsequently Lisa married a Christian man, and found her way to this church through a series of job-related moves. She'd been in a variety of twelve-step and New Age groups before discovering that she needed "something more intimate, something that would hold me accountable. Something that if I didn't go, I'd be missed." Tall and dark-haired, elegant even in thrift-shop clothing, she was one of the liveliest members of the group, bringing an infectious sense of humor to all discussions. She was admired by both the younger mothers and the older women. "I love those women," she exclaimed. "They are like an extended family, one that you don't have to keep explaining yourself to over and over again." When, beset by unemployment and bankruptcy, Lisa and her family had to move back to Michigan, the group took up a collection for them.

Roberta, thirty-three, is tall and soft-spoken. She and her husband had "planted" an evangelical church in California and came to Springfield Evangelical Church looking for a similar intimate experience. They and their four small children lived in an older two-story house in a historic village about a half hour from the church. Roberta provided day care for some children; she also taught her children at home (not an unusual practice for mothers of this group and this church). When Roberta had the time, she would attend the WBS meetings. The East Coast proved to be so different that, although she participated in WBS and started a couples Bible study with her husband, Roberta still felt rooted in California; in fact, she frequently said she was homesick when she attended the group. She was in the group only three years before her husband was transferred back to the West Coast.

Then there is Amalia, thirty-six, who with her husband and small daughter lives in a townhouse about a half hour from the church. Her parents divorced when she was nine, and that experience devastated her.

As she explains, "I never really feel secure, and that has a lot to do with my relationship with God. It was like there [was] no one to protect me, no one to watch over me, and no one to champion my cause. Even as a young child, I felt so vulnerable and unsafe. There [was] only so much my mother could do, and she was raising two little children and trying to make it on her own. . . . I've always felt that God has kind of watched over me. I just really felt that somehow he's kept me safe in so many ways." Together with her mother and sister, she moved around so much between the Bronx and Long Island that by the time she got to high school, she had attended six different schools. She was raised Catholic, but attended the church only sporadically because of the frequent moves. When school friends took her to their Baptist church, she remembers, "It was wild because when you're brought up Roman Catholic, everything is always the same every week and everything is very quiet and sedate. People don't say 'Hallelujah.' They don't sing loud. But when [I went to] a Baptist church, they were very friendly. 'How are you doing?' And they would sing out loud and stand up and clap hands, so that was kind of like culture shock for me. But I enjoyed it because a lot of adults started paying attention to me. It was nice to have someone care." When a woman there befriended her, she joined Pioneer Girls, which is a Christian version of Girl Scouts, and "that's really kind of the anchor that held me. I went through rebellion in college, even wondering if God was even there. It was those roots of people really caring for me that, in the long run, made me come back to actually becoming a born-again Christian." In college, she experimented with Transcendental Meditation, the human potential movement, and the occult, always "searching." And, in a sense, she is still seeking answers, but now the women of WBS are her traveling partners on her spiritual journey.

These, then, are a few representative members of the group. They come from different parts of the country, from different religious backgrounds, and from homes that have exposed them to different sorts of problems.[6] Some have changed churches because they wanted something

---

6. For example, Rachel is one of the most fundamentally religious and stalwart members of the group. A 28-year-old full-time mother of two, she and her husband and small children live in a second-floor apartment. Her husband drives a delivery truck. Rachel's recounting of her memories of her alcoholic father's abuses and her continuing struggle to maintain a relationship with her parents provide a stimulus for many of the group members to recount similar experiences and to demonstrate

more biblically grounded. Others were raised as fundamentalists and find the atmosphere at WBS refreshingly tolerant. All are quite serious about their faith. They want Jesus to guide them. They are also deeply in need of a warm, caring community in which to find support and encouragement. They are especially attracted by the fellowship the group offers, but also by its Bible study and prayer.

Fellowship

According to Susan, the cofounder of the group, fellowship — building relationships and providing encouragement — was the critical reason for starting the group in the first place.[7] "We started it," she explains, "as a way to bring in people who were in the church, but who weren't building relationships, and didn't have the opportunity to spend discretionary time with each other because they didn't know each other well enough. We felt it would help us get to know each other better. And [the group could offer] encouragement, mutual encouragement about colic and

the salvation of Jesus Christ. Rachel was raised a Catholic, became a Baptist, and then was born again; she was looking to religion to provide all her answers: "I looked to God to be the father my own father wasn't." She gives the group a lot of credit for helping her: "My childhood background was terrible; my father was an alcoholic. It was tough, it was really tough. Just in the past three years, since I've been going to the Bible study, I've been able to deal with a lot of issues from my childhood and come to terms with being an adult child of an alcoholic and seeing things that I do, the compulsive behaviors. The Bible study has helped me grow and come out of that." The entire group gave Rachel encouragement through prayer during the year it took her to lose a hundred pounds, and several of the older women have nurtured her and become her mentors. Rachel is extremely active in the church: she's a deaconess, a member of many boards and committees, and generally is the first to volunteer for everything. She formed a young-couples Bible study with friends she made in WBS. The group has influenced her worldview — she no longer permits anything but sacred media into her home.

7. Susan credits Ann, wife of the then-assistant pastor, with having the idea for the group. "Ann was involved in Campus Crusade in college. I'm on the staff of Campus Crusade, so we had a lot of experience with small groups. And she had some experience from her college days. We were good friends; we spent a lot of time together. The book we used to start the group, *The Master Plan of Evangelism* by Robert E. Coleman, is very commonly used in ministry. It uses Jesus' pattern with his disciples as the pattern for discipleship in small groups. Another book we used was *Disciples Are Made, Not Born.*"

diapers and how hard it is to make that adjustment, and then once you make it, what a joy your kids are."

Ten years later, the group still holds to the importance of deepening relationships and providing encouragement. When I talked with Roberta, for example, she emphasized the need to build relationships. "Just to come [to church] on Sunday and go home doesn't fill the need for that family, the closeness and knowing each other. [The group has helped me in] not just realizing that yes, we share the same beliefs, that's why we're here, but going beyond that and really having people become my friends."

Others feel the rushed atmosphere of Sunday morning, too. "Even with friends my age," one older woman admits, "we don't get a chance to talk to each other on Sunday morning. They all have their own things that they do and grandchildren that they help with. So for me it's just to get to know the ladies."

And the group is still a place that offers encouragement for young mothers. One speaks for many when she talks about her reasons for joining WBS three years ago:

> First off, I'd say I was looking for the Bible study part of it, which was really lacking in my life. Second of all, I was looking for a break. It was something I needed to give to the Lord. It was an hour for me to have a cup of tea without a crying baby. And thirdly, I really so needed the support of young mothers. I didn't know any. A lot of my friends aren't even married, never mind having babies. I needed some friendships [with women in my situation].

In a similar vein, Amalia admitted that "after having a baby and feeling so isolated, I wanted some place to go where I could connect with other women that believed what I believed." Many women said they would never have taken the time to get to know each other were it not for the group, because their paths otherwise crossed only superficially.

Having the time and the space in which to meet and intentionally share at a deep level is significant to these women. Roberta summed it up best when she said, "Bible study is an activity that doesn't occur in any other part of my life. [The meetings provide] a time to be together with other women and talk about our lives and our roles as women, as wives, as mothers, and all the things that revolve around that life and how it relates to our faith." She went on to explain, "I don't have that opportunity on Sunday morning, listening to a sermon or in an adult Sunday school class, or even in a mixed [Bible study] group. [In WBS meetings] I'm more free to discuss things that are really important to me and to hear other women's viewpoints on these things."

Women also seek out this group because they've moved to the area from another community and have given up close friendships and proximity to family.[8] This change means that they have to start from scratch to seek out and cultivate a new set of friends. As one of the members explained, "We had just moved here. We were only here about a month,

---

8. Much scholarly literature suggests the need for surrogate families, and explores the dynamics of friendships as they apply in this situation. For example, Lopata (1971, 250) observes that "Middle- and upper-class women are aware of organized groups as a resource for social contacts and future friendships . . . and usually join voluntary associations upon movement to a new area. Organized activity outside the neighborhood may bring together people living near each other. Churches are the most frequent source for building sound relations." Gouldner and Strong (1987, 152) talk about building new relationships: "American women of the migratory middle class have suffered from the depersonalizing effects of urbanization and residential mobility. In making the transitions from one place of residence to another the women are always forced to put together a new scaffolding around which they can build a network of social relations for themselves and their families. In these activities of taking down old frameworks and constructing new ones, they are the prototypical modern members of the family unit, the ones who are confronted with rapid social changes affecting their personal lives. Although they may acquire the skills and orientations to enable them to accomplish the tasks of reconstruction through repeated training, *they do the usual female work of managing the social and emotional welfare of the family members without the traditional support of their mothers, sisters, aunts, cousins and female in-laws* [my emphasis]. They straddle the old and the new world, not necessarily giving up the strong attachments to relatives living elsewhere, but often becoming estranged from their more traditional way of life through the broadening access to the fruits of upward mobility." Lipps (cited in Andersen, 1993, 93) shows why women gravitate toward social groups: "Men . . . are most likely to emphasize the significance of concrete helping as central to friendship, *while women emphasize talking, sharing, and comforting each other.*" And Rubin (1982, 149) writes that because "the suburbs have long been known as friendly places, the split between the groups of working and non-working women has been a particularly painful one. . . . With half of the women at work and many others in school, it's harder to find people at home anymore. . . . Today nobody seems to have time for anybody else. Years ago, there was always somebody out in the yard or down the street you could talk to, somebody you could share your problems and ideas with. And while you didn't want to be in each other's homes all the time, it did give you a warm feeling about your neighborhood. Today, that warm feeling seems to be gone."

and I didn't really know many people. The first thing we did was find a church we really enjoyed. Then these two women approached me about joining Bible study. I was really just looking for fellowship, for other people to be with, and to get to know more closely and more intimately the other women from the church."[9]

The group is a source of close friends. But it is no accident that these women selected a church Bible study group to find friends: it is a context that works for them. In their study on friendship, Gouldner and Strong (1987, 37) observe that friends "were likely to frequent places and settings in which their relationship could be pursued conveniently and where they both enjoyed spending time." Many of the women involved in WBS are also quite actively involved in the wider programs of the church.[10] And this forges deeper bonds, as one member explains: "I think it's because all of us have so much in common, as far as our concerns for our church, for our pastor, for the programs of our church [go]. And a lot of times a lot of our discussion and a lot of our outside conversation before the Bible study is about a concern we have about a church program or something else we're involved in."

Mentoring is a major feature of this surrogate family of women. As I mentioned, a number of the older women function as role models

9. Kraft (1992, 3) comments, "In previous generations women did things together — cooked, sewed, quilted, canned, raised children, and mostly talked. We have largely lost that sense of community and today the church must step in and help women get to know and love each other, filling the gap left by the disappearing extended family. Serving on committees and boards together, taking an elective together, going on retreats, praying together — all provide opportunities for friendships to develop. Fellowship is more than coffee and cake; it is working together toward a common goal."

10. The women who attend WBS are involved in a number of other activities: Bible Study Fellowship, a highly organized study of the Bible that is completed in five years; Camp Henley, a district evangelical retreat camp (21 WBS members attended Camp Henley this year); church choir (3 WBS women participate); church softball (7 WBS women cheer on the team); Friday Night Couples Bible Study (11 WBS women participate); Homebuilders, a group of couples that meets socially once a month (8 WBS women participate); Inspirational Speakers (4 of the older WBS women attend inspirational lectures that are given in Collegeville every other Friday by a nationally famous religious leader); Ladies' Night Out (8 WBS women attend); MOPS (Mothers of Preschoolers; 6 WBS mothers participate); Pioneer Girls (4 WBS women make up some of the staff: two are teachers and two are Pals); Play Group; SEC Small Groups; Sunday school classes; and Women's Ministries (22 WBS women attend).

for the younger women, and provide them with motherly encouragement. Why is this dynamic so strong here? Because this group does what an extended community used to do. An old African proverb says, "It takes a village to raise a child." In earlier times, generations of women commonly worked side by side, helping and encouraging each other through the daily challenges of marriage and child-raising. Today, with extended families scattered, it is almost impossible for most women to enjoy a nurturing, discipling relationship with other women in their families. "Therefore," writes one author, "women must look outside the home to find multi-generational relationships that offer wisdom, encouragement and fellowship. And what better place to start looking than at church" (Kraft 1992, iii). Indeed, in this group both generations interact on a deeply personal level: the young women look to the older women for spiritual focus and role modeling, and the older women offer the younger women guidance as they face the challenges of homemaking and dealing with difficult childhoods. This intergenerational interaction makes the group unique and sets it apart from other small groups such as twelve-step groups, mixed-couple Bible studies, and community groups.

Lisa, for example, tells why her favorite part of the group is learning from the spiritually mature women. "I want whatever I do to be at its richest, to be as best as I can do it, and I know that I'm not going to be able to do that alone, especially with the wisdom that I [have] now. I can draw from the wisdom of the older ones who have gone through it before and who have the joy of the Lord and are mothers. I enjoy listening to them. . . . They have such wisdom, they have such balance." She adds, "They're not worried about the things that I'm worried about. Those things are trivial. They're more in tune with what God has for them in their life and they're more content with what they have. And I want that. I want to be able to incorporate what they have into my life now, to be able to give to my children and my husband and be as rich . . . a woman as I possibly can."

The biblical directive for mentoring is found in Titus 2:3-5: "Bid the older women . . . to be reverent in behavior, not to be slanderers or slaves to drink; they are to teach what is good, and so train the young women to love their husbands and children, to be sensible, chaste, domestic, kind, and submissive to their husbands, that the word of God may not be discredited." Modern sociology reinvents this same principle: "Religion is among the foremost of institutions which conserve society,

111

encoding stabilizing world views and values and transmitting these from generation to generation" (Falk 1985, xv).

Arlene interprets this principle at the group level: "Those of us [who] are older feel very strongly that there is a need for the older women and the younger women to get together because it's a biblical principle that the older women should teach the younger women how to be a Christian homemaker and wife." Then she explains what the biblical directive means to her personally: "That's another big reason why I'm there, because I feel I've made enough mistakes in my lifetime that I might be able to help a younger woman avoid them. I really believe that this is something I want to do."

The role of the older women is key to this group. Those younger group members who moved away miss their former support system of older women. According to Lisa, "There have been years where there have been no older women, and it has just been us mothers who have the same problems, but no answers." Arlene underscored the importance of the older women encouraging the younger ones. "Today, . . . one of our members [offered] a fervent prayer: 'Lord, I need help to raise this child. I'm having a difficult time.' Now after the prayer, people can go up and encourage this girl in the situation she's in." And the older women are eager to share their spiritual and practical knowledge. Ruth acknowledges that "as an older, more mature person [I see] that you do get through these crises and problems in life. I think we need to share that with younger women who probably don't see it because they haven't experienced it yet."

This group helps make up for the lack of role models in other areas. Amalia, one of the younger women in WBS, envisions the ideal group as one "where there would be a mix of older women and younger women." She would like to be under the tutelage of an older woman who would help her learn how to organize her home and how to be a good wife. "I'd love to have someone take me under her wing, kind of like a mentor," she says. Indeed, these relationships *are* developing outside the confines of the group. One older woman, for example, explains, "I'm everybody's mother. They all call me Mom. Most of them I've been with at least three years on retreat. I usually drive, and I've got five young women in the car with me. We talk about everything from breast-feeding to menopause. . . . It's fun. I enjoy it — I love it." Rachel, whose parents live in Florida, is one of the younger women with whom this woman has formed a special bond outside the group. Rachel talks about their relationship: "She is almost like my mom. Bible study is the only reason that she and I are as close as we are. There would not have been another area in church where I would have met her and had a relationship in that way. She's almost like a best friend and a mother together."

For many of the women, the group also defines who they are as Christians. Their walk with God is enhanced by the group discussions, in which they are encouraged to talk about their lives from a religious perspective. This helps them personalize their Christianity. "My faith is deeper because of being in the group," says one woman, "because you get to see it lived out in other people, too." And being in the group gives members an opportunity to put their Christianity into practice. One woman, for example, says that the prayer requests help her to respond to others' needs with specific acts of compassion: "I hear things [in the group], and then I'm able to go up to that person privately later. I remember [to send] cards, think of [giving] food more often than I would think of [otherwise]. It sensitizes me."

In fact, through some of my interviews I learned that some of these women experienced dramatic changes and personal growth as a direct result of participating in this group. One of the changes that these women talked most about was the increase in self-esteem and self-confidence that they felt as a result of sharing in this safe environment. For instance, one woman remarked, "My self-esteem is so much better now. I'm more confident. I'll say what I feel. I don't just 'yes' people to death. I used to be what they call a people pleaser, and I would just kind of go with the flow and roll with the punches; that's what you do when you grow up in an alcoholic family. You just are quiet and don't have an opinion, and you don't have a statement. Now I've learned to know who I am, what I'm about, my likes, my dislikes, and I can express those things, whereas before I didn't. The group has really helped me with that, building my self-esteem and my confidence and just helping me to be what Christ wants me to be."

One woman found the courage to accept the leadership of another group because of her experience in WBS. "We used to take turns leading the Bible study, and even though I was a little uncomfortable with it at first, I did lead the Bible study. And as a result of that, when the opportunity came and I was asked to be the president of the Women's Ministry group, I felt more comfortable being able to say yes, I was willing to do that. The Lord gives you smaller stones to step on."

These women also believe that the group has increased their in-

113

terest in and understanding of Scripture and deepened their spiritual lives. Some explained that the group simply made reading the Bible more interesting. One woman said that her "desire for Scripture" had increased, "because it is made so fun in the Wednesday Bible study and because of everybody else's input." She added, "I go home sometimes with questions that will make me seek the Word more." Others emphasized that group discussions helped them see the meaning of Scripture more clearly. "I'm amazed at how interpretation of the Word will all of a sudden become the light," one group member commented. "It's like 'Oh!' You can see how they've applied it. I like [it] when the Scripture comes alive that way."

Being in the group has also influenced the values and personal relationships of these women in interesting ways. Many of the women said that they had become more loving and tolerant toward other members in the group itself. One older woman frankly confided that "I would have been a lot more impatient and intolerant of some of these younger women had I not been involved with them in this Bible study." Another woman said the group had helped her be more accepting of others: "It's made me more aware of things that I was doing that really weren't Christian, really weren't Christ's walk. I have a terrible time [with] being judgmental of people and thinking that my way is the only way. It's helped me to understand that we're all individuals and that just because somebody does it different than me, it's not wrong. We're all made in God's likeness, and Christ loves every one of us."

However, membership in the group also erected barriers between group members and people in the wider world. It wasn't that members became less tolerant of other people. But they did worry more about the differences between Christians and non-Christians. They became more fully committed to living out their Christian beliefs, and this in turn sometimes meant associating more with Christians or deliberately shielding themselves from non-Christian influences. One member, for example, came to feel that she should not let non-Christians take care of her children, and this led her to decide not to work outside her home. She explains: "I've grown in the sense that before I became a Christian and before I was involved with other Christian women, I felt you could leave your children in day care and it wouldn't be a big deal. But now as I've gotten older and really looked at what it means to be a wife and a mother and to be a godly person, I'm affirmed in that [my choice] through the group, knowing that I'm doing the right thing." Another

114

woman decided to filter out all nonreligious media, including cable television. Now she only listens to a Christian radio station. In addition, she says, "All my books are now Christian-based. My magazines even aren't secular anymore. I'll go to the Christian bookstore and pick up novels. Because of becoming a Christian, I just want to be the light in the world. I want to stand out and be different than other people."

Clearly, fellowship is a significant aspect of the group. It undergirds all the members' activities, not simply the brief minutes they spend sipping coffee together but also their Bible study and prayer time, and the friendships that extend into other church activities and that connect these women in invisible webs of interaction during the week. Because the group is theirs, they feel a certain pride of ownership. Because it indeed functions as a surrogate family, they feel they need it, and they depend on it. And because they depend on it, they allow it to shape their beliefs and values, and to feel good about those influences. One member summarized what the group meant to her this way: "I feel like a vital part of it. I feel like it's my group, and I like to be there. I feel like I *need* to be there, although the group certainly wouldn't fall apart if I weren't. The fact that it's right in the middle of the week is such encouragement to just go, get the fellowship and the input from the Word from people who've had more experience than myself."

Bible Study

The group is a fellowship, but it is also a Bible study. Studying passages from the Bible, biblical themes, or inspirational books based on the Bible composes the core of its weekly activities. The study is what makes the group distinct, what gives it a reason to exist. It is also something that the members take seriously. They describe their own experiences in ways that parallel biblical passages. They make God's Word come alive in the stories they tell about their everyday lives. Their control over the group extends to what they study, and just as their self-governance gives them a sense of ownership over the group, so their relating the Bible to their own experience gives them a sense of owning Scripture as well.

From the outset, whatever the lesson material used, the method of study has been Socratic. Susan, one of the cofounders of the group, says this was intentional, that the goal from the beginning was to give members more than "head knowledge":

> We modeled the group after the Bible studies that we'd been in in Campus Crusade. Just action-oriented open questions where you try to get people to think, rather than just "Where was Jesus headed? . . . He was headed to Lystra." You know, not closed questions like that, but open questions, so that you teach a person to study the Bible and make observations, interpretations, and applications, so that you can see an encouragement for your own life as a result at the end.

In fact, this interactive style of study has not changed in ten years and is one of the primary reasons for the group's growth and success.

I asked Susan why she thought the meetings had gone so well. "I think mostly it was people's attitude," she recalled. "People did not come there to show what they knew. They came there to learn something. They came to grow." And the women do grow in this group. As each woman links her life with the Bible passage or other material being studied, either by contributing to the discussion or listening to someone else make the biblical/personal connection, she gains a sense of ownership, not only by applying the passage to her everyday experience, but also by participating in the group's business.

Examples of how the group studies the Bible can be found by randomly sampling almost any of the tapes I made of the group's weekly meetings. At the fifth meeting I attended, for instance, the study for the week was based on a chapter in a book by a prominent evangelical theologian. After summarizing a story from the chapter (about the death of the author's father) and summarizing some of the hardships that the Israelites experienced under Pharaoh, Arlene asked the group to think of "the most life-changing experience" they had ever had, and whether this event had caused them to think about God. In response, several women mentioned childbirth or marriage, one commented on the death of her sister, and another mentioned the death of her parents. Then the comments turned to how God had helped them through these events. One woman said she had been sick not long ago and that reading the Bible had helped her make it through the night. "Sometimes you feel heaven has a brass door and you just can't get through," Arlene interjected, but she assured the group that "the knowledge that God is there" would carry them through even when "the emotion of God in your heart" might not. Others mentioned times of feeling vulnerable or weak, but realized that God would protect them. After a few more testimonials, Arlene directed the group to think about funerals they had attended and

116

how they had felt about them. Several mentioned the deep sadness they had felt. Others said they wondered whether the dead person was a Christian, but figured the important thing was that God knew. Eventually Arlene brought the discussion to a close, pointing out to the group that "God's existence gives meaning to our lives" as Christians.

Discussions of this kind have provided group members with new insights into how to live and how to think. For example, some of the meetings have generated ideas about how to relax, how to enjoy one's children more fully, and how to be a more patient mother. These are what members described as practical applications. Scripture, they see, can make a real difference in their lives.

For these women, however, the main result of studying the Bible is not gaining some insight that inspires them to live in a fundamentally different way than they have lived the week before. Instead, their discussions make them feel better about what they are already doing and who they already are. One of the things they like most about the group is that it validates their own unique perspective on life. The group cultivates a stance that in fact tries to accept all points of view, and this is comforting. As one member explained, "It's great to hear how one question can have so many right answers or appropriate answers. Then you take out of that what fits your particular life needs."

If it is comforting to have differences affirmed, it is even more comforting to express opinions that others share. The group emphasizes its diversity and its acceptance of different backgrounds and interests. And yet it clearly is a select gathering in which not everyone would be comfortable. Its members are in basic agreement, for example, that conservative, evangelical Christians have more going for them than liberal Christians or non-Christians. They share an implicit conviction that abortion is wrong and that most brands of feminism are leading women astray. They respect women with small children who work outside the home, but they also believe strongly that staying home with one's children is a virtue.

Knowing that these values are controversial, that they are not shared by many people in the wider community (or in the mass media), these women are comforted by having a group of like-minded people with which to discuss their beliefs. As one observed, "It's a real encouragement to me to have a place to share similar beliefs and similar values and to discuss issues from a biblical viewpoint and relate them to everyday life, applying the things that I believe in to where I live."

Most importantly, the Bible study is comforting because it affirms that the WBS members are indeed living good Christian lives. They might not decide to make difficult life changes, like selling all their goods to feed the poor, or going to a distant land as a missionary, or even to school their children at home. But they can see in the passages they study that in smaller ways what they are already doing is consistent with God's Word, or can be with perhaps a slight adjustment in their attitude. With this perspective, the Bible ceases to be a book of ideas, something that other people believed, and becomes a guide that these women can use for their own lives. "When you study the Bible," one member explained, "you learn to put feet to all those things you read. It's not just here [in the Bible], it's how it affects you, how it affects your walk." Through this process, the Bible becomes more meaningful to them, and their personal lives are enriched. The Bible becomes more meaningful because its principles seem to work. They are truths that are practical, that can be implemented. And the meaning of the women's personal lives is enriched because the study helps them see their small acts and ordinary activities in a divine context. A simple phone call to a friend is an act of Christian love. Reading one's daughter a bedtime story is an act of Christian mothering. The group fulfills what one woman described as the "quest for meaning in our spiritual lives."

Prayer

No single activity is more indicative of the group's character and nothing this group does has more of an impact than its prayer. It is the spiritual glue that binds these women to each other. It is what sets this group apart from a coffee-klatsch, a self-help group, or even (in their eyes) a mainline religious study group. Without prayer, this group would be only two-dimensional: the women would be only superficially aware of each other's needs and joys; there would be no proof of how God reveals himself and answers prayers; and no one would feel connected to anyone else spiritually or feel cared for and uplifted by other members throughout the week.

The group tries to go beyond just paying lip service by praying "for so-and-so." It attempts to galvanize members into action, encouraging them to perform acts of caring, and it consistently tracks prayer concerns, with the results being "God's scorecard." Deep prayer, both that offered in the meeting itself and by these women in their daily lives, is at the very core of their spiritual journey and helps them interpret God's plan for their lives.

To realize the importance of prayer in this group, one only need look at the prominence it is given in the meeting format. A full one-third of the meeting time is regularly designated for prayer. There is a set ritual: the first half hour is devoted to expressing and recording prayer requests and then praying for them out loud. As if she is conducting a business meeting, the leader first reviews "old business" by following up on prayer concerns from previous meetings and personal answers to prayer that can be moved over to the "praise column." When, for example, the group has prayed for someone undergoing surgery and that person has recovered, this news is recorded in the "praise column." "Any time God has answered prayer, that's a praise item," says Arlene. Each prayer concern receives significant attention. First, a woman voices her prayer concern or praise. After she explains the concern or the cause for praise, the group usually asks questions or makes comments. Then the leader writes the item on a big tablet in one of two columns — the one marked "petitions" (predominantly regarding health concerns, church needs, and employment and housing needs, occasionally involving a political item) or the one marked "praise" (this includes answers to prayer — e.g., someone getting better — and various kinds of good news — a good report from a church meeting, someone's selling a house, someone's husband getting a job). Many of the women take notes so that they can pray specifically about these joys and concerns during the week. (When I analyzed transcripts of the meetings, I found that about two-thirds of the prayers were about the individual needs of group members themselves; the remaining third were for others: family members, neighbors, friends, church members. Health concerns were brought up most often, followed by employment needs of spouses, business difficulties, selling or buying real estate and moving, and church activities and the general operation of the church. Occasionally prayers were offered in support of social or political issues.[11])

11. At the final luncheon, Arlene summarized how God had answered prayer during that year. Following is an abridged summary of her comments: "Our Bible study group has had many prayer concerns throughout this past year. We have seen many things happen in answer to our prayers, for which we thank God. Probably the single most significant and meaningful answer to prayer was the staff of nursery workers which the Lord sent to us through the efforts of Kim. It has greatly enhanced

119

When the list is finished, the leader asks for volunteers to pray out loud for certain things on the list. Then the group "goes to prayer." Someone offers an opening prayer. Next, the members offer spontaneous prayers for the items on the list. When all the items have been prayed for in this intercessory fashion, the leader closes with a prayer, and the lesson portion of the meeting begins. When the meeting concludes at 11 o'clock, the leader offers a benediction.

Everyone is encouraged to pray publicly. At the March 11 meeting, for example, Ruth nudged people to pray out loud: "Who would like to open with praise items and anything else that they would like? I know it's difficult to pray publicly, but if you've never done it before, remember you're amongst sisters who care, and they would not embarrass you in the least if you take one or two [of the prayer items]." The feeling is that if a group member prays out loud, she translates her struggles into spiritual language, thus invoking an answer on a spiritual level. In these meetings, prayer is an elastic element: it helps these women praise God but also share out loud their hurts, needs, and joys.

---

the effectiveness of our study to have the mothers freed up to attend each week. Our attendance remained almost consistent, with the same group of women coming from week to week. There were many specific things which we prayed for and [we] saw some very specific answers to those prayers: We prayed for Kathy through her difficult pregnancy and then for the health of her twins after they were born, as well as praying for them through their bout with pneumonia. These were very specific answers. We prayed for Marilyn's mother, who needed heart surgery. The surgery was successful and we were able to minister, not only to Marilyn but to her mother as well, as Marilyn shared with her that the women in the Bible study group were praying for her. There were concerns for employment and for housing needs. We saw answers to prayer in those areas, most outstanding in the area of housing. Sales came from the most unexpected places and at a time when the market has made it almost impossible to move real estate. We prayed for business difficulties that some were experiencing and saw, over the months, God's hand moving in those instances: the Berkeleys' new garden center, the Donaldsens' slowdown in income over the winter. During the year there were various health concerns that we shared just within our group. Nora Larsen [the mother of two group members] had serious surgery with some complications, but we saw evidence of God's hand on her life and body as she recovered. Lucille had surgery; Walter Hinkle had surgery for a broken hip; John Brooks continues to struggle with his cancer, but we have seen evidence of God's care and strengthening for both [him] and Valerie. We found God to be a faithful Guide and Friend during these times of prayer and, over the course of the months, learned to share more openly and pray more personally as we met together. We learned about faith in a great God!"

The ritual of sharing concerns through public prayer helps these women open up about their needs. One member illustrates the spirit of acceptance that prevails:

> I like the process of prayer. When you do have something that you need to pray about, you don't feel . . . like, "Oh, here I go again with another request." The women are genuinely concerned about everything. . . . It's allowed me to have needs, and not just constantly be sure that I meet everybody else's. [I know] that this is a place where it's okay for me to say "Help."

Prayers about personal struggles are especially appropriate and create an atmosphere of intimacy and shared concerns. One woman, for example, notes that prayer "gets me in touch with what's really going on with people."

Maintaining a Sense of Ownership

By June, at the end of my observation year, group attendance was up, averaging twenty to twenty-five women a week, and there was a lot of talk about splitting the group up. That month, the pastor of the church talked with me about the group's size. He made a strong case for dividing up the group based on diminishing opportunities for relationship. His observations about intimacy levels could hold true for any small group trying to preserve its sense of connectedness:

> The group is over capacity for a small group. The intimacy level is going to cap at where it is. It can't go deeper; there's too many people shut out of the discussion process with 26 people. You're going to have three or four talkers and the rest listeners, because that's the way groups work. Break the group up and you create more opportunities for people to be enveloped by other people. Then there's more places for people to bring their friends and to grow.

Any group that wants to foster church growth and community outreach will realize that, while the division process may be difficult, the maintenance of a certain level of intimacy is key to their goals. The more chances there are in a group for people to participate, the greater their sense of ownership of and involvement in the group. This fosters in-

121

dividual spiritual growth and creates more opportunities for a greater number of participants to have a satisfactory small-group experience. Groups like this one — successful, "open" groups that continue to attract new members — have to deal with the diminishment of intimacy levels as they grow.

This group held a planning meeting during the summer of 1992 with representatives from both subgroups — young mothers and older women — to tackle the problem of the group's size. There was disagreement about how the group should be divided. The older women wanted the division to be based on age. They felt a need for mutual support on issues specific to their life stage (e.g., living with retired husbands and caring for aging parents). They claimed they would have a better chance of receiving scriptural guidance for their concerns without having to compete for time with the young mothers. (This was in some ways surprising, given how positively a number of them had spoken to me about their role as mentors in the group.) By contrast, the young mothers did not want to divide the group by age. In the end, the younger mothers' need for mentoring won out over the older women's desire to isolate themselves. They reached a consensus to divide into two mixed-age groups (chosen by lot). They also reached consensus on another major point: to preserve a sense of community, the women would meet together for prayer and petition time in one large gathering for the first thirty minutes, then break into two discussion groups for the lesson. With this format, each group member would be able to stay informed about the important events happening in other members' lives.[12] The women thus

12. A mission statement was also drafted at that summer planning meeting and handed out at the opening fall session; this was the first time a formal purpose had been put into writing. Nothing in the document was new; the group had always functioned this way. But just putting the purpose into writing was a sign of the group's maturity. The document charged each woman to emulate and embody Jesus. It was drawn up in the form of a "voluntary covenant," with a place at the bottom for the member to sign "in recognition of her commitment to God and the members of the study group," a form congruent with the self-governing nature of the group and its emphasis on participatory ownership. The language of the six covenants included in the document is highly participatory and stresses accountability:

"For our individual benefit and accountability, let us each prayerfully consider making the following covenant with the Lord.

1. Regarding the interpersonal relationships established within this group, I covenant and pledge to accept my friends here at the Bible study, no matter

found a way to stay together, to retain small-group intimacy, and above all to retain control over their group.

As I see it, the sense of ownership is at the heart of the group's success. The group's autonomy is a recurring theme. To begin with, the women themselves decided to form this group. In addition, they run the group democratically, taking no specific direction from the church hierarchy. They find leaders in their own ranks, choose their own study guides, hire their own babysitters, and do their own setting up for meetings. Shared responsibility is not unique to this group, but it does add to the sense of ownership that these group members feel.[13]

Each member decides how big a helping of ownership she will take for herself from the smorgasbord of opportunities for participation — whether or not she will participate in group prayer, share personal experiences, care for others outside the meeting time. And the group gives her a sense of participatory ownership in deeper ways too. On a spiritual level, she is given the opportunity to "own" a Scripture passage when she internalizes it and interprets it through her everyday experi-

---

> what has been in their past, what is happening now in their lives, or what may occur in the future. I may not agree with each and every action, but I will attempt to love each one as a child of God and do all I can to express God's affirming love. I need each one of you.
>
> 2. I pledge to make myself available — as personal needs may arise within the group — to the limit of my resources. As a part of this availability, I pledge to meet with you on Wednesday mornings on a regular basis and to arrive on time at 9:30 a.m. ready to begin, to the best of my abilities.
> 3. I promise to pray for you regularly.
> 4. I agree to share my true opinions, feelings, struggles and joys with you.
> 5. I pledge to be sensitive to you and your needs to the best of my ability, as I trust you will to me. I will try to hear you, see your point of view, understand your feelings and draw you out of possible discouragement or sadness.
> 6. I promise to keep whatever is shared within the confines of this group. I vow to not push you to share things about yourself that you would prefer to keep undisclosed."

13. In a paper on feminist spirituality groups, Lummis (1992, 7) concludes that "whether women's groups are spiritual feminist groups or more traditional church women's groups, they are similar in exhibiting shared responsibility for meeting agenda, space and food provision. Also in most of these women's groups, decisions are not made autocratically or even authoritatively by leaders after discussion with group members, but at least democratically if not consensually, and rather informally."

ences. In addition, the group provides an important benefit by validating her thoughts and actions, which encourages her to validate them and thus develop "personal authority," which is something she can exercise in the group.[14] This too gives her a sense of ownership. On the whole, this Women's Bible Study remains true to its purpose: "to provide a place where the women of the church and community gather together to develop a personal relationship with Jesus Christ through fellowship, prayer, and Bible study." Yet it is not without its flaws. A primary weakness of the group is leadership development. It is ironic that the group, although it expressed concern about its becoming so large that it would have to divide, made no provisions to develop new leaders. And, like all groups, this one also suffers to some extent from the fact that study materials are subjected to a great deal of individual interpretation that sometimes weakens their intended message. This is related to the issue of ownership, which is a weakness as well as a strength for the group. However, the women involved would not retain this sense of ownership if their leader prodded them too hard or their pastor decided to intervene in the group's discussions. To its credit, the group does an excellent job of supporting its members and of affirming what each person has to say. And it provides an occasion for members to offer short testimonials about the goodness of God and for them to express their needs in a context of prayer and thanksgiving. But it probably does less well at offering them challenges — to take a hard look at their short-comings, for example, or to discuss the prevalence of sin and the need for forgiveness, or to look at their biases and attempt to understand better how people with different religious perspectives might think.

The discussions of an autonomous Bible study group like this one probably help to place Jesus at the center of participants' lives, thereby making them feel better about who they are. Whether these discussions can also do more to help each participant face the challenges of God's will is undoubtedly still a point at issue.

14. Young-Eisendrath and Wiedemann (1987, 1) define personal authority as "the ability to validate one's own thoughts and actions as good and true. It develops gradually, as others recognize and communicate the value of one's ideas and contributions. Our society designates authority symbolically by conferring decision-making influence, social status, and power over material resources. These are typically not associated with women or women's work." Attneave and Speck (1974, 166) state that "groups provide a context within which an individual can look more deeply into himself and at the same time validate his observations by communicating with others."

Making Disciples in a
Liberal Protestant Church

DANIEL V. A. OLSON

Compared with conservative Protestants, lay members of liberal Protestant churches are, on average, less committed to their church and their faith. In surveys they claim to attend church less frequently, pray less frequently, read the Bible less frequently, have less knowledge about the Bible, and give a smaller percentage of their income to their church. In addition, liberal Protestants are also less likely to identify themselves as "strong" members of their church and less likely to say their faith has an important impact on their life decisions and their daily lives (e.g., Stark and Glock 1968; Roof and McKinney 1987; Olson 1993).

Some suggest that little can be done to increase liberal Protestant commitment. They argue that the commitment of the average member tends to be diminished by the very features of the tradition that many members find most attractive — for example, the unwillingness of liberal churches to make strict demands in matters of lifestyle and belief (Kelley 1972), demands that would screen out less committed members (Iannaccone 1989); their openness to social and theological diversity, diversity that undercuts the basis of shared community (Wagner 1979); and their less supernaturalistic interpretations of life, death, and the hereafter, interpretations that provide less justification for life-changing commitment (Stark and Bainbridge 1985). Such arguments suggest that liberal Protestantism is, by its very nature, incompatible with a high level of commitment from its members.

The "Disciple" group examined here is part of a denomination-wide effort by the United Methodist Church intended to increase biblical knowledge and religious commitment among small groups of lay members who, the designers of the program hope, will then influence other members by example. Through disciplined Bible study, regular prayer, and focused group discussion, the program aims to make "disciples" out of ordinary Methodists, disciples equipped for ministry both in the church and in the world.

Based on my assessment of the group I observed, the program appears to be moderately successful. The group members pray and read their Bibles regularly. Many claim to have found a new, more personal relationship with God, a relationship that influences their daily lives, making them more compassionate, sustaining them in difficult times, and helping them to overcome personal obstacles. Some have begun, almost unintentionally, to witness to others about their faith. Most are active church leaders.

How is this achieved? Has the program simply turned these Methodists into pious conservatives? Or is it possible to build religious commitment and piety without forsaking core elements of the liberal Protestant tradition?

In discussing their devotional life, their relationship to God, and the impact of their faith upon their lives, the group members sound much like the evangelical Protestants among whom I was raised. But, like most liberal Protestants, the group members maintain a very open stance on theological and social-moral issues. On the other hand, certain group members rejected and effectively blocked discussion of liberal social-justice issues during meetings, even though this was an important theme in the Disciple materials.

The experiences of this group highlight the key ingredients involved in fostering spiritual growth and religious commitment within any religious tradition: knowledge of the religious tradition, and regular social contact with others who by example help one to interpret its meaning for daily life. While these conditions are more likely to occur naturally in conservative church settings (Olson 1993), the experience of this group shows that they can be intentionally created, even in a liberal church.

The Disciple Program

The Disciple program, which began in 1987, was created by the Board of Discipleship of the United Methodist Church. Methodist Bishop Wilkie, who played a key role in its development, felt a need to (1) raise the levels of biblical literacy among Methodists, describing the current situation as "a wasteland," and (2) "equip the laity for ministry" both in the church and in the world.[1]

"Disciple groups" are formed in the autumn and consist of no more than twelve "disciples" and a "teacher," a size intended to remind participants of Jesus and the twelve disciples. Group members publicly commit, before their congregation, to thirty-two weeks of intensive Bible study, which every week involves four to five hours of preparation and a group meeting that lasts for about two-and-a-half hours. Members are allowed to miss only four meetings. During the first year of the program, titled "Becoming Disciples through Bible Study," participants read through most of the Bible. They do this with the help of a detailed study guide and a workbook complete with daily reading assignments and questions to be answered prior to each meeting. Meetings follow a highly structured discussion format. At the end of the year, a ceremony is held during a Sunday worship service. During the ceremony, a small wooden cross attached to a leather necklace is hung around the neck of each new "disciple."

During the initial years of the program, its designers were, according to Bishop Wilkie, "caught off guard by the tremendous spiritual power of the group experience." They found that people in the groups really "bonded together" and were hungry to continue their study together. Moreover, "whole congregations were being revitalized" through the influence of the new disciples, who began taking on leadership roles in their churches. This led to requests for more materials so that graduates of the program could go further. The result is the Disciple II program, begun in the fall of 1991 and used by the group I observed.

The Disciple II program is titled "Into the Word, Into the World," a title that emphasizes its twofold purpose. Whereas the Disciple I program covers the entire Bible, the Disciple II program gets "into the Word" in greater depth, focusing only on Genesis, Exodus, Luke, and

---

1. Wilkie's comments, here and elsewhere, come from a video tape shown to all Disciple II group members during their first meeting of the year.

Acts. According to Wilkie, the creators of the program did not want people to just go on "studying the Bible forever and ever." Clearly, the Disciple II program does not view Bible study as an end in itself. Rather, the study guide is structured to challenge people to get "into the world." People should "hear what God is saying" and this should "lead to a change in their lives."

The Disciple II program maintains its commitment to core liberal Protestant values but also incorporates elements usually associated with conservative Protestantism. For example, liberal Protestants sometimes argue that Christians should be more concerned with changing the world and worry less about inner spiritual development. But the Disciple II program stresses both and insists that an individual can give "witness and service" only when he or she has experienced an inner transformation.

The Group

The Setting

Our group met every Monday night from September through mid-May at Trinity United Methodist Church,[2] one of the larger Methodist churches (with about 1,000 members) in Morgantown, a medium-sized midwestern city. We met in a basement-level Sunday school room in the church's educational wing. The room, which measures about 25 by 15 feet, has fluorescent lighting, an acoustical tile ceiling, gray wall-to-wall carpeting, dark wooden wainscoting, and white-painted walls. On the walls are several posters showing dogs and cats in unusual poses with humorous captions; another picture shows the little children coming to Jesus and sitting on his lap.

During the meetings we sat around three long tables with Formica tops and collapsible legs, the type used to serve people at large church banquets. But these tables were always pushed together, side by side, to form a large conference "table" that was almost square (about $9' \times 10'$). Bill, the "teacher," always sat alone on one side of this table at the front of the classroom. The rest of us sat around the table in padded folding chairs, three to a side. During the meetings, this table was almost

2. All proper names that might help identify the participants have been changed to protect their anonymity.

completely covered by open Bibles, workbooks, notepads, and various reference works. In the center of the table was a three-inch thick, slow-burning candle that was lit at the beginning and extinguished at the end of each meeting. This same candle was used throughout the year. At the front of the room, next to Bill, was a portable whiteboard as well as a VCR and a television monitor on a rolling stand. In the back there was a table with coffee and "goodies" brought by a different member each week. Dress was casual: blue jeans, T-shirts, sweatshirts, and running shoes were common attire.

The arrangement of the "table," chairs, and whiteboard suited the discussion–seminar format of the meetings. The candle at the center of the table, which was Bill's innovation, served to remind participants of the religious purpose of the meetings.

The Members

Only graduates of the Disciple I program are eligible for the Disciple II program.[3] In the fall of 1991, nine of the 30 eligible graduates at Trinity signed up for the Disciple II program. Our group had ten people (including me), six women and four men. These members ranged in age from 34 to 80; the average age was 52. They (excluding me) have, on average, 17 years of formal education. All have graduated from high school, and all but one have at least some college education. Two have master's degrees. Seven (including me) are married, two are widowed, and one is divorced. Four have children living at home. The members are unrelated, with the exception of Fred and Jean, who are married. All of the members under age 65 are employed full-time. Their homes, most of which I visited during my interviews with them, suggest a middle- to upper-middle class lifestyle. All of the members are white. Their religious backgrounds are typical of other Methodists I know. Only four were raised as Methodists; three were raised in fairly inactive Protestant households, one was raised as a Catholic, and one as a Baptist.

3. The Disciple II program assumes knowledge of the Bible gained in the Disciple I program. The church made an exception in my case because the Disciple I class, which met just down the hall, already had twelve members and because I already knew most of what was covered in the Disciple I program.

In most ways the members seem fairly representative of Trinity, whose members tend to be white, middle to upper-middle class, well educated, and "semisuburban." The exception is that all but two of the members now have tasks or hold positions on committees in the church.[4]

Study Materials

During the first meeting of the year, each Disciple II participant receives a 256-page softcover study manual. The manual contains 32 chapters or lessons of about eight pages each, one chapter per week of the program. Most of each lesson describes and explains the assigned reading for the week. The lesson is divided into two parts: "Into the Word," which explains more about the background and interpretations of the biblical readings, and "Into the World," which is shorter and usually consists of a series of fairly pointed questions asking how the individual, the group, the church, and the community could respond to "the Word." Both parts of the lesson contain blank space for participants to write in their answers to questions raised by the study manual. These questions are often the source of group discussions during the meetings.

So that they can get further "into the Word," each Disciple II group is provided with copies of several books and reference works intended to be shared among group members. Each week, in addition to the regular Bible reading, members are assigned specific pages in one of these texts. These include *Genesis and Exodus* by Everett Fox, *Jews and Christians: A Troubled Family* by Walter Harrelson and Randall M. Falk, the Harper's Bible Dictionary, the Oxford Bible Atlas, and William Barclay's commentaries on Luke and Acts.

"Teachers" receive additional materials that provide a schedule for weekly activities, lists of questions and activities to facilitate discussion, and additional background information on the weekly readings. All leaders of Disciple groups, clergy and lay, must attend a weekend training seminar conducted by the Board of Discipleship.

4. As I explain subsequently, this is partly because an attempt was made during the early years of the Disciple I program at Trinity to recruit people who were either currently involved in church leadership or people who were likely candidates for such positions. But it also reflects the success of the program.

Group Meetings

Most Bible studies that I have observed struggle with the tension of trying to be both a "class" that focuses on study and learning and a "fellowship group" where people discuss personal concerns and provide emotional support.[5] The two goals are often, though not necessarily, in conflict.

The Disciple program leans heavily toward the class model. The result is a highly structured discussion-seminar. An introductory video warns participants to keep the prayer time "brief," no more than five minutes, because it's easy to "get carried away." However, it also tells leaders that meetings should focus on "discussion" and should not become "lectures." The program structure encourages participants to share their personal experiences as a way of helping one another see connections between the biblical tradition and daily life, but the program designers want to avoid making interpersonal support the main function of the group.

Every week the meetings had the same six-part structure: (1) opening, (2) getting "into the Word," (3) break, (4) encountering the Word, (5) getting "into the world," and (6) prayer/closing.

The "opening" (my term) usually began about five to ten minutes after the official meeting time of 7 p.m. and followed a period of informal conversation as people filtered into the room. When Bill lit the candle, this was the signal for everyone to quiet down. Next, Bill played recorded music, using his own tape recorder and playing songs he had quite carefully selected from his personal tape collection. These songs always had religious lyrics and often related directly to the readings for the week.[6] During the music, members either bowed their heads in an attitude of prayer or listened attentively to the words of the song. This simple ceremony was effective in marking off the time ahead as special and religiously serious.

5. During the past fifteen years I have lived in six different cities, and I have been involved in six different Bible study and fellowship groups based in church settings ranging from Baptist (evangelical) to Presbyterian.

6. Bill mentioned that many of the pieces were performed by members of a Catholic charismatic group known as "People of Praise." The playing of this music, like the candle lighting, was another of Bill's innovations. Bill told me that he often spent quite a bit of time finding songs that fit the readings for each week. In the interviews I had with the group members, all of them mentioned that they especially enjoyed the opening music.

The purpose of the first discussion segment, "Into the Word," was to expand members' understanding of the historical, geographical, and theological context of the previous week's readings. This always began with a fifteen-minute "video presentation" played on the VCR/TV from tapes provided with the Disciple II materials. The presentations were by prominent biblical scholars or well-known ministers who provided background information or an interpretation of the readings.

Next, Bill assigned us tasks and questions to answer. Sometimes we read a Scripture passage quietly to ourselves and then reported to the group what we found. Often we broke into small groups of three, with each group responsible for answering a different question.

Group members enjoyed these activities. It seemed to excite their curiosity. Often someone would spontaneously blurt out a question, and the rest of the class — despite being broken up into smaller groups with different assignments — would dig into their Bibles and reference materials until they found the answer. One week, for example, as we were trying to reconstruct genealogies of the twelve tribes of Israel, someone asked if Tamar, through whom came David's lineage, was a Caananite. If so, how did this square with later prohibitions against the Israelites marrying Caananites? Members seemed pleased that they could use their newfound skills and knowledge in Bible reading (along with the reference materials provided by the Disciple program) to answer these questions for themselves.

Around 8:30 p.m., we took a break (lasting from five to fifteen minutes) to stretch, use the bathroom, and eat the "goodies." This time, along with the brief period preceding the opening and the brief time following the closing prayer, was important because it provided one of the few opportunities for unstructured conversation among group members. Often these conversations had nothing to do with the explicit goals of the group, and might involve an exchange of jokes or a discussion of recent church or news events. But on other occasions these periods provided an opportunity for the members to talk about personal concerns and events in their lives. Members would show support for each other by asking about prayer concerns mentioned the previous week. Sometimes the break would be used to continue the discussion that had been going on before the break, or someone would raise a question that had occurred to them during their previous week's studies. The break ended when Bill would say, "Let's get started now with our encounter of the Word."

The "Encounter the Word" segment began with Bill or several people in the group reading a short passage from Scripture while the

132

rest of us followed along in our Bibles. Then Bill would ask us questions about the passage. Unlike the questions we dealt with during the "Into the Word" period, these questions focused less on background information and more on interpreting the personal meaning of the passage. For example, after reading about God calling Moses from the burning bush, we were asked questions like these: "Why do you think God chose Moses?" "Have you ever felt God is calling you to do something?" "How do we know when God is calling us?" "Is there anything in the passage that can help us know?" and "How have you responded to God?"

The ensuing discussions were sometimes very rich. People gave examples from their lives showing how their faith influenced their life decisions and outlook. In response to the questions at the end of the previous paragraph, Bill began the discussion by explaining how God's call often came through the "opening and closing of doors" (life's opportunities). He described how devastated he had been after being fired from a previous teaching position because of his union activities. He had been blacklisted in most of the state. He had taken his current teaching position in Morgantown because nothing else was available on such short notice. Nevertheless, he now believes that God used his firing to bring him to his current position, where he feels he can be a force for good helping Hispanic junior-high students adjust to adulthood in Anglo society. Rob then told how, after reading the book of Jonah, he realized that he should no longer avoid God's "call" to lead a church prayer group. Matilda mentioned that while at the shopping mall she felt God calling her to help a stranger in a wheelchair who was having trouble putting his coat on.

At other times the discussion quickly moved away from the topic, often through the use of jokes or puns. For example, at another point in the same meeting, Fred commented that today God wouldn't be allowed to speak to someone from a burning bush unless God first got an environmental impact statement. This led to a mostly negative discussion of government regulations. In interviews at the end of the year, most members acknowledged that the group discussions often wandered away from the assigned topic.[7] While some, including Bill, felt this joking

---

7. During interviews, several of the members — especially those who took the first Disciple I class conducted at Trinity — noted that this wandering away from the topic happened more frequently in the Disciple II class than in the Disciple I class. This class had been taught by Julia Asplund, who at that time was the associate minister. Those who took Julia's class agreed that it was much more intense and

around was good because it fostered group bonding, others felt that it prevented discussion of certain topics, especially social justice issues, and wished that Bill had been more assertive in keeping the group focused on the assigned topic.

Next Bill asked us to turn to the "Into the World" section of our study manuals that asked us how we planned to respond to what we had learned during the week. These questions focused specifically on changes that members could make in their lives, their church, and their community.

The ensuing discussions varied greatly from week to week. Sometimes people became engaged with the questions and struggled to find meaningful answers. During one meeting one of the questions had to do with how we could witness to our faith. Several people commented that they felt bad that their grown children seldom attended church. They wished that they could speak more freely to their children and grandchildren about the importance of faith, but they said they had learned not to be "pushy" lest their children get upset with them. Rob also said that he was careful, but when important life issues came up during informal conversations with coworkers, he was not ashamed to talk about his beliefs and the role they played in his life decisions. Others felt that they witnessed through their actions. Jean described how that very day a customer with a severe speech impediment had come to her office. She said that some people would have just tried to get rid of him, but that she tried to treat each person as if he or she were Christ. So she gave this man special attention, for which he was very grateful. Alice said that the idea of being a witness used to bother her, but she felt differently about it now. Although she pointed out that she wasn't "a Bible thumper," she said that she tried to set an example and that people seemed to notice. They would tell her that she had a "glow," and would comment, "I wish I had that." In response, she would tell people how God had changed her life.[8]

---

focused and made a bigger difference in their lives than did the Disciple II class. They disagreed on whether this was due to the different materials used in the Disciple II class, or if it was due to Bill's more relaxed, less assertive leadership style. Most of the members who claimed that the Disciple program was responsible for major changes in their lives thought that these changes were mostly due to the influence of the Disciple I class with Julia.

8. While Alice made these points during this particular discussion, some of the quotations come from her elaboration on these same points during my interview with her.

On other occasions, members had difficulty responding to the questions, and there would be almost no discussion. People would say something like, "Gee, that's a hard question. I don't know what to say." This happened most frequently when the questions concerned topics that seemed distant from the daily lives of the participants. For example, after reviewing a chapter that dealt with the Hebrew bondage in Egypt, we were asked what we could do about several other types of "bondage": illiteracy, drug addiction, and political enslavement. While there was some brief discussion of drug addiction and the fact that the church provided meeting space for an Alcoholics Anonymous group, there was no discussion of political enslavement. None of the participants had experienced political enslavement, nor is it likely that they knew anyone who had.

On still other occasions, the "Into the World" discussions took a very conservative turn not intended by the program designers. This was most likely to happen with regard to social justice issues. For example, one evening we discussed the following question: "Most years in the United States, a great deal of grain is stored up. Yet in some parts of the world, including the United States, hunger prevails. What ideas do you have that would help Christians become better providers for hungry people?"

There was a brief discussion of a church program that collected canned goods for a local food bank. But then the discussion turned to the question of whether we should distinguish between the deserving and the undeserving poor. This led to a long series of tirades against those who abuse welfare. Alice told of an eleven-year-old who got pregnant and was really proud of it because it was the "in thing to do." The grandmother was taking care of the baby and getting paid AFDC. As Alice explained it, she "just sits home taking care of these babies while the money keeps flowing in." Others spoke of the cycle of dependency, "generation after generation" of people who live off welfare. Several times Bill asked, though not very assertively, how we as Christians could do something about this. Fred said, half jokingly, that the best solution would be to drop a huge bomb on Washington, just wipe the whole thing out and start over again from scratch. Jean said that we needed to go back to an earlier time when we had a sense of pride in this country. The "solutions" focused more on who not to help than on how we could be better providers for hungry people.

The last few minutes of the meeting were used to quickly share personal prayer requests. During the beginning of the year, almost all of these requests pertained to medical problems (e.g., an acquaintance was in the hospital, someone was facing cancer, surgery, etc.). Later in the year, the requests began to include other things of a more personal nature (e.g., prayer for God's help as Linda's son faced his first finals week in college; prayer for Jean's sister, who was in the midst of a court battle for custody of her children following a divorce; prayer for Barbara prior to Christmas because her husband had died several years ago and she was lonely at this time; and prayer for Alice as she organized the orientation class for new members at the church). As members shared prayer requests, each of us copied them down in the space provided for this purpose in the study manual. Each day, before beginning our Disciple studies, we were expected to pray for the concerns mentioned during the previous meeting.

In other Bible studies I have attended, members have shared concerns and then prayed aloud for one another, a practice that often leads to strong interpersonal bonding. By contrast, Bill ended our meetings with a prayer in which he briefly mentioned the concerns that members had shared with the group. This prayer was usually very brief and seemed to serve more as a marker that the meeting was over than as a deeply significant time of sharing or worship.

Immediately after the prayer, we shuffled a set of Polaroid snapshots, one of each group member, and passed them around face down. We each took one and were expected to pray for this person each day before beginning our Disciple studies. Given how late it was at this point — between 9:35 to 9:45 — people usually picked up their materials and left quickly after cleaning up the room. Informal conversations, when they occurred at this point, were brief.

Evaluating the Group and the Program

How well does the Disciple II program attain its goals? I can best answer that question by looking at several key characteristics of and developments in the group I studied.

Reading the Bible

Consistent with the first goal of the Disciple program, group members read their Bibles regularly and read with understanding. During the meetings I was impressed by the members' serious approach to Bible study. Their study manuals were usually heavily marked up with notes that they had taken during the previous week's studies.[9] I was also impressed by the breadth of members' knowledge regarding both basic and sometimes esoteric aspects of the Bible. Their spontaneous questions revealed both a curiosity to learn and sufficient background to ask intelligent questions about the Bible. One week someone asked, "Who is this Melchizedek guy, anyway? Isn't he mentioned in Hebrews too?" One member then turned to a Bible dictionary while others used their concordances to locate all of the biblical references to Melchizedek.

While three group members had previously been involved in many years of Bible study,[10] four members admitted that they had begun the Disciple I program with very little knowledge of the Bible. Alice, aged sixty-five, told me that despite having attended Methodist Sunday school classes for most of her life, she had previously believed that the twelve disciples wrote all the books in the Bible. She also claimed that she had "never really understood before that Jesus was God's son." The more she learned, the more excited and curious she became. This led her to read the historical accounts of Josephus in parallel with the Christian Gospels.

A Relationship with God

The Disciple materials stress that individuals can offer "witness and service" only when they have experienced an inner transformation. During my interviews with them, many group members told me that as a result of the Disciple program, especially the Disciple I program, they had developed a much "closer relationship with God." For example, Alice said that she had always believed in God but now found God to be "a personal friend." "I talk with him every day," she explained. As a result, she now has an "inner peace" that she has never had before, a

---

9. During the interviews, most of the participants indicated that there were some weeks during which they had not done the assigned reading. However, most of the time they came to the meetings prepared.

10. Matilda and Elizabeth, both women of retirement age, had completed four to five years of Bible study in the nondenominational Bible Study Fellowship (BSF) program prior to beginning the Disciple program. BSF is a national program with a local "chapter" in Morgantown. Rob, aged thirty-four, had been heavily involved in the Navigators (an evangelical campus ministry) during his college years.

peace that makes it easier for her to be outgoing and helpful to others. "I used to be a sour pickle on the inside, always filled with envy, 'til I took the Disciple program." This peace, she told me, is "a gift from God," a gift "I never want to lose."

Elizabeth, aged seventy-two, noted that regular Bible study has made her more aware of God's presence in her life. "Every time you study, you realize you are never alone." Elizabeth, who lives alone, feels that being aware of God's presence helps her cope better with situations that come up each day. It also makes her more willing to reach out to others. If she misses this study time, for the rest of the day she feels there is "something missing."

Several group members emphasized that they had always believed in God, but that it was an impersonal, distant God with whom they had one-way communication. For example, Jean, aged forty-two, said that prior to her involvement in the Disciple program she had often prayed, "but now I wait for an answer." She claims that she learned this patience from the biblical examples of Job and Paul. They "went through a lot, yet they kept going in spite of it all." She has learned that "It's OK to yell at God" or be "grumpy," but also that you cannot bargain with God. Linda, aged forty-one, told me that she had always relied on others as intermediaries between herself and God — for example, she would ask a minister to pray for her. Now, she says, "I am in touch with God. God has always been there, but before it was a one-way conversation. Now it's a two-way conversation, a personal relationship."

Stronger Faith, Inner Peace, Transformed Relationships

How does this changed relationship with God affect participants' lives? Most of the life changes that group participants reported are of an inward, personal nature. During the interviews, six of the members told me that their participation in the Disciple program had given them a stronger faith, an inner peace, and a greater ability to cope with stress. However, many also claimed that these inward changes spilled over into their relationships with other people, making them more loving, accepting, and forgiving.

Linda said that she first became involved in the Disciple group because she wanted a "stronger faith." Her faith "wasn't that personal." It wasn't something that she "could hold onto in a crisis." Now she feels that her faith is supporting her as she faces several (unspecified) difficulties with her teenage children. It keeps her from "going crazy." She relaxes more, worries less about tomorrow, and feels a sense of peace knowing that "somebody else is in charge." Barbara indicated that she had been quite self-critical, feeling that she "had to do it all and do it all well." She now feels more at peace with herself, more willing to accept her own limitations. She admits that she has a lot of questions that God hasn't answered yet (e.g., Why did her husband die five years ago, when he was only in his mid-forties, and leave her alone?). She is often quite lonely, she told me, but added that she is beginning to feel an inner peace partly as a result of the Disciple program. She is now "more comfortable with not having all the answers."

Many participants told me that their experience with the group had changed their relationships with other people, helping them to be more accepting, forgiving, and willing to reach out. Matilda gave an example of how a neighbor, who tended to be a hypochondriac, called her, saying she needed a ride to the emergency room right away. At first Matilda was reluctant, but then she thought, "That is not what a Disciple should do!" So she drove the neighbor to the hospital. Barbara feels that her studies have made her more tolerant of others and their shortcomings. "I realized what Jesus went through for me — he gave up his life. If Jesus can be forgiving to me," she reasons, "then I can be more forgiving to others." Apparently this change is quite real. During one of the meetings, Barbara explained that for many years she had harbored negative thoughts about her mother. She went on to say that her mother had told Barbara's daughter that she (Barbara) had "really changed since she started going to that group."

Into the World?

Undoubtedly the program designers would be pleased with the participants' increased biblical literacy and with their reports of inner spiritual transformation. Yet, as Bishop Wilkie points out, these changes are not ends in themselves; they are intended to "equip the laity for ministry" both in the church and in the world. Methodist ministers with whom I spoke see the Disciple program as a way of revitalizing congregations through the influence of reinvigorated lay leaders. Having been "into the Word," are participants now going "into the world"?

None of the members said that they had joined the Disciple group in order to become church leaders. Nevertheless, all but two are now involved in church tasks or leadership positions. This is partly because an attempt was made during the early years of the Disciple I program at Trinity to recruit either people who were currently involved in church leadership or people who were likely candidates for such positions. Even so, four of the members claimed that they had become more involved in church service since joining the Disciple group. For example, Alice said she was once "a pew warmer" but that now she is the director of outreach to prospective new members, a job for which she is paid a part-time salary but to which she gladly "contributes" up to forty hours a week.

During my interview with Alice, she listed the names of seven other people from her original Disciple I class who she feels have become much more involved in church as a direct result of the program. Several Disciple II members told me that at the end of the Disciple I program, the group discussed each member's "gifts" and the areas where he or she could best serve. Fred told me that this was a powerful personal affirmation for him. Without it he would not have become a member of the Christian Education Committee.

Both Alice and Bill feel that the members of the Disciple classes are now influencing the church as a whole to become more involved in helping others. For example, Linda helped get Trinity, along with other churches, involved in starting a home for unwed mothers. She says that this is something she might have done anyway, but the Disciple program helped her get started. Alice mentioned her own Sunday school class, which was getting together for a lot of social activities but "wasn't doing anything Christian." She explained how former Disciple group members took the lead in convincing the class to start supporting a Christian summer-camp program for inner-city kids. Now the class gives the camp financial support; in addition, several CPAs from the class now donate their accounting services to the camp.

In a few cases, group members say that their participation in Bible study encouraged them to volunteer their time in nonchurch settings. Elizabeth, aged seventy-two, indicated that she now volunteers at a local hospital and at a local elementary school library because she learned that "this is something God wants me to do."[11] She feels that she should

11. Elizabeth began these activities after becoming involved in Bible Study Fellowship and prior to her involvement in the Disciple program.

give back some of the good things she has received in life. She said she feels better inside when she does this. Even Fred, who in meetings often spoke forcefully against giving welfare to the "undeserving poor," volunteers occasionally at a homeless shelter in Morgantown.

While the Disciple program does not encourage aggressive evangelism, it does encourage members to talk about their faith. As noted above, some of the members, especially Alice, have found that they have begun to do this, almost unintentionally, as a natural result of their new relationship with God. Others, like Bill, indicated that the Disciple program has made it easier for them to talk about their faith because they are now more sure of what they believe and what they don't believe.

As I mentioned before, perhaps the biggest failure to go "into the world" from the point of view of the program designers is that certain group members, especially Fred, have rejected and effectively blocked discussion of liberal social-justice issues even though this is an important theme in the Disciple materials. Indeed, four of the members hold quite conservative views on welfare, social spending, taxation, economic regulation, and crime and punishment. They often expressed these conservative viewpoints so forcefully in meetings that the two or three members with more liberal views — including Bill, Linda, and me — became reluctant to speak up.[12] (See, for example, the discussion of welfare issues described above.) As a result, there was little sustained discussion of practical actions that the group or the church might take to alleviate suffering or halt injustice.

Conservatives in Disguise?

If one looks only at participants' knowledge of the Bible and levels of church involvement, one might suspect that these are really evangelical Methodists, not typical of the denomination as a whole. Indeed, their "personal" relationship with God sounds a lot like evangelicals' "personal relationship with Jesus Christ." The only difference is that for these Methodists, this "relationship" is the result not of a dramatic, identity-changing conversion, but of a concerted effort to draw closer to the God who has always been there.

---

12. During my interview with Linda, she told me that she often kept her views to herself but left the meetings feeling frustrated and angry.

Despite these similarities, the group members are not religious conservatives. Nor is Trinity markedly more conservative than other Methodist churches. During the meetings I attended, members frequently made disparaging remarks about "fundamentalists," Baptists, Mormons, Jehovah's Witnesses, Seventh Day Adventists, and several other groups they perceived as being "too conservative" or too "rigid." Group members reject the need for strict doctrinal standards. During the interviews I conducted, I asked what sort of person would have difficulty fitting into the group. Many said it would be difficult to accept someone who was "really rigid" or "literalistic" in their biblical inter-pretations, someone who wouldn't accept other valid points of view. Bill admitted that as a science teacher he sometimes has serious doubts about whether there is a "hereafter" and whether there really was a bodily resurrection of Jesus. Nevertheless, he knows he has a personal relation-ship with God, a relationship that is changing his life.

Group members also reject strict views on social-moral issues. One evening, near the end of the break, Alice commented on how the church had changed "over the years." "I realized the other day that we have a lot of people in this church who are living together and are not married and the church doesn't say much about it." The responses ranged from "So?" to "Who are we to judge?"

As I mentioned, some of the group members are quite conservative on social justice issues. However, even though the group as a whole is more conservative on these matters than are most Methodist clergy, denominational leaders, and designers of the Disciple II materials, the members are probably not much different from most Methodist lay-people, who tend to be moderate to conservative on economic and social justice issues (Hadden 1969; Olson and Carroll 1992).

Pros and Cons of the Class Model

By design, the Disciple group is more like a class than a fellowship group. This was especially true of our group.[13] This became clear one night

13. During the interviews, nearly all of the members said that they felt that this particular Disciple II class was more of a "class" than a "group." Most said there was less fellowship and bonding than they had experienced in their Disciple I class. This was especially true for people who had taken the Disciple I class with Julia

following the unexpected death of Jean's thirty-five-year-old brother from a rare virus that destroyed his heart in a matter of weeks. When I arrived for the meeting, someone in the group told me that he had died on the previous Tuesday or Wednesday. We were just getting started five or ten minutes late when Jean arrived. As she entered the room, Alice got up and gave her a hug, but nothing was said about her brother's death. Bill then said that we needed to get started with the meeting because we were late. At the end of the meeting, someone commented that we should pray for Jean and her dead brother's wife, but little else was said.[14] I was quite surprised. I felt that something important was missing. The Disciple program views Bible study primarily as a means to an end, and one of these ends is to make participants more caring persons. It seemed to me that here was an obvious opportunity to care for a fellow member, yet the requirements of the "class" seemed to displace the ultimate goal of caring for others.

While the class-like structure of the meetings limited members' opportunities to show emotional support for one another, it helped focus the meetings on the study goals of the program. Members learned a great deal about the Bible — not just the facts, but also the implications for daily life. This was partly a result of the deliberate two-part structure of the class and the workbook. The "Into the Word" sections, including the speakers featured in the video segment, focus on getting the facts straight and providing adequate background for understanding. This helps avoid situations where group members construct elaborate and highly personal biblical interpretations based on misunderstandings of the text. And, indeed, in the group I attended, the group members readily drew upon the commentaries, workbook, and video presentations when they had questions about a confusing passage.

The "Encounter the Word" and "Into the World" sections of the

---

Asplund. Julia's class had shared many meals together and had undertaken several class projects, including the planning of an Easter sunrise service. The members of this group thought that Julia's enthusiastic leadership style was partly responsible for the cohesive, family-like quality of the group. "We were a family," they said. "We could share anything."

14. During the interviews, a number of people said that they had expressed their sympathies to Jean the day before at church. When Jean recalled the meeting, she said that she thought that people probably felt awkward and didn't want to arouse powerful emotions when they supposed she might be struggling to retain her composure. She didn't feel that the group members were uncaring.

workbook and the meetings served as an important complement to the "Into the Word" sections. They prevented an exclusive focus on historical, geographic, and textual minutia. They pushed members to draw connections between their personal experiences and the assigned Bible readings (e.g., "Have you ever felt God is calling you to do something?").

The stories that people told in response to these questions were perhaps the most valuable part of the meetings. They helped the members come to know and trust one another on a fairly personal level, and they provided concrete models of how they could live their faith "in the world." When, for example, Jean explained that she witnessed by treating each person as if that person were Jesus, others could envision themselves witnessing in a similar fashion. Even though the group frequently wandered away from the topic of discussion, such times of focused sharing might have happened even less frequently with a less structured format.

As noted above, the group failed to discuss social justice issues in a meaningful way. This failure was partly due to Bill's less assertive leadership style and the very conservative economic views of some group members. However, the class-like structure of the program made it difficult to overcome these obstacles. The program was most successful in areas where members were able to draw upon and share relevant personal experiences. But the discussion of social justice issues seldom elicited such sharing. This probably happened because most members had little personal experience with social injustice or the concerns of the oppressed. And what experiences they did share tended to reinforce negative stereotypes. To overcome this difficulty, the program designers might need to find ways to give members greater personal exposure both to people engaged in social justice ministries and to people who benefit from such ministries. This might be accomplished by incorporating a practicum or field-experience element to balance the current seminar-study-discussion activities.

On the other hand, I expect that there would be significant resistance to such a change. Fred told me that unlike the Disciple I program, the Disciple II program tries to push a liberal "political agenda." Not only does he disagree with this agenda, but he feels that "politics" has "no place" in the program because it works against the cohesiveness and thus the effectiveness of the group as an instrument for personal spiritual transformation. Given that many Methodist laypeople probably share Fred's definitions of politics, religion, and their separation, he may be right about its effects on group cohesiveness. In order to better incorporate social justice issues into the Disciple program, the program designers may first need to address members' conceptions of politics, religion, and their appropriate interpenetration.

How the Disciple Program Fosters Spiritual Growth and Commitment

Unlike Jesus' disciples, no one in my Disciple group left home and family or gave all their possessions to the poor as a result of the program. Nevertheless, the program appears to increase biblical literacy, encourage spiritual renewal, and increase levels of church leadership and volunteer work. While some members began the program with a broad knowledge of the Bible and some were already actively committed to their church and their faith, others were not. The experiences of this group suggest that it is possible to foster meaningful spiritual growth and higher levels of religious commitment even in a liberal church setting. How does the Disciple program accomplish this?

My observations suggest that it is accomplished in much the same way it is accomplished in any religious tradition. In order for a religious tradition to become "real," in order for it to have an important influence on one's daily life and the decisions one makes one needs a working knowledge of the religious tradition, and regular social contact with others who by example help one to interpret its meaning for daily life.

The first goal of the Disciple program is to increase biblical literacy. Since for most Protestants the Bible is, officially at least, the primary source of spiritual and religious insight, knowledge of the Bible is critical for spiritual development and maturity. How can one apply the religious tradition to one's life if one does not know that tradition? Among the members of my group, Alice gained significant knowledge. Not only was it helpful for her to learn that Jesus' twelve disciples did not write the entire Bible, but it was critical for her to understand that "Jesus was God's Son." Similarly, Barbara was able to be more forgiving of others once she understood what Jesus had gone through for her — "he gave up his life" to save her.

Yet for most people, knowledge of the religious tradition is not enough to stir commitment. Emile Durkheim (1915) and Peter Berger (1967) argue that people need regular social contact with others who share their beliefs. Without such contact, people slowly forget the vitality of their religious experience, their religious identity begins to blur, and their beliefs lose much of their plausibility and relevance for life. Most people need help to see the connections between their daily lives and a religious tradition that may be thousands of years old.

The structure of Disciple meetings encourages members to share stories from their lives, stories that show how they are interpreting and applying their newfound knowledge of the Bible. Hearing others use religious language and religious analogies to describe their life experiences makes it easier for members to interpret their own lives in a religious framework. It may be helpful to read that God called an outlaw like Moses to lead the children of Israel out of Egypt, but it is even more helpful to hear how God "called" an unemployed and blacklisted teacher like Bill to his current position, where he now helps junior high students prepare for adulthood.

In this way group discussions in the Disciple meetings function much as they do in more conservative churches. There they are much like testimonies: they make the tradition more plausible and real. When others describe the struggles they are going through and tell how they "really feel God's presence" helping them, listeners are more likely to feel that they can call upon God when facing similar problems. According to Berger (1967), the group discussions function as "micro plausibility structures."

Elsewhere (Olson 1993) I argue that there are sociological reasons why this social reinforcement of belief naturally occurs more frequently among members of more distinctive, often conservative religious groups than among liberal Protestants. Comparatively strong, religiously based, intra-group social ties provide conservatives with many opportunities, both inside and outside of church, to discuss the meaning of their faith. By contrast, liberal Protestants discuss such matters less frequently. The lack of such discussion becomes especially critical when these believers face crises such as divorce, illness, and death. When they are unable to discuss personal crises with others who affirm their religious interpretation of and response to these experiences, religious beliefs and the religious tradition begin to lose plausibility and relevance for them. And a tradition that becomes distant, implausible, and irrelevant is unlikely to arouse deep commitment.

While the conditions favoring spiritual growth and religious commitment are more likely to occur naturally in conservative church settings, the experience of the group I attended shows that they can be intentionally created in small-group settings even in a liberal church. Conservative theology is not a requirement for religious commitment.

Without borrowing conservative theology, the Disciple program intentionally creates some of the elements that foster commitment in more conservative groups. There are "strict" standards (Iannaccone 1989) for membership — not theological or lifestyle standards, it is true, but standards that nevertheless screen out those unwilling to commit to regular attendance and completion of reading assignments. The content of the program forces members "into the Word," thereby increasing their knowledge of their religious tradition. Finally, the program creates regular social contact among people who help each other, by their life examples, to see the connections between the biblical tradition and their contemporary lives. Only when people see and understand the personal implications of these connections are they likely to heed the call to go "into the World."

Sacred Space on Tuesday: A Study of the Institutionalization of Charisma

ELFRIEDE WEDAM AND R. STEPHEN WARNER

Introduction

The Oakley Prayer and Sharing Group consists of sixteen adults in a large midwestern city who meet for two hours every Tuesday evening for the purpose of praising God and sharing what God is (or is not) doing in their lives. Every week the meeting is held at a different member's house, so everyone equally bears the burdens and enjoys the privileges of hosting. Yet complicated travel is not involved because all the members live in the same neighborhood, that surrounding St. Hildegard's Church. Most of the group members send their school-age children to the parochial school. (In 1992, the members ranged in age from thirty-three to forty-five, and among them they had brought twenty-eight children into the world.) On Sunday morning, most of them attend the charismatically inspired "alternative mass" at 10:30 in the parish's gymnasium, across the street from the main church; there a conventional mass begins at 11:30. The masses are well attended, perhaps in part

The authors wish to offer their thanks to the Gallup Institute for financial support, to Robert Wuthnow for methodological guidance, to the members of the Oakley Prayer and Sharing Group for their generous cooperation, and to each other for many things. This project has been in every sense a joint effort.

because many who attend this urban Catholic parish can walk to church. During our year of observation, the group members marked their seventeenth anniversary of meeting together. The parish pastor, Father Byrne, has said that the members "model what it means to be in your thirties and go to church."

In one way, the Oakley group can be seen as a success story of the incorporation of youthful post-charismatic energies in the post–Vatican II Roman Catholic Church, since it appears on the face of it that the church, as represented in this one parish, has made room for baby-boomer spirituality. To be sure, most members of the prayer group were educated in Catholic schools and CCD classes. Several went to seminary. Many report having been profoundly influenced by clergy, from members of religious orders to diocesan priests.

Yet the center of our story is not the receptivity of the church but the independent institution that the Oakley group created. In fact, technically, most of the Oakley members live outside St. Hildegard's boundaries. Moreover, they did not grow up in the neighborhood but moved there as adults.[1] At the time of our observation, they had been attending mass regularly at St. Hildegard's for only seven years, since shortly after Father Byrne arrived. They had spent the years before worshipping with St. Francis's parish nearby (though also not the one in which most live), and for a while they had also attended a Mennonite fellowship, whose practices influenced them deeply. While all are now registered members at St. Hildegard's, they are spiritually heterogeneous. Some are Orthodox Trinitarian Christians; others resonate with the goddess; one prays to trees. That they have persisted so long together — losing some members and picking up new ones along the way — is attributable to dogged persistence, to good luck (perhaps Providence), and to a protracted, painful, and creative process of institutional evolution.

The group began in the mid-seventies. During the first four years, members of what is now the prayer group were leaders of an unbounded, open, charismatic prayer meeting with as many as 150 occasional participants, mostly single students living in a university neighborhood on the other side of town. For the past eight years, they have been a committed, closed, collegial group with rotating leadership. Most of the

---

1. They provide an example of "elective parochialism" (Warner 1988, 86-87, 201-208, 292-293). See also the discussions of Catholic "floaters" in Warner (1994) and of "loyalists" and "returnees" in Roof (1993).

current members are married and have children. They are homeowners with college degrees (sometimes higher degrees), employed in the helping professions, who work and live in the central city. The time they spend together on Tuesdays allows them to explore the religious meaning of their busy, people-centered lives. In between these two phases — the open meeting and the collegial group — was an extended period of transition. It is with an eye to this outcome that we will analyze their experience and achievement.

We — in this report we'll use our first names, Elfriede and Steve — were members of Robert Wuthnow's research team studying spiritual small groups, and we used the observational and interview protocols discussed elsewhere in this volume. We are indebted to Professor Wuthnow for the care with which these protocols were developed. In a sense, though, our research began much earlier, during Elfriede's doctoral dissertation project (Wedam 1993). When she was doing her field research between 1984 and 1986, we first learned of the Oakley group and met some of its members through "Peaceful Solutions," a "seamless garment" pro-life, anti-war group. After Wuthnow had contacted Steve in 1991 about joining the research team, he asked Elfriede if the long-running prayer group she had told him of years before might welcome us as researchers and her as an observer. We took this request to the Oakley group, and they took it seriously (as they tend to do everything else). They devoted one business meeting, in lieu of a week's sharing, to the issue, and Elfriede was asked to make a formal presentation. Their answer to our question about participation was "yes," and we are grateful to the group for their welcome and cooperation.

Our data are drawn from observations, interviews, and documents. Elfriede, herself a forty-something cradle Catholic, was a regular participant-observer in the group from September 1991 through June 1992; Steve joined her and the group for two meetings in May 1992. We have attended the 10:30 alternative mass and the 11:30 parish mass on several occasions. Elfriede interviewed all current members of the group, and Steve interviewed the parish pastor. We also drew on a 14-page booklet called "History of the Oakley Prayer and Sharing Group" (written by group member Matt O'Connell in 1983 and revised in 1987), and a 24-page booklet called "Diamond Jubilee of St. Hildegard's Parish" (1987), as well as various parish bulletins and brochures.

What we did not do was track down and interview the many scores of individuals who were at one time involved with the Oakley group but are no longer. We are aware, then, that our retrospective is constructed from the point of view of survivors. Only six of the 1991-92 members go back to the early days of the mid-1970s; one had joined as recently as 1990. The notion that "the group" has a seventeen-year history is thus to some extent an idealization. In the section that follows, we will detail the structure and norms of the Oakley Prayer and Sharing Group as we observed them and were told about them in 1991-92; we will also mention specific accounts and events. In the subsequent section, we will recount, in abbreviated form, the group's history as members tell it. In later sections we will analyze aspects of Oakley's religious and social constitution, their notion of "god talk," the relation of members to the group, and the relation of the group and the wider society. In a final section we will reflect on the theory of institutionalization. Throughout our discussion, names of group members, clergy, churches, and places are pseudonymous.

The Setting of the Oakley Prayer and Sharing Group, 1991-92

On Elfriede's first visit to Oakley — on the September evening when she presented our research proposal — the harmonious sound issuing from the open windows of the hosts' living room confirmed that she had found the right place. Group members — seated on couches, stuffed chairs, dining chairs, and a piano bench — were ending their "prayer" session, the first half of the regular two-hour weekly meeting. During this time — through songs, formal prayers, *sotto voce* praise, speaking in tongues, readings from Scripture and spiritual literature, guided meditation and contemplative silence — they invoke the name of God and become open for the second half of the meeting, which is devoted to "sharing."

Music is central to the group's history and liturgy. They own a dozen each of two charismatic renewal songbooks.[2] (A few months ago they sent a cassette of their "greatest hits" to a former member who had moved away.) Some members have trained, solo-quality voices; others provide ad-lib harmonization. For longtime veterans of the group, sing-

---

2. They are *Songprayers,* rev. ed. (Phoenix: North American Liturgy Resources, 1979), and *Songs of Praise,* combined ed. (Ann Arbor, Mich.: Servant Publications, 1982).

ing invokes memories of common experience going back to their college days; for all of them, singing helps concentrate, or "center," their thoughts on God.

The year before we arrived on the scene, the group had decided on an option for the prayer session, an alternation, depending on who was hosting the meeting, between the "old format" of spontaneous praise-and-prayer inspired by the 1970s charismatic movement, and the "new format," when hosts would designate a prayer "theme" and assign texts to be read during the meeting. For the Tuesday that happened to be St. Patrick's Day of 1992, the new format was used. Katy assigned readings with Celtic resonance. George, who had just spent two weeks in Ireland, read an explanation of the Celtic symbols of sword, stone, lance, and cauldron. Sara read a meditation on the book of Ecclesiastes published by the Christian Appalachian Project. Katy herself read her favorite Dylan Thomas poem, "Vision and Prayer," which, she said, interweaves Celtic Christian and pagan symbolism.

The prayer session ends at about 9:00 p.m., when there is a short break. Sharing begins when members come back, coffee cups filled, to tell and hear stories. During this time, those who want to explain how they feel God has been manifest (or missing) in their lives, especially in the areas of work and family.[3] During the year we were involved in the group, George worried about the viability of his small business venture, while Dennis worried that his successful corporate career threatened to draw him away from his family. Margaret, a new first-grade teacher, worried about how to combine a full-time job with taking care of her and Ralph's three children. And Julia, a home health nurse, confessed her fear of violence in the public housing projects where she visited her patients. How to find the time and money to provide the right kind of upbringing and education for their children concerned many of the parents; at the same time, many of their own parents were aging and ailing. Several of the women were coming to grips with memories of abuse as children, and members' marriages were a frequent topic of concern and celebration. In all of these matters, members tried to discern the presence and the will of God.

3. "Growing numbers of Roman Catholics, Muslims, and Jews are turning to small groups. For Catholics, many of these small groups are far more than Bible studies or prayer groups. . . . They function as faith communities that come together to enrich each other's family and work lives" (Roof 1993, 254). See also Prell (1989).

The group has rules for sharing. Unlike the prayer session, when murmured prayers may be addressed to God, those sharing are obliged to speak up so that everyone present can hear. Sharers are supposed to talk about personal, immediate things (this caveat may have been inspired by the "new format" theme); "head tripping" (or intellectualizing) is frowned upon, if not always avoided. The earlier readings, scriptural or otherwise, are used to illuminate life; they are a springboard for personal disclosure, not the focus of discussion. Whoever has the floor is supposed to (and, to a remarkable extent, does) have the undivided attention of the group. No one is ever cut off, nor do people try to "top" one another. Rather, they listen, offer supportive comments, and, when it seems appropriate, give advice. The norms of the group proscribe too much "advising," and we heard in interviews that members have to restrain themselves from giving more advice than is wanted. Not everyone will have something to share every time, and the hour may be taken up by the stories of only two or three members. On the rare occasion when no one seems to have anything to say, someone may joke, "Does anyone have a life?"

Some members are known to be reticent, and, over the months, they can expect encouragement and coaxing. When we asked one of them, Ralph, if he is ever uncomfortable with the group, his answer was revealing:

> The group makes me uncomfortable every week because I'm being challenged to give a little more and grow a little more and become a little more honest with myself and a little more intimate with God or other people. And that's what I need very much. When I want to be comfortable, I go to bed with a good book. That's comfortable. I'm not sure that faith and sharing faith should be too comfortable.

The sharing session ends near 10 p.m. when the host-leader reminds people of the time. If sharing has focused on someone's illness or distress, such concerns may be remembered as the group joins hands for a final, soft-spoken prayer.

People don't leave right away, because they look forward to a half hour of dessert (often a homemade specialty of the host) and frequently high-spirited socializing. "Sharing" within the group is intended to be relevant to all participants, present-oriented and focused on faith experiences. But after that people gather in small groups of twos and threes, relate news of absentees, and read letters from former members. Sometimes they discuss differences that came up in sharing, or make general-interest announcements. Conversation is ebullient, yet this time is not technically part of the meeting, not at its heart.[4] One member told us, "Small talk is nice, but it's not at all why I . . . go."

Members let us know in many ways how central these weekly meetings are to their lives, especially the sharing. They respect each other's thoughtfulness and frankness and value the energy they collectively generate. One member observed, "People have really busted their butts to get there. They have emotions and time invested into it." Another said of herself and her husband, "We moved here on the street because of the prayer group. We bought this house as a result of the prayer group. We're different parents, we're different people as a result of these people in our lives." Yet another said that the group was the anchor that kept her and her husband living in the city.

The group is enmeshed in the city, and from week to week the meeting moves from one member's house to the next. Their homes are, for the most part, the sort of airy, two-story houses with a lived-in look that are typical of aging midwestern urban neighborhoods dating from the turn of the century. Despite the spacious houses, the neighborhood has smaller lots, more apartment houses, and higher population densities than you would find in nearby suburbs and small towns.

The members of the group — predominantly Irish-American Catholics but also Italian, German, and Polish Catholics — live in what has always been a mixed neighborhood. Before World War I, there were the Irish, Germans, and Luxembourgians who built St. Hildegard's; now there are Hispanics; Chinese, Koreans, Filipinos, and Vietnamese; African-Americans, Afro-Caribbeans, and Africans; Indo-Pakistanis and Arabs. The huge public high school at the end of the street where five families live is one of the most ethnically and racially diverse in the city.

Those five families in particular worry about the city. The other side of their street has large apartment buildings, with many transient tenants, some of whom deal drugs. Crime seems to be increasing, and group members are concerned for their kids' safety. Last year an elderly member of the parish was abducted during a robbery of her local convenience store; her bludgeoned body was found in a downstate cornfield a week later.

Closer to the quiet, tree-lined heart of the neighborhood, away from

---

4. Thus the group does not *formally* "break bread together," in contrast to the theories of Dick Westley (1992), an influential friend, fellow parishioner, and former professor of some group members.

the busy arterials that form the parish boundary, sits the large, well-maintained plant of St. Hildegard's — which includes a 1,200-seat sanctuary, a school, a gymnasium, a rectory, and a social hall. This is the sort of complex that so-called megachurches are building today, but St. Hildegard's was constructed between 1912 and 1950. The parish is a healthy, stable, busy operation. The present pastor is only the fifth in its eighty-year history, and the fourth Irish-American. An official directory lists forty-four parish organizations, such as a Divine Mercy Prayer Group, the Friday Men's Faith Group, Heart to Heart (serving the homebound elderly), Hope and Help (start-up assistance for twelve-step groups), Legion of Mary, Our Lady of Penafrancia, Pax Christi, Rite of Christian Initiation of Adults, the Rosary, Theology on Tap, and Women's Spirituality, and a theater group. Oakley members are active in many of these organizations.

The Prayer and Sharing Group itself does not appear on this list. As we shall see, its history and identity are independent of the parish. What does appear in the parish directory is the "10:30 Gym Mass Core Group," with group member Matt O'Connell listed as "contact person," because the Oakley group provides the initiative for the alternative mass.

The 10:30 mass is distinguished not so much by its folksiness and informality (these days it is easy to find Catholic masses where guitars are played and blue jeans are worn[5]), as by liturgical dance, piano jazz, individual prayer requests, a hand-to-hand prayer circle, generally high levels of participation and, most notably, dialogue or "talkback." When the priest has concluded his homily, the floor is open for discussion (a microphone is available), and this is no mere gesture. About a dozen people, men and women both, will endorse, add to, qualify, or disagree with what the priest has had to say. Time for the lectionary readings may be sacrificed to make this discussion possible, but the result is a genuine alternative to the often perfunctory feel of the standard parish mass. Father Byrne told Steve that the 10:30 mass has drawn scores of younger people into St. Hildegard's, and all but one of Oakley's members are regulars.

The Group's Story

Drawing on our interviews and the booklets, bulletins, and brochures provided us, we will sketch the story the group tells about itself, from

5. For a satirical view, see Day 1991.

its beginning in 1974 to our last contact with it in 1992. We will focus on its changing structure.

1974-75: A New Pentecost

The story begins in 1974 with Dave Kern's road-to-Damascus experience. A Roman Catholic seminarian in high school, Dave had dropped out of religious life years before, turned off by the rigidity and dogmatism of the church. But, despite his indulgence in the freedoms of the 1960s, he had found nothing more satisfying. He remembers himself, a year after his college graduation, as a "lost soul." At this juncture, Dave's curiosity was piqued by a chance encounter with Father Bill Sawinski, the former rector of the seminary, who had been a particular source of Dave's dissatisfaction with the church but who now, five years later, seemed a radically changed man. Father Sawinski told Dave that he had had a new experience of God, and that he knew God differently now. Eventually Dave invited Father Sawinski to talk about his spiritual life with several friends. It turned out that Father Sawinski had been touched by the Catholic charismatic renewal.

The friends met with the priest over wine in Dave's College Park apartment. During the third meeting, Dave accepted Father Sawinski's invitation to experience God anew and instantly had a life-changing experience. He remembers a rushing in of energy, better than "sex, drugs and booze," which left him practically speechless. He felt "a force bigger than life" in the apartment, permeating the very fabric of his being. Looking back, Dave says with certainty that he "encountered God." He later recalled a statement attributed to Carl Jung, who, when asked if he believed in God, replied, "I don't believe. I know."[6]

Dave's friends in the room felt something fleeting, but Father Sawinski felt the holy presence and took Dave into another room to explain what had happened to him. Dave felt cleansed and healed. When the two returned to the others, Father Sawinski suggested that it was time to hold a liturgy, and he said the mass for the day. Even the lectionary readings, Dave felt, spoke directly to his heart for the first time in his life. Later that evening, Dave's girlfriend, Naomi, came by

6. We have heard a version of this story in which Jung's certainty pertains to the afterlife, not God *per se*. What is important is Dave's conviction.

after work and remarked on an extraordinary change in his appearance. Dave counts that evening, November 13, 1974, as the central moment in his life.

The small group of friends agreed to meet again to discuss Dave's experience, and, at the next meeting, Dave's friend, Tom, had a similar encounter with God. At this point they decided to meet for discussion and prayer every week. After a few months, Naomi was able to rearrange her work schedule to join them, and, as the word spread about this group, others came as well.

1975-78: The College Park Prayer Group

The group soon outgrew Dave's apartment and found meeting space at the Augustinian friary in College Park, where the average weekly attendance was two dozen or more. The group attracted a variety of people, younger and older, married and single, religious and lay, some Protestants but mostly disaffected Catholics. Among them was Matt O'Connell, who had heard about the group from his fiancée, Darlene. Connecting with other charismatic groups, the College Park group held its first of several "Life in the Spirit" seminars, structured programs offered through the Charismatic Renewal movement to help more people "release the Spirit" in their lives.[7]

The College Park prayer group was open, and many people came and went. Dave estimates that about 150 people were involved at some point during that time. As the meetings grew in size, planning was required to accommodate all the participants, and planning meetings fostered the talents of particularly committed members who could give "teachings," play music, join a prayer team (in which people were prayed over while others practiced the laying on of hands), provide refreshments, and plan further events. Thus, one of the results of the planning meetings was the formation of a strong core group, among them Dave and Naomi and Matt and Darlene, who developed a desire to share in a deeper way in one another's lives. So they held their planning meetings every other week and met during alternate weeks for personal faith-sharing.

Soon these same core members began to get married and settle down, and several chose the affordable but pleasant vicinity of St. Hilde-

---

7. See McGuire (1982), chapter 3.

gard's on the other side of the city. At first they drove the thirty-mile round trip to the College Park friary for group meetings once a week. However, as they began having children, earning graduate degrees, and entering careers, the commute became burdensome. Eventually, in 1978, they decided to dissolve the College Park group and invited all those interested to join them in their new neighborhood.

1978-84: "Kernell Acres"

The next six years were a time of intensive commitment to and experimentation with community. The new geographical location of the prayer group was the Oakley Street residence shared by Dave and Naomi Kern and Darlene and Matt O'Connell. Because of their friendship and their desire to share in community with one another, they purchased and lived in a two-flat together. Few other members were homeowners with the freedom to invite over whomever they wished and make as much noise as they wished, so the meetings were usually held at "Kernell Acres," the name for the two-flat that combined the couples' last names.

For two years, the group continued to have weekly open meetings and smaller core meetings that alternately focused on "business" and sharing. Because of an unwelcoming atmosphere at St. Hildegard's, the parish church for Oakley Street, many of the members became active in the life of nearby St. Francis, where two Jesuits on temporary assignment became their mentors. But then a long period of struggle ensued.

Kernell Acres increasingly became the focal point for group life, particularly once the friendly Jesuits left St. Francis and the group was without a church home. New people joined the group who did not share the legacy of the College Park years. Few of them had the time to devote to the business and planning side of the group. Some of the newcomers had dysfunctional family histories and looked to the group and its leaders for psychotherapy and fulfillment of basic needs. (Dave was by then a social worker and Matt was studying for his doctorate in psychology, and their wives were training to be, respectively, a nurse and a teacher.) The Kerns and the O'Connells and other core members began to feel burdened by the expectations thrust upon them, and their own relationships were strained. But some of those outside the core felt that they were being left out of key decisions. Subgroups were formed and then dissolved. Some people left.

Group members thrashed out these issues in many meetings, a weekend-long retreat, and counseling with Jesuit spiritual advisors. Talk of the charismatic gift of "discernment" (of the will of God) became prominent in their discussions. At length, the group decided to seek advice from and worship on Sunday with Urban Place Fellowship, a nearby charismatic Mennonite community,[8] but also to attend the brief Saturday vigil mass at St. Hildegard's, the parish church for Kernell Acres. The group established Pentecost of 1984 as a decision date, and they expected guidance from the Holy Spirit.

1984-90: "A Ministry to Each Other"

As a result of the experience with Urban Place Fellowship, which itself had recently moved from a strictly communal to a more associational structure, the Oakley group refocused and shed ambitions that had become burdensome, including the ideas of building an outreach ministry and forming a tightly knit surrogate family. They concluded that a formative spiritual life could be achieved simply by gathering each week, sharing their faith, and trying to apply the resulting lessons in day-to-day life. Not all the members were willing to abandon the search for an all-encompassing community, and they began to leave.

Those who stayed also learned from Urban Place that holding the prayer group meetings continually at the same core members' home helped fuel suspicion of oligarchy. So the Oakley group decided to meet at a different member's home each week. Meanwhile, within two years, the O'Connells and the Kerns moved into separate homes. In effect, the group turned inward, decentralized, democratized, and limited its scope. As Naomi recalls the Kernell Acres days, the group "really was a kind of ministry. It was there *for* people, anybody who was interested, anybody who needed or wanted to come." Since the transition, "it's certainly still a ministry to those of us who are there, but it's more of a time to nurture. I think it's still a ministry to each other, but it's not an outreach."

Despite the nurturance and support that the Oakley group members received from Urban Place, they discovered their need for meaningful Catholic worship, especially celebration of the Eucharist. And just

---

8. See Harris (1973). Some of the advice they would have received is presented in Jackson and Jackson (1974).

as their Mennonite sojourn drew to a close, the diocese sent a new priest to St. Hildegard's: Father Frank Byrne. He knew and respected the spirituality fostered at Urban Place, and, soon after he took charge at St. Hildegard's (a month before Pentecost), a friend[9] told him about the remarkable bunch of young people known as the Oakley Prayer and Sharing Group. Byrne welcomed their overture when they asked the new pastor how they could be of help.

Oakley's gift was the establishment of an alternative mass, which, with its homily and subsequent dialogue, was designed to reach out to alienated Catholics and other unchurched Christians. In this mass, Oakley members could experiment with new forms of worship such as jazz, dance, and drama, to which they had been introduced at Urban Place. Over the years following Byrne's arrival, Oakley members have helped launch the parish's RCIA program (Rite of Christian Initiation of Adults), a Friday-morning Men's Spirituality Group (to which the pastor also belongs), and a Women's Spirituality Group. Several group members are now parish employees. Sara, who joined Oakley in 1980, is a parish pastoral counselor; Margaret, a group member since 1984, is a teacher in the parochial school; Martha, a group member since 1986, is social service director, a position previously held by Katy. Several members have become active in parish committees and outreach programs.

Thus St. Hildegard became the larger, formal community to which the prayer group members could meaningfully relate. Their Catholic identity was reaffirmed as they embraced the local parish, which came to serve as a channel for outreach and a resource for people in need. Eventually, the 10:30 mass became a function of the parish, no longer expressing the distinctive Oakley style. But the Tuesday-night experience itself provided the spiritual nurture and discovery that the members craved.

1990-92: "The New Format"

In the charismatic years of Kernell Acres and before, group meetings began with the kind of free-flowing praise-and-prayer session that members had learned in the charismatic movement: it included loud singing and speaking in tongues with arms raised skyward, spontaneous Scripture

9. As Father Byrne told Steve, the friend was Dick Westley.

readings, dancing, and prophetic utterances. For the members of longest standing — especially Dave and Naomi, Darlene and Matt, Julia, and Jim — "prayer" of this sort was and is satisfying. Still, their own settling down and the loss of some key instrumental musicians in the exodus of the early 1980s meant that the praise-and-prayer offerings became less rousing. In addition, newer members who had not had the charismatic experience or whose theology was less orthodox found the prayer hour less satisfying and often wondered and waited in vain to receive the Spirit. Sometimes they fell asleep and only rejoined the group when sharing began.

In late 1990, the newer members articulated their dissatisfaction through a series of business meetings. In response, the group agreed to change its format once again to allow for a more directed, intentional way of starting things off, which became the "new format" option. Hosts using this option would announce a theme and assign appropriate readings. Members were also to take a more directive role in prayer; the perception of some was that certain members had been merely acting as passive receptacles for the action of the Spirit. Nevertheless, some continued to prefer the old format.

This group history — told by some, told to others, shared by all — provides a context within which members can be "elbow to elbow" with each other each week. The group memory contributes to the trust the group has developed, on the basis of which issues can be addressed and further longevity built. Nevertheless, the changes in membership over time demonstrate that despite Oakley's own persistence, not everyone's needs have always been met.

God and Life, Life and God

We have seen that a group which began with one young man's personal Pentecost eventually became a regular meeting of a half-dozen married couples and a few single people setting aside Tuesday nights to get together in one or another's living room and talk about God. Under the assumption that God is a living presence in the world — the conviction that came to Dave Kern on November 13, 1974 — the prayer group collectively dedicates a space and time to recognize their encounters with God.

In the intervening years, they have changed and the world has changed. Most of them have married, had children, moved to a new neighborhood, launched careers, bought houses, and embraced or re-embraced the Catholic Church. The church itself has changed and is far more open to signs of the gifts of the Spirit, both in the U.S. generally[10] and, after 1984, in the parish of St. Hildegard in particular. Women in the church, with or without permission, were making their presence felt.[11] Thus in 1992 the church more effectively met the religious needs of Dave and Matt (who had returned) and Sara and Katy (who were converts) than it had in 1974.

Despite the Catholic Church's greater openness, the Oakley group persists in collectively dedicating a space and a time to God. Indeed, this recurring dedication lies at the heart of the group. Matt made this point when he explained what he valued about the group:

> The shared commitment to God, the collective experience of just praising God. . . . One of the things I always found interesting about being a Christian is that you're drawn together to people, not necessarily that you're naturally attracted to but because you share this thing in common. I wasn't immediately happy about the great friendships or relationships [in the group]. I was much more excited about an opportunity with other people to praise God, and then the relationships developed over time. . . . If you get the right frame of reference you get to encounter God there.

Getting into "the right frame of reference" is something that occupies the group's attention, particularly in the "business meetings" they have several times a year to discuss and decide on rules and format (as well as to consider suggestions for new recruits). As we have related, a year before we came on the scene, the group deliberated at length before adopting the "new format" of optional prayer-hour "themes." Nonetheless, the first hour is still referred to as prayer time and is still, both in

10. See Neitz (1987).

11. For the church at large, see Wallace (1992) and Weaver (1985). At St. Hildegard's, Katy, the only prayer group member who regularly attends the 11:30 mass instead of the 10:30 mass in the gym, has become chief lector, training other lay people to read Scripture at mass and herself prefacing readings with learned commentaries presented as engaging stories. At the combined mass for Pentecost 1993, she was one of four persons to be honored with a "spirit award" for her storytelling gifts.

concept and in execution, more meditative than dialogical. (Indeed, often the prayer time still follows the spontaneous, nontheme format that has come to be called "traditional.")

To move from the older, ostensibly spontaneous but in fact codified and charismatic prayer session to the newer, more structured but more religiously eclectic one was risky, but we felt that the result was distinctly religious. As we saw it, the prayer time was clearly dedicated to God, as the individual members understood God. When the host opted for the new format and announced a theme, it more likely than not corresponded to an event on the liturgical calendar (e.g., Advent, Epiphany, Holy Week) or had some other clearly Christian resonance (e.g., Martha's session on devotion to Mary, mother of God; Ted's on favorite Scripture passages; Naomi's on living the Gospel). In other words, as the group moved closer to the church, its prayer could more easily derive from institutional religion. The members also seemed to find it easy to respond in their own religious ways to less conventional themes, such as Sara's session on death, Helen's on tragedy, and Katy's on marginality.

Only a year or two before the change to the new format, the group accepted Martha's suggestion that nonscriptural readings be incorporated into the prayer time. During our observations, we heard readings from Carlos Castaneda, Nikos Kazantzakis, Morton Kelsey, Thomas Merton, Henri Nouwen, Dylan Thomas, Henry David Thoreau, and Jim Wallis, among others. But the group also meditated on countless Scripture passages, whether or not they had been chosen as part of someone's theme.

We were aware of no attempts to impose religious uniformity, and, despite the fact that all of the group members were members of a Catholic parish, we knew from what people said to each other in meetings and from what they said to us in interviews that there was a wide range of personal religiosity among them, from near agnosticism, to orthodoxy, to near pantheism. Naomi, one of the more orthodox, often opened the prayer session with an extemporaneous but carefully composed and articulated invocational prayer. By contrast, Katy told us, "You breathe God. You're born God. You are God. You live God. You see God. So how can you ask God to be with you?" One night, when the spirit led Matt to burst into a solo song about Jesus as the rock, Katy picked up the same melody to sing about the goddess within each of us, picturing the goddess as a river. In an aside to Matt, who was sitting next to her, Katy said, "I just wanted to balance that off a little." Matt said, "Cool."

Although occasionally heard in song, the name of Jesus was seldom invoked in prayer. But in a prayer offered during Lent, the sacrifice of Jesus was raised as a theme for meditation. This prompted Katy to leave hurriedly at the end of the prayer hour. The next day she explained to Elfriede that after all this talk about the sacrifice of one man long ago, she needed to attend to someone she knew nearby who was sacrificing herself at that moment. She went on to explain that "that man Jesus" only suffered for three hours, whereas most human beings suffer much more in a lifetime. Yet during the same session, Margaret was moved by the realization that Jesus can understand our suffering because he too has suffered. In our opinion, this doctrinal independence is a source of the Oakley group's capacity to grow.

Elfriede heard some revealing God talk during one meeting that had the fewest participants she had ever seen — five in addition to her. They were four of the most orthodox believers — Matt, Darlene, Jim, and Martha — plus one of the least orthodox, Sara. Martha was the host, and she had prepared some readings, including the *Magnificat*, centering on Mary, mother of God, to whom she is particularly devoted. The music was good. The sharing was about the presence or absence of God, and Matt cited a column of Andrew Greeley's in which Greeley said that people don't talk enough with others about the experiences of God that they claim they've had when an individual inquires. The group agreed that one reason for this phenomenon was that most people don't have a trusted group like the Oakley members do that they can confide in and share with.

That led Sara to talk about how she discovered God talking to her through trees. She could confide that to the group only because she had known them for years, had worked on relating to them, and had learned to trust them and they her. Without that relationship of trust, she would never have told them about how she talks to trees, or how God talks to her through trees, which is very significant in her life. Matt responded that his weekly two-hour walk in the nature preserve, during which he contemplates its beauty, is essential to his spiritual life; yet he is frustrated that the nourishment he experiences there doesn't stay with him when he returns home. Sara responded that she has learned to internalize some of the beauty of the scenes she sees, to drink it in and put it in a place in her memory where she is always able to recall it and re-experience it.

As far as rules for faith sharing went, we were aware only of the ideal, articulated by our interviewees and invoked once or twice as a controlling norm in group meetings, that faith sharing, or "God talk," must be present-oriented, personal, and daring, not academic, gossipy, or safe.[12] They agreed that their Tuesday-night meetings provided an opportunity to share experiences, not expound on beliefs; to talk about oneself, not one's neighbor; to risk disclosure, not get off easy.

During our year of observation, we saw what such faith sharing looked like; we offer two examples. One long-running story was Darlene's complaint about being "on the outs with God." The story began, a week before Christmas, with a lament. Having placed her life in God's hands, Darlene was finding that things were not turning out to be as satisfying as she had hoped they would be. She was not dissatisfied with her marriage or her children, but for about a year she had been wondering whether she had been wise to be so unconcerned about material things. Now the nice, large houses in the suburbs, the kind she had grown up in, were looking attractive to her; her six children were growing up in a less safe neighborhood than she had. These doubts made her feel that she was angry with God, and she stopped talking to God. Maybe she didn't want to hear what God had to say. Maybe she was having a spiritual midlife crisis, yearning for the certainty and excitement of ten years ago.

During Holy Week, Darlene recounted that her feelings about God had changed because of Lent, during which she made a practice of going to the daily mass held at seven in the morning, a very small, very quiet liturgy. Being in the presence of the ritual helped her understand that it is necessary to be open to God in order to accomplish anything; so she was opening the door to God just a crack, to listen to God again. She drew an analogy to her marriage: "If I stopped talking to Matt for months, what would that do to my marriage?" she asked rhetorically.

Group members responded to Darlene with encouragement, advice, gratitude, and, at the close of the meetings, prayer. A few days after Pentecost, Darlene reported briefly that she had not made much progress in her struggle with God and felt that she should be "wooed" or "courted" by God. In response, Matt said, "If I were God, I would woo Darlene."

On several occasions during our year of attendance, Katy talked, without going into much detail, about pain in her own marriage, and she wondered whether she was having her own midlife crisis. Late in the

12. These principles are also articulated by Westley (1992).

year she reported that she and her husband, who was not a member of the group, were seeing a counselor. During the meeting immediately after Easter, she reported that on Holy Saturday she had gone to the Salvation Army and bought a bunch of cheap china plates, taken them home, and then smashed them one by one against the garage wall, yelling epithets at her husband. Feeling partially cleansed, she went to Easter mass and heard a homily about the empty tomb in which the priest focused on the fact that year after year pilgrims come to the Holy Land to experience precisely the emptiness of that particular space. Feeling the emptiness within herself, Katy was very moved and asked for a copy of the homily to bring to her husband.

Despite these revelations — or more likely because of them — Katy said in her interview,

> [The prayer group experience has] made me see that marriage itself, the institution of marriage, can be as important [as], if not more important than, the two individual people coming into marriage. The synergy is more important than the two pieces of it. We as individuals need to commit ourselves to a thing larger than us, I think, in order to be whole people, and that thing which Rick and I have committed to is our marriage.

The group clearly values commitment. Indeed, for them, dedicating Tuesday nights to faith sharing is an act of will, not a natural inclination. Ralph, whom we have mentioned, always found the meetings "uncomfortable" and challenging. Although an experienced teacher, an amateur actor, and an articulate person, Ralph is one of the least active in discussion because of how unsure he is of his faith and how much he feels he risks by faith. Although his wife, Margaret, confidently sees the hand of God in their lives, and although he knows that the prayer group began with Dave Kern's road-to-Damascus experience, Ralph does not have that conviction himself. He told us that he would like some day to be "walking down the street sort of minding my own business and, Boom! God says, 'Hey, here I am, you schmuck!'" But he immediately added, wistfully, "That will never happen, I don't think."

Talking with Elfriede about how the group has affected his faith, Ralph said that during one particularly intense group session six years earlier, he was challenged by Dave and found himself "forced to conclude that I believe in God." But that was by no means the end of it:

For me, it came to a point of actually openly articulating and being able to admit faith. And then from that point — when I said that night, "Okay, all right, all right! I believe in God!" — the whole thing from that point up to this very night is saying, "So what does that mean?" and "What is that faith?" and "How far do you go?" and "How does it affect me?"

Ralph describes Oakley as "the *catalyst,* the *forum* through which questions have been asked, through which faith has been an issue. . . . It's probably still the main *fulcrum* of my faith" (emphases added). Having been a group member for seven years, Ralph cannot imagine a reason that he would not want to continue, unless the group were to disband. "I mean, that is one way I can identify myself, that I am a member of the Tuesday-night prayer group."

Intimacy and Its Limits

Oakley is not primarily a group of friends. It is rather a group of people who share the goal of developing their spiritual lives. Spiritual meanings take precedence over the social interactions in which they are embedded. As valued as the personal ties within the group are, the group's reason-for-being demands that they be subordinated to the spiritual journey.

Nevertheless, Elfriede saw that a context of personal intimacy is the necessary means to the spiritual experiences that group members seek. One of her most moving experiences came about midway into the nine-month observation period. The rhythm of the Tuesday-night meetings had become comforting to her, a welcome respite. This particular evening, however, she was moved to tears during the prayer time when she felt engulfed in the deep sharing of experiences among the members but realized at the same time that *she could not take part in this sharing.* While the emotional impact of this realization took Elfriede by surprise, it must have been anticipated by the members themselves. During the negotiations for Elfriede's being able to observe the group, the group decided at the outset that Elfriede would be invited only to observe, not to participate. Members felt that full participation required a commitment on both sides, and they were not sure they wanted to extend that level of commitment to a relative stranger. Indeed, during the first few weeks of our research, the group reached a decision to formally withdraw membership from a couple who had ceased participating. The group has no room for the uncommitted.[13]

Members have no sure way of separating the spiritual from the social when intimacy is deemed necessary to achieve spiritual goals. Indeed, when group members complain about each other's holding back from self-revelation, it appears sometimes that intimacy is its own goal. Given the group's long history and the trust inspired by the group norm that things shared within the group are not to be related outside it, the reticence of some members exasperates others, like Matt: "The need to keep their distance bugs me. This isn't a group that barely knows each other. . . . I feel like 'Take a risk, tell us about your life, Chrissake. Tell us about your fear of telling us about your life, but shit, just talk.'" Matt, who works as a clinical psychologist, also best articulated how the spiritual goals of the group depend on interpersonal intimacy: "I'm not really looking for an encounter group. The only person I want to encounter is God, and I feel like I encountered God if you tell me about your life and your experience of God or the absence of God in your life. I encounter both you and God."

Elfriede saw the vulnerability of intimacy in the group one night in January. For the meeting nearest Epiphany (January 7, 1992), the host, Katy, prepared a theme for the prayer session, beginning with her rendition of a child's story about listening to the sounds of nature. This set off a series of observations on the meaning of "epiphany," and two of the men who were good at such things offered learned etymologies of the word's Greek roots. Elfriede was already identifying enough with what she felt to be the group's ideals that she found herself becoming impatient for meditation. We quote from her field notes:

> I felt like I needed that time, that quiet time for thinking before I could really understand what people [were] saying. So I did feel just a little bit of spiritual information overload. . . . I noticed [that] a couple of people were trying to put up a barrier for themselves during the time others were giving their reflections. They were sitting with their heads back, their eyes closed, looking like they were trying to concentrate on their own prayer.

The next day, when Elfriede met Matt to complete the interview they had begun a week before Christmas, he said that, after Katy's reading

13. See Iannaccone (1992).

from the children's book, the previous night's meeting was one he "could have gone without absolutely." Asked to elaborate, he said,

> I don't especially like irrelevant, bullshit talk. I don't go there for small talk. I don't go there for any intellectual discussion of anything. . . . I don't go there for an exchange of ideas.[14] . . . It cuts into the time when we do what I'd like to do, which is basically just share our faith on a very personal level and pray.

Two weeks later, in her own interview, Katy told Elfriede that she and the other women felt that they were more inclined to be personal while the men were more inclined to be "intellectual."

The object of the group is to support each person's experience of God, and this support is manifested in the sharing sessions that provide the opportunity and the challenge to reveal oneself. When one participates in this sharing, one's spiritual life can be articulated, observed, and sometimes guided. During our year of acquaintance with the group, we were struck by the forthrightness with which members came to grips with childhood traumas, family problems, and their own fears.

One evening a member said that her marriage was in crisis. Without giving details, she told the group about her pain. She said that she urgently needed to share this part of her life with the group because she needed their prayers and concern. She admitted that she didn't know what to do or how the problems of her marriage could be overcome. One member, speaking from her own experience, said that you took more risks in deciding to stay in a marriage and try to work at it than in leaving it behind. Another member, herself a divorcée, pointed out how the typical action-oriented approach to every challenge in life had, in this instance, eluded this woman in crisis. Consequently, she was more open than she might otherwise have been to hearing God's message for her. The woman's sense of immobility, confusion, and inclination to think and pray instead of charging ahead with decisive action was deemed by the group to be "great spiritual progress."

One night during Lent, Ralph spoke frankly about coming to grips

---

14. As we have seen, Matt violated his own anti-academic strictures, even as he reiterated his point about the importance of faith sharing, when, several weeks later in the group, he cited Andrew Greeley to the effect that 85 percent of Americans claim to have had an experience of God but almost that many have never told anyone else about their experience.

with the imminent death of his mother. He had come to recognize that a lifelong pattern of self-pity and denial of pain had led to his putting people who should be closest to him at a distance. Separating himself from pain, he separated himself from others, including his wife, Margaret. For Ralph, this confession was anything but glib.

On another occasion, Ted agonized over his parenting. He was reassured by Julia, Darlene, and Debby that his son was probably more normal than he and his wife, Helen, thought, that the two of them were loving people and must be doing what was called for, that children are by nature a problem. During the final prayer, Ted asked for grace to be a better parent, and Darlene prayed that Ted would receive the grace to recognize what a good parent he was.

Yet for all the importance of this kind of self-revelation, the members put limits on the forms that intimacy can take. At the same time that they value personal self-revelation, they also value personal integrity and a certain level of personal independence and separateness that conform to the way they live their lives.

First of all, Oakley is not a commune — one is required to share one's faith journey, not one's home or material substance. When, after the crisis of the early 1980s, the members resolved the issue of what type of community they ought to become, there was an exodus of those members who felt that the group should be a "total community." George told us that Oakley had had some members who seemed to be "very needy." These people found that despite the group's best efforts, the support and exchange of sharing time was not enough for them. They eventually got frustrated and left.

Second, those with serious personal problems are advised to seek professional help (and relevant suggestions may be made during the aftertime). No one is exempt. Despite Dave's standing as the founder of the group and one of its leaders until the mid-1980s, he himself recognized at one point that he was facing a personal crisis which the group could not fully share in nor help him resolve. Consequently, he took a leave of absence from the group in the late 1980s in order to seek professional counseling. The membership includes therapists, but Oakley is not a therapy group.

Third, while the members have an obligation to share their lives, they are not required to abide by anyone's "advice." In fact, they are not required even to welcome anyone's advice (although the obligation to listen to the speaker is most serious — it is the reciprocal of sharing).

Members vary on the kinds of response they prefer to get to their stories. Sometimes members preface their sharing with statements such as "I just want your prayers about this" or "Please just hear me out." Katy told the group that she often wants only a "spiritual-emotional-physical hug." By contrast, Darlene told the group that she shares in order to get a response from them. If she didn't receive one, she would wonder what was wrong with what she said. But the members agree that "over-advising" is to be avoided.

When Elfriede shared her impressions of the group during her last meeting with them, she remarked that she had witnessed few overtly challenging responses to peoples' sharing, and group members agreed that it had been a long time since "we have . . . given each other permission" to be very critical of one another. They said that in the "Kernell Acres" days they were less patient with each other's evasions and more likely to confront contradictions.

Finally, though it is not part of the group's explicit constitution, the fact is that the members do live challenging, rewarding lives and are willing to delve into the spiritual dimensions of those lives. People do not "join" this group; they are invited to become members. And part of potential members' attractiveness is the competence they express in their work and their personal lives. When Elfriede first met the members of the group, she was struck by how "healthy and slim" all of them were, and Steve affirmed these impressions during his visits in May. Most members work in the helping professions, several in entrepreneurial fashion. They are well educated and well informed, and their conversation is enjoyable. Wit, good humor, and story-telling are valued skills. On one particularly engaging and high-spirited evening, Jim called out, "Who writes the script for this group, anyhow?"

Sacred space provided by a conventional institution — in this case, the Sunday-morning Roman Catholic mass — does not provide the intimacy that the Oakley members desire. While it is a protected space, the mass cannot accommodate the kind of sharing that these individuals do during the deep and thoughtful time they spend together on Tuesday nights. Like partners in a marriage, Oakley members have freely chosen their association; having made this commitment, they accept the obligations entailed. They are bonded to each other and know each other's lives intimately. However, their bond is unlike that of marriage in that their choice of partners is not purely personal or based primarily on shared common values, although clearly they share many. The members

171

are not all close friends with each other. Their choice is based on only one goal: to support each other in their relationship with God. And, while they have self-consciously formed a community, they have put limits on the claims of that community.[15]

Selves in Society

In the move a decade ago from regular meetings at "Kernell Acres" to rotating meetings, Oakley turned away from communalism; at that point the group also abandoned any aspiration to function as an organ of social justice, despite the members' religiously influenced social liberalism. Helen, whose own opinions would place her on the left of a generally liberal group, said that members are not influenced politically by the group because they tend to agree already (though they do have disagreements over abortion). Yet "political" issues had no place in group discussions, because, she said, "I don't think that's what we're about. I think we talk about stuff as it relates to our lives." Once again we see that the group accepts and respects the privacy of individual members.

Nonetheless, the lives of Oakley members typically put them on the frontier of urban society. Not only do they live in a metropolitan inner city, but many of them are in the helping professions: four are teachers in public and parochial schools, three are nurses, one is a clinical psychologist, one is a social worker, one is a physical therapist, one is a pastoral counselor, and one (Martha) is in charge of social services at St. Hildegard's. Jim, who works in the computer field, spends most of his off hours volunteering. Thus many of them *as individuals* regularly address the needs of society.

This social involvement — and the boundaries of it — was the focus of articulate self-examination during a meeting near the end of our observation period. Naomi, who is one of the nurses, hosted this particular meeting. Months earlier, she had mentioned in her interview that she and Dave subscribed to the magazine *Sojourners,* but that she was ambivalent about the magazine's uncompromising, communal commitment to social justice:

---

15. Wuthnow (1991) reflects at length on the boundaries that Americans establish between themselves and their voluntary altruistic activities.

I don't feel like in my life right now it can be my primary focus, but I would like it to be *a* focus. . . . and this is the thing I want to pray about and figure out: Have I just kind of sold out to the American way of life — upper-middle-class lifestyle, a house, three kids, two cars? Going about our business and not really being concerned in particular about anybody else's business — the poor, the disenfranchised, the homeless, the poverty-stricken, all the kinds of marginal [people], the thirsty, the hungry? I don't feel that I can frame my whole life around that, and these aren't the choices we've made. But I also don't want us to totally ignore that or do nothing.

For the meeting in May, Naomi had copied a series of statements on the relation of faith and social responsibility from a recent issue of *Sojourners,* and she gave them to the group to read, round robin. These readings were followed extemporaneously by others' readings from Scripture. Naomi began the sharing session by asking what people thought about her theme, and many people responded that the theme spoke deeply to them.

Helen said that she was particularly struck by this passage: "We must place the Word in the most intimate and tender center of our lives."[16] She and Ted were close to deciding whether or not to take up a long-standing call to join the Maryknoll sisters in Nicaragua (who work with the poor) in order to do mission work themselves. But they were wondering if this might not be the best time to go — because Ted's career was going well, because their spiritual mentor was going to Rome shortly, and especially because Helen was doing some long-delayed self-exploration (having, the group knew from earlier disclosures, to do with abuse as a child). In fact, she was exploring what was precisely a "most intimate and tender center" of her life. But at the same time, she hated the thought that she was just absorbed in herself and escaping commitment. Matt strongly affirmed the providential nature of her decision not to join Maryknoll, and many others offered supportive comments. Later, during the closing prayer, someone prayed for her.

Matt's response to the statements from *Sojourners* was an admission that when he becomes too busy to take his two-hour prayer walk every week, he gets out of touch with God. As a result, he becomes — well,

16. This and subsequent quoted statements are taken from "Our Life at the Foot of the Mountain: Sojourners Community Statement of Faith," *Sojourners* 21 (February/March 1992): 22.

not racist exactly, but unaccepting of other people, "icky" people (especially the new Asian immigrants he meets at the bank and the grocery store), people unlike himself. This is particularly a problem because many of his patients are not very likeable people, and his job is to provide them with quality care. Thus he particularly resonated with the line that immediately followed the one cited by Helen: "We must always touch the face of God before we stretch out our hands to the work of the world, and we must reach back to God again and again."

On the other hand, Martha's response to the statements from *Sojourners* was that an individual-to-God relationship isn't enough. Martha's own faith demands that she reach out to others in some way, be it small or large. Martha is deeply involved in parish life, and while she is aware of her need to maintain boundaries and not to get overinvolved, she said she is always on the lookout for ways that the parish can address urban problems.

Julia, however, said that as a single working mother, she cannot get involved, and she tries to "screen out" a lot of what she hears about problems. She is a visiting nurse, and she mentioned her recent visit to a patient in a chaotic housing project. She realized from the patient's history just how bad the project was ("Someone was shot here last week!"), and that she, Julia, *wanted to be out of there.* With that kind of job and her inevitable involvement with "icky" people, Julia wanted to ask, how could she be asked to do more, as Martha does? She expressed thanks that she belonged to a group that has Martha so that the need to reach out does not rest on her shoulders individually but on the group's shoulders collectively. Several others assented to this idea, and during the closing prayer someone gave thanks for Martha's service.

Several months before, the group had discussed how much they identified with a poem by Thomas Merton that Darlene had brought out one evening when the sharing turned to questions of overinvolvement. Merton made the point that being overextended in the work of caring killed "the root of inner wisdom which makes [the] work fruitful." That evening Jim and Martha were singled out for their continual giving to others in need, and they were encouraged to pull back. In particular, Matt advised Jim to avoid letting dependent, needy people continue to impose unreasonable demands on him. On an earlier occasion Martha had told the group that prayer sustained her so that she could reach out to help others. Yet at this meeting she admitted that she too needed to limit her giving as parish director of social services.

From our observations and our interviews (with group members and clergy), Matt's observations sound right. About the group, he commented, "I would say it's a direct fruit of our experience . . . to become more involved in the parish." About himself, he said, "I am definitely more compassionate," particularly toward those who do not enjoy all the rewards of our society, the unrich, the unthin, the unintelligent, the unattractive, those whom he and Julia had called "icky."

At the same time, group members recognize that they must balance their outside involvement. They realize they need this balance in part because many of them are in the helping professions, and they need to invest their after-work time in themselves and their families, not the larger community. And they recognize that meeting their own spiritual needs, "touching the face of God," is the wellspring of their being, of their nurture of both themselves and others.

The Institutionalization of Charisma

The eighteen-year history of the Oakley Prayer and Sharing Group testifies to many things, but as sociologists we are particularly struck by the group's institutionalization. The members are committed to providing time and space in their lives for the group every Tuesday evening; indeed, their children (many of whom are "younger" than the group) have grown up with the understanding that their parents will be out this one night every week. Members are committed to following the format agreed upon collectively and to make changes only as a group. At the same time, they share the commitment to respect the theological diversity among them, even though it is often not fully understood. Like a church, the group has no foreseeable end and is, for practical purposes, an end in itself. Katy said, "I would call it more of a religious community than I would a religious prayer group."

Being members of the Tuesday-night prayer group thus describes not only what members do but also who they are. Like an increasing number of American church members,[17] they are individuals whose identities as Oakley members are achieved — through affiliation with this group as young adults and adults — rather than ascribed through parental determination. They are the collective authors of their spiritual

17. For a discussion, see Warner 1993, 1074-1080.

biographies. This became evident in a number of ways. We heard Ralph — in some ways the most ambivalent member — describe his connection to the group in terms of identity. Even though Darlene has been experiencing a crisis in her faith, it is clear that her life has been significantly framed by her commitment to the group. Several members, particularly some of the women, found the courage to face deeply disturbing events from their childhood because the group provided the emotional and spiritual support they needed to do so. The group has helped a number of members to make significant life choices.[18]

The group has become an integral part of the members' identity because it has fulfilled profound spiritual needs. Through their intimacy and bondedness, the group members have focused much of their energy on meeting each other's spiritual needs and, within limits set by the group, their emotional needs. And the collective prayer of the group nurtures individual prayer lives. Jim, one of the more pious members, told us that the group relieved him of feeling that he had to be original in prayer. "I don't have to do *everything* about prayer, in order to pray at all." He had been a member since the College Park days and rarely missed a meeting. Clearly he felt that his spiritual contribution was important to the group, yet he was confident that, when he was "dried out," he could be "carried along by the efforts of the other members . . . as part of the prayer." As his story indicates, members are not spiritually on their own.

We have also seen how the Oakley group directs its collective spiritual energies to the parish and how the individual members direct their spiritual energies to the wider world. Most of the members have jobs that strive to meet the needs of urban people, especially in central city areas. They live in one of the most ethnically and economically diverse sections of the city, and some, despite their worries about crime, stay there because of the group. Their outreach to the parish has been extensive, and, as Father Byrne told Steve, the parish recognizes it. Like other social institutions, Oakley is valued by its own members and by those who know it.

In retelling the group's history, we glimpsed something of Oakley's early charismatic excitement and how that changed over time. The excitement generated by participation in a new social movement can

18. Pizzorno (1986) reflects on the fact that people make decisions not as isolates but as members of past, present, or future collectivities.

176

translate into enormous investments of time. The early Oakley members frequently found themselves spending two evenings each week in group sessions and activities in addition to the time they spent in communal morning prayers. Several members also met with individuals who needed attention outside the group. Dave recalled somewhat ruefully, "I wonder now why we met so often, but I guess we thought it was important at the time." Rather than die a "natural death" when that early excitement waned, the prayer group determined to find a way to preserve a space in their lives in order to continue to confront the ultimate reality that had drawn them together in the first place.

The group seems to accept what we call the institutionalization of their charisma (Eisenstadt 1968). Rather than seeing the loss of the spontaneity and freedom of their charismatic origins as a process of rigidification or routinization, they celebrate their capacity to grow and change. Rather than feel, like *Big Chill* baby boomers, that in settling down they have sold out, they prod each other to apprehend and enhance the sacredness inherent in life.

The members are all Catholic, whether raised as Catholics or converted to the faith, and Andrew Greeley's concept of the "sacramental imagination" may help us understand their capacity to embrace, in their words, "God and life, life and God." Inspired by theologian David Tracy, Greeley (1990) distinguishes the sacramental imagination, which sees the world filled with God, from the "dialectical imagination," which sees the world as God-forsaken. Like Greeley's Catholics, the Oakley members tend to have androgynous images of God, to find religious meaning in poetry and narrative rather than in doctrine, to have liberal attitudes on economic and foreign-policy issues but moderate ones on sexual and familial matters, and to portray moral decisions in shades of gray rather than black and white. Unlike radical Protestants with their "dialectical imaginations," they do not have to withdraw from the world or radically transform it to see that God is immanent in it.

The Oakley group is a both/and rather than an either/or culture. The members have families (large ones) and jobs (demanding ones). They live in the city and love nature. They respect intellect and feeling. They value personal privacy and communal intimacy. They think it is important to help others and to nurture themselves. Every week they go to church for the Eucharist and to each other's homes for prayer and sharing. They are Catholic in spirit as well as in denominational affiliation.

We have written in the present tense about Oakley's practices and

177

norms, but it is important to conclude with the observation that Oakley is a group in process.[19] We were among them for only nine months, and if we were to return to do more research, we would undoubtedly have to add not only length but also new phases to their story. Indeed, we were told several times that our presence affected the group. Because of Elfriede, members were more prompt, more faithful in attendance, and more articulate in sharing. But in the end, we were part of their process, another encounter with the world, like Dave's chance meeting with Father Bill Sawinski in 1974, the group's mentoring by the Jesuits of St. Francis and the Mennonites of Urban Place, the bishop's appointment of Frank Byrne as pastor of St. Hildegard's, and the changing demography of their neighborhood. Sara told us that when the group considered our request to observe them, they discussed how they might use our presence as an opportunity for self-examination, possibly as a catalyst for further growth. Since our departure, we have heard that the questions we posed in our interviews foreshadowed questions that some of the members asked each other after we left.

Ralph expresses well the group's faith in its own flexibility, and we call on him to conclude our story:

> I expect [Oakley] will change. It seems like the only way that anything can remain stable is through change. That's why the group has remained a group. . . . Change has been explored and . . . discussed and argued [about] and discerned and eventually incorporated in some way — which has allowed the group to remain a group.

19. Van Maanen (1988, 65, 72) explains the significance of the "ethnographic present" and how historical ethnographies require new writing practices.

Working the ACOA Program:
A Spiritual Journey

SARA WUTHNOW

"This is basically a spiritual program, and those of us who have been in the program a long time will tell you that. But I don't think that a lot of the newcomers recognize it for what it is. They are in too much pain, and all they can see is darkness. Later on, if they keep working the program, they will look back over this step 1 period and realize it's the beginning of a genuine spiritual journey. It takes a lot of hard work, but it's worth it!"

Margie, ACOA member

Margie is a middle-aged social worker who attends Adult Children of Alcoholics (ACOA) meetings at the Marysville Presbyterian Church. She has attended ACOA meetings there for six years and credits

---

I attended the Marysville ACOA meetings as a participant-observer-researcher. The group had given me permission to fill that role in meetings so long as I respected their tradition of anonymity, one of AA's twelve traditions. Ten of the members agreed to be interviewed outside the meeting. With their permission, portions of those interviews are recorded here.

the group with giving her the support she needed to start on a long, hard, and eventually rewarding spiritual journey. She is currently exploring her relationship with God with a traditional Christian spiritual director.

As I sat with Margie and her friends week after week, I had no doubt that I was in the presence of a group of people who knew what it meant to start on a spiritual journey, who knew how to be honest, how to be vulnerable, how to stand in need of love, and how to give love. The group has its problems, but it also has some valuable lessons to teach churches about spirituality in small groups.

The Spiritual Basis of Alcoholics Anonymous

The Marysville ACOA group is part of the widespreading twelve-step umbrella of Alcoholics Anonymous (AA). The term "twelve-step" refers to AA's famous twelve steps to recovery from alcohol addiction. It is helpful to review briefly the history of AA in order to understand the spiritual underpinnings of any twelve-step group.

The story of the founding of AA is familiar to growing numbers of sober Americans who refer to themselves as "friends of Bill W." (Stafford 1991; Nace 1992; Kurtz 1979). Bill W. was Bill Wilson, the man who, along with Dr. Robert Holbrook Smith (Dr. Bob), was responsible for starting AA in 1935 in Akron, Ohio. Bill W., a New Yorker, was an alcoholic who had deteriorated to the point where he found it difficult to cope with life. One day in 1934 he was visited by an old alcoholic friend, Ebby Thatcher, who claimed he had become sober through the influence of the Oxford group led by the Episcopalian pastor Sam Shoemaker. The Oxford group was a nondenominational evangelical movement that attempted to recapture the first-century Christian experience with an emphasis on personal conversion rather than doctrine. After attending a meeting, Bill W. went on a drinking binge and was hospitalized. When he called out to God, he had a dramatic conversion experience complete with a white light and a feeling of ecstasy. He never drank again.

A few months later, when he was on a business trip to Ohio that went badly, he was tempted to drink, but he reached out to the local Oxford group instead. He was invited to the house of one of the members, and there he met another alcoholic, Dr. Bob Smith. Out of this meeting, AA was eventually born, based, according to Bill W., directly on the

ideas of the Oxford group and Sam Shoemaker. The fellowship of alcoholics formed was less religious than the Oxford group but incorporated
key concepts such as "powerlessness," "surrender," and "higher power."
Bill W. published an elaboration of these concepts in 1939 in what has
become known as the "Big Book." The twelve steps are the core concepts.
They are as follows:

1. We admitted we were powerless over alcohol and that our lives
   had become unmanageable;
2. Came to believe that a power greater than ourselves could restore
   us to sanity;
3. Made a decision to turn our will and our lives over to the care of
   God as we understood Him;
4. Made a searching and fearless moral inventory of ourselves;
5. Admitted to God, to ourselves, and to another human being the
   exact nature of our wrongs;
6. Were entirely ready to have God remove all these defects of character;
7. Humbly asked Him to remove our shortcomings;
8. Made a list of all persons we had harmed and became willing to
   make amends to them all;
9. Made direct amends to such people whenever possible, except
   when to do so would injure them or others;
10. Continued to take personal inventory and when we were wrong,
    promptly admitted it;
11. Sought through prayer and meditation to improve our conscious
    contact with God as we understood Him, praying only for knowl-
    edge of His will for us and the power to carry that out.
12. Having had a spiritual awakening as a result of these steps, we tried
    to carry this message to alcoholics, and to practice these principles
    in all our affairs.

When Bill W. sat down to codify the process of recovery from
alcoholism, his understanding was influenced by the perspective he had
been given by Sam Shoemaker. As a clergyman, Shoemaker conceptual-
ized the "conversion" process in traditional Christian terms; thus, it is
not surprising that the twelve steps are consistent with the writings of
Christian saints over the centuries.

In general, the saints saw the struggles of life as opportunities rather
than guarantees for spiritual growth. The difficulties of life merely gave

them opportunities to observe what blocked their relationship with God. The saints practiced what have become known as "spiritual disciplines" to remove these obstacles between themselves and God. Although restated over the centuries to reflect different cultural contexts, the traditional writings on the spiritual disciplines are difficult for the modern reader. The modern rewriting of the spiritual disciplines in the form of the twelve steps serves as a translation. In order to appreciate the tradition upon which the twelve steps are based, it is helpful to review briefly some of the major contributors.

One of the early Church Fathers, St. John Cassian (360-430/35), wrote two books on the Christian spiritual journey; the first is an introduction to the inner life and the second traces the path from first purifications to perfection (Hamman 1993, 111). His writings inspired almost all monastic rules in the East and the West. Cassian had visited the monks in the Egyptian desert and was as influenced by their exercise of repentance (metanoia) as by their asceticism. In the desert, the interior life was central to a relationship with God. According to Benedicta Ward (1980, 33) one of the Desert Fathers, John of Lycopolis, ". . . describes the rooted selfishness that coils round the heart like a serpent, continually burrowing deeper and creating a false and illusory self which is continually restless and unstable. The restless heart is contrasted with the inner well of peace and stability which is the work of the Spirit of God." The same message resounds through countless AA meetings around the globe.

About the same time as Cassian, St. Augustine (354-430) was writing in his *Confessions* about his tortuous journey from being a great sinner to a great saint. With passion and honesty, he told of a search for "God and the self" (Miles 1992, 9). Augustine's seductive prose has influenced the church over the centuries and still has the power to influence modern readers. One can imagine his story of sex addiction being told at a twelve-step meeting today.

The Rule of St. Benedict, written about 535, was influenced by Cassian. It became the pattern for the religious life for most of Western monasticism. According to Benedict, the key to learning how to be in relationship with God was humility. Indeed, in Chapter Seven of "The Rule," Benedict offers a series of twelve steps to humility by which one could develop the proper attitude about the self in relation to God (Taylor 1989, 49). One wonders if Bill W.'s choice of twelve steps is coincidental.

One can also find parallels between the twelve steps, especially step 11, and the musings of the fourteenth-century mystic (a woman?) who wrote *The Cloud of Unknowing.* In this text the more advanced pilgrim enters a period in which the mystery of God is experienced at deeper, more intimate levels. The author of this contemplative work cautions that it is not a book for "the merely curious, educated or not." Rather, it is for those "who feel the mysterious action of the Spirit in their inmost being stirring them to love" (Johnston, ed., 1973).

Over the years the spiritual disciplines have at times been expressed through metaphor. One thinks of Renaissance writers such as St. John of the Cross and his "dark night of the soul," and St. Teresa of Ávila exploring her "interior castle" (Walsh, ed., 1985; 334, 416). The "dark night" image is a powerful way of speaking about the lost, confusing period known to people in twelve-step programs as step 1. A person's ability to exert some control over life disappears. God also seems to disappear, and all is darkness. Then, in the midst of that darkness, a new relationship with God is forged. This new relationship is described in steps 2 and 3.

The "interior castle" image is particularly helpful when thinking about steps 4 through 7. At this stage the individual looks deep within, exploring and bringing to light that which had been hidden. The saints found, however, that interior exploration did not lead them permanently inward and away from other people. St. Teresa wrote that after she had explored her "castle," she found herself "back out on the street." This eventual development is noted in step 12.

The spiritual disciplines are also explored in *Spiritual Exercises,* written by St. Ignatius of Loyola (1491-1556). Ignatius divides the journey into four "weeks" (Barry 1991, 8-9). During the first week the pilgrim asks God to reveal his/her sins so he/she can repent and be converted. During the second week he/she desires to know Jesus better in order to love and follow him more closely. During the third and fourth weeks, the pilgrim, who has come to know and love Jesus, shares in his passion, death, and joyful resurrection.

Bill W. understood alcoholism as a spiritual disease that went beyond physical addiction. Echoing the Desert Fathers, he wrote in the "Big Book" that the root of the problem was selfishness or self-centeredness, and to get well, alcoholics "had to quit playing God" (1984, 62). What he communicated in the twelve steps introduces the spiritual disciplines to yet another group of pilgrims. It has obviously found a hearing in twentieth-century culture.

Adult Children of Alcoholics and
Other Dysfunctional Families

The AA organization has grown to include two million men and women worldwide. Today there are 63,000 groups in 114 countries. Bill W.'s wife, Lois, started the first spinoff organization, Al-Anon, for the families of alcoholics (Robertson 1988). Al-Anon, with over half a million members, has been joined by other groups targeted at families and friends of alcoholics, such as Alateen for minor children and Adult Children of Alcoholics (ACOA or ACA) for adult children and grandchildren. In addition, there are now many other groups that focus on addictions other than alcohol, such as Narcotics Anonymous (NA), Overeaters Anonymous (OA), Gamblers Anonymous (GA), and Co-dependents Anonymous (CODA).

Adult Children of Alcoholics groups are growing very rapidly. In 1981 there were only eleven groups in seven states listed in the World Directory of Al-Anon Family Groups and Alateens; today there are over a thousand ACOA groups listed with Al-Anon in New York and Adult Children of Alcoholics (ACA) on the West Coast. In addition, there are many more groups that are independent and not listed with any organization. ACOA groups usually add to their title "and other dysfunctional families." This legitimates the presence of adult children from families that abused narcotics, shopping, food, religion, and so on.

Individuals who have been raised in addictive situations do not escape unaffected. Many develop addictions or exhibit addictive behaviors. The spiritual writers of old would probably have used the word *attachment* or *sin* instead of *addiction*. But for many today, *sin* is an old-fashioned word that makes them uncomfortable. In his book on the twelve steps for traditional church members, J. Keith Miller relates the concepts of addiction and sin: "Sin is like compulsive or addictive habits that seem to control our actions even when we don't want them to and after we swear we will 'never do it again'" (1991, 4). In the twelve-step program, these behaviors are often referred to as dysfunctions or character defects — language influenced by the recent self-help movement.

As someone who grew up in an alcoholic family, Thomas Perrin describes a number of experiences, feelings, and behaviors that he uncovered during his process of "recovery" (1991, 10). He suggests that these dysfunctions or character defects interrupt the lives of countless Adult Children, bringing them into twelve-step programs. (In the ACOA program, a list of similar character defects is referred to as the "laundry list.") Perrin has recorded his list of Adult Child character defects as "I" statements so that the Adult Child can keep the focus on him/herself and make personal applications:

> I guess at what is normal. I have difficulty following projects through from beginning to end. I lie when it would be just as easy to tell the truth. I judge myself without mercy. I have difficulty having fun. I take myself very seriously. I have difficulty with intimate relationships. I overreact to changes over which I have no control. I feel different from other people. I constantly seek approval and affirmation. I am super responsible or super irresponsible. I am extremely loyal in the face of evidence that loyalty is undeserved. I look for immediate as opposed to deferred gratification. I seek tension and crisis and then complain about the results. I avoid conflict or aggravate it, rarely do I deal with it. I fear rejection and abandonment, yet I am rejecting of others. I fear failure, but sabotage my success. I fear criticism and judgement, yet I criticize and judge others. I manage my time poorly and do not set my priorities in a way that works well for me.

The Marysville ACOA Group

The Marysville Adult Children of Alcoholics group meets on Sunday evenings in a small town in central New Jersey. The meeting site is a large Presbyterian church on the main street. Although the group uses the building, there is little contact between the church members and the group members other than the yearly donation the group makes to cover the building utilization costs. None of the church members attend the group. Group members could remember only one contact with the pastor of the church over the years: the group was locked out one night and went to the parsonage to see if they could get a key.

According to the oral history provided by group members, the Marysville ACOA group was started sometime in 1985 by a few ACOA members who wanted an additional ACOA meeting available to them on Sunday nights. None of the original members are currently active in the group. Although the Marysville group never registered with one of the Adult Child organizations, it identifies itself as an ACOA group and has the common ACOA structures and functions.

The Marysville group has survived over the years with uncanny tenacity. Over the years the group has fluctuated in size, from a gathering of five or six to a group of over twenty. There is a very loose core of half-a-dozen people who have been attending the Marysville group for the past four or five years, people who show up once every couple of months. There is also a group of five or six newer members who have been coming weekly or biweekly for the past six months to a year.

A typical attendance pattern is easily sketched. An individual comes to the group at the height of a personal crisis and continues to come weekly for a number of months. After this initial period, he or she may stop coming altogether, reappear during the next crisis, or continue attending on an irregular basis. At one meeting during the past six months, a young man who had not attended for a year could spot only two people he recognized in a group of about twelve. This pattern of attendance is consistent with the "minimal consistency of attendance at ACA groups" noted by Charles Whitfield (1992, 828).

There is a great deal of tolerance in the group for such irregular attendance. The hoped-for commitment is to recovery, not to the meetings. Those who attend are expected to figure out for themselves what they need to do to "take care of themselves." No judgment is passed on who is there and who is not there. People who reappear after long absences are greeted with great warmth. Some evenings by chance there might be five or six "old-timers" present, which usually stirs some excitement in the group.

The types of people coming to these meetings have stayed fairly constant over the years. Most are people who have been struggling with the effects of some kind of dysfunction in their background that is causing them trouble in their adult life, and they are ready to "work on themselves" or are in need of emotional support. Some people come after talking with a friend or reading an article on Adult Children in a magazine. This group of beginners, who are often at a loss for a few months, are encouraged by the leader in the opening comments to "come at least three times before you decide if this is for you or not." Others start attending meetings at the urging of their therapists. Therapists tell clients that ACOA meetings are a safe place to talk out their family-related "issues" between sessions. Many of these people come to see the Marysville group as their "home" group.

Still others who attend meetings are individuals who, after several years in AA, OA, Incest Survivors, or CODA, come to ACOA to work on the "family of origin" problem uncovered in the other program. If their primary addiction becomes hard to handle, they retreat into their primary program. This relationship with other twelve-step programs is endorsed in one of the opening comments made at meetings: "You are encouraged to match this meeting one on one with another twelve-step group or organization." Again, there is very little possessiveness or concern about how many people attend.

On any given evening there is also the person who drifts in because he or she "needs to pick up a few more meetings this week because my life isn't working for me." The Marysville ACOA group is certainly part of the larger twelve-step network. Its meetings are listed in the combined list of "Anonymous" meetings in the area and so attract people who need a few more meetings to make it through a hard week. There is one other twelve-step group, an Al-Anon group, that uses the church on Wednesday evening; however, there is rarely crossover between the two groups. There are many twelve-step groups in the immediate area, enough that someone noted that if you needed to, you could probably find a meeting at least twice a day on any day of the week.

The Marysville group attracts larger numbers of men than some of the other ACOA groups in the area. Although most evenings the women outnumber the men, on some evenings there are equal numbers of them. There is a limited mix of socioeconomic backgrounds in the group. Although the meetings are "anonymous," people give many clues over the weeks about their economic and educational backgrounds. Many are professionals — social workers, teachers, nurses, therapists; others have jobs in the business community or are blue-collar workers. A high number are writers, poets, artists, and musicians. A safe guess would be that the majority are college-educated, with perhaps 15 percent holding graduate degrees. There is practically no racial mix. Over the years an Asian or an African-American has drifted in but has not stayed more than a few weeks. (This is true of many of the twelve-step groups in the area.) There is some diversity in religious upbringing. Some members have no religious background, but the faiths represented within the group include Roman Catholic, Presbyterian, Reformed, Baptist, and Jewish. However, few of the members speak of regularly attending church as adults.

The Meeting Space

The Marysville group has always met from 8:00 to 9:15 p.m. in the church lounge, a rather large room with a few easy chairs and an available stack of folding chairs. The person who has signed up to be the leader for the evening arrives early, unlocks the building, sets up a dozen or so chairs in a circle, and sets out the reading materials for sale. Since this is not an official ACOA group, it is free to promote "non–conference approved" literature — in other words, literature not officially sanctioned by the parent organization.

The lounge is connected by folding doors to the dark, silent, cavernous sanctuary. Usually the doors are shut, but some evenings they stand open. One evening, while someone was telling an especially heartrending story, something airborne emerged from that gloomy expanse and buzzed the group several times like pain personified. It took a few shocked minutes for the group to recognize the attacker as a bat, and the meeting stopped while the heavy folding doors were drawn to trap the bat in the sanctuary. Although the bat has visited more than once, the lounge usually has a warm, welcoming feeling.

Many evenings the ACOA group is the only group meeting in the Marysville church. But occasionally a group of young people meets in the church at the same time. Before that meeting starts, some of the young people have been running and shouting in the sanctuary and connecting passages. That has annoyed the ACOA group at times, and it has asked the youth leaders to exert better control over the young people. When there are other people present in the building, it makes some group members noticeably nervous and hesitant to share. One group member explained that, given the nature of what members are divulging, it is of utmost importance that the space where the meeting is held be perceived as safe.

Occasionally, the group will meet outside the lounge. Sometimes, on hot summer evenings, the group has sat outside on folding chairs. Twice, when the person with the key didn't show up, the group sat on blankets on the grass in the old graveyard next to the church. These outside meetings produced some interesting results. Margie, the social worker introduced above, commented, "I remember the meetings in the graveyard. Since the meeting started at 8:00 p.m., dusk fell during the meeting, and by 9:30 the group was sitting in the dark. It was the strangest thing. I can't remember any time when the sharing was more intimate. Perhaps people felt freer to share really personal stuff when it grew difficult to see each other. Even more anonymity, I guess."

The Structures

The opening of the meeting is similar to the opening of every twelve-step meeting across the country. The agenda for the opening, which takes about fifteen minutes, is typed up for the leader to follow. The leader begins by saying, "Hello, my name is ___. Let's open with the Serenity Prayer." This is the famous prayer attributed to Reinhold Niebuhr that reads, "God grant me the serenity to accept the things I cannot change, the courage to change the things I can, and the wisdom to know the difference."

The leader then identifies the Marysville group as being a twelve-step program based on the twelve steps and twelve traditions of AA, and he or she suggests that participants compare this meeting with another twelve-step program. Next the leader reads a descriptive paragraph to remind members and visitors why they are there:

> We are a fellowship of individuals who believe that surviving an experience is more than just living through it — we must learn from it. We gather to share our strength, hope and experience to learn how we were affected by growing up in an alcoholic or other type of dysfunctional family. Whatever your problems, it is likely that there are those among us who have them too. This is a journey, and a journey starts with a single step. Coming to this meeting is such a step.

Then, they go around the circle. Each person says, "Hi, I'm so-and-so" (a few add "and I'm an adult child of an alcoholic," which echoes the famous AA introduction). Since this is an anonymous program, people give only their first names. In fact, most people don't know each other's last names even after four or five years of being together in meetings. After introducing himself or herself, each person then reads one of the twelve steps. Sometimes a version of the twelve steps for Adult Children is read, but typically the original version is used. Sometimes the "laundry list" of common ACOA character defects is also passed around, or a list of affirmations for ACOAs.

A series of housekeeping details follows. A basket is passed for voluntary contributions. Most people put in a dollar bill. The money is use to make a yearly donation to the church. Next a book is passed around so that those who would be willing to be leaders in the future can sign up. There are no restrictions on who can lead, but newcomers are advised to wait several months before they volunteer. Also circulated is a phone list with members' first names and last initials. Individuals are encouraged to call each other if they need support during the week. The group is then reminded about the books available for purchase on the literature table. Next, recovery anniversaries are acknowledged. Someone will say she's been in recovery for six months; someone else will say he's been in recovery for a year, and so on; these victories will be greeted with applause. (Problems are to be brought up at a business meeting held during the last meeting of the month.)

Next, a page-long list of the group's rules is explained rule by rule. These rules are discussed below in the "Group Problems" section.

After working through the preliminaries, the leader usually talks for about ten minutes about some issue or topic that has been of concern to him or her during the previous week. (The exception is the first Sunday of the month, when the leader reads the step of the month — step 1 in January, step 2 in February, etc. — and presents it for discussion.) The leader presents the topic for discussion with the understanding that anyone who has something different to say can change the topic.

The meeting lasts until 9:15 p.m. and usually breaks up right on time. At this point the leader invites the group to stand and repeat a prayer. (In years past, the prayer was always the Lord's Prayer, but for the past few months, the Serenity Prayer has been repeated. Some of the group members are unhappy about this change.) Group members hold hands during the prayer; afterward they give each other's hand a quick squeeze and chant, "It works if you work it!" At this point the newer people leave, and the rest stand around for about half an hour for "the meeting after the meeting." This is a time when there are a lot of one-on-one conversations and a lot of hugs are exchanged. About once or twice a month someone suggests that they go to a nearby ice-cream store; about five or six people usually go. The conversation at the ice-cream store is notably more social, focusing less on problems. These individuals stay until the store closes and then retreat to the parking lot, where they exchange more hugs.

Three Members

Before describing the sharing part of the meeting, in which the real work of the group takes place, I will introduce three members of the Marysville ACOA group. Since it is an anonymous group, the quotations I use come from interviews I had with these individuals outside the meetings. These individuals represent a cross section of the Marysville group.

John M. is openly acknowledged as the elder statesman, a fact that has begun to bother him. He started attending the Marysville group in

1986, one year after the group organized, so he was able to provide historical information about the group as well as a thoughtful perspective on it. Although he is middle-aged, John is short, trim, and boyish looking. He dresses casually; his taste runs to corduroy pants and flannel shirts, which tend to soften his erect, almost cocky carriage. He exudes self-confidence and a consistent happiness. When I asked him if the family he grew up in was close and supportive, he answered, "Hell, no." He went on to explain that his father was an alcoholic, "a discreet alcoholic, not the drunk-every-night, smashing-up-the-furniture type of alcoholic." His father had converted to Catholicism in order to marry, so the children were raised in the Catholic faith. John attended Catholic schools from grade school through college. He attended church until he was a sophomore in college, then dropped out permanently. After college he went on for a master's degree and subsequently got his Ph.D. After two short teaching stints in the South, he headed for a job in Arizona, "the perfect position at the perfect place," and promptly started having regular panic attacks. A therapist taught him stress reduction, but a magazine article that listed the characteristics of an Adult Child made him suspect that his problems lay deeper, and eventually he began going to ACOA. When he failed to receive tenure in Arizona, he moved East; he recently received tenure at a small suburban college. Although he doesn't attend church, John is a student of mysticism, both Catholic and Eastern. In recent months John has been attending meetings very infrequently.

Rose P. was selected to represent the incest survivors who have found their way into the Marysville group. She has been attending faithfully for the past seven or eight months. Her therapist suggested that she attend ACOA meetings in addition to an Incest Survivors Anonymous group. Rose is in her thirties, married, and the mother of several children ranging in age from three to eleven. Rose is a pretty woman with dark hair who dresses in fairly trendy clothes that look good on her medium-large frame. But she has a sad face, and she sighs often. Even when she does not speak, her face speaks for her; when she does share, it is with such feeling that it touches the entire group. The oldest of three children, Rose grew up in a large midwestern city. It was not an easy childhood. "My parents are both active alcoholics. My parents are abusive people — verbally, emotionally, and sexually abusive. As an adolescent I became an addict myself." She stated that she was able to get herself off drugs after seven or eight years by bringing into her life

191

over-controlling people like her husband. She is celebrating eleven years of sobriety this year. Her mother came from a very strict Catholic family who disowned her when she married a Presbyterian. Although she was baptized a Presbyterian, Rose also attended a Roman Catholic church with her girlfriends from the neighborhood when she was growing up. But she has not attended church in her adult life. After she got married she moved East, where she has spent her time raising her family. She is currently a student at the local community college.

Steve W. is a young man in the process of discovering himself. He is in his thirties but appears at first glance to be much younger. He wears his sixties-looking shoulder-length hair pulled back into a long ponytail and usually wears rather scruffy clothes. In meetings he frequently expresses strong emotions, sometimes about what's going on in his life, sometimes in reaction to what someone in the group has said. He cries, talks loudly, shouts angrily. Steve has an undergraduate degree from a prestigious university and a master's degree but dropped out of school three years ago to devote himself to his music. His father converted from Catholicism in order to marry a girl from a very religious Presbyterian family. His family went to church every week and took him to Sunday school, but Steve doesn't attend church as an adult. His grandfather was an alcoholic, and he thinks his father is one as well. The net result of his upbringing was "dysfunction . . . I mean, not being able to cope as an adult, going from job to job, having no sense of direction, no career . . . getting enmeshed in relationships." Steve sought the help of a therapist who suggested some group therapy. He decided to try ACOA instead after talking with a friend, who happened to be one of the founding members of the Marysville ACOA group.

Working the Program

One of the purposes of the group is to provide a safe place for Adult Children to come and tell their stories. In his book entitled *Healing the Child Within* (1987), Charles Whitfield suggests that it is by telling your story over and over to safe people that healing eventually takes place, and ACOA functions on that premise. Week after week men and women tell difficult stories, stories of family secrets. As an individual tells his or her story, he or she often relives what happened, experiencing sometimes for the first time the emotions that go with the story. There are also memories stored in the person's body that resurface, especially if he or she was the victim of incest or physical abuse. Being able to "betray" one's family and tell the family secrets to strangers takes an enormous amount of courage. If the teller is to endure these memories, he or she needs the loving presence of another person or persons. Providing this kind of supportive presence is what the Marysville group usually does well.

Revealing the life struggles and the stories of family secrets presents an opportunity for — rather than a guarantee of — spiritual growth. What happens after that initial crisis is over? It appears that some people drop out of the program entirely while others continue on at their own pace. Members often refer to continuing in the program as "working the program." No good definition of "working the program" can be given. However, the implication seems to be that one would not only come to meetings but would attempt to apply the basic principles of the program in his or her disordered life. The following section describes how Steve, Rose, and John, introduced above, "work the program" and what the results have been for them spiritually.

Steve, the long-haired musician, entered the program when he found his "life had become unmanageable," as the first step suggests. He has responded angrily to the dysfunction he experiences in his adult life as a result of the alcoholic family he was raised in. During his interview he explained why he started coming to meetings: "This summer I had sort of several crises hit, one after another. I was living out of my car for a while and that was just so embarrassing for me, because that was something that was the crystal evidence of how dysfunctional my behavior was. I didn't know how to take care of myself enough to provide myself a place to live. But people listened to me and they didn't recoil . . . in horror when I related these stories, and that really helped. I felt these people didn't want to see me like that, but at the same time they were accepting."

What Steve is doing is identified in the ACOA program as step 1 work. He is aware only that he has problems which have overwhelmed him and are creating a confusing, unfamiliar personal situation for him. His limited perception is evident in the following quotation: "I go to meetings because I have a problem, and I am trying to take care of that problem and improve my behavior so I can function better. . . . I mean, I don't go to tag along like a puppy dog to some spiritual leader."

Steve is not totally without spiritual awareness, however. He has some beginning notions about the spiritual nature of the program, which he seems to equate with getting in touch with feelings. For example, when responding to a question about the spiritual aspect of the meetings, he stated, "The beautiful spiritual stuff comes out when people start to get in touch with what they are feeling." He illustrated his point by describing what happened in a meeting when one member was very upset: "There were two people that comforted that person, and the meeting just took on this air of real tragedy. . . . We all recognized what had happened to us. We were all helping each other, and that was a family of choice. And at the end of the meeting we usually hold hands, and instead of holding hands [at this meeting] we put our arms around each other and that was a really beautiful thing. And nobody said, 'Let's do this.' It just happened, and that was important. It felt Big." He then mused that he experiences the same thing when he plays the blues. "I try to just get in touch with how I'm feeling and not so much thinking about what I'm playing as how I'm feeling."

Regardless of how much self-awareness Steve has, he is living out a process that has been identified by spiritual writers for centuries, a process that starts when a person has his eyes opened, is able to admit that he has a problem, and begins to get in touch with the inner self. At this point Steve uses the word *feelings* to describe what is happening internally. It is reminiscent of St. Augustine's self-awareness, which started him on a journey inward.

The abuse that Rose experienced growing up in her home was unusually severe. When I interviewed her, she appeared sad most of the time, and several times she had to quit talking because she was in tears. When I asked her about her family, she answered, "Well, recently this past year I've gotten on the tack about my father sexually abusing me. That was something I really had no memory of at all. I mean, years have been blocked from my memory. It was also many episodes of severe physical abuse and very severe verbal abuse. . . . I've had times recently when I wouldn't have the visual memory, but I would just feel afraid for my life, especially in the middle of the night. I would hear sounds in my house like wood creaking and the heat creaking, and the creaking really triggers that terror for me." There have been times when she was so lost in pain that she was suicidal. Truly a "dark night" experience.

Rose also talked about her relationship with God, which has developed during this period. She told me that she experiences God in the meetings through the group itself and through group prayer. "It feels real good to hold everybody's hand and pray. It feels really good to me. I don't like it when someone says, 'Let's not say the Lord's Prayer.'" She is also aware of what the group has to offer her in terms of support. "The first time I shared with the group that I was an incest survivor . . . after the meeting I felt so warmly received and I'll never forget that. That really meant a lot to me. I think from that moment on I felt okay. I felt good there. I really wanted and needed to be there."

When I asked her how she knew she was experiencing God in the group, she explained that God speaks to her through her body — that is, she has bodily sensations. "I really believe that. [I] listen to what's going on in here [my body], and that's how God answers my prayers."

Rose also spoke of her dependence on God outside the meetings. She described the panic she sometimes felt at night and added, "What really helped me through is that I could really visualize God holding me, and I could visualize God holding that little girl in me, too. He kept us safe. He kept us warm and loved, and that's what's really given me my faith." She thinks she is lucky that God has given her a chance for recovery as an incest survivor; others have not been so lucky. "I am who I am because of incest, and I think I'm a better person, and God chose me."

She had a lot to say in the interview about incest and spirituality. She also attends a twelve-step incest survivors group and thinks the spirituality in that group is even greater than that of the Marysville group. "I would say that there is more spirituality in that group than there is in the Sunday-night group. I think every single person in there really leans on the higher power a lot. Almost everyone in that group . . . goes to church." Later in the interview she said she has recently had the urge to go to church, a new feeling for her. She attributes this new feeling to two things: her newfound comfort with being in a group of people, and her habit of daily prayer. She thinks it "feels really good to pray with other people."

In terms of the ACOA program, it seems obvious that she is moving past the confusion spoken of in step 1 and is discovering God, the process recorded in steps 2 and 3: "[We] came to believe that a power greater than ourselves could restore us to sanity" and "[We] made a decision to turn our will and our lives over to the care of God as we understood Him." Or, to use the traditional language of spiritual journey provided by St. John of the Cross, Rose's internal desolation is being replaced by contact with divine love.

John, the group's elder statesman, is well past his desolate days of regular panic attacks. That period has given way to four or five years of focused attention on the shotgun effect of alcoholism on his personality. He is chipping away at the "laundry list" of inherited dysfunctions that he experiences. He does so in a rather intellectual, detached manner. During the interview with me, he discussed how difficult it has been to discover his true self, partly because his parents did not present their own true selves to him as a child. He talked about it in an amusing way. "One of my persistent fantasies from childhood . . . was that my parents were really animals, like the Three Bears; they always show you Papa Bear wearing pants and a coat, and Mama Bear's wearing a dress. Only I thought they not only wore human clothes, but they had to have these masks made so that their faces would look just like mine. I remember thinking, 'Boy, it must get awfully hot for them wearing these rubber masks all the time . . . so they must like to take them off when I'm not around.' I would never rush into a room unexpectedly — I'd always make some noise coming down the hall — and I always thought I was giving them time to get their masks back on."

The discovery of a true self is part of a spiritual journey. The language of true self/false self appears notably in the twentieth-century writings of Thomas Merton, who was influenced by the psychologist Carl Jung. As John works on finding his true self in addition to working through other related "laundry list" issues, he is, in program language, "taking the fourth step" (making "a searching and fearless moral inventory" of oneself). Then, when John talks about these issues in meetings, he is taking the fifth step ("Admitted to God, to ourselves, and to another human being the exact nature of our wrongs"). Put in the more traditional language of St. Teresa, John is in the process of exploring his own "interior castle."

John has been in the program long enough to have a number of insights into how he goes about making "conscious contact with God," the eleventh step. First, like Rose, he experiences bodily sensations during the meetings. "I experience physical sensations — the words that seem to fit them best are *warm, golden, light, pulsating* — in the sense of highly energetic, and yet at the same time serene." He said that he experienced these sensations particularly during the moments in the meetings when nobody was talking, when there were stretches of silence. Second, outside the meetings he has been seeking God in traditional Christian ways, including meditation. He is especially interested in mys-

196

ticism and has done a great deal of reading on the topic. He stated that although he grew up in the Catholic Church, he never heard about the mystical tradition in Catholicism, but his academic research led him to find Julian of Norwich and many other medieval mystics. Third, John has also sought God in traditions outside Christianity. He has, for example, read a lot about Zen Buddhism and frequents a nude beach at a Zen monastery in the high deserts in California. John believes that when he visits that beach he has corporal spiritual experiences similar to those he has in the silence of some ACOA meetings. The experience is similar to the stripping down, the anonymity of an ACOA meeting, but it's more pronounced and powerful. "There is something in being there and looking around, and there's a bunch of other people, and they're all nude. It's very anonymous. . . . Even in meetings when people walk in and sit down, you look at them and you think, 'Hmmm, work boots, jeans, and a flannel shirt, [or] Gucci loafers and slacks and an alligator sweater.' There's a powerful kind of anonymity [at the beach]. And it's just a feeling of connectedness." He also practices tai chi, which he says he likes more than meditation.

When I pressed John to explain what he finds spiritual in meetings and in going to the nudist beach, he replied, "It's not always spiritual; sometimes it's just going to the beach." He went on to explain, "My definition of spirituality is when mind and body are no longer separated, but you're right there at a point where you're not particularly aware of any difference between the two." He then mentioned Thomas à Kempis, Julian of Norwich, and Margery Kempe, and said that his ideas about spirituality are full of erotic imagery, that a spiritual experience is very much like making love. "Is one aware of oneself as separate from the other person? I mean when it is really good. Yes, it's a wonderful paradox."

John's sensual language is not much different from that used by many saints in their writings. It is well known, for example, that the writings of St. John of the Cross contain sensual images. According to Margaret Miles (1992), St. Augustine's *Confessions* are also full of "desire and delight." *The Cloud of Unknowing* is also surprisingly intimate. It would appear that John has traveled far in his spiritual journey, thanks in part to his participation in the Marysville group.

However, John seems to have outgrown the Marysville group. He has started attending another ACOA group that is more grounded in the twelve steps and the twelve traditions. He told me that he wanted a "group which is connected in closely with the Al-Anon Intergroup

197

Agency or the AA World Service Organization which keeps the twelve step tradition to its original intent."

Group Problems

John's comment about needing to get back to the twelve-step basics indicates what is perhaps one of the chief problems encountered in the Marysville group. According to John, this particular ACOA group has always been very relaxed about things, and when the question of becoming an official group came up in 1985, nobody did anything about it. This has allowed the group to ignore the rules prohibiting "nonconference" literature and references in meetings. For a number of years John himself enjoyed the luxury of bringing in outside articles to read to the group. According to Margie, however, that has also allowed the group to drift away from a narrow emphasis on twelve-step language and allowed the program to get watered down: "There has been a tendency for a lot of trendy self-help and New Age ideas to creep in. It weakens the spiritual base of the program." A good example is the substitution, at the end of the meeting, of the more neutral Serenity Prayer for the Lord's Prayer. Margie is thinking about leaving the group.

Talk about God or a higher power is at a minimum during the Marysville meetings; recently the meetings seem to be focused more on the telling of painful stories than on stories of how God has been working in their lives. This could be related to the increased number of beginning members who have come and shared long, dismal first-step stories. As a consequence, longer-term members like Helen (an artist in her sixties), who are looking for something beyond that first step, are not coming as often. When I asked why she had started coming to the Marysville group, Helen said, "It just seemed to be a very holy little group, and I don't mean because it was in a church." But things seem to have changed, and she is concerned. "There seems to be an awful lot of dumping in this group," she explained, "and I know that's necessary because I did the same thing myself. I hear a lot of problems being expressed, but in my other meetings I hear a lot of joy and a lot of gratitude, and a lot of thanksgiving for the program, and a lot of actual demonstrating what has happened that has made them move from one step to the next step — sharing it in such a way that some people that are in a lot of pain can see it and maybe move to the next step too."

As the older members participate less or leave the group, there are fewer and fewer present who talk about the twelve steps, who point the way out of the darkness. It seems that the more advanced members are deserting the younger members to find themselves a better situation — and that seems to contradict the injunction in step 12 to help others. Margie, however, had an explanation straight out of the self-help movement: she said that it was *codependent* to take care of someone else's needs before your own. Adult children of alcoholics have to be very careful, Margie explained, because of the dysfunctional family dynamics they grew up with. In an alcoholic family, the ministrations of family members "enable" the alcoholic to continue in his/her alcoholism. This reasoning — avoiding codependent behaviors — seems to legitimate a lot of self-serving behavior.

I observed much caring behavior going on during and after the meetings, but when I asked about expressions of caring and concern in between meetings, I got little response. Members have each other's phone numbers, but as far as I could determine, they rarely call each other. In addition, there is no emphasis on sponsorship (a big part of AA) in the Marysville group. A person can regularly attend meetings for months and then disappear for weeks, and no one will ask where that person is or phone to find out. The focus, as they say, is on themselves.

According to the older members, the focus of the meetings has been changing as more and more incest survivors attend. Indeed, on many evenings, incest seems to be the dominant theme. The stories told by incest survivors are intense and powerful and have an influence on everyone present. Margie commented, "Recovery work can be very tricky. Feelings are coming up, stuff you don't understand, and it's easy to start to 'remember' things that 'happened' to you which in actuality maybe happened and maybe didn't." Steve, for example, is in the process of trying to sort out what actually happened to him in childhood. When the subject of childhood punishment came up in an interview with me, he said, "My mom spanked us with a wooden spoon." Then he paused and added, "It's hard not to make some of this stuff up. . . . You hear so much in the group of the way people were treated, and sometimes you think, 'Yeah, I was treated that way,' and then you're not really sure." Later in the interview he mentioned that he has started to go to incest survivors' meetings even though he has no memories of incest. "I get feelings. It's more of a feeling than an actual memory, and that's a difficult thing because then I don't like telling stories about my family because I feel unsure how much of an effect those incidents really had on me. In a sick sort of way, I'd like my life to be much more tragic than it was, so I could point to it and say, 'Look, that's obviously tragic. That's what happened.'"

Influence isn't all bad; in a way the positive influence of one member on another is what a twelve-step group is all about. Margie stated that the group becomes a substitute family where people can get the unconditional love they never got at home and can also have and express feelings that had to be repressed at home. However, she went on to say, "It is real easy for the group to become dysfunctional, given all the dysfunctional people that are there. Some of the problems with mother or father get worked out almost unconsciously in the group because it is a safe place to do that." For example, Steve had problems with his mother discouraging the expression of anger. During the interview he started to talk about the problem of women in the group who are comfortable with crying but not with anger. He commented, "There are certain issues that are a little bit more difficult to get brought up in that meeting because of that [the women]. I mean, it's safe. It's calm. It's reassuring. It's comforting. . . . Maybe there's a group sense of keeping it safe and protected and also quiet. . . . It's okay to cry, but don't get angry. It's almost encouraged that you get to the root of your problem and cry. But sometimes the root of your problem might be anger."

Another indication of how issues are being worked out in the group is illustrated by the recent changes in the opening statement of the group's ground rules. What for years had been a simple statement about anonymity ("Who you see here, what you hear here, let it stay here when you leave here") has been expanded to include a single-spaced page of rules for the meeting. The author of the new opening explained that the purpose was to make the meeting run more smoothly and provide a safe space for people to share their family secrets. He felt that too many people were new to the group and didn't understand the rules, and that made people feel unsafe.

Two of the added rules have to do with expressing emotions and touching one another. The latter is an addition obviously related to the special needs of the growing number of incest survivors in the group. This section reads, "Sometimes people may cry or express other strong emotions while sharing. This is as it should be. Recovery is not possible without experiencing painful feelings. It is important to respect these feelings and not try to 'cheer someone up' or 'get them to look on the bright side.' Similarly, we feel that touching can be viewed by some as threatening and should not take place unless permission is given. Many of us grew up in families where we were not allowed to be sad, angry, scared, or ashamed. In recovery we have learned that we have a right to all of our feelings. Only by owning our sadness will we come to know joy." But now the new rules are read at the beginning of every meeting even if only "old-timers" are present. It seems obvious to me that this change reflects the troubled side of the group. When read aloud, the rules sound like declarations from an angry Old Testament prophet.

Another difficult issue for the Marysville group is the "no crosstalk" rule. No crosstalk means there are to be no conversations between two individuals during the meeting, no "feedback." The idea is to give people a place to say difficult things, to externalize thoughts and feelings but not to have a conversation about them. The no-crosstalk rule is qualified by the following statement: "It is, however, appropriate to say that some-one else's sharing prompted your own thoughts and feelings about a similar issue. If we need to ask someone about something they mentioned while sharing, we do so after the meeting and then only after asking their permission first." "No crosstalk" functions as an informal rule in many ACOA groups, but it is a bitter issue for this group because some want to supersede the rule while others do not. One evening, for example, one member had shared some difficult emerging memories about his family. The next person to speak, a woman, addressed her comments to him directly in an attempt to comfort him instead of focusing on her own issues. He was furious at the unbidden intrusion and did not return to the group for a month.

Closely related to this rule are two other rules that are in turn related to each other: the rule about not giving advice and the rule about keeping the focus on yourself. Since many individuals don't want anyone to give them advice, there is not only the rule about advice-giving but also the corollary rule about focus. The idea is that if you focus on yourself by making "I" statements, you are less likely to fall into the error of telling someone else what he or she should be doing. The word *should* is taboo. Yet there are some in the Marysville group who have broken these rules. One member, an incest survivor, left the group and never came back after someone suggested he should forgive the "per-petrator." The adjunct statement now stresses the importance of uphold-ing these two rules: "We do this because as children many of us learned to 'take care of' other people, focusing on their lives rather than our own. We need to share our own feelings and experiences and listen to and learn from others sharing their, without trying to give advice or otherwise take control."

It is ironic that this new set of written rules illustrates some of the very behavior patterns that Adult Children are trying to break. It is a perfect example of the tendency of Adult Children to give advice and try to control situations — basic character defects of the Adult Child.

Conclusions

There are several observations to be made about twelve-step spirituality in general and the Marysville group in particular. It seems obvious that the twelve steps outlined by Bill W. provide the framework needed for a genuine spiritual journey. In some groups this nonreligious approach works well; in other groups, such as the Marysville group, it doesn't work as well.

On the positive side, the nonreligious phrasing of the twelve steps makes the spiritual disciplines accessible to many individuals from non-church backgrounds. They also help individuals who are alienated from the church and church language to seek God without the old associations. The use of the term "higher power" seems to help many who would never visit a church.

The twelve-step program also allows individuals struggling with their interior lives to be vulnerable. Many churches do not create an atmosphere in which parishioners can honestly express their weaknesses. In fact, churches are very often places where keeping up appearances is the norm. It is true that when someone is in crisis, the good people of the church will rally round him or her in a paternalistic kind of way, but shared vulnerability is rare. A number of those in the church see genuine struggles with the interior life not as a sign of strength but as a sign of weakness. By contrast, at a twelve-step meeting, individuals can feel surrounded and supported by fellow pilgrims.

The twelve-step meetings are also set up to provide guides along the way. Ideally, guides are those who have been down the path themselves and haven't just read about the path in a book. A basic principle in AA is that an alcoholic is never fully recovered and will need to practice the spiritual disciplines of the AA program for life. Ideally this keeps a fair number of older members active in the program, ready to be sponsors of newer members. Indeed, for generations of pilgrims, being held accountable has been vitally important.

Given these structures and traditions, there is a tremendous potential for spirituality in any twelve-step group. The Marysville group has certainly benefited from being associated with ACOA, as evidenced by the spiritual development of its members. However, in many ways the group fails to live up to its potential.

One of its most critical flaws is its lax attitude toward the twelve steps. As noted, this attitude has characterized the group from its inception, and has allowed such things as discussion of "outside" ideas and the display of materials not approved by the AA organization. In many ACOA and Al-Anon meetings, sections of conference-approved twelve-step literature are read and become the focus for the ensuing discussion. In the Marysville group, however, the discussions are based on individual life experiences, on "sharing," which means that no study of the twelve steps is involved. For many years the presence of experienced members who also attended other twelve-step meetings kept the group clearly within the disciplines of the program. But the influx of many new members who are in the early stages of recovery and the exit of many older members has created a shift in focus away from the basic twelve-step principles.

Allowing "outside" ideas into the group has functioned to water down the original twelve-step spirituality. With the departure of members steeped in the twelve steps, more self-help and New Age ideas are heard. Many of these ideas are in subtle conflict with the traditional spiritual disciplines that underpin the twelve steps. For example, the self-help notion of escaping codependence is given equal weight with following the twelve steps, even though selfishness seems to be at its core.

The infrequent attendance of the more experienced members has also left the group with too many individuals who are just beginning their recovery and are still clearly dysfunctional in many aspects of their lives. As indicated above, many times these dysfunctions are acted out in the context of the group. In some meetings it seems to be the blind supporting the blind.

At this juncture the Marysville group does provide individuals who are in a great deal of pain and confusion a place to talk and receive support. As noted, this period of confusion can be the beginning of a genuine spiritual journey. However, it is also a time when many do not have a clear concept of the spiritual journey. One of the newer members of the Marysville group, an outspoken atheist responsible for eliminating the Lord's Prayer from the closing, is aware only of working on personal character defects. Another cannot conceive of a higher power any greater than her teddy bear, so allows her teddy bear to love her. These individuals need structure and guidance to help them advance in their spiritual lives.

But this help is minimal in the Marysville group. According to Margie, who also attends other ACOA groups, the Marysville group is notably weak in providing help beyond the beginning steps, although she noted that most ACOA groups fail to provide guidance in the spiritual life after a certain point. Through the interviews I conducted, I learned that many of the more experienced members have sought help outside the twelve-step structure. John, the elder statesman, has sought help from sources both inside and outside the traditional church. Two other more advanced members have begun sessions with a Roman Catholic spiritual director. Rose, the young incest survivor, is thinking of attending church.

It would seem that the richness of the Christian tradition of spiritual disciplines is embedded in the twelve steps ascribed to by the Marysville group, but that the group lacks the support structures it needs to follow these steps as rigorously as it could. The departure of more experienced members has hurt the group, as have the dysfunctions of the newer members. However, this group is helping a number of individuals whose needs would perhaps not be met anywhere else. What they do in terms of supporting each other as they share painful stories, they do well.

Cathedral Nights:
A Group in Creation

WENDY YOUNG

This is the story of a small group within a large Episcopal cathedral. Cathedral Church of St. John the Divine is famous (or, to
some people, infamous) for its unusual combination of high church
liturgy and provocative use of the arts as expressions of spirituality.
The Dean, the Very Reverend James Parks Morton, S.T.B., M.A., is
vivacious and welcoming, and in twenty years of tenure, he has transformed what was an empty cathedral into a vibrant place of worship
and creativity.[1]

A person living in New York City will find both the pleasures of
a rich cultural milieu and the harsh truths of a big city with problems.
In the case of the Cathedral, these are strikingly juxtaposed. Outside on
112th Street and Amsterdam, most signs of urban decay are clear: there
are homeless people, drug dealers — and rats. But the Cathedral — still
growing, as the scaffolding around it attests — stands tall, pigeons and

---

1. The Episcopal Church is headed by the Archbishop of Canterbury. Serving
directly under him are the bishops of each diocese, which are made up of a collection
of parishes. Each diocese has one bishop and one cathedral. The bishop appoints a
dean to serve the cathedral, and canons, ministers, and deacons serve under the dean.
Dean Morton was chosen by Bishop Moore in 1973. (The present Bishop of New
York is the Right Reverend Richard Frank Grein, D.D.)

205

all, and upon entering its doors, most people are awestruck by its extraordinary size and beauty.[2]

Dean Morton first trained as an architect, and was attracted to the priesthood because of the mission the Cathedral presented. The design of the building inspired him, as did his good friends Canon West and the Right Reverend Paul Moore, Jr., S.T.D., Thirteenth Bishop of New York. These friends began the project of making the Cathedral a house of prayer for all people, the Cathedral of the United Nations.[3]

The Cathedral holds popular public events, attracting eight thousand, for example, for Christmas Eve services. A large number of occasional worshipers attend the Cathedral; they include people from other faiths and avowed atheists. An average of 300 people attend the weekly service at eleven on Sunday mornings. The Cathedral also serves the community at large in a variety of ways: it runs a recycling center and a soup kitchen, and it offers language classes, job training, legal aid for senior citizens and others in need, and pastoral psychotherapy.

The Cathedral is unique in its combination of radical spiritual expression and orthodox Anglican liturgical traditions. People visiting the Cathedral for the first time often assume it is a Catholic stronghold, because of the long services, the chanting of plainsong, the use of formal language, and the burning of incense. But supplementing the very orthodox form of

---

2. The design of the Cathedral is eclectic, including Byzantine, Gothic, and Romanesque elements. A visit to the Cathedral today amounts to an education in cathedral building, because the structure is still being worked on. The architects of the Cathedral, first Heins and LaFarge, and later Cramm and Ferguson, believed that the Cathedral was to be the symbol of the kingdom of God on earth, a concept of "sacred architecture" no longer held by twentieth-century architects. This concept derived from medieval times. Everyone was welcome in a medieval cathedral: the minstrels, the traders, the gardeners, the artisans, the wealthy, and the indigent. Similarly, all are welcome in the Cathedral Church of St. John the Divine in the 1990s.

3. The mission statement of the Cathedral reads in part:

The Cathedral of St. John the Divine in the City and Diocese of New York is the mother church of the Episcopal Diocese of New York and the Seat of its bishop. In this international city and home of the United Nations the universal need for world peace and reconciliation is addressed powerfully by the Cathedral's three-fold Charter: "to be a House of Prayer for all people ... a center of intellectual light and leading ... an instrument of church unity." It is a place for preaching the Gospel of Jesus Christ and for Christian worship, based on the Book of Common Prayer and the breadth of the Anglican liturgical tradition.

liturgy influenced by the Russian Orthodox tradition in which Dean Morton was trained is an eclectic range of practices. The high altar holds symbols from the other world religions, services start with the Beatitudes, and communicants receive communion standing in a circle around an altar that is set up in the crossing, a practice designed to encourage intimacy. Native American prayers may be read, and at times the politics of freedom and environmental concerns are heard from the pulpit. This church is an example of the liberal side of the Episcopal Church.

The Dean's creative touch and all-encompassing passion have attracted a large following. People might first attend a free concert and then return to find out what the Cathedral offers on Sundays. Because of its size, a visitor can observe the goings-on from a distance and then step closer when he or she chooses to. Beverly, one of the women I interviewed, explained her response this way:

> Because that Cathedral is so large, somehow you can find *your* God lurking around some pillar, or in the light of a window, or a special painting. It is the gift of a cathedral, that the sheer space of it gives you space to look at your life, and to feel God. I joined the evening group because I wanted to be in that space more. It's so *public* on a Sunday, with busloads of tourists arriving, even during services. Cathedral Evenings were the time when the Cathedral was all ours.

Another person I talked with, James, also believes the sheer size of the Cathedral has something to do with its success:

> I think the Cathedral can hold a large number of potentially incompatible people because of its enormity. I mean, if Ben has a fight with Ellen, let's say, they can sit on opposite sides of the Cathedral without much trouble until tempers cool. Other churches can be more claustrophobic. Also, you are *obligated* to shake the minister's hand after services if he stands at the only exit! The Cathedral allows people to be anonymous if they choose to be, to come and worship quietly.

Perhaps the most apt image of the Cathedral's daily routine is that of a circus.[4] The Dean is the ringmaster, overseeing the various acts and making sure the performances come off, making sure all the balls are in the air.

---

4. In fact, the Big Apple Circus, with Phillipe Petit and his tightrope act, first began rehearsals in the crypt of the Cathedral. This circus is now a New York institution, performing in a tent next to Lincoln Center every year.

The small group that I focus on in this chapter was very much in the Dean's style: each of its meetings had several different activities that made it extraordinary. Cathedral Nights, as it was named, continued in various forms for nearly ten years, eventually ending in 1992, and can be considered a microcosm of the Cathedral at large. That the group was successful for ten years was largely due to the Dean's extraordinary energy and his ability to orchestrate unusual and thought-provoking multisensory events. These included annual Sunday services such as the St. Francis Day Celebration, when people brought their pets to be blessed and to listen to Paul Winter's *Gaia Mass,* a composition with animal calls in the melodies. There were also regular classical music events, dance concerts, and art exhibits. The complex issues surrounding the decline of the group during the period I studied it provide a useful glimpse of the challenge of urban ministry in today's society, and of the problems that small groups may face when carrying on the work of a visionary.

The Birth of the Group

Cathedral Nights was a small group — small by Cathedral standards — that began meeting on Tuesday evenings in 1982. The stories that center on the ten years of the group's existence provide an insightful picture of the Cathedral as a whole. When some of the group members tried to recall how the group began, it was difficult to separate fact from fiction. One thing is clear, however: this extremely diverse group of people shared a devotion to Dean Morton and felt that the Cathedral was their true home. The Tuesday-evening meetings were the highlight of their week. These meetings attracted the core group, the inner circle, within the Cathedral, including those who considered themselves close personal friends of the Dean. These people volunteered a great deal of their time and energy to Cathedral work.

Like most things within the Cathedral, the Tuesday-evening group started with the inspiration of the Dean. The group evolved over ten years, its shape depending on the Dean's ideas and the volunteers available. The first incarnation of the meetings focused on discussion about the previous Sunday's sermon, led by the speaker who had given the sermon. The Dean invited the speaker to elaborate on his or her ideas to the group; sometimes he or she explained the subject of the sermon on a more personal level. Then there would be an opportunity for questions and comments, when the group would break into smaller subgroups of about six people. These smaller groups ensured that even if the group attracted forty or fifty people on a particular evening, there would be a context in which everyone could participate in the discussion and feel included. The evening also might include a procession, a musical presentation, or singing, and it always included prayer and the celebration of the Eucharist. Deacon Minka Sprague offered these comments:

> The Dean likes to invite his friends to the Cathedral. Each Tuesday night was like a party for him. He could introduce people and ideas, and each week was unique and exciting. He is a genius with public relations. He has extraordinary energy, and enjoys helping to orchestrate thought-provoking and multisensory events. The evening group meetings were, in a very special way, even more his style. Always ready for the unexpected.

Each year the group's makeup changed as people left the city or had scheduling conflicts; there were also personality conflicts. So each season the group became a different combination of new blood and old-timers. The group began as an invitation-only event; later all churchgoers were invited with an announcement in the weekly bulletin.[5] For them, the evening group felt like family rather than a maddening crowd.

Celebration of the Eucharist was the single most important part of the evening. The intimate celebration during Cathedral Nights was a time of reflection on the meaning of the experience: participants expressed the importance of this ritual in their personal lives and saw how their understanding of this rite was essential to their commitment to the

---

5. The following mission statement was distributed:

Cathedral Nights is dedicated to enriching the community life of its participants through interaction with and exposure to committed individuals, concepts, public issues, private concerns, spiritual quests, profane and profound — whatever touches the mind and soul of humankind in these complex, rich and troubling times. . . . Among the congregation and visitors to the Cathedral there are so many remarkable individuals whose talents and ideas serve to enhance the experience and knowledge of everyone. Cathedral Nights has explored a range of topics limited only by our imaginations — from the immediate crisis in our communities wrought by AIDS and homelessness to the philosophic substrata of the world's major religions, from the higher arts to the garden arts, and — along the way — the many paths to commitment in a fragmented, secular world.

Episcopal Church. In Beverly's words, "One of the ministers put together a special ritual for the evening's Eucharist which added to the standard liturgy. There was a prayer for the environment, and different people were handed the Bible to read each week. People participated more. It was *ours*, very personal." Lay ministers would carry the wine and bread — in this case, pita bread — to the group, and people who had never read the Bible aloud could be called upon to read. Participants found this the most deeply meaningful part of the evening. They understood that, like much of what went on in the Cathedral, this liturgy was "in process." It defined the uniqueness of the group and the nature of the evening itself. The group's identity was formed around it.

The special quality of sharing the Eucharist,[6] of experiencing community, was brought home because the group itself resembled a global community: it included men and women; old and young; blacks, whites, and Asians; gay people and straight people; people with drug problems and people who were drug-free; professional people and the homeless; the athletic and the physically challenged. The group probably could not have existed without the leadership of the Dean, given its substantial diversity. Still, the fact that such different people could sit side by side and communicate in any context is itself reason for hope.

As one indication of the diversity of the group, consider Stanley, a man who began attending Cathedral Nights because he was looking for a place to celebrate the Eucharist. He recalled,

> At one point in my life I thought that if you're ever going to get over any of these things, you're not going to be able to do it alone, no matter what it is in your life. . . . Soon after I was diagnosed [with the HIV virus] I started going to daily Eucharist. I searched for places where there [was] a tightly knit group that [gave] me that feeling of being in Christ's presence. One of the ways of going to daily Eucharist was Cathedral Nights.

Providing Nurture and Education

Throughout its history the group was shaped by a variety of influences and emphases. During the third year of its existence, the group was joined

6. Eucharistic Prayer C was especially popular because of the references to people's responsibility to care for the planet.

by several newly confirmed members of the church. They wished to continue their confirmation-class discussions of what it means to live as Christians. For most of them, this matter was compounded by the added stress of what it means to live as Christians in New York, where the issues of homelessness, environmental pollution, illegal immigrants, gay rights, AIDS, and violent crime confront you when you walk the streets, and the stench of urine can be distinct when you walk up the steps of the Cathedral. Beverly commented,

> Living in New York takes a lot of energy. You feel constantly bombarded, harassed, and sometimes you feel like your spirit can be drained by the huge needs of the city. It sounds trite, but you can be terribly lonely in the crowds. And unless you have some balance, it is easy to burn out.

Later on the group also welcomed guest speakers from various disciplines, not necessarily someone who had delivered the previous week's sermon. Tuesday nights were thus an opportunity for the Dean to introduce prominent visitors to the Cathedral. In addition, the group was a deliberate experiment that developed out of a need for an educational program in a context where a conventional Bible study would have been unsuccessful. When asked what was wrong with a Bible study, the individuals I interviewed answered that the mention of "Bible study" reminded them of bad Sunday school experiences. One participant commented,

> I guess when you think about it, all Christian education really is a form of Bible study. Cathedral Nights was certainly dedicated to bringing Scripture to life. But the term "Bible study" to me brings back terrible memories of dreary Sunday school classes with bad teachers. Maybe we New Yorkers think we're too sophisticated for an ordinary Bible study!

The church leaders knew that the people needed both nurturing and education, and the Dean made sure they got both one evening a week.

The Dean also encouraged expressions of the spirit in the arts, so he featured expressions of spirituality in music, dance, painting, and writing (via discussions with writers). The Dean was also known to bring surprising guests, guaranteed to stir the intellect of a sophisticated Episcopalian and even the emotions of the most jaded New Yorker. Some of the visitors included a representative of the Onondaga tribe, a Muslim cleric, a psychic, and a Dominican friar. Sometimes there would be an appearance by a circus troupe. Interwoven in the schedule was always prayer and time to discuss references from the gospel.

A "Typical" Meeting

In the later years, the meetings often began near the main doors to the Cathedral, at the peace altar, which was a favorite symbol for participants. A prayer would start as people lit candles and a Xeroxed sheet with the special liturgy was distributed to everyone. A leader for the evening, previously selected by the Dean, had chosen the prayers and songs on the sheet. One of the participants, Fred, offered this basic description of a meeting:

> We assemble at 7 o'clock, and generally we've had somewhere around 30 people on the average. We start out at the peace altar, and we say a prayer and so forth. And then we process up the aisle singing a song until we come to the choir of the Cathedral. And our program generally takes place there unless we go into another chapel or something for a distinct reason. . . . And then we . . . have the Eucharist and go home, or usually, go over to the pizza parlor and socialize a little bit.

The other leaders of the Cathedral gave their perspectives on the meetings, which also focused on spiritual journeys. Canon Gibson, for example, made this comment:

> What this group discovered was that there were a number of issues that they could talk about, other than simply the sermon, that really helped them move out of their individual private quest for an understanding of God in their life to the next step, which was the understanding of God in the community.

In other words, how was one person's spiritual journey like that of the others in the group? How could they mutually enable each other's spiritual journeys? What resources would help them along that journey? As Canon Gibson explained, many of the group's activities emphasized the communal: celebrating the Eucharist together, studying art, discussing crises in the city, and so on. Through these activities, individuals could mature in their faith and understand that they belonged to this community, that they were a vital part of it, and that the group as a community had a life of its own.

The following list of activities and special events from the fall of 1991 illustrates the diverse array of ideas and subjects presented to the group:

- The showing of a video about the similarity between Christianity and Judaism, followed by a discussion led by a student of Jewish history
- A Halloween event put on by the Cathedral: the showing of the silent film *Nosferatu*, the first Dracula movie made, accompanied by live organ music. This was followed by a choreographed march of ghouls, with costumes and special effects provided by a famous professional designer. Cathedral Nights participants were given free entry in return for assisting with the show; a dozen dressed up in masks and robes as nightmarish creatures and marched down the aisle.
- A presentation about Buddhism by a follower of the Dali Lama (The Dali Lama had visited the Cathedral in an interfaith celebration held the previous week.)
- A discussion by Canon John Luce about prayer and spirituality
- A talk by one of the participants about his ministry in Australia
- A dance presentation illustrating the spirit of St. Teresa of Ávila, followed by a study of and meditation on her work
- A presentation by Johanna Young about her retreat in Scotland
- A presentation by Canon Broderick-DeGuerra about her trip to Israel with a group of black priests
- A personal testimony by Reverend Bob Castle about his ministry in the Bronx
- A presentation by a missionary nun about the life of Iraqi women during the Gulf War
- A discussion led by Reverend Peregrine Murphy about her work as a pastoral counselor to patients with ALS (Lou Gehrig's disease) at Columbia Presbyterian Hospital

Each of these events interested the group. Indeed, the group seemed drawn by the opportunity to learn something new, to have their minds challenged and their experience broadened.

The last event on the list — Reverend Murphy's discussion about the challenges facing patients with ALS — made for a particularly memorable evening. Her description of this tragic disease and the effects it has not only on the patient but on his or her caregivers encouraged the group to meditate on issues of disease and death. After some moments of silence, Stanley, the group member who has been diagnosed with HIV, shared his perspective with the group, explaining what it felt like to have this incurable disease. The group was visibly moved but very uncomfortable, because many in the group hadn't realized that Stanley was HIV positive. When the group was silent, Reverend Murphy suggested that the group could pray. Then an older member of the group felt he needed to express his opinion about AIDS: he claimed that it was a plague sent by God to punish homosexuals. At this point Reverend Murphy thanked both Stanley and the older gentleman for their thoughts and led the group in prayer. Later that evening there was a heated discussion when the group adjourned to the pizza parlor. This evening clearly revealed the wide range of opinions and perspectives in the group.

Sister Rosemary represented another manifestation of the vast diversity that the group tried to embrace. A fixture in the daily life of the Cathedral, she regularly attended Cathedral Nights. Her participation was symbolic of the inclusive nature, the tolerance and love of the Cathedral. Sister Rosemary, who has a strong Caribbean accent, carries with her at all times a large Bible, a South African flag, and large bags filled with clothing. She wears various colored turbans, and has what to her are very clear ideas about prophecy. To an untrained eye, Sister Rosemary resembles a street person, and those unfamiliar with her find her keen stare disconcerting. During a typical meeting, she seemed to listen to the discussion intently; then she would stand up in the middle of it to pray out loud. She would walk to different areas of the room and bow, kneel, and quote various Bible verses. She would participate in discussions by suggesting that the group read a particular passage of Scripture. New members of the group found it difficult to understand her meaning, as did most of the older members. Still, Sister Rosemary was treated with respect during the meetings, and was often escorted home when meetings ran late. There is speculation about her emotional balance, but most people who have spoken to her over the years believe that she has a wisdom about the workings of God that is quite beyond that of the average person.

Cathedral Nights is thus a study in inclusion. When it flourished, it did so by articulating a vision of New York City as a microcosm of our planet—that is, by promoting an understanding that the problems experienced in the Cathedral community are those shared in every country, city, and small town in the world. And in every family. This vision was especially evident in the group's commitment to "earth ministry"—that is, taking responsibility for stewardship of the planet, which Dean Morton explained as an awareness of the earth as the body of Christ. In this view, all aspects of human life must be considered sacramental, not just the seven sacraments designated by the Book of Common Prayer. Essential to this theology, considered New Age by some, is an awareness that we are interdependent with all life on our planet. (Accordingly, the reading of the Gospels takes on a decidedly "green" tinge at Cathedral events, and attendance guarantees an education in ecology, feminism, and peace-and-justice issues.)

As this description indicates, the Dean's shaping of Cathedral Nights and of the general program of the Cathedral involves using symbols that reach beyond the traditional boundaries of Anglicanism, and this remains a controversial subject.[7]

The Group's Strength: Teaching Acceptance

The people I interviewed explained that they attended the Cathedral and the group meetings on Tuesday nights because they felt they were accepted for exactly who they were. They had not found this at other churches, and most of them had tried several (as many as six) other churches in their lives. This appreciation for the great tolerance of the Cathedral is a theme I found repeated in every interview, and a primary reason for participants' commitment to it.

The majority of participants in the group were committed Episcopalians, some "from the cradle," others newly confirmed. Some members had left Catholicism or Judaism.

Beverly was active in the group for about six years. She explained that Cathedral Nights allowed her to "recharge her batteries" so that she could live as she felt a Christian should:

7. For his understanding of earth ministry, the Dean credits the work of Réné Dubos and Paul Gorman, William Irwin Thompson, and many other artists and thinkers.

We are all God's children, one in the Holy Spirit. But it is so hard to live by this. Living in the City, it is easy to fall into one's prejudices for a feeling of safety.

I grew up in an all-white community, and until I went to college, it didn't occur to me that this was a problem. But when I became aware that the world is made up of many, many types of people, I consciously sought environments where I could learn about diversity.

I came to the Cathedral because it is the only church I have found where there are equal numbers of black and white people, and of men and women. I need to be reminded that God's Kingdom is not a whites-only club, which I see so often in churches. It is surprising how little progress we have made since the days of slavery in our country. Frightening, really. And what is my role, as a white woman? I started to see the importance of my part ten years ago when I met the Dean. When I see the extraordinary compassion the Dean brings to his work, I think I can live the vision, the belief that we are all one under God, for another day.

Participants reported that seeing each other in the intimate setting of the group helped them get to know one another. They saw that they needed to address the serious problems of the city by having dialogues and learning to understand each other's needs. Because speakers and presentations varied from week to week, and because issues of social concern were addressed most of the time, everyone was able to participate, regardless of background.

Janice explained that the Tuesday-night group played an important role in making the city feel like home to her:

To be honest, when I first came to the City, I would have crossed the street out of fear when encountering some of the people I now sit next to on Sunday mornings. The reason I'm no longer afraid is that I got to know them during the years I participated in Cathedral evenings, and I now realize that despite our incredible differences — in education, lifestyle, dress, whatever — we are all God's children.

I am profoundly grateful for the Cathedral because of the opportunity I have been given to experience this. Now, I still have limits.... I'm not saying I would invite everyone to my home any night of the week....

Many of the group's participants moved to New York City from another state or another country, so the friendships that they developed during these evenings were particularly important, providing them with a foundation for their lives. Many of the participants saw the group as a guiding force in their spiritual development, and they considered part of that development to be learning to see all types of people with compassion.

Cameos of Spiritual Development

In all, forty or fifty people were part of Cathedral Nights at one point or another between 1982 and 1992. Following are the stories of five people who participated in the group and were active in the Cathedral when the group stopped meeting. Each of them has a slightly different perspective on the group and its importance.

Soon after moving to New York City from Jamaica, Howard joined the Cathedral and then began attending Cathedral Nights. He is thirty-nine years old and has never married. He has completed a degree in electronics, and now works as an administrator for a distributor of building materials. He has been a committed Episcopalian since his youth, and has served on many church boards and participated in many groups, including sports and social clubs, for as long as he can remember. He found it difficult to establish a niche in the city, and didn't find community with any of the black groups he initially encountered. Howard is shocked by the fact that white people often think that all black people are the same and don't understand that a black person from the West Indies will have entirely different opinions about things than a black person from Jamaica.

He committed himself to the Cathedral because it felt open and welcoming, unlike the other churches he attended in the city. He is now one of the most active members of the Cathedral. The meeting of the Tuesday-night group was one of the most important events of the week for him because it gave him the opportunity to hear many points of view on important subjects.

Howard values the community he finds within the Cathedral. Like most of the people I interviewed, he often spoke of the Cathedral and the Cathedral Nights group interchangeably:

> The main purpose is for Christian group fellowship. It's a way of preparing you for services in the Cathedral and the life of the church.

217

... Cathedral Evenings for me — it's an area of the Cathedral community life that brings you to meet people at the Cathedral and to know the clergy at the personal level. That's one thing. The second point is when Cathedral Evenings was just beginning, I had an opportunity where I could meet the preacher after the Sunday service.

. . . that was one of the main focuses — education. It's also what you'd probably call Christian growth. So we need to grow spiritually, grow more knowledgeable about the ways of the Episcopal Church. And it would be a time to know the people on a one-to-one basis, including the clergy.

... until you go back to church on Sunday.... Cathedral Evenings is additional spiritual food that you get.

. . . People are willing to listen and to hear where your point of view is coming from. Even though you may not agree with their point, they're willing to accept your point of view and believe in your right to believe in that. It can be almost the same at other places, but it's a very unique place where people come to know you so well on a one-to-one basis. It's a very personal place.

For Howard, then, Cathedral Nights provides fellowship, a place where he can feel accepted because, he says, it's not "a very high, aristocratic place."

Stanley, whom I have already mentioned, is thirty-seven years old and works as a domestic aide. He is gay, and was diagnosed as HIV positive several years before. He grew up in the Midwest and attended the Lutheran Church. Participation in small groups has been important to him ever since he joined the Boy Scouts. Stanley remembers a heterosexual Scout leader who became a positive role model for him, and he remembers attending meetings to learn from him. Stanley also remembers most of his youth as traumatic. He was beaten up regularly because he was gay, because he was "different." He explains that he has been searching for self-acceptance for most of his life and only recently realized that; he thought he was looking for a place to belong.

Stanley is also an alcoholic and used many of the practices he learned in AA to communicate with people in Cathedral Nights. He says he was angry at the world for most of his life, and he blamed the world for his problems. Now he thinks he is slowly learning to acknowledge his responsibility for his problems. He says that groups have helped him learn these important lessons by providing a close circle of people he could reflect with. Cathedral Nights provided a focal point for his involvement with the Cathedral. Stanley saw the group experience as being a process of "calling spiritual gifts out of one another":

> I remember a sermon given by the bishop when he said you call people's gifts out of each other. That's what Cathedral Nights was to me. . . . The others called gifts out of me, and I called gifts out of them.
> I went to Cathedral Nights for three years. But [at first] I took part in it from a high-handed point of view, projecting myself on them. I was not able to be honest with myself and let myself be vulnerable at first. After a year or so, I was able to relax a little bit and let them beam in.
> Now I'm kind of known as the loudmouth. I'm not afraid to pipe up when no one else will. I suppose I annoy people.

Martin is forty-seven years old and divorced. He is a lawyer who has his own practice. He lives in Connecticut but commutes to the Cathedral. He has been attending services at the Cathedral for eight years. Although he is an active member of the Greek Orthodox Church, he also considers himself an active Episcopalian. He sees that his involvement in the Cathedral has filled needs for intimacy that aren't met by the Orthodox tradition. He is a member of the Cathedral Council and works in the soup kitchen occasionally. He considers Cathedral Nights to have been one of the most important groups within the church. He supported it to the very last. He explains how he came to be involved:

> I went to an inquirer's class at the Cathedral, just to learn about the Episcopal Church. And after that I started going to 11:00 services regularly. There was a Bible study class on the book of Revelation, which I was always interested in because it was a very bizarre book of the Bible which fundamentalists really get into. I was just very curious how this very liberal church would be teaching a course on it. I didn't know much. But I got into it, and I got to meet a couple of the people who were active in the congregation there, and then eventually one of the people, after a service, told me about Cathedral Nights.

In addition to its younger and middle-aged members, Cathedral Nights also included several older people. One is Beverly, who is now sixty-seven. She has two adult children and three grandchildren; she was widowed several years ago. A musician, Beverly lives in an apartment on Fifth Avenue. By most standards, she is considered wealthy. She started attending the Cathedral about five years earlier, after having been counseled by the Dean during a very troubled time in her life. She was inspired by the fact that blacks and whites, men and women, joined equally in Cathedral services. Soon after this, she started to attend Cathedral Nights and found that the personal tone of the meetings helped her to examine her own spiritual life and gave her something to do on lonely nights. Beverly is very active in the Cathedral; she is a member of the Council and heads various committees. Cathedral Nights meant a great deal to her, both because of the presence of the Dean and because it was a context in which she could consider spiritual truths more deeply than she ever has before:

> The Cathedral Nights group was the most important evening for me, because the Dean was present. I know he cannot always be there for everyone — he is only human — but I felt that at least on that one evening, I could see him in action.
>
> I came to Cathedral Nights because it was not just theological. What is important is encouraging people to understand where the spirit operates, which is in mystery. It cannot be pinned down. It cannot be manifested in concrete things. That's what I liked about Tuesday nights: the Dean and most of the Canons, too, emphasize the side which is mystery. I wanted to study Scripture, but I didn't want pat answers. I wanted to be guided in finding my own answers.

Finally, there is James, who provides yet another illustration of why people came to Cathedral Nights. He is fifty-three years old, and has been active in the Cathedral for seventeen years. He grew up in the metropolitan area, and now lives near the Cathedral. James is a visible part of daily life at the church, since he spends part of each day there. He also checks on the activities at various churches "downtown," to keep tabs on what is happening in the city. He claims that Cathedral Nights was something he could take or leave, depending on his schedule and his interest in the topic for the evening:

> I am skeptical of anything that rings of groupie-ism. I respect the Dean deeply, but I think it is important for people to realize that he cannot please all of the people all of the time.

The Cathedral is unique in that we do indeed have homeless persons join us for services and coffee hour, and even for Cathedral Nights and other smaller services. Not everyone is comfortable with this. And we can never tell if someone's handbag will be stolen, or [if] one of our friends will have a psychotic episode and need to be taken to the Emergency Room. Seriously. These are risks, and these things happen when we're dealing with the street people. There was a discussion in a Vestry meeting the other day about these problems, and someone commented that these people have *forgotten how to be social.* I believe it is our task to remind them how to be social.

The Problems of Co-existence

Despite conflict, the Cathedral is known as a place where contradictions can co-exist in peace. The people I interviewed explained that they attended the Cathedral, and also Cathedral Nights, because they felt they were accepted for exactly who they were; the Cathedral was re-markably unprejudiced. But this unifying factor — the commitment to diversity — also presented problems because it made communication more difficult. People could become offended, and often did. For ex-ample, several people left Cathedral Nights during its ten-year existence because they felt that their expertise was not appreciated. As a body, the group had many emotional needs, and it was clear that these needs weren't being met.

The strains of tolerating such extreme diversity, as well as the problems associated with wounded egos and unmet emotional needs, were kept at bay as long as the Dean was actively involved in Cathedral Nights. He provided a center of gravity that held the group together. Gradually, however, the group lost that center. After about six years, the Dean stopped participating in the meetings regularly, apparently because he was busy with other projects and felt that he needed to move on. Many people wished to carry on with the group despite the Dean's absence, though there were varied opinions about this. Canon Gibson noted that by 1988 the group had started to "spiral down." Some members of the group still hoped that the Dean would return. Others believed that the spirit he had instilled in the group would live on without his actual presence. But the sense of cohesion and identity that had made the group succeed seemed to be lost.

221

The Last Days

In 1990, Canon Cecily Broderick-deGuerra was hired via a special grant for a two-year tenure, and she was assigned the job of guiding the group to an existence independent of the Dean. Some group members were indignant about this; they felt abandoned. This confusion about the identity of the group and the crisis of leadership opened new wounds and allowed new emotions to surface; the "darker" sides of personalities emerged. The organizational meetings that Canon Broderick-deGuerra held during 1991 were marked by dissension, blaming, paranoia, and general disappointment.

Since there was no precedent in the group for an alternate power structure, there was no adequate source of unity. Several individuals volunteered to lead the group, but no clear leader was accepted by the entire group, and a system of alternating leadership proved impossible to implement.

When I studied the group, it was still experiencing feelings of abandonment. Canon Gibson summarized the mood this way:

> Yes, issues revolving around Cathedral Nights lifted up unhealthy aspects of our community, some fault within the community. And nothing is wrong with that. All groups have faults. . . . But it is understandable that people feel abandoned by the Dean when he tells them, "Hey, I love you, but I can't come anymore. I've got to do these other things." I think that what the Dean was really saying, though, [was] "I cannot always be there to hold your hand." What the group is experiencing is about growing up, moving on.
>
> I think something was not accomplished in that group so that the Dean couldn't freely move on. Now, maybe he didn't move on with integrity. Maybe he didn't say openly, "I can no longer be with you." Maybe he didn't know that. Maybe he doesn't want to say that, and maybe that's hard for him to say. But somehow there's a minor dysfunction in there which allows them to feel abandoned.
>
> The fault here is not understanding the gift of giving life and the nature of the life and death cycles of everything. We need to understand when our mother or father figure can no longer be with us. My son is seventeen and about ready to leave home, and I have real regrets about that. But if I don't let him go or if he's afraid to leave, then somehow as a family we haven't accomplished something.

Several people in the group remained quite bitter about the decline and eventual dissolution of Cathedral Nights. Some people believed that Canon Gibson was at fault for not encouraging the Dean to rejoin the group. Others felt that the Dean was irresponsible to leave the group; they believed that it was his job to be its shepherd. There was a general consensus that Dean Morton's weaknesses might lie in his inability to delegate power to others, and in his insatiable interest in the new and different. One member put it this way: "I don't know why he gave up Cathedral Nights. Maybe he had too many other things to do. Maybe he no longer enjoyed it. He was probably bored with it, and wanted to move on to other things. Maybe he didn't realize what he had created."

Around Christmas of 1992, the group disbanded. There were about twelve people who continued to support the group, and although they were very disappointed, they did not leave the church. The Dean and other ministers felt relieved that the matter had been laid to rest, and they explained that by letting go of the past, the group members could sooner move on to new groups that were forming.

The period immediately following the group's dissolution was a time of emptiness, of waiting, and of learning. In Canon Gibson's opinion, it was like the vigil after the death of Christ:

> We have been at the moment of essence in the Christian community. There appears to be no group. What happens if you go to that grave and it is empty? They have a tomb, but it is empty. No one is there. People complain, "We wasted all our time believing in this place!" It isn't taking the form they want. But the spirit isn't dead, just the form. So now we must wait to see what form it might take.
>
> We are wandering now with respect to this group, trying to figure out what we are left with. We were left with the spirit. The proof of this are the stories people keep telling. *Remember when . . . Remember when the group gave us this, remember when the group made us feel that way?* This is the proof that the spirit is alive.
>
> I don't know what form it will take, but we are all waiting and watching.

One of the many offerings of the Cathedral was its Lenten Meditation Series, a tradition of discussions with Madeleine L'Engle, the Cathedral librarian and resident spiritual guide, in the company of the Dean and other friends. During the last year of Cathedral Nights, the subject of these meditations was "Spirituality in Our Depression." This caught the mood of both the group and the members of the Cathedral at large. A series of single-evening workshops organized by Canon Gibson included one entitled "The Use and Abuse of Religion in Grief," led by the Reverend John Bauman of the Center of Pastoral Psychotherapy. The series was particularly appropriate for the group because it was experiencing a time of mourning.

Soon after the final meeting of Cathedral Nights, a retreat was also organized, and a Thursday-evening series was established. Each series, which lasted from four to six weeks, was led by a different minister; series titles included "Issues of Peace and Justice" and "St. Paul." A group of about twelve attended these classes, which met in a room in Cathedral House, a building next to the Cathedral. The meetings were intimate. Some people began to refer to them as "Bible study," which seemed like a peaceful step back to basics rather than an attempt to choreograph a Dean-style performance.

As my period of research came to an end, members of the group were busily discussing possibilities for the next calendar year, and were beginning to focus on the community's needs. Leaders were trying to balance favored traditions with new inspiration. Said Canon Broderick-deGuerra, "There is an opportunity here. If it is successful, we would be a model for all successful interracial co-existence. It could be a model of community for every city. If it is not successful, it is still a model. We have to start somewhere."

Praying for the Saints: Single Mennonite Charismatics and the Conundrum of Community

COURTNEY J. BENDER

Introduction

Mennonite charismatics founded the Worship Center in 1976 as an alternative to the mainstream Mennonite Church of Lancaster, Pennsylvania.[1] The charismatic movement[2] emphasized the baptism of

1. I interviewed Mennonites who grew up in a number of Mennonite subgroups and conferences in the Lancaster area, and also a number of Amish and midwestern Mennonites. In this essay I will use "Mennonite" broadly to describe those who identified themselves to me as such. In the sections in which I discuss Lancaster Mennonite life, I refer more specifically to the Lancaster Conference, as the majority of Mennonites in the area were affiliated with it. All of the names of Worship Center members have been changed for this essay.

2. Charismatic renewal was felt in a wide range of denominations. Most notably and most widely researched is the Catholic charismatic renewal, which started with charismatic prayer groups (see Neitz 1987; and Lawson's essay in this

I would like to thank Robert Wuthnow, Gary Wheeler, Matthew Lawson, John Schmalzbauer, and participants in the Religion and Culture Workshop at Princeton University for their helpful comments on earlier drafts of this paper. Research for this paper was funded by the Joel Dean Summer Research Fund (Swarthmore College, Swarthmore, PA) and by the Center for the Study of American Religion (Princeton University).

the Holy Spirit as a necessary aspect of Christian life, giving individuals spiritual authority and an intimate relationship with God. The movement appealed to some Mennonites in Lancaster who in the early 1970s were alienated from the structures and rules of the Mennonite Church, and it made its presence felt in ecumenical retreats, revivals, and tent meetings. Many charismatic Mennonites, once they felt filled with the Holy Spirit, left the Mennonite Church to begin charismatic congregations where they could retreat from the restrictions of Mennonite liturgy. A typical example is the Worship Center.

In its first decade it grew tremendously (from 35 to over 1700 weekly attendees). It grew no doubt in part because of its popular emphases: it placed a high value on individual expressions of faith and privileged the single subject over the group experience. These emphases allowed members to demarcate the charismatic community itself with a variety of committees, programs, and small groups.

Small groups were started at the Worship Center by the growing group of young single adults who met every week, following the organizational patterns they had learned at youth group meetings, Christian summer camps, and college prayer groups. These groups paid special attention to their needs as young adult charismatics, most of whom were from Mennonite backgrounds. They became places where young Mennonites could evade the social pressures of single life.

Eventually the small-group program became institutionalized. As the Worship Center continued to grow, leaders and members sensed a loss of the intimacy that originally had attracted so many people to it. Accordingly, the successful model of the young-adult program was implemented for the entire congregation; the leadership trained lay members to be group leaders and encouraged broad participation. These groups, called "CARE groups," became a permanent fixture when the

---

volume). Mennonites refer to the movement as the Holy Spirit Renewal. Its first influences were felt in the late 1960s and early 1970s, when issues of the second baptism became part of the Mennonite denomination's discourse in official church papers and conferences, and when the Lancaster Conference adopted a position on the Holy Spirit (1971). In 1974, Mennonite churches in Lancaster sponsored charismatic renewal meetings. The denomination also encouraged charismatic renewal through a denomination-wide forum in 1975, through several books produced by Mennonite publishing houses, and through church-sponsored meetings held in 1976 (Bender 1991; Bender 1992).

congregation approved the appointment of a minister to coordinate the group program.

These groups provide a space where Mennonite charismatics can reformulate the meaning of religious life, leaving behind the "community" ethos that permeates the traditional Mennonite *Weltanschauung,* with its narrow boundaries and implicit judgments of social and religious life.[3] At the same time, the groups help provide bonds among a very large number of congregants. According to an assistant minister in charge of CARE groups, small groups are an integral part of the Worship Center's ministry: "We're so big that without the small groups, we wouldn't have a church. We like to think of it as a two-horse team. Both the big-group meetings and the small-group meetings are indispensable."

Over time the small groups have become particularly important to the single people in the church, who view themselves as increasingly marginalized because of a significant change in the focus of the Worship Center. This change came about when the Center affiliated itself with Ken Hagen Ministries by hiring a graduate as its senior minister and consequently incorporated a theology that speaks primarily about "family" life. Given this emphasis, the singles' groups at the Worship Center serve as essential spaces for singles to assert their roles as Christian adults in ways not otherwise fulfilled in church settings. Cut off from the corporate emphasis on the nuclear family, they create spiritual families of their own that give them nurture and support.

3. The dominant Mennonite ethos or story (and definitely its predominant paradigm) is "community." Traditional communal aspects of Mennonite life are embedded in its rituals (foot-washing as a mark of servanthood, closed communion for congregational members only), in its theology (adult baptism and membership are by ascription only; the congregation is seen as the locus of biblical interpretive authority), and in its sectarian restrictions (distinctive dress codes and lifestyle restrictions, which declined in the 1960s). On this subject, compare Redekop (1989), Beulah Hostetler (1986), Kraybill (1979), and Nolt (1992). Community as it has been constructed in the Mennonite Church has helped to distinguish those who are in its center from those who are on its margins. Nevertheless, the recent decline in the salience of traditional markers of community has made the definition of Mennonite community nebulous and the defense of its boundaries more obviously arbitrary—the results of which have been felt in part in the success of the charismatic movement and in the more general malaise among Mennonites, which has been called an "identity crisis" (Peachy 1968; Redekop and Steiner 1988).

The CARE Groups:
Creating Community at the Worship Center

I got an opportunity to get involved in a singles' CARE group when Mel, a man in his early thirties, invited me to his CARE group meeting. His small group (I noted later) usually sat in the particular section of the church where I happened to venture that day. Because I was alone, he told me later, he thought I might need a group like his, made up of young to middle-aged unmarried people. His group was a descendant of the initial young-adults program, and although most of its original members had left the church or married and joined other groups, it was led by one of the original leaders, Janet, and her husband, Phil (the only married couple in the group). The group had ten or eleven regular attendees, and loose connections with about twenty others. Most of those in the group had never been married, but there were also single mothers, divorcées, and widows who ranged in age from the mid-twenties to the early forties. They met with the group to express their happiness with their church and with their lives, even though they did not fit the church's explicitly upheld norm of the middle-class family. That they were not "mainstream" church members aggravated the struggles they faced as charismatics establishing a new religious community.

Accepting Mel's invitation, I arrived at the right address a little before seven o'clock. Mel welcomed me in and introduced me to Phil and Janet. Several people sat in a small circle in the living room, and I sat down next to Marge, who introduced herself before continuing to talk with Mark, Dorothy, and Janet. As twelve people filled the chairs, Phil took a seat next to Janet and asked if anyone had anything exciting to tell about their week.

Mark and Phil said that they had gone "street-witnessing" in Lancaster. Mark had been walking with a group on Queen Street and had met Salome, a Zambian minister who was in Lancaster for a conference. He was wandering the streets, looking for some music to listen to, but after hearing about the group's mission, he decided to join the street team. Together they "led a Hispanic girl to the Lord."

Marge asked about the girl they had helped save. The girl was sitting out on the front porch of her house with some other people, Mark said. When the team of six came up to her, most of the people with this girl laughed and walked away, but the girl sat there and listened. "We knew she felt convicted when she kept listening," Mark said, "and then

[she] called one of her kids to come over and take the alcohol that was sitting next to her into the house." Minutes later, she recommitted her life to the Lord.

Phil had been with a second group of street witnessers. This was the first time he had gone into the city to witness — he usually witnessed at the malls, which he considered much safer. They began walking down one street but saw that it was dark and inhabited only by groups of young black men, so they decided to go where it was better lit. On another street they talked to a young black man whose father was a preacher. He told them that he was under the conviction that Jesus had a plan for his life, but he was resisting it. He explained that he was not yet ready to give his life to the Lord because he loved to drink and he knew that he would have to give that up if he "committed." Phil said that he told the man that "Jesus would take him wherever he was." The man made no commitment, but he was impressed with the witnessers and thanked them for coming. Phil felt frustrated by the experience. "I thought maybe he would call me this morning so I could pick him up and take him to church, but he didn't."

Next Phil asked if there was anything else to mention. Marge said that she was trying to get a promotion and that she had had an interview that she thought had gone well. "Everything was just so smooth, I could tell the Lord was with me," she explained. Cheryl was smiling at Dorothy, who returned the smile, laughing. "Cheryl and I went to a concert last night, and it was really a blessing."

When no one else volunteered anything after this, Phil stood up and, rubbing his hands together absently, said, "OK, why don't we do worship?" As the group rose to its feet, stretching, Cheryl closed the front door. "Don't you want my neighbors to hear our good singing?" Mel asked. The group laughed, and John asked if he should shut the back door too. "Nothing out there but the cows," Mel said. Phil told us to begin with a verse or a song or a prayer. People closed their eyes, and Mark started saying "Thank you, Lord" over and over. Everyone else was quiet, until Janet started a song that we had sung that morning in church: "I Will Call upon the Lord, Who Is Worthy to Be Praised." We all joined in, the women echoing the men through the verses.

As the song broke off, a hush fell over the group, although individuals continued humming. Some raised their hands or rocked back and forth on their heels. Everyone else had their eyes closed, except Sylvia, who looked detached from the worship. Over the rhythmic ebb and flow of the sounds of "worship," Marge started to whisper, over and over, "Thank you, Jesus," until Jacob started to pray. He thanked God for the day and for friends and for the opportunity to worship in a free country. The others affirmed his praise: "Yes," they whispered, or "Thank you, Lord," or "Hallelujah." As Jacob finished, Nolan began to pray for Sam, the senior minister. He prayed that he would be hungry for the Word and continue in God's ways. Two others prayed for Sam's health; then the room was quiet again.

When there was almost complete silence, Marge and Mel, who were standing on either side of me, started speaking in tongues, raising their arms so that their fingers brushed against my upper arm. Others followed their lead. Nolan and Jacob kept their hands clasped in front of them; Janet and Dorothy each raised one hand. Soon everyone was speaking in tongues. Then Cheryl started singing "I Will Call upon the Lord" again. All of the singing and praying lasted about forty-five minutes, ending when Phil thanked God for friends, religious freedom, and the freedom to worship. Phil also prayed for forgiveness for not taking the Lord seriously enough. This was met with loud amens.

After the worship period, we sat down, and Phil asked for specific prayer requests. The next hour of the meeting was devoted to stories and requests and prayers.

Cheryl raised her hand to get the attention of the group and mentioned Linford, a group member who was spending the evening with his twelve-year-old daughter, Karen, who was about to leave for the summer to stay with her mother in California. There was a general concern that Karen might be wooed to the "California lifestyle" and decide to stay there. The group prayed for Linford and his daughter — first that he would be able to offer her and her future to the Lord's will, and second that the Lord would take care of her, that "the seeds of the Word sown in his heart would have taken root and been in Karen's heart as well." Mark prayed that she would experience a "faith that was her own and not her father's" by seeing all the sin in California for what it was. Dorothy prayed that Karen would find Christian friends and not be scared.

When the prayer was finished, Mel asked if it was really possible that Karen would not return. The consensus was that the temptation existed for her, even though Linford had bought her a round-trip ticket. Cheryl then recounted a story about the Marshalls, a married couple at the church. This was a second marriage for both of them, and Mrs.

Marshall was always afraid of letting her two daughters visit their father for long, because she was afraid of incest. She had finally "given the children over to the Lord" and realized that although she could do nothing about their safety, the Lord could.

Sylvia spoke up next, thanking everyone for their prayers for her grandmother, who had died that Monday. Sylvia said that it had been easier for her to deal with the death because she had felt all the prayers lifting her up. She also said that the Lord had been working in her life in another way. She had been laid off from her managerial job, but this had cleared the way for her to go back to college full-time, something she had been considering doing but had never had the guts to do. "God is such a good God, I never cease to wonder . . .," she said, tears welling up in her eyes. She asked the group to pray that the transition period in her life would not be too hard. Mark quizzed Sylvia on how she had come to the decision to go back to college full-time. "Oh, I didn't hear any voices or anything like that," she said. "I just felt a real strong desire in my heart, and it didn't go away, so I thought about it, and thought that going back to school wouldn't hurt anyone. . . . So I'll be back at school full-time starting in January."

"When you were laid off, did you know it would be this way?" Mark probed.

"No. . . . When I heard it, I was very upset," Sylvia said. "They shuffled a whole lot of people around and found replacement jobs for almost everyone. I felt rejected. So I called up Janet and she came over and I told her the whole story. I felt like crying. I guess it was a slow realization that this was what God wanted for me. The hardest part of it all was telling my parents what all had happened."

Next Phil asked her if she would like to go to the "hot spot." She said yes and stood up and walked to the middle of the circle. Everyone gathered around her and put a hand on her; Marge held one of Sylvia's hands. Then the group started praying. Dorothy prayed that Sylvia would make good grades in school and would make friends and have good professors, and she thanked God for the seeds that Sylvia had planted in people's hearts at her old job. In a little while we sat down, and Mark paged idly through his Bible until Nolan cleared his throat for attention.

Nolan asked members to pray for him because he was having foot surgery that week on an ingrown toenail. Nolan was promptly invited to stand in the hot spot, and after we had gathered around him, Mark started the prayer for Nolan by reading from Colossians "because that's what the minister suggested we do when we pray for the saints." The saints, Mark reminded us, are not just biblical figures; they are all of the holy, including those of us who stood around Nolan in the hot spot. Next Dorothy knelt and picked up Nolan's foot and prayed for God to give Nolan a new, perfect foot, praying that God would heal the whole man.

As we were resettling ourselves in our seats, John, a Nigerian man, walked in just in time to hear Marge begin explaining that the last year had had its problems, but that things seemed to be getting better. For one thing, she had disliked her job. "I said, 'OK, Lord, I'll stay here if you show me why I'm supposed to be here. . . .' And soon after that I started getting the hours that I wanted, and everything else, the benefits that I wanted. Then this past fall I was supposed to go back to school, and I was all set to go, but then Mom had a heart attack, and there were lots of problems that were related to that in my family. So I didn't go back like I thought [I would]. I still wanted to get out of those working conditions, so I kept praying, and then all of a sudden I started noticing job offers in the papers, lots of them. There have been all kinds of openings, there were even two that I saw today in the Lancaster paper, which means I could move closer to church. But now, even though there are all these jobs, things are getting better [at my job]. I went home on Friday and for the first time I said to myself, 'Gee, I really enjoyed myself at work today.' But I keep on seeing these jobs, and I don't know what the Lord wants me to do, to look around or to stay where I am."

Even though her life was on the upswing, the group offered Marge the hot spot. Once she was there, Mark prayed loudly that God would answer her question "right now" and thanked God for the answer that Marge was being given, even as he prayed.

Next we sat down and prayed for Darla, whom no one had heard from in a long time. She was back in college, and the group raised questions about whether she was "struggling with too much knowledge." Mark and Nolan prayed that she would not join the groups that would confuse her, and that she could find a good church that would counter the doubts that the devil put in her mind.

By then Phil thought it was time to start a short lesson, so we talked about the sermon preached earlier that day. Dorothy had the most to say. She was very impressed that the minister had put in her mind the idea that she was just to talk to God and not to worry about the spiritual warfare going on all around her. This comment made the group sit in

232

reflective silence for a moment. Next Sylvia suggested that it was time for a snack. The group broke out of the circle and moved to the kitchen, where everyone stayed and talked for another hour, eating cake and drinking soda.

As I had stood in this meeting, I had tried to imagine what early meetings at the Worship Center were like: informal gatherings where everyone shared personal concerns, troubles, and "praises," people singing and praying in the Spirit — followed by more fellowship and reflection on Scripture. In their meetings now, the CARE group sings without instruments, which facilitates a flow from song to prayer to speaking in tongues without breaks. Silence is rare in CARE group worship; almost always there is at least one person singing or humming or whispering, contributing to the rhythm of sound and word. Women begin singing songs, usually from the morning's worship service, which ensures that at least the tune will be familiar; the lyrics of these songs are a mixture of Scripture and simple praises. Ecstatic speech like the repetitious "Thank you, Jesus" and praying in tongues (without interpretations) are accepted as easily as singing; one person begins and others join in.

CARE groups exude intimacy and connectedness in ways that the mass worship services cannot. Long-term members describe the long, caring prayers and personal prophecies that occurred at the Worship Center before the congregation grew to its current size. Now that the church is larger and the mass meetings are orchestrated to fit into a schedule of events, small groups provide personal affirmation in spiritual development and the time to address individual needs in prayer and discussion.

CARE group leaders are called "touch pastors," which suggests the physical quality of their position and their accessibility in contrast to the seeming distance of church leaders. (Indeed, the attendance records and notes that touch pastors send to the administration of the Worship Center exemplify the distance between laity and clergy. The lack of personal experiences and discussions with the congregation's ministers accentuate the dynamic qualities of the senior minister and establish an aura of reverence that inhibits personal spirituality, a problem that the CARE group system attempts to allay by encouraging personal encounters with God. In a CARE group, the deeper role of the touch pastor and individual relationships between members allow the single adults to maintain spiritual independence and to skirt the otherwise typical deference given the leadership's decisions.) Members of my group were used to calling Janet, not one of the ministers, when something unexpected arose. Janet, a longtime leader of small groups at the Worship Center, is clearly a trusted friend. In this regard, I expect that Janet's role is different from that of many touch pastors: many simply fulfill their perfunctory roles of taking attendance, leading the worship and discussion, and noting prayer requests for the assistant minister. Perhaps the members of Janet's group are closer to her because of the nature of the group. Since they are single, they have fewer ties outside the group and so have a greater need for connection within the group; in this context, the role of the touch pastor becomes more significant.

Although Janet is a longtime group leader, the group is in no way dependent on her for affirmation; she typically does little in the meetings to mark herself as leader and remains silent through sharing time. The group appears confident that they can trust each other to empathize and remember events from meeting to meeting. During my first meeting, it was clear that they knew about Sylvia's grandmother's illness (many had also heard that she had died), and they were affirming of Sylvia's occupational changes. At times, however, the group seemed much more intent on finding out what a person had learned from any given experience than what he or she was actually struggling with at the time. Mark's persistent questions about whether Sylvia had heard God's voice demonstrate the fact that the group wants to hear certain types of stories, particularly those in which God is present.

The confidence that God is present in all such life circumstances ensures the continued attention of the group. Yet, the group plays a passive role in listening, offering few challenges or suggestions. During my first meeting, the group was satisfied to hear that Sylvia was going back to college to enter a psychology program at a state university despite the fact that many of the group members are vocally against the "teachings" of secular colleges, as their prayer for Darla and their discussion at the following meeting (see below) demonstrated. Furthermore, the focus on individuals' problems left little or no time for discussion of local concerns or the national and international problems so frequently cited and prayed for from the pulpit. The division of labor between the small group and the mass meetings of the church underscores the therapeutic and inward focus of the group program.

The individualistic nature of the group does seem to tie its members together. During my first meeting, rituals like Mark's earnest prayer for the saints enabled the group to reassert their identities as specially marked *individuals* brought together with a holy purpose. (Members are encouraged to share every week, or to join in prayers. I was given two weeks' grace before I was actively encouraged to share my own story of the week so that the group could pray for me. I never made it to the hot spot, and by not partaking in those "blessings," I remained an outsider in the group.) The requests that Marge and Nolan made for healing and the group prayers that followed helped group members to articulate their common identity as saints, living out holy lives.

When I arrived at the next meeting, Marge, Nolan, Mark, Jacob, and Mel were already deep in conversation. John was talking about his wife. He explained that because she is Nigerian, she has to have a letter of invitation before she can come over to the States. That morning at church, John had asked the senior minister to write one, and he had referred John to an assistant minister. John was happy that the senior minister had smiled at him, but he expressed disappointment that the senior minister wasn't handling the matter himself. Mark said, "Well, on Sundays he is wrapped up in his responsibilities." And Jacob added that it had been such a busy month that not even the assistant ministers had seen him.

Marge told us that she had gone to a revival in Philadelphia that Tuesday. Her eyes darkened and her voice lowered as she told us that the revivalist had said that he felt a lot of resistance on the East Coast and had remarked that "There are many strongholds [of the devil] here." Jeb said that he believed that the great number of strongholds of "the enemy" in the East were due to intellectualism. Mel attributed the problem to materialism, but Nolan agreed with Jeb, noting the problems of higher education. "Humanism is horrendous," he said, citing as an example a college he had attended briefly. "When I was going there, I wish I had had a better sense of discernment, because when I look back, I see all the ungodly professors I had . . ."

At this point Mel interrupted and asked Marge about her job. She explained that the Lord led her to 1 Peter 5:10 earlier that week and then had given her a promotion at work. "The Lord gave me a sense of contentment, that everything would be all right in my life as regards my job, and then I received the promotion, and that means more money and different people, probably better people to work with." At this point group members opened their Bibles and turned to the verse that Marge said the Lord had given her: "And the God of all grace, who called you to his eternal glory in Christ, after you have suffered a little while, will himself restore you and make you strong, firm, and steadfast."

Since Phil and Janet were at a family reunion, Mel started the worship time by asking Nolan to lead the group in prayer. Nolan said a long prayer, taking up the earlier theme of the dangers of humanism, praying that God would not let it take over the country. John chimed in next, praying for the minister. Then we sang the songs that had been sung in the morning service. Some people clapped their hands; others lifted their arms. When we finished these songs, we paused momentarily, waiting for something to happen. Marge started singing "Holy Spirit, You Are Welcome in This Place." Marge's voice started strong, but weakened — we were all getting quieter, and ended up murmuring again. Then, out of the quiet, Marge started speaking in tongues. Her voice grew louder and her syllables more distinct. As Marge's voice rose and fell, Mark began speaking in tongues; his voice, unlike Marge's, was even and insistent. Mel and Jeb also began to speak in tongues, but Mark's loudness overpowered the other voices. Sylvia was also speaking in tongues, with her eyes open and her hands together in front of her. Sylvia spoke in a more repetitious form than the others did. She was the only one in the room besides me who kept her eyes open. As this subsided, Cheryl started a song, and when we finished singing, Mark told us that we could be seated.

Jeb started the prayer request time by asking that we pray that he get his plane tickets in time. Jeb had mentioned earlier that he was going to be a counselor at a camp, and he was particularly concerned that the religious training there would be led by "a New Age woman." He disagreed with the goal of the training, that "other people could understand each other's culture and each other's God" — he was concerned that it didn't say "*the* God." Nolan reminded us that the New Age movement was very subtle. He had been in the army for three years before he had realized that his commanding officer was part of the New Age movement.

Breaking this mood, Jacob said that he felt the Lord was leading him to pray for Sarah. Sarah was at the CARE group for the first time. She had been invited by Mel and Jacob, who were friends of hers from other singles' activities. Even though few people in the group knew her, she spoke up about her problem: "Six years ago I had a baby and was flat on my back after that. I've had trouble with my back since — sometimes it flares up, and I must have done something today to put it out, because it feels like I'm in labor again." The group quickly decided that she should kneel in the hot spot.

Group members laid hands on her and most people spoke in

236

tongues, and then Marge prayed that Sarah's spine would line up and that she would be healed and relieved of pain. Either the tongue-speaking of earlier that evening or her knowledge of medicine made Marge's prayer long and loud and forceful. She talked to Sarah's body, commanding it to be better. Sylvia followed Marge, praying that Sarah's nervous system wouldn't give her any more trouble. We stood up, and Marge and Sylvia hugged Sarah. No one asked her if she felt better, and she didn't volunteer anything, but she did look happier and sat through the short Scripture lesson with the rest of us.

Later, during the social hour, I asked Sarah how she was feeling. "Oh yes, I feel fine for now. I don't have any pain. I wasn't sure I was going to come over tonight, it hurt so bad — before the meeting I was down in the basement, lying flat on my back on the floor. I'm glad I came, though. It's one of those things I'm going to have to get used to, I guess."

As this meeting indicates, the group believes that the Holy Spirit grants each member the authority to speak about his or her devotional life as a series of "words from God." Marge, for example, shared the message that God showed her one morning in First Peter. Despite the verse's context in a passage that discusses the persecution of a congregation, she interpreted the verse as a moral for her own life. She believed that it told her that her former indecision and lack of answers to her employment changes were a gift from God to make her stronger and "more steadfast" in the Lord. The rest of the group dutifully underlined the passage in their Bibles and noted the date in the margin, reinforcing the passage's special significance as an answer to prayer. The reinterpretation of a communal verse into a personal message that was then shared with a group and confirmed by their action exemplifies the path the group takes to find community. This circuitous route — taking a communal ritual and focusing it on the individual, which then serves to reinforce the group — is common, evident also in healing rituals.

The uses of charismatic gifts in the CARE group's "hot spot," for instance, do more than help an ailing individual. By bringing the group together physically and spiritually as they place hands on their kneeling friend and pray in tongues together, the "hot spot" further signifies the group's trust in their ability to tap into the Spirit's resources. Although I was surprised by Sarah's remark after her "hot spot" experience — "It's one of those things I'm going to have to get used to, I guess" — I later realized that the essential part of the experience for her was the "gift" of healing from the group, and not the actual "healing." In fact, after this evening Sarah became a regular in the group: she attended the meetings and sat with group members during Sunday morning services.

Cheryl: One Member's Experience

The spiritual community in Mel's small group was encouraged by the members who were Mennonites — Mel himself, as well as Janet, Cheryl, and Jacob. Their experience as Mennonites gave them an appreciation of the particular freedoms of the Worship Center and a vocabulary of community. Of all the Mennonites in Mel's CARE group, Cheryl was the most articulate about the ways the small group helps create a spiritual space and a community.

Cheryl was a newcomer to the charismatic movement when she started attending the Worship Center in 1982; her path to the Worship Center had included several years of churchless Sundays. She had gotten tired of "going through the motions" and concerned that "people were doing one thing and the ministers another," so she stopped attending church and took a job that required her to work on Sunday mornings. When Cheryl decided to go back to church after a conversion experience in 1980, she didn't know where to go. "I'm sure I would have been welcomed back to the Mennonite church, but — well, I would have felt guilty. I think what would have been hardest was the questions people would have asked, like, 'Where have you been, and what have you been doing with yourself?' and I just couldn't have dealt with that. I decided that I wanted to go to a church where no one knew me." But when she first went to the Worship Center, to her surprise she did meet people that she knew — and that turned out to be a positive factor:

> For the first three or four Sundays I met people who I knew, but didn't know were going there. First, I met the fellow I worked for at [the] market, and his wife and family were going there. Then, the next Sunday I met a woman who had graduated with my brother, and she and her husband were going there. And then the following Sunday I saw a cousin of mine and his wife and family, and I hadn't known that they were going there. So I just really felt like those were signs that it was the place I was supposed to be, and it really assured me. I took that as affirmation. And I've been going there ever since.

Meeting people she knew at the Worship Center made Cheryl feel at home there. In the beginning, these friendships were enough for her; she didn't feel ready to make additional commitments. After several years, however, she attended some special meetings organized for "the singles group" that led her to CARE group participation. She explains the history of her involvement:

This is the third CARE group I've been in. The first time [I was in a singles group that grew too large, and] they switched us into a new one; it wasn't as though we split up. But the second one I really didn't like. The husband-wife team that was leading it — I didn't see any unity between them. By that time my current singles group was forming, and that's when I decided to switch. I didn't want to hurt the feelings of anyone in my old group, and I didn't want to tell them the real reason why I was leaving, so I called everybody in the other group and thanked them for their support — not their monetary support, of course, but their support in my life. I told them I was becoming part of the singles, as I was participating more with them. And there were not hard feelings between us, as there have sometimes been — sometimes there's bitterness when someone changes groups, but as far as I know, my case hasn't been that way. I discerned that I was really not in a position to bring my personal feelings about their [the couple's] relationship out in the open, as a single woman who doesn't really have a position to do that. So, I felt pushed by the Spirit to switch over.

The CARE groups have been my first extracurricular [involvement]. I would like to be involved more in the church and be more disciplined, and maybe I will be soon.

As a single woman in the church, Cheryl sensed the marginality of her role when she felt awkward criticizing a married couple. Rather than speaking up, she found a group where, if such a situation would arise, she would be free to speak her mind. The singles group allows her to share openly, something she has a hard time doing even within her own family. Like many other single adults, she is loathe to call on her parents for guidance and assurance for fear of seeming dependent and instead leans on the group. The group, as part of the church body, is part of a hierarchy that Cheryl appreciates in certain ways:

Each of the CARE group leaders [is] responsible to someone, who, of course, is responsible to someone else. Just like me, they are all accountable to people for their own marriage and family problems, because we are all human and have those problems. . . . You know, we all need God, and we all need to be accountable to God. But we also need to be accountable to somebody with skin on. Sometimes people get really caught up in the idea that it's just them and God.

I can think of an example of this, actually. There was a youth minister, and he wasn't doing something that he should have been — I think it was something like a program format or something. And they approached him in a biblical way, like it says in Matthew, I think. The first time you go to him in a group of two or three, and then you take it in front of the body, and there were some statements made, and everything got messed up — I don't know what role [the senior pastor] played in it, but the youth minister got up in front of the church and repented, and the senior pastor did too. It was a real tough time for the church. But there was a real sense of forgiveness there.

This really impressed me, because I know that I would be treated in the very same way that the youth minister was. And I — well, I don't really have anyone I can talk to about this stuff, you know. I don't have the covering of a husband, and I really can't discuss this stuff with my family, it's — you know, not important to them, they have their own church lives.

The spiritual and moral hierarchy in the Worship Center reassures Cheryl that egos and bad ideas are held in check in a variety of cases. But accountability does not end with vertical lines of accountability. There are also horizontal lines of accountability, which Cheryl feels very strongly in her group, because she values it as a space where she can reflect on the meaning of her everyday experiences and draw on the group's understanding of her worldview as a single person. So to a certain extent her emphasis on accountability to the group displaces the hierarchical accountability of the Worship Center. Interestingly, she came to the Worship Center because of her previous negative experience with the Mennonite church hierarchy, which she said "was doing one thing while everyone else was doing another." The disunity between word and deed drew her to the charismatics:

The charismatic expression of faith really speaks to me. I'm past the point where I do things just because everybody else does. Charismatic things can be taken to an extreme, I know. There are some who think that everything is caused by a demon, and those people cast them out. . . . I can't quite understand it, personally. . . . I used to think that God allows illness to happen, that there is a reason God did it, for his glory, or whatever. I still think it is God's permissible will to have some people be sick, because we are of this world and we do die sometime, that's a fact. Yet, God does heal people. My dad had cancer. He didn't die a traumatic death like some; it was a lingering death. Well, the elders of our church came and anointed my father with oil like it says in James about two weeks before he died and, well, he was pretty far gone by then. Now, they're not to blame, but I just have to wonder what would have happened had they come six months earlier. Then he was still in chemotherapy, and he could still walk around.

I've never been instantaneously healed and I've never thought, "Why can't I have this or that?" or "Why aren't I married, Lord?" With my father, though — he had to *ask* the elders to come and perform their duty, the duty of the elders to anoint with oil. If they had just come six months earlier, what would have been the result? And I don't know, but it would have been more of an act of faith, I think. I'm not blaming them, though, for him dying.

Cheryl's experience with the Worship Center stands in marked contrast with her earlier church experiences: she sees the Worship Center as a vibrant place where she finds commitment to Christian action. Yet the small group particularly is where Cheryl finds a place to be accountable for her actions and finds real fellowship. Her story is typical of many other Mennonites at the Worship Center who left the Mennonite Church and found a better community than they had hoped — in small groups. Cheryl's comments demonstrate a concern for continued accountability and community, two elements of the traditional Mennonite *Weltanschauung* that many charismatics found restrictive. Although these ideas have been antithetical to the religious experience promoted by Mennonite charismatics, they have been resurrected among the groups of single adults. The ambiguous role of community in the charismatic congregation and in the small group is best illustrated by an exploration of the Worship Center's hybrid Mennonite and charismatic origins.

Changes in the Mennonite Church
and the Charismatic Alternative

Janet, the leader of the CARE group I attended, told me how her path of religious inquiry led her to the Worship Center:

> I distinctly remember one Sunday.... It was really funny, because the Sunday school superintendent didn't know what to do with us, me and my girlfriend. There were classes for the young marrieds and the youth group, but nothing for us. We were single and professional and we didn't know anyone. The way they set up their classes, though, didn't make us feel too welcome there.
>
> We went around to different Mennonite churches for about two years. I guess then a friend, an older woman, took me under her wing and asked me to go to the Worship Center. They were starting up a singles group there, so that's where I went. And I've been going there ever since.

In the early 1970s, young, unmarried adults like Janet were forming a new, dissatisfied social group in the Lancaster Mennonite community. They returned home to Lancaster after going to college or doing missionary work to find their Mennonite churches failing to provide resources or programs for them. As Janet saw it, the Mennonite churches in the area were not equipped to deal with her as a young single woman — there weren't even Sunday school classes for young singles. This lack left Janet without a social network and a way of getting involved in these churches. When Janet went to the Worship Center, however, she found many other young single Mennonites there and was encouraged by the ministers to organize a singles' group.

Interest in the charismatic movement among singles and other young adults highlighted the kinds of social changes the Mennonite community faced in the early 1970s; dissent over issues of religious authority and an increasing lack of adherence to dress codes were just two flags of the growing resistance to Mennonite traditions. Despite the Mennonite leadership's continued emphasis on sectarianism and separation, Mennonites had, following World War II, forsaken the farm for the city and taken up new occupations, particularly in small businesses; in the process they had amassed new kinds of wealth. New occupations, money, and education led to new assumptions about the way the world worked — and to new behaviors. Not as many young people got married, and those that did married later, which created a social group of single adults with more on their minds than their wedding day. All these factors weakened the social ties that bound Mennonites to their traditional interpretations of ethics and community.

While the Mennonite Church was slow to respond to changes in the Mennonite community, the charismatic movement justified and facilitated new social interactions.[4] The charismatic movement had many celebrants, but it appealed particularly to Mennonites with families who were moving into semiprofessional, nonagricultural occupations, and to college-educated single adults who did not marry immediately upon graduation. Young adults at Mennonite colleges joined charismatic prayer groups and participated in campus-wide charismatic revivals; after college, they found a place for fellowship in nondenominational charismatic groups. Mennonites on their way up came into contact with evangelical Christians rising to middle-class positions and joined them in nondenominational ecumenical prayer groups like the Full Gospel

4. The Mennonite Church in Lancaster County has stood against religious and secular currents in popular American culture and so to some degree remains communal, sectarian, and pacifist. But continued influences from outside the bounded Mennonite sphere (antisectarian impulses, revivalism, and missions) have impinged on the Mennonite sense of separation. In addition, schism and conflict within the conference have reinforced a growing sense during the twentieth century that the Mennonite way of life has been under siege and have indeed worked to alter definitions of Mennonite life and thought. (On church disputes in the Lancaster Conference, see Kniss 1991; on the controversy over fundamentalism, see Schlabach 1980; on the Franconia (PA) Conference's struggles with a host of American Protestant movements, see John Hostetler 1987.) Most boundaries were clearly marked in the Lancaster Conference: all members were expected to dress alike, think alike, worship in the same way on Sunday morning, and were forbidden to join other organizations. The emphasis on correct behavior and dress codes focused on the restrictive aspects of community.

In general, the Mennonites who came to the Worship Center believed that too much stress on conformity in religion had undermined the value of worship, and they sought to make a place where worship could be "free." Negative Mennonite reactions to charismatic worship focused on its expressive style and involved criticism of individuals who disrupted church services. In addition, many of the spiritual gifts that charismatics held as central to the life of the Spirit-filled Christian (speaking in tongues, prophecy, and healing) were gifts they saw as bestowed on the individual, which contradicted traditional Mennonite teaching. These charismatic emphases worked against Mennonite practices of "community," which assume that a communal emphasis is better than an emphasis on individuals when it comes to worship styles and theological interpretations.

Businessmen's International Association and Women's Aglow. Two Mennonite businessmen involved in such organizations started the Worship Center because they didn't know where to send the people they healed on their weekly visits to hospitals.

The emphasis on individual decision-making and sanctioned expressionism in public services (highlighting personal religiousness) drew Mennonites to the Worship Center and other charismatic churches. Mennonites made new commitments that downplayed the communal aspects and morals of their tradition.[5] They emphasized the availability of the gifts of the Holy Spirit, which led undeniably to an ascriptive definition of Christian commitment, which in turn prompted many excluded from the traditions of the Mennonite lifestyle to join charismatic churches that stressed both freedom and an understanding of their ethnic Mennonite backgrounds. People once on the margins of Mennonite society could move to the center of their new charismatic churches, where expectations of involvement were nominal.

Yet despite the Worship Center's motto, "Where Everybody is Somebody and Jesus Christ is Lord," it is not the same haven for all. When Mennonites moved to the Worship Center, they separated themselves from their original religious group, its networks, and its ideals. Once outside of the Mennonite world of family and church, Mennonite charismatics constructed different ideals of the Christian life that reoriented the places of spiritual authority. The Mennonite Church ascribed authority to the community and the conference; Mennonite charismatics ascribed authority to individual leaders and individual heads

---

5. The Mennonite Church's emphasis on group decision-making and community discipleship was challenged by the charismatics, who claimed to have revelations from God contrary to tradition. Mainstream Mennonites quickly turned the tables on religious personalism, stating that although the manifestations that the charismatics pointed to were certainly from the Spirit, they were by far the lesser of the Spirit's functions. According to mainstream Mennonites, the Spirit was much more interested in promoting the attitudes or fruits of the Spirit that included patience and self-control.

The fruits of the Spirit are listed in Galatians 5:22-23: love, joy, peace, patience, kindness, goodness, faithfulness, gentleness, and self-control. Although the virtue of humility, highly prized by the Mennonites, is not listed in this group of nine, it is included in this same passage: "Let us not become conceited" (v. 26). The manifestations of the Spirit are listed in 1 Corinthians 12: wisdom, knowledge, faith, healing, prophecy, miraculous powers, discernment between spirits (good and evil), speaking in tongues, and interpretation of tongues.

of households. Yet at the Worship Center they eventually embraced the model of the family as structurally and religiously significant. They saw the spiritual hierarchy ordained by God on earth as clearly and unquestionably that of the nuclear family: father, mother, and children.

At the Worship Center, "the family" is both a goal to strive toward and a metaphor affirming the cosmic positions of God the Father, Jesus the Son, and the bride-church. Translated into human terms, the father is the unquestioned spiritual leader of any household, the mother is the caring "helpmate" with secondary authority, and the children kind and obedient. This understanding is a recurrent theme in sermons, liturgy, Sunday school lessons, and school curriculum. While such an interpretation of spiritual and everyday life encourages men, many of whom are highly involved in business, to be more attuned to spiritual matters and home responsibilities, it also tends to make married women less active in leadership roles. At the Worship Center, women do participate in corporate activities, but they rarely preach or teach in public meetings. The church celebrates individuality and the variety of gifts that God gives indiscriminately to all, but at the same time it underlines the fact that women in general have the "spiritual covering" of men.

The messages of family have become an integral part of the Worship Center's self-definition. Single adults do not fit easily into this ethos, and the dominant ideology can be a problem for them. It is a rare occasion when singles are included in the tales and examples of moral accountability taught by ministers in sermons and Sunday school classes. Single adults do not fall within the bounds of standard moral discourse here. It is the consequent dislocation they feel that strengthens their CARE group ties.

Although single adults are on the margins of Worship Center cosmology, they are not entirely outside its focus. After all, the early singles' groups gave the church its original small-group program, and singles' groups continue to appeal to young adults who join the church and eventually marry. Still, singles are on the sidelines. This explains why the CARE groups have become increasingly important for singles at the Worship Center — because they provide an institutionalized space supported by the church for single adults to cultivate trust, accountability, and fellowship, as other members do in nuclear families. Mel's group demonstrates the process by which a group uses spiritual language and experience to create a community bound together by its members' marginalization: just as they were on the edges of the traditional Mennonite world, so they are on the edges of the Worship Center world. Small groups like Mel's are tailored to the needs and lives of singles: they provide a place where a new understanding of charismatic Christian experience can be formed, where accountability is experienced in a group instead of a hierarchical relationship, and where the cosmology of the family is rarely invoked.[6]

The differences between the dominant ethos of the church and the ethos of the singles' group became conspicuous during what was billed as "Singles' Weekend." The Worship Center, operating on its best intentions, invited a special speaker for singles who gave a morning message and an evening service. To make a day of it, the singles groups planned picnics for the afternoon; our small group was meeting at Sylvia's house for pizza.

"Singles' Weekend" at the Worship Center: An Example of Marginality

On Sunday morning I walked almost to the front of the auditorium to sit with the group. Mel, Sarah, Sylvia, Cheryl, Mark, and the rest of the group were discussing plans for the afternoon. As we were chatting, the senior minister introduced the guest speaker who would be leading the singles' seminar that weekend. The speaker then turned on an overhead projector, and began by telling us that he had saved 243 marriages from divorce over the summer, and that he had written two books in eight weeks while holding six marriage seminars. This, by way of introduction, included an apology to the married people, who he thought probably wouldn't get much out of his sermon. As he continued over the next ten minutes to tell the audience about his successes with marriage counseling, I realized that the other group members were only barely listening. Activity on our two benches was constant. Phil and Janet passed around a sign-up sheet to see how many were coming for pizza that afternoon. Sylvia noticed that Sarah

6. Mel's group was not in any sense a place for finding a future mate. It was tacitly agreed that using the group in this way was inappropriate in the context of the group's formal meetings. Despite some of the members' assertions that they would someday be married, they didn't seem to be searching for partners. This makes sense, given the group's identity and the practices it considered important. Looking for a partner would disrupt the spiritual communion in the group, which was considered very significant.

thought she might be bringing two kids, and groaned. "Maybe I can lock them in the basement," she whispered. Marge and her friend wrote notes to each other, and Mel stood up and went to the back of the auditorium to stand with Jacob. Eventually the speaker did talk about single people's lives, focusing on their freedom to experience the world, pointing to biblical examples like Paul and the other missionaries, and glorifying the single lifestyle as one that was pleasing to God. Nevertheless, my group seemed happy when the service was over.

Afterward, I followed Sylvia to her home, and we talked about women's issues until the others arrived. Although we didn't start out talking about that morning's service, we soon strayed to the subject. Sylvia was irate that the speaker had been so chauvinistic, indicative of what she considered to be the prevalence of chauvinism at the Worship Center. I wasn't quite sure what she meant by chauvinism, and asked — she replied that women have different ways of thinking about things, and that she was disappointed that more women didn't get a chance to preach at the Worship Center because they had things to say that would speak to her in ways that men's comments sometimes didn't. She cited examples in the New Testament of women speaking and preaching, but noted that that didn't happen at the Worship Center. Cheryl appeared at this moment, and the discussion broke off, leaving me with more questions than answers about Sylvia's views on single life and chauvinism.

More of the regulars arrived soon, including Sarah, Mel, Jacob, Mark, and Salome, but some of the people who showed up I didn't know. Dorothy arrived on the heels of Phil and Janet, who carried in eight pizzas. Next came the setting up for lunch: the rescuing of some spilled iced tea, the bringing out of paper plates, napkins, and chairs. During this activity, Dorothy came over and said hello, and asked me how I had liked the morning's message. I asked her if she had noticed how much the speaker had focused on marriage, even though his talk was meant to be for singles. She said that she had noticed, and she seemed perplexed about whether or not being single was a kind of deficiency. "I don't really worry about marriage, because I know that the Lord knows what is best for me, and that someday I will be married. But that's in the future, and right now that's not my issue.... Sometimes I do want the freedom of marriage, though." On some issues, she vehemently disagreed with the speaker, who had asserted that single people were free to travel and "follow God's call." "That may be true if you are a man," she commented, "but not if you are a woman, because women can't just pick up and go somewhere." Like Sylvia, she believed that many of the speaker's remarks were chauvinistic and didn't take into account the difference in social position between men and women. This difference would someday be altered for her, when she found someone to marry. She paused, and then added, to repeat her earlier point, "I know that someday I'll be married."

In all, twenty-five people prayed before lunch. After getting our pizza, we found places to sit in the house and the yard. I was introduced to Theresa, who asked me how I came by my name. When I said that my parents had picked it out for me by chance, Dorothy countered with an alternate explanation. "Courtney," she said, "God picked out your name. God, and the Holy Spirit. Even before the world was created, God and the Holy Spirit and Jesus sat down and said, 'OK, let's get to work.' And they wrote down everything that was going to happen, and put your name in the Book of Life." This fact, she said, reassured her that she was saved. This mystical cosmology helped me to better understand the position of single women attending the Worship Center. They used this concept to explain both the ordained nature of their entire lives and their single status, as well as to help them find an alternative to the hierarchical definitions of spiritual authority that focused on men.

When most of the pizza had been eaten, people gravitated to the living room. They were talking about the singles' seminar and whether or not they were going to the service that evening. Another singles' CARE group was having a carry-in meal beforehand; some were going to that, and would decide with that group whether or not to go to the service. As it turned out, most people were going to the evening's service, even though the majority had expressed dissatisfaction with the morning's sermon. Mark argued that by arranging for the speaker, the ministers were acknowledging the presence of the singles; the least the singles could do to thank them was attend the events. Someone remarked that since the majority of the morning's worshipers were married, the speaker had probably wanted to say something for their benefit too. "Well," Janet said, "then he shouldn't have kept on telling the married people to bear with him as he talked to the singles."

On this Sunday afternoon and for months afterward, I would reflect on the single adults' groups to try to make sense of their place in the Worship Center's theology and structure. For, despite the Worship Center's best attempts to include single members, the church openly embraces the so-called nuclear family as the epitome of Christian life and as an allegory for the order of the cosmos.

This interpretation of Christian authority stands in contrast to the traditional Mennonite emphasis on congregational authority; it is lauded by those who wish to be free from responsibility to these traditional emphases. The majority of Mennonite families who joined the Worship Center fit well into the new pattern of spiritual authority: they discarded the religious aspects of kinship ties and set up spiritual authority in the nuclear family almost by default. Mennonite singles made their way out of the Mennonite Church into the Worship Center only to discover a "spiritual" ethos that privileged marriage over the single life and the life of the nuclear family over extrafamilial relationships. Although the Worship Center still promotes individual spiritual authority and personal autonomy, these emphases are severely mitigated by its focus on the family.

In this context, small groups have become highly valuable to single people, who use them to form their own families of support. The small group becomes the equivalent space of the nuclear family for singles, giving them room in which to interpret their lives and be accountable to others. Although "touch pastors" in the singles' groups play prominent roles in caring and counseling, for the most part the single individuals themselves retain spiritual authority; that is something rarely ceded to leaders. In addition, the freedom to belong allows the groups to continue to grow as spiritual communities. In all these ways, the singles' community subverts the hierarchical authority and family order that have combined to form the status quo of the Worship Center.

Small groups at the Worship Center provide different things to different groups. In general, they allow the large church to maintain intimacy and allow for some limited communication between laity and clergy. For Mennonites who joined the Worship Center, the groups provide fellowship with others who had similar experiences growing up in the Mennonite Church and allow for a continuing therapeutic discussion of the meaning of the restrictive community they left. For single adults, however, the small groups do more than reaffirm the charismatic values of intimacy and provide space for discussing life experiences. The small groups of singles actually form an alternative expression of charismatic faith and community that is based not on cosmological allegiances to leaders or fathers or husbands but on allegiances to each other. They come together to sing, to pray, to heal one another, to support one another. The tenuous place they occupy on the edge of the Worship Center community is in many ways far from ideal, but the continuing conflicts they experience establish and strengthen a community rising out of a hierarchical congregational ethos. Their struggle points the way to a communion of the saints.

Small Groups in a Campus Ministry: Shaping the Future

ANTONY ALUMKAL

One of the most important though seldom discussed types of small groups is the kind that ministers to young adults. Young adulthood is a critical life stage, a time of transition during which individuals must prepare for their roles in the adult world. In addition to choosing educational and career goals, young adults must answer questions about the meaning of their existence, the moral values they will embrace, and their beliefs about the nature of ultimate reality and/or the divine — in other words, determine the type of faith[1] that will undergird their adult lives. Many young adults find that small groups — whether formal or informal — provide valuable support during this often difficult period, as well as a setting for asking questions, hearing others' viewpoints, and working out their identity.

Small groups for young adults have a long history in the United States. As one might expect, these groups have frequently thrived at universities (institutions whose traditional mission was to instill character and virtue as much as it was to impart technical knowledge). The earliest groups of this sort were voluntary student religious societies founded on college campuses during the eighteenth century. These societies generally were of two types. On the one hand were devotional groups that

---

1. The term "faith" here refers to broad patterns of meaning rather than cognitive assent to particular doctrines. Cf. Parks 1986, xv.

provided mutual support and encouragement in practicing the Christian faith. On the other hand were groups committed to discussing and debating controversial theological and ethical issues of the day (Shedd 1934, 15). Both types of societies reflected an inadequacy on the part of churches and universities to deal with young people's spiritual needs and their questions about how faith should be translated into action in the world.

The nineteenth century brought the formation in England of the Young Men's Christian Association (YMCA), an interdenominational organization that sought to minister to city youth, carrying religion into the sphere of daily work. After the movement spread to the United States, it was not long before students began forming YMCA chapters on their campuses. This followed from the students' recognition that, in spite of the YMCA's urban orientiation, it could easily be adapted to the needs of students (Shedd 1934, 100). In addition to performing social-service projects, these campus chapters maintained small groups of various sorts — including Bible studies and prayer meetings — in order to meet the moral and religious needs of students that universities were not adequately addressing (Shedd 1934, 119).

With the growth of secular public universities and the relative decline of church-supported colleges in the twentieth century, mainline denominations saw the need for establishing ministries on public campuses. This involved the recognition that traditional congregational structures could not adequately deal with the special needs of students, a fact demonstrated by the popularity of student voluntary associations. Yet the voluntary associations could not provide the specific pastoral and sacramental functions associated with a church (Hargrove 1976, 207). Denominational campus ministries sought to form student congregations that, while bearing a denominational affiliation, still maintained a sense of distance from the church at large (Underwood 1969, 14-16). Like the YMCA and the other ministries before them, these ministries sought to nurture the spiritual and intellectual lives of students through Bible studies, vespers, theological discussions, and a host of other small-group activities. And though denominational campus ministries have had to adapt to ever-changing situations in the churches and universities, their basic functions have remained largely the same.

In order to further explicate the phenomenon of small groups for young adults, in this chapter I will present a case study of an Episcopal campus ministry at a northeastern university. I will detail how this ministry uses small groups and what impact (if any) these groups have on the spiritual lives of the students. I will also describe some of the conflicts and other difficulties that a campus ministry must contend with in the course of its activity. Finally, because no group operates in a vacuum, I will analyze how the ministry's use of small groups is influenced by its institutional and social milieu.

An Episcopal Campus Ministry

The Episcopal Chaplaincy (EC) is the oldest campus ministry at its university. Its roots stretch back to the 1870s, when a nearby Episcopal church began outreach to the campus. In the 1920s, the local bishop, an alumnus of the university and an heir to a considerable fortune, created a foundation to support the ministry. He set up a chaplaincy advisory committee and began hiring chaplains to serve five- to ten-year terms. He also purchased a house next to campus (Episcopal House) to serve as the chaplain's residence and the center for the chaplaincy's activities.

Chuck Stranton, the current chaplain, is an alumnus of the university from the class of 1967 (according to him, the year before anything resembling activism appeared on campus). Prior to his work as a campus minister, he worked first as a boarding-school teacher and then, after going to seminary, as a minister in a parish. He was contacted by the chaplaincy advisory committee when the chaplain position was to become vacant, and he took over the job in 1986.

EC underwent a big change in the fall of 1991, when it hired an assistant chaplain, Jan Middleton. For a number of years, Chuck had been increasingly aware of the importance of gender issues in ministry and the inability of a male pastor to handle them alone. Accordingly, the chaplaincy began searching for a woman chaplain to provide an alternative perspective to Chuck's and to lead a support group for the women members. Although Jan had not originally planned to work with college students, she found appealing the chance to work in a ministry where her gender was an asset rather than a liability (as it sometimes had been in her parish work) and where she could speak openly about her feminist views. She accepted an offer for the position and has since added a dynamic presence to the ministry, though not without causing at least some controversy (to be discussed below).

The ministry has several activities throughout the week, the most

253

important of these being the Sunday Eucharist service, which draws, on average, fifty to sixty students. The service, which follows a conventional liturgy as outlined in Rite 2 in the Book of Common Prayer, is held in the university chapel at 10 p.m. Those involved are fond of the dark, contemplative atmosphere of the chapel at night. One student said about the service, "It's a quiet time, an hour where you can really sit down and just think." Given the hectic pace of most students' lives, this opportunity for quiet reflection is one of the most important contributions that the ministry makes.

Yet, the Sunday service has certain limitations. The dark, quiet atmosphere makes it an anonymous experience, not one suitable for getting to know others or discussing the issues addressed in the sermons. For those who desire more intimate fellowship and a setting for exploring spiritual issues in more depth, EC offers several small-group meetings. These include the Wednesday-night dinner/discussion meetings at Episcopal House and the newly instituted women's group meetings led by the assistant chaplain, as well as various retreats and special events.

Wednesday-Night Meetings

Episcopal House sits opposite a group of dorms on the west side of campus. Its bright yellow exterior hints that it is somehow distinct from the other houses lining University Avenue. A sign next to the door, bearing the symbol of the Episcopal Church, indicates for what purposes the house is used.

The interior looks like a typical family house. A short hallway leads from the front door to the living room and kitchen areas, where the group's Wednesday-night activities take place. By a few minutes past six, a dozen or so people are gathered inside the house, either helping to prepare the evening meal or relaxing on the living-room couches. The presence of Chuck's three young children (and occasionally the family dog as well) reinforces the "homey" quality of the setting, sharpening its distinction from the self-contained world of the campus.

Conversation comes to a halt when the chaplain ushers everyone into the living room for the informal Eucharist service that precedes dinner. The service follows Rite 3 in the Book of Common Prayer, which specifies the minimum elements necessary for a eucharistic celebration.

The liturgy follows either a traditional form or one of the inclusive-language versions that Jan has been introducing to the group.

The service begins with a few moments of silence as the participants clear their minds of everyday concerns. The presiding chaplain then reads a passage of his or her choosing from the gospel, after which everyone is seated for a brief homily on the reading. The homilies, which are simpler and more to the point than typical Sunday sermons, often relate to the evening's topic for discussion or some other long-term issue facing the ministry. After this, all stand and pray both silently and aloud for their own personal concerns and those of the world. When the prayers have ended, the participants are ready to greet one another with "the peace." This usually involves an exchange of hugs rather than the standard handshakes; many consider this to be their favorite part of the service.

After the peace comes the celebration of the Eucharist. Everyone gathers in a semicircle around the altar as the chaplain recalls the Last Supper and consecrates the bread and wine. On most occasions, the participants administer the sacrament to each other, moving clockwise around the circle. This begins with the presiding chaplain giving the elements to the person on his or her left, who then administers them to the next person, and so on. People in the group find this communion more "personal" than that at the Sunday service, and find that by getting more involved in the celebration of the sacrament, they are better able to grasp its significance.[2] When communion has ended, members join hands and sing the doxology "in celebration of the meal we have just eaten and the one we are about to eat." The chaplain then gives the dismissal, signaling the end of the service, and everyone heads for the dining room.

The food, which is prepared by the students, is considered by most a welcome break from dormitory fare. The participants serve themselves in the dining room and then return to the living room to sit and eat. Dinnertime conversation ranges from bits of personal news to matters concerning the university to current political or social controversies. Participants have about fifteen to twenty minutes to eat before the discussion begins.

---

2. Robert Bellah argues that much of contemporary worship fails in its goal to transport the worshiper out of "the straight and profane world of everyday pragmatic common sense," instead becoming part of this world (Bellah 1970, 209-10). Perhaps EC's Eucharist service is successful because it presents a familiar ritual in an unfamiliar manner, forcing participants to take another look at the ritual and its meaning.

The discussions involve either an outside speaker addressing the group or simply an issue that the participants debate among themselves. One of the best-received speakers of the year was a former hostage in Iran who gave an account of his ordeal and the spiritual resources that helped him get through it. Another evening featured two Episcopal clergymen, one liberal and one conservative, debating the merits of the Baltimore Declaration (a conservative theological manifesto) and the question "Where does the Episcopal Church stand?"

One typical Wednesday-night discussion was part of a series entitled "How much questioning does the Christian faith allow?" The previous week, a professor of religion from the university had given a lecture on the great questioners of the Christian tradition, including Rudolf Bultmann, Paul Tillich, and Bishop John Robinson. This week, the group was ready to discuss questions of their own. Jan, who presided over the meeting, began by giving participants pieces of paper and asking them to spend a few minutes jotting down some questions or areas of doubt they had concerning Christianity. After this, the participants gathered into several groups of two to three people to discuss what they had written before sharing with the whole group.

One member shared that doubt was as much a part of her faith as belief, and that the process of searching was as important to her as finding answers. Others began debating what constitutes the essential or core beliefs of Christianity, with some admitting that they were not sure if they accepted any such beliefs.

At this point, one person raised an interesting question. Considering the number of questions and doubts that people had, was it appropriate for the ministry to recite every Sunday the Nicene Creed, which begins, "I believe ..." and then gives a detailed list of doctrinal statements? One member replied that during the service she would recite only the lines in the creed that she agreed with. Another added that, while he believed the entire creed and considered it important, deleting lines was an honest course of action for those who had doubts. Finally, someone suggested that even if one does not believe the entire creed, perhaps reciting it could be a step toward believing.

This discussion is characteristic of the group in several ways. First, diverse points of view are shared with no attempt at reaching a consensus or resolving the question at hand. Second, group members are free to express unorthodox opinions without eliciting sanction either from other group members or from the chaplain. Third, the very topic of discussion reveals a willingness to engage difficult or controversial issues head-on. All this helps to ensure that the Wednesday-night discussions remain thought provoking. On the other hand, this type of discussion is not suitable for everyone, particularly those seeking affirmation of their faith within an unstable campus environment.

People in the group gave different responses when asked why they come to Wednesday nights and what they appreciate most about the meetings. One woman told me that she thought the fellowship was the most important part. "I think people come to be with each other, and the dinner is the focal point. Sometimes the discussions are not very good, and some of the guest speakers do not know where students are at." Others said that they enjoyed discussing various issues and especially valued hearing people share "deep things" about themselves. But people in the group generally did agree on the importance of the informal Eucharist. Anglicans, along with Catholics and Lutherans, have always counted their liturgical and sacramental emphasis as one of their strengths. The informal Eucharist service successfully draws on this tradition in a manner well suited for a campus ministry setting, providing both continuity and differentiation with respect to the larger Episcopal Church. But perhaps most importantly, the service allows an infusion of the sacred into the "world of everyday" of university life, preventing the latter from going unchallenged in the lives of the students.

The Women's Group

One of EC's most dynamic ministries is the women's group, led by Jan, the new assistant chaplain. The group was formed in response to a feeling of alienation among the women in the fellowship and the realization that they needed some type of support network. As Jan explained, "Women need time apart in order to empower each other and to recognize what is happening to them, but also to affirm themselves in a world that says, 'You are not quite as good as men.'"

The group meets early Sunday evenings in the chaplain's office on campus and involves six to eight people. Jan usually brings tea and food, and often will light candles. According to the participants, the "homey" atmosphere increases the intimacy of the gathering. The meetings normally begin with the chaplain leading a relaxation exercise to help participants get focused and overcome any restlessness they may be experiencing. Sometimes the group will have a particular discussion planned, with topics ranging from theological issues, such as masculine and feminine images of God and the church's traditional separation of body and spirit, to more personal issues, such as the women's experiences with their families. At other times, group members will have personal problems they need to talk about, and the planned discussion will be dropped. At still other times, the group members are simply given time to sit and meditate quietly — a necessary counterbalance to their busy lifestyles.

Crucial to the functioning of the women's group is the high level of trust that the members have developed for one another. Only when there is an atmosphere of trust can members feel comfortable sharing their intimate thoughts and concerns. As one member commented, "The women's group is a very safe environment for sharing personal stories. You can share things knowing that everything will be kept private and you won't be criticized." But trust here involves more than confidentiality and the withholding of judgment. There is also the confidence that group members are willing to put aside their own concerns in order to care for others. One member explained that the busyness she sees affecting much of the ministry's life, particularly the Wednesday-night meetings, is absent from the women's group. "Being busy and pressured doesn't seep into the women's group. You can really be open and caring about other people because you have the time."

Members had no trouble describing the impact the group has had on their lives. Many of them mentioned that the interchange of ideas has helped them broaden their perspective, especially the way they view God. "Without realizing it," one woman said, "I used to picture God as a big man in the sky with a white beard and a staff. The women's group made me think about how I picture God and realize that God has both masculine and feminine aspects." Others mentioned that the group has helped them work out their identities as women, specifically as "women of faith in a patriarchal church." All of the members value this setting where they can share their experiences and come away "empowered."

Conflicts and Challenges

The descriptions above illustrate how, under ideal conditions, a campus ministry can effectively meet its objectives of enriching the spiritual and intellectual lives of its members. Real conditions, however, rarely remain ideal. Conflict of one type or another is an inevitable part of group life. One potential source of trouble for a campus ministry can be personality conflicts, either between students or between a student and the chaplain. But in addition to personality issues, there are social forces that affect campus ministries in problematic ways. Three sources of difficulty common to campus ministries are (1) friction between liberal clergy and conservative students, (2) student opposition to the tendency of ministries to question rather than affirm belief, and (3) religious individualism. I look now at how these affect EC and some possible ways in which groups with similar conflicts can respond to them.

Liberal-Conservative Friction

One source of conflict in a religious group of any size, from a small group to a denomination, is differences of opinion over what the faith means and how it should be practiced. This can be particularly problematic when the differences exist between clergy and laypeople, as is the case in many denominations.

Ideological differences in campus ministries between chaplains and their students have been common for some time. In a major study of campus ministry, Kenneth Underwood observed in the 1960s that campus clergy "are more liberal than the students they most attract; they are more flexible in the relation of their religious views to their social and political opinions and more open to varied activities in the churches than are the students who participate most regularly in their services" (Underwood 1969, 170).[3] These differences are probably even more pronounced today, given the relatively conservative nature of youth in recent years and the fact that many of those currently working as chaplains formed their opinions during the late sixties and early seventies. Not surprisingly, an ideological gap between the chaplains and at least some of the students is evident in EC.

---

3. Phillip Hammond's explanation for the prevailing liberalism among campus ministers is that "for Protestant churches the campus ministry serves as an organizational device for segmenting radicals" (Hammond 1969, 5). According to Hammond, many clergy who feel constrained in their parish ministries because of ideological differences with their congregations find "retreat" in the campus ministry. Some clergy make this move voluntarily; others are "eased out" of parish positions by church officials (Hammond, 8).

One manifestation of Chuck's "liberal" attitude is his practice of addressing political issues both in his sermons and during Wednesday-night discussions. He considers this to be an integral part of the church's mission. "The church is an inherently political institution because it is about people ('the polis'). When you talk about 'love your neighbor,' you are talking about politics." Like many mainline campus ministers, Chuck espouses political attitudes that are quite liberal.

Reaction to the inclusion of politics is mixed. Some participants would rather have the church concentrate on purely spiritual matters and leave politics to other institutions. One member complained, "I can hear a political discussion anywhere on campus. I expect to get something different when I go to church." Others, though, appreciate the political sermons for making them think about how faith can be applied to the real world.[4]

Another area of concern among the more conservative members of the ministry was the decision to hire the female assistant chaplain and her subsequent use of inclusive language and other nontraditional approaches to ministry. One EC alumnus wrote Chuck a letter expressing concern about the direction the ministry was taking. Chuck sent a reply explaining that the decision to hire a woman came not from a desire to pander to the women of the fellowship but from a desire to deal better with the spiritual needs of the entire congregation — men and women. He further explained, "I think the reason [women's ordination] has been so controversial is that it raises questions about the nature of God, the nature of human beings, and the nature of the Church." By the end of her first year, Jan was generally well-received by the fellowship, particularly by the women. This was helped in part by Jan's efforts to befriend anyone whom she thought might be uncomfortable with her presence, assuming they were accessible.

Chuck is aware of the differences that separate him from certain members of his ministry. In response, he emphasizes that the Episcopal Church has always been characterized by diversity of opinion on a wide

---

4. Jeffrey Hadden argues that in the American churches the basis of conflict between clergy and laity over political and social issues is that "the clergyman's new theology has moved him beyond the four walls of the church to express God's love in concern for the world, while the layman comes into the sanctuary of God to seek comfort and escape from the world" (Hadden 1969, 280). A similar dynamic may exist in campus ministries, though college students are probably less "escapist" than their older parish counterparts.

range of issues and yet has managed to stay together as a communion. The ministry, like the denomination, can simply agree to disagree on political and theological issues. The diversity of the denomination was the topic of a number of Wednesday-night discussions, including the debate between the conservative clergyman and the liberal clergyman. Making diversity in the ministry into a strength rather than a weakness is the challenge that lies ahead.

It is also necessary to mention that campus ministries, like other religious collectivities, have a safety valve for minimizing conflict — exit from the group. Given the usually large number of ministries on any particular campus, and the fact that these ministries welcome people from diverse religious backgrounds, anyone who finds a particular chaplain intolerable can go elsewhere. It is not suprising, therefore, that some of the more conservative students have left EC to join evangelical ministries. The fluid nature of campus ministries lessens the potential for conflict by separating those with extreme differences of opinion.[5]

Radical Questioning

Related to the liberal orientation of many mainline Protestant campus ministers is their tendency to encourage the questioning of religious beliefs (Hammond 1966, 48). In this respect, Chuck gives a characteristic description of his job: "The purpose of any campus ministry is to help students make the transition from their adolescent faith to their adult faith, whatever the adult faith turns out to be." In this vein, EC is a fellowship where people are free to ask difficult questions about faith and share diverse viewpoints. However, not everyone in the group is pleased with this. There are some who feel that the ministry spends too much time raising questions and not enough time doing what (in their view) a church is supposed to do — affirming belief in Christ.

5. It is not clear what impact liberal campus ministers have on future denominational membership. On the one hand, they discourage conservative students from participating in their own denominational ministry, causing some to seek out evangelical and other ministries. On the other hand, Hammond (1969, 11) suggests that liberal campus ministers encourage participation by more radical students who would normally avoid institutional religion. The issue is further complicated by the fact that involvement in a particular campus ministry is not necessarily a sign of any long-term religious affiliation.

As mentioned earlier, young adulthood is a time of social and psychological transition when individuals must construct a worldview. Some are comfortable with the rootlessness of this period in life and enjoy the unfettered exploration of ideas. Others find the experience distressing and seek stability in their lives. This second tendency helps to explain the popularity on many campuses of "cults" that offer students a rigid framework for their lives.

Not as extreme as the "cults" are evangelical groups that take a less ambiguous approach to faith than mainline groups, proclaiming Jesus as "the solid rock." Those seeking a conservative and affirmative approach to Christian faith will most likely join one of these groups. But there remain within mainline ministries those who, though not driven away, are at least uncomfortable with its questioning nature. These people will often be "moderates" who are not quite conservative enough to belong to an evangelical group but not quite as liberal as most campus ministers.

There is not much vocal opposition in EC to the ministry's approach to faith because those most bothered by it either have left the group or have marginal involvement in it. But at least a few active members have quietly expressed dissatisfaction. One person I talked with complained, "The church seems to be trying more to question and shake my beliefs than to strengthen them and build them up." He also accused the church of having a "watered-down" version of the gospel and of failing to hold up biblical principles for members to believe.

Others in the group resented the chaplains' assumption that those in the ministry have an unexamined or transitional faith. Several people maintained that their adult faith (one they claimed for themselves) began several years earlier with confirmation, the church's rite conferring adult religious status. The chaplains should recognize this, they argue, rather than assuming that all young adults have a less-than-mature faith.

In fairness to the chaplains, it must be acknowledged that even if young adults have committed themselves to a particular faith, the details of what this faith means in practice have yet to be worked out. It is possible that those who believe that they have achieved a mature faith may be in the midst of a transition that will become apparent to them only in hindsight. And individuals at any stage in their faith journey can continue to learn from asking questions and listening to other people's perspectives.

The ministry has yet to resolve this issue because those uncomfortable with the chaplains' approach have not spoken up. But, assuming the issue is raised, a satisfactory solution will depend on the chaplains' ability to strike a balance between questioning and affirming faith, and the ability to encourage young people to grow in faith while respecting the growth they have already achieved. One possible stategy toward these ends would be to have different small groups taking different approaches to ministry, with some oriented toward questioning and others toward affirmation. Alternatively, the chaplains could give "equal time" to different concerns during the small-group meetings.

Once again, it is clear that the success of the ministry depends on its ability to encompass diverse people and still manage to find sufficient common ground to hold together as a group. But if one threat to group unity is separation into factions, a second is an individualism that sees the community as superfluous.

The Group and the Individual

Many observers of American society, beginning with Tocqueville in the nineteenth century, have taken note of Americans' high degree of individualism. In *Habits of the Heart* (1985), Robert Bellah and his colleagues argue that Americans' primary moral vocabulary (their "first language") is that of utilitarian and expressive individualism, a vocabulary which makes it difficult for people to articulate commitments to each other and to the public good.

In the sphere of the church, individualism manifests itself in the form of religious privatization, the tendency to see oneself as having a direct relationship to God unmediated and unsupported by religious community. In *American Mainline Religion* (1987), Wade Clark Roof and William McKinney describe this phenomenon:

> Custom and tradition play less of a role in shaping what an individual believes; religious feelings and meanings become, or can become, more a matter of choice and preference. Privatized faith is subjective, often concerned more with style than with substance, and more with sensibility and taste than with shared meanings and shared realities (33).

This tendency presents a clear challenge to the churches whose biblical and liturgical traditions emphasize the union of individual believers in one body.

263

Although all denominations in the United States are affected to some degree by privatization, those most affected are what Roof and McKinney call the "liberal Protestant" churches, including the Episcopal Church. Concerning these, they write,

> Drawing off upper-middle-class constituencies, their clienteles are the most exposed to the currents of modern individualism and the pursuit of self-fulfillment. Boundaries between the religious community and the larger culture are often vague, and commitment to the church as a gathered community of believers in which faith is shaped and nurtured is noticeably lacking (87).

The problem is especially acute for campus ministries. For if Americans are individualistic in general, they are even more so during young adulthood, when they are consumed with the task of working out their identity and carving out a niche for themselves in the world. It is not surprising, therefore, that in EC there is a tension between individualism and the communitarian tendency of the group. Individualism, religious and otherwise, was a topic that regularly came up in conversations with EC members.

Perhaps the tension between individualism and community identity can best be illustrated by looking at portions of an interview I had with one particular member. Candice has been an active member of the ministry for several years, and participates regularly in both Wednesday-night meetings and the women's group. She explained that she first became serious about her faith as the result of a "semi-conversion" experience that she had at an Episcopal conference she attended while in high school. She related that this experience put her in touch with "both personal spirituality and community spirituality." She was involved in church groups while she was in high school and subsequently became involved in EC. Assessing these experiences, she told me, "I have found Christian small groups very good for me in dealing with my faith and myself."

These comments seem to indicate that Candice has a good understanding of the importance of community in Christian faith. But further questioning revealed a different, more individualistic perspective. I asked her if she thought she could practice her Christian faith alone, apart from any church or group. She responded, "Yes, particularly my personal brand. A lot of times I tend to be a lot more mystic about my Christianity than I am institutional."

I asked if this didn't contradict her previous statements about the importance of groups. She paused for a minute before responding. "I guess . . . I don't know if I could practice my Christianity alone because a lot of it comes from group activity and fellowship." Finally, she brought the individual and communal aspects of faith into a dialectic relationship: "There is continually personal faith going on, but always built up and helped out and clarified by other people."

Some others in the group were much less qualified in their individualism. Another active member, when asked if she could practice her faith alone, responded, "I think that theoretically I could and ideally you should be able to just have this personal relationship with God, and you should be able to go to a mountain with your Bible and be okay. . . . But for most people, they need the support of the church."[6] Another person in the group went so far as to compare the role of the church to that of a study group which helps an individual prepare for a test. Both of these people expressed the idea that the church's role is to help "weak" individuals who do not have the discipline to maintain their faith on their own.

My argument is not that the members of EC are merely self-interested or unwilling to care for others. Indeed, some of the most individualistic rhetoric came from members of the women's group, which, as we have seen, involves high levels of commitment. Rather, my point is that those involved in the ministry seem unable to articulate the basis of their commitments to each other or even, on occasion, to give reasons why the ministry should exist at all.

The best course of action for a group like EC would simply be to have the members discuss together their understanding of what it means to be a fellowship in light of the biblical and liturgical traditions of the church, and how a group can be cohesive and still respect diversity. As the co-authors of *Habits of the Heart* argue, individualism and group commitment are not mutually exclusive; rather, "a strong group that respects individual differences will strengthen autonomy as well as solidarity" (1985, 307). A campus ministry that can bring about this understanding will help not only itself but also its denomination in the future.

6. Another member answered the question using almost identical language: "I think you can go sit on a rock with your Bible and be okay." Apparently this is a commonly held image.

Two Modes of Ministry

At several points I have already mentioned that mainline denominational groups exist beside evangelical groups that provide an alternative for those seeking a more conservative religious environment. But this has not always been the case. A few decades ago, a much different situation existed on college campuses. At the time of Kenneth Underwood's study in the 1960s, campus ministry at non-church-affiliated colleges was being performed almost exclusively by the denominations. Since then, the denominational campus ministry has been equaled if not surpassed in popularity by the ministries of evangelical parachurch organizations. Two of the leading organizations of this type are InterVarsity Christian Fellowship and Campus Crusade for Christ, both of which are experiencing rapid growth on many campuses.

Relations between the evangelical and the denominational groups have often been tense, sometimes even hostile. The evangelicals accuse the denominational ministries of being more concerned with intellectual exercises than with proclaiming the gospel. Denominational ministries, disturbed by the swelling ranks of the evangelical groups, accuse them of using slick recruitment techniques, of obscuring the ambiguity of religious beliefs by speaking in absolutes, and of generally lacking intellectual and theological rigor. Some of the tension can be traced to competition for members, though most of it can probably be attributed to the general ill will between liberal and conservative Christians in American society (Wuthnow 1989, 22-23).

For our present purposes, it is important to understand how differences in the mission and general ethos of the two types of ministries translates into differences in their use of small groups and how features of the Episcopal Chaplaincy can be understood in light of this classification. The discussion that follows is general and, like all generalizations, does not do justice to the diversity of individual cases. There are likely to be major differences between, for instance, a Presbyterian and a Baptist ministry, and evangelical organizations range from having fundamentalist to more moderate orientations. However, this discussion highlights some patterns common to the two types of ministry.

The denominational campus ministries have the obvious function of representing their denominations on campus and providing those students who wish to continue in their denominational tradition with the means for doing so. But denominational campus ministry tends to attract "unorthodox" clergy who are rarely interested in being apologists for their denominations (Hammond 1966, 42-48). As the chaplains of EC illustrate, most campus ministers are not primarily interested in drawing members to their particular tradition, or even of retaining those members presently in it. Rather, their primary concern is helping students explore spiritual issues and move toward their adult faith, even if this means changing religious affiliations. The ministries' understanding of faith is "subjectivist"[7] — that is, each individual must find his or her own religious truth. Denominational campus ministers thus encourage students to ask "difficult questions" about religion without presuming that there will always be answers.

In contrast to their denominational counterparts, evangelical parachurch groups do not serve any particular church but seek to advance the cause of evangelical Christianity in general. As the term "parachurch" implies, their purpose is not to replace the churches but to serve them by producing mature evangelical Christians. But the absence of denominational ties does not translate into a freer agenda. On the contrary, these organizations operate with specific objectives, the primary one being evangelism.[8] Additionally, evangelical organizations are concerned with "discipleship" — that is, helping young Christians mature in their faith through prayer, Bible study, and other activities. The two objectives are not unrelated, for witnessing to nonbelievers is seen as an important means of deepening one's faith. These organizations adhere to strict doctrinal statements affirming the infallibility (or inerrancy) of the Bible and the divinity and atoning death of Christ. The statements are taken with utmost seriousness, because false doctrine is seen as a danger to the ministry.[9]

7. The "liberal" campus minister's view of religious truth is similar to the neo-orthodox position described by Hunter: "It is only when the individual reads or hears the Scriptures through the eyes of faith that the text becomes the Word of God. . . . [T]he meaning of a text or a story would necessarily vary for each believer since everyone would be approaching the Bible from a different life situation" (Hunter 1987, 26). The "liberal" perspective differs from the neo-orthodox in that the Bible is not considered the sole authority for religious faith.

8. As Campus Crusade founder Bill Bright argues, "Our priority commitment as Christians must be to disciple and evangelize in obedience to our Lord's command" (Bright 1985, 250).

9. A recent history of InterVarsity, written by two of its staff members, blames the decline of twentieth-century Christian student movements on the spread of "liberal" doctrine among campus ministers. They warn their contemporaries, "Un-

If the denominational ministry's approach to religion can be described as inquisitive, the evangelical ministry's approach is declarative. This is related to the "objectivist" nature of evangelical theology, in which the Bible is regarded as the source of ultimate truth (Hunter 1987, 27). Both InterVarsity and Campus Crusade place a heavy emphasis on apologetics, and each organization employs at least one traveling evangelist who visits college campuses to make the case for Christianity. These ministries thus encourage students to ask difficult questions about Christianity, but with the assurance that they can provide (at least some) satisfactory answers.[10]

Finally, the two types of ministries tend to have different attitudes toward the relative importance of social justice issues and activism on behalf of these issues. Mainline denominational ministries have typically been sympathetic to campus activists and their causes. During the 1960s, many campus ministers engaged in antiwar protests and developed good relations with the countercultural elements on their campuses (Hargrove 1976, 211-13). More recently, campus ministers were among the few voices of opposition to the Persian Gulf War, and they continue calls for a society purged of racism and sexism.

The evangelical ministries, while embracing a range of views on activism, tend to emphasize changing individuals rather than social structures. As Bill Bright, the founder of Campus Crusade, argues, "The most important way to solve our social ills is to change the hearts of men by introducing them to our Lord Jesus Christ" (Bright 1985, 252). InterVarsity took a strong stand on the issue of social activism at its 1970 Urbana missions conference. A delegation of black students wanted to change the emphasis of the conference from missions to addressing the social issues of racism and poverty in the inner city. But David Howard, the

---

swerving loyalty to an unambiguous biblical theology is crucial. Otherwise it could be said of us that 'The reason we do not learn from history is because we are not the people who learned the last time'" (Hunt and Hunt 1991, 55). Clearly, this historical analysis is also meant as a critique of current mainline campus ministers.

10. This attitude is illustrated by two popular apologetic works: Cliff Knechtle's *Give Me an Answer that Satisfies My Heart and My Mind* (1986) and Josh McDowell's *Answers to Tough Questions Sceptics Ask about the Christian Faith* (1980), published by InterVarsity and Campus Crusade respectively. Both Knechtle and McDowell, with their frequent references to the "evidence" supporting Christianity, display the rational, empiricist cognitive style that Hunter (1983) argues is typical of contemporary evangelicalism.

keynote speaker, had recently completed a book on the Student Volunteer Movement in which he argued that the movement's decline was a result of its departure from an evangelical emphasis. The InterVarsity leaders decided to retain the emphasis on missions, thus demonstrating that evangelism rather than social justice was their primary concern (Hunt and Hunt 1991, 276).

The differences in orientation between evangelical and mainline denominational ministries result in differences in how prominently the Bible figures in fellowship and the structure and function of small groups. For evangelicals, Bible studies are the principal type of small group. In addition to providing fellowship and instruction for group members, these Bible studies usually are meant to aid evangelism by providing nonbelievers with a setting for exploring "the truth" proclaimed in the Bible (Hunt and Hunt 1991, 250). For many mainline campus ministries, by contrast, the Bible figures less prominently — or hardly at all — in their small groups. EC is typical of the latter case. Members of the ministry have periodically attempted to start Bible studies, but these groups have always collapsed from lack of interest. And while discussions at both Wednesday-night meetings and the women's group often involve reference to the Bible, neither group resembles a Bible study as it is usually conceived.

There are not only quantitative differences in the ministries' use of the Bible but qualitative differences as well. For evangelical groups, the Bible is the infallible Word of God. Accordingly, discussion concerns the proper way to interpret and apply a biblical text. Questioning the veracity of the text itself, while permitted for those yet uncommitted to Christianity, is considered out of bounds for regular members and may provoke group sanction. When the group does deal with a non-Christian, the assumption is that if the person is persistent in asking questions, he or she will eventually discover the truth of biblical Christianity (although the conversion process is ultimately attributed to the action of God rather than to persuasive arguments).

The approach that mainline denominational groups take toward the Bible varies, but for most, inerrancy is not assumed. Among these groups one is more likely to see criticism (both scholarly and otherwise) of the Bible and the expression of unorthodox opinions by members; this was the case during Wednesday-night discussions in EC. This is not to say that more orthodox forms of Christianity will be without defenders, but that people holding different views are free to voice their opinions without fear of group sanction.

Additional differences between evangelical and denominational ministries exist in the way groups of each type formulate their mission to the campus. For the evangelical group, the members' primary task is evangelism, or "outreach" as it is often called. The group's commission —in keeping with the Great Commission—is to bring the gospel to the campus community and make new disciples for Christ. Members are encouraged to invite their friends to group meetings, which they try to make receptive to outsiders. Often an evangelical group will have specific outreach weeks during which it makes a concentrated effort to evangelize the campus.

The denominational campus ministries also see themselves as fulfilling a mission on the campus. They seek to be a prophetic voice in an otherwise secular environment, confronting the university with the challenge of Christianity (Hammond 1966, 9). It is not unusual for these groups to participate in campus demonstrations regarding political or social issues or to engage in other types of social action. On the day-to-day level, however, these ministries are probably more concerned with helping those inside the group than those outside it. Although newcomers are always welcomed and people regularly invite their friends to group meetings, these groups do not seek out new members in the systematic manner characteristic of evangelical groups.

Finally, there are likely to be differences in the level of social cohesion found in each type of group. This stems from the different ways in which the groups function to support religious beliefs within the secular, pluralistic environment of the university—that is, to act as "plausibility structures" for Christianity. In *The Sacred Canopy*, Peter Berger argues that a religious institution which finds itself in the position of a "cognitive minority" within a pluralistic environment has two options:

> They can either accommodate themselves to the situation, play the pluralistic game of religious free enterprise . . . or they can refuse to accommodate themselves, entrench themselves behind whatever socio-religious structures they can maintain or construct, and continue to profess the old objectivities as much as possible as if nothing had happened (Berger 1967, 153).

These are only ideal types, and they are meant to apply to religious institutions within an entire culture rather than a university "subculture." Yet Berger's description sheds light on the character of campus ministries, with the denominational ministries coming closer to the former option and evangelical ministries coming closer to the latter.

There are different forms of "social engineering" associated with each type of strategy. In general, the closer a group is to the second option (entrenchment), the higher its level of social cohesion will be (Berger 1967, 164). This tends to be the option of evangelical campus groups, and the consequent higher level of social cohesion produces several differences between its groups and mainline denominational ones: group members spend more time with each other, more of their friends belong to the group, and membership entails higher levels of commitment to the group and its goals. Evangelical group members are also more aware of the boundary separating them from those who do not share their beliefs, a boundary signified by the frequent use of the term "non-Christian" to describe people and concepts outside of the evangelical milieu. Finally, the entrenchment orientation helps explain the evangelicals' enthusiasm for apologetics, which serves the double function of helping convert those outside the group and helping maintain the beliefs of those inside it (Berger 1967, 50).[11]

Perhaps the difference in orientation described above is best illustrated by comparing EC with an evangelical ministry I observed at length, both of which on separate occasions gave a presentation of the controversial movie *The Last Temptation of Christ.* Although each group chose to show the same movie, each had decidedly different objectives. EC showed the film, appropriately enough, as part of its celebration of Holy Week. The purpose of the event was to provide a "fellowship" activity and generate some interesting discussion. A small group of the ministry's members gathered to watch the movie and afterwards dis-

---

11. In a study of evangelical college students, Phillip Hammond and James Davison Hunter found that those attending evangelical colleges experienced a slow erosion of their beliefs, while those on a secular campus developed even more strongly evangelical beliefs. In explaining the latter case, they argue, "Mere recognition of the minority status of one's convictions relative to competing perspectives may ... foster a 'fortress mentality' among those determined to maintain the integrity of their worldview. ... In this situation, the believer's identity *qua* believer is accentuated and reinforced; one' worldview is annealed" (Hammond and Hunter 1984, 232-33).

This "fortress mentality" was notably lacking in EC. None of the members I talked with found the university a difficult place to practice their faith, and attacks on their beliefs by professors and fellow students were minimal.

cussed its theological implications. Although not everyone agreed with all the movie had to say, people were at least receptive to its message.

The evangelical ministry that showed the movie took a different approach. The event was organized by one of the ministry's Bible study groups that was concluding a yearlong study of the Gospel of Mark. The event, like many of the ministry's activities, was oriented toward evangelism. Group members invited their non-Christian friends to the movie and then, at a later time, discussed with them how the film's Jesus differed from the "real" (i.e., New Testament) Jesus. These discussions were meant to get the members' friends to think about who Jesus was and eventually to "make a decision" whether or not to follow him. The movie's viewpoint, judged to be in obvious conflict with the Bible, was not seriously engaged.

From the very different treatment each of the ministries gave the movie, we can see some of the aforementioned features of each. The evangelical ministry demonstrated its concern for evangelistic outreach, while the mainline ministry showed a more inward focus. The evangelical ministry's approach underscored its "objectivist" theology, in which the Bible serves as the absolute standard of truth, while the mainline ministry's approach underscored its "subjectivist" theology, which tolerates a plurality of views. Finally, the evangelical ministry's approach served to dramatize symbolic boundaries — Christian versus non-Christian, orthodox versus heretical, and church versus world, while the mainline ministry's approach left all such boundaries blurred.

In summary, the mainline denominational campus ministry can be described as pluralistic and more interested in helping individuals explore religious issues than in asserting religious claims. The evangelical ministries, by contrast, are based on the Bible as infallible truth and seek to proclaim this truth on campus, trying to bring "unbelievers" to conversion and strengthening the faith of those already in the fold. The differences in purpose and orientation are seen in the different ways these ministries utilize small groups. Mainline denominational ministries offer students a context for asking questions about faith and a liberal doctrinal approach, while evangelical ministries offer the affirmation of faith and a conservative doctrinal approach.

Although on some campuses the two types of ministries have developed unhealthy rivalries, in general their co-existence best serves the interests of students, ensuring that different religious options are available to meet different needs. And although this kind of competition has its downside, it at least forces ministries to be responsive to the needs of students lest they find their members have all gone elsewhere.

Conclusion

This case study of the Episcopal Chaplaincy demonstrates some of the ways in which a campus ministry can use small groups to nurture its members' spirituality. One such way is by having discussions of issues relevant to students' religious lives. Both the Wednesday-night meetings and the women's group meetings feature such discussions. They allow members to ask difficult questions, hear other people's perspectives, and, in the process, to come to a more mature understanding of their faith.

Small groups can also nurture spirituality through worship and meditation. Whether taking the form of an informal Eucharist service or an opportunity for quiet reflection, these provide a "pause" from the world of practical activity, a pause necessary for personal growth. As Sharon Parks argues in *The Critical Years*, "The modern academy had its genesis in the contemplative monastic tradition, but we have in large measure lost the essence of our heritage through our inattention to the power of pause. . . . Although the academy engenders a good deal of conscious conflict, it often fails to allow the pause so necessary to the gestation of new images and insight" (1986, 145-46). The opportunities for worship and meditation provided by small groups allow for the reflection on the sacred missing from contemporary university life.

A third way small groups can nurture spirituality is by providing a supportive environment where members can safely share their fears and vulnerabilities. This is illustrated by the women's group started by EC. In that context, members feel safe sharing the difficulties associated with being female in the male-oriented worlds of church and university and, through sharing, are able to forge a positive self-identity.

The Episcopal Chaplaincy also demonstrates that conflict, whether personal or theological, is a normal part of the life of a ministry. In almost any small group, one is likely to find differences of opinion. A successful small group must find ways of turning these differences into an asset rather than a liability. This involves fostering respect for all points of view and emphasizing members' commonalities more than their differences. EC has made some progress in this area, but the long-term stability of the ministry depends on the chaplains' ability to address the needs and concerns of conservative members. Failure to do so could result in some members leaving, which would mean a loss of ideas and perspectives as well as "numbers."

I have described how EC's approach to ministry is influenced by its affiliation with a mainline Protestant denomination, and how campus ministries associated with evangelical organizations operate in a much different manner. The challenge ahead for both types of ministries is to overcome the mutual suspicion that (on many campuses) separates them, replacing name-calling with constructive dialogue. These conversations would dispel the various myths each side has of the other and, by forcing mainline liberals and evangelicals to articulate their positions, would reveal the implicit assumptions behind each side's view. Most importantly, dialogue would perhaps make both sides realize that they have significant goals in common: to nurture students' spiritual lives and to challenge the prevailing secularism of the university.

Finally, there is the question of what implications the activities of campus ministries have for their denominations. Those concerned about the unfettered questioning that many campus ministers encourage should be comforted by the fact that almost all the members I talked to — even conservative critics of the chaplains — felt that their experience in EC made them more likely to continue in their denominational tradition. Moreover, young adults who have engaged in discussions of difficult theological and social issues will become more thoughtful adult members of churches that themselves are grappling with thorny issues. And from their encounters with "radical" campus ministers, students can take with them a critique of where the church is and a vision of where it can go in the future.

Jesus and Self in Everyday Life: Individual Spirituality through a Small Group in a Large Church

GEORGE M. THOMAS AND DOUGLAS S. JARDINE

Driving home tonight, I realized that over the six months [I had attended,] this group had become a family to me. I knew my life would be emptier now. What I had gained, and was now losing, was this special group of people who really seemed to be able to love God and love their neighbors; and I had been a recipient of this love. In their farewell card, the leaders had said, "Thanking God for you. . . . May you be richly blessed as you walk with the Lord." And I *had* been blessed — and inspired — even though my "walk" was different from theirs. [Jardine's field notes, last meeting]

How do people in a large evangelical church pursue spirituality in their everyday lives through a small group? How do people who would be labeled broadly as evangelicals pursue a personal relationship with Jesus through participation in their small group? This is a case study of "Lars' and Ann's First Group," based on in-depth personal interviews and participant observation in twenty-four of the group's twenty-nine weekly meetings. We use the group members' practices, what they said to each other, and what they said to us in interviews

---

This study is dedicated to those involved in small groups at Desert Evangelical Church. We especially wish to thank Pastor Dave and the members of Lars' and Ann's group, who welcomed us into their midst.

to present many of the particulars of the group and to discuss a number of patterns and themes, including (1) how people in the group worked out their understandings of individual spirituality, (2) how individuals expressed themselves within the context of biblical truth, and (3) how praying, sharing, and the telling of stories made God more real to them in their everyday lives.

People joined this group and remained committed to it because of their understanding of what it means to be a spiritual Christian. Their understanding of spirituality was a complex integration of individual spirituality and group spirituality informed by the concept of "walking worthy with God." Members also attained a level of intimacy within the group that they regarded as deep and sincere. It felt very much like a family or other primary group, with little conflict manifested at the meetings.

As evangelicals,[1] their final authority was the Bible. They also saw the head pastor as having great expertise and authority, and they held implicitly to absolute truths. Nevertheless, within these boundaries, members tolerated — if they did not always appreciate — differences in each other's opinions, and they manifested a markedly high degree of tolerance for ambiguity and unresolved questions. Documenting this "bounded subjectivity" at the personal level gives an innovative view of evangelicals and their spirituality.

The content and style of members' sharing, requests for prayer, telling of personal stories, and praying together focused on Jesus' presence in all aspects of their lives — their relationships, their work, their health. Through these activities, they brought all areas of their everyday lives into their relationship with God. They attributed the source of their spiritual growth to their relationship with God, but they saw the group as playing a significant role. Within this context, there was little organized outside activity — neither their getting together socially nor their pursuing political and social causes. Each member seemed to assume that the others were involved in the world in their own ways.

In this essay, we first describe the function of small groups at

---

1. Nearly all of the people we talked to balked at labels such as "fundamentalist" and "evangelical" and even "born-again" because they thought such terminology hindered others from understanding Christianity. They preferred to be called just "Christian" or "Bible-believing Christian."

"Desert Evangelical Church."[2] Next we explain how Lars' and Ann's group developed and describe a typical meeting. Finally we analyze the characteristics and dynamics of this group.

Small Groups in a Large Church

Lars' and Ann's first group was part of the small-group ministry of Desert Evangelical Church, a rapidly growing, 3000-member evangelical church located in a large southwestern city. A detailed welcome packet designed for new attenders explains that the goal of the adult ministry "is to help everyone involved with our Church to find a group to which they can belong and a place where they can serve. We have found that when people are committed to these two areas, they tend to be healthy, growing Christians." The small-group ministry is a well-worked-out program, involving approximately 1,500 people in about 120 groups of varying sizes. It is headed by Pastor Dave, one of nine associate pastors at the church. He typically screens and trains all group leaders and coordinates formation of the groups.

The small-group ministry is designed to achieve three basic goals. First, a small group is meant to provide close, weekly contact among the church attenders — to "make the big church small." Second, it is meant to "edify and strengthen Christians in their walk with the Lord" — or, as group members and church officials often say, to help them "walk worthy [of having been saved by Jesus]." The third goal is to identify and begin training couples who can lead groups of their own. Perhaps the most succinct statement of purpose came from Pastor Dave: "A person in a small group is going to be growing, more like Christ would have them grow, than if he wasn't in that group. God designed us to be in a group like that of some sort." He elaborated, "In our society, it happens to be a Christ-centered small group of ten to twenty that meets in a home."

At Desert Evangelical, midweek groups fall into one of two categories: First Groups and Home Fellowships.[3] Home Fellowships are

2. We have changed the names of the church, of all individuals, and of identifiable programs. All other information is factual. Undocumented quotes are from church publications, including bulletins, pamphlets, and newsletters.
3. Sunday groups at Desert Evangelical include one-time Welcome Classes for newcomers, six-week Membership Groups to prepare attenders for full voting

groups of twelve to twenty people that provide a continuing "opportunity to be more deeply involved in the Word and in each other's lives." These groups meet weekly in members' homes. While they usually have no official life span, Home Fellowships tend to last about a year.

Before joining a Home Fellowship, people usually join one of the so-called First Groups, such as Lars' and Ann's. The purpose of a First Group is to provide people with a short-term small-group experience with the hope that they will then move on to a Home Fellowship group, which is longer term. First Groups are defined as "twelve-week discussion-oriented Bible Studies designed to discuss the previous Sunday's sermon."[4] When a first group completes its term, it may decide to extend its meetings, its participants may join a Home Fellowship, or its participants might be selected as candidates for leadership training with the goal that they will eventually start groups of their own.

Group Leadership

Pastor Dave said that the secret to the consistent success of the groups is carefully recruiting leaders, offering a clear and consistent statement of doctrine at all levels of the church, and then displaying trust that the leaders will do a good job. "When I recruit," he explains, "I don't throw out a blanket and let everyone come in. In that sense, I'm very controlled. I'm responsible . . . to the elders here at the church for what goes on in these groups — because we're a church and because there

---

membership, and ongoing Enrichment Classes (which have from 25 to 100 members) designed "for fellowship, growth and to minister to each other in a casual atmosphere"; often a given class is aimed at a homogeneous group (e.g., young marrieds, empty nesters, or single adults). In all of the Sunday classes, attenders are encouraged to join one or more of the small midweek groups. In addition to Sunday and midweek groups, Desert Evangelical attenders may also participate in accountability and/or support groups focused on specific topics such as grieving, addictions, parenting issues, and financial difficulties.

4. At Desert Evangelical, the pastor will typically preach a long series of sermons focusing on a single book of the Bible. Thus, in studying the sermons for a twelve-week period, members conduct an in-depth study of a particular book. In the case of Lars' and Ann's group, this was a book in the New Testament, and except for some special readings prior to Christmas, all sermon discussions focused on that book.

is a doctrine that people have to agree to. Otherwise we're pretty loose in our leadership."[5]

Lars and Ann, like almost all the group leaders at Desert Evangelical, were provisionally selected by Pastor Dave based on the recommendation of the leader of a previous group they had participated in. They were then trained for three ninety-minute sessions held during a three-week period. Subjects included the dynamics of a Bible-study group, leadership methods, what to do in difficult situations, how to start a group, and how to keep it going.[6] After they were trained, Pastor Dave decided that the couple would make a good leadership team, and said that Lars could lead a group.[7] In separate interviews, both Lars and Ann reported that the leadership role was initially uncomfortable for him. When asked about the possibility of coleadership in the group, Ann said unequivocally that Lars was the leader. After some prodding, she did acknowledge that she had special functions in the group. Among them were using her teaching background to help Lars and keeping track of prayer requests.

After their group began, the church made available to Lars and Ann "motivational and nurturing" meetings about once a month. Pastor Dave also touched base with Lars two times to see if there were any problems in the group. There weren't.

Pathways to Group Membership

At Desert Evangelical, it is easy for a person to join a group. Small-group membership is routinely advocated by the pastors in sermons, by example

---

5. Jardine saw clear evidence of the trust placed in leaders. Pastor Dave said he had talked to Lars only once before Jardine joined the group and only twice during the six months of his participation, even though there was presumably some sensitivity about Jardine's role in the group.

6. The leadership training program included materials designed by Pastor Dave. At the time of Lars' and Ann's training, he was also using several well-known books: Lyman Coleman's *Serendipity Training Manual for Groups* (Littleton, Colo.: Serendipity House, 1987); Robert E. Coleman's *The Master Plan of Evangelism with Study Guide by Roy J. Fish* (Tarrytown, N.Y.: Fleming H. Revell, 1963); and Carl F. George's *Prepare Your Church for the Future* (Tarrytown, N.Y.: Fleming H. Revell, 1991).

7. At Desert Evangelical, men exclusively fill the positions of leadership. All ten pastors are men, as are all other leaders, except in women's groups.

(the senior pastor and most of the nine associate pastors are themselves in small groups), by regular articles in the church's newsletter, by prominent mention in the Sunday bulletin, by descriptions in at least three different brochures, and by the staff of an information booth.

Smooth "entry paths" are provided to lead the less involved into fuller involvement via a group. As Pastor Dave explains, "It has to be easy for them. You've got to be able to move people from point A to point B. If we believe that small-group participation is something we want them to do, then we have to walk them through it." He went on to summarize, "So a person is going to get it from every single direction."[8]

People desiring to join a group fill out a card and place it in the Sunday-morning offering plate. Names are then sorted by preferred meeting night, location, and general age group of prospects. A list of about twenty are given to new group leaders, who then contact them.

Assembling the Group

This description of the larger church organization and the consciously constructed pathways into small groups suggests a level of social engineering and control. Most of those in Lars' and Ann's group, however, experienced all of this as a well-organized facilitation of what they wanted to do in the first place.

Lars and Ann were given the names of about twenty people ranging in age from the mid-thirties to seventy years old. The couple then contacted them and invited them to the First Group they were forming. The result: eighteen individuals (eight couples and two single people) showed up the first night the group met. Over several weeks this evolved into a core group of twelve active members, plus the participant observer.[9]

8. To support the group-involvement effort further, Desert Evangelical does not schedule any major events on the midweek days when small groups meet.

9. Of the original eighteen, two couples, one single mother, and an unmarried woman attended the group a few times, then stopped coming. The single mother said she needed to be with her teenage sons. The other single woman claimed excessive work and too long a drive. The wife in one of the couples who dropped out told Ann that her husband — who sat silently throughout the meeting — was not yet ready for a First Group. The other couple simply drifted away. One other woman (who was married to a Buddhist) dropped in for just one meeting, "to learn about Christianity." She was a co-worker of Ann's and had heard Ann talk about the group at the retail shop where they both were employed.

280

Excluding the first two and the last two meetings (when the participant observer was not in the group), attendance ranged from seven to ten.

The twelve core members ranged in age from the late thirties to the late sixties. Renee was Native American; the others were white.[10] There were five married couples and two widows. With the exception of the youngest couple (Hank and Amanda), all (including the participant observer) were parents. Three of the five couples were also grandparents. Of the men, one was self employed, two were managers for small local companies, one worked for a company that sells businesses, and one was a senior executive in a transnational firm. All of the women were employed in positions ranging from bookkeeper to retail clerk, with about half of them working full-time. Five members (including Lars and Ann) had four-year college degrees, six others had some college training, and one — one of the widows — was a high-school graduate with accounting training in a technical school.

As would be expected in First Groups, most of the regulars were fairly new to Desert Evangelical and had been part of the congregation for six months to less than two years. One couple, John and Joanie, was an exception, having belonged to the church for "four or five years." Joanie would have joined a group earlier, she said, except for John's reluctance.[11] They became the most regular attenders. Lars and Ann had belonged to the church for about six years.

Lars' and Ann's group began in the early nineties; it started in the fall and lasted through the following spring. The group met regularly on Tuesday nights from 7:15 to about 9:45 p.m. (meetings were called off twice because of holidays and once because of illness) — a total of 29 times. When the group was formed, the members agreed to attend twelve meetings, although there was a strong indication that they would go beyond that time frame. At about the thirteenth meeting, Lars told them that they had fulfilled their agreement. At that time they all said that they wanted to continue meeting as long as possible.

At the twenty-fifth meeting, Lars announced that the group would

---

10. Jardine was also within the age range of the group and was also white and middle class. Unlike the others, he had converted from being an Episcopalian to being a practicing Reform Jew, a fact he made known to everyone at his first meeting.

11. John's reason for joining the group was to support Joanie after she took the initiative to submit a membership card and promised that he could drop out after a few meetings if he wanted. As it turned out, he said he loved the group immediately.

be disbanding. He reminded the members that the purpose of such groups was to help participants "grow and go" (a popular phrase at Desert Evangelical). He added, "All of you have been recommended to Pastor Dave as qualified to lead groups of your own." The group ended four weeks later, with many members expressing interest in joining a new Home Fellowship group that Lars and Ann planned to start in the fall.

A Typical Tuesday Evening

We meet in the warm and inviting living room of Lars and Ann, a nicely furnished, two-bedroom 1,000-square-foot apartment at the top of a flight of exterior stairs. We start to arrive around 7:00 p.m., about 15 minutes before the group is scheduled to begin. I (Jardine, the participant observer) usually look forward to the drive to the meeting even though it takes about an hour. In these fall and winter months, I walk from the parking area up the stairs underneath a clear, starry sky. On the landing I look out at a beautiful desert landscape bounded by mountains — a view also visible through the large picture window in Lars' and Ann's apartment. When I climbed those stairs to attend the meetings just before Christmas, I could see the holiday decorations through the window. They reminded me of the warmth, family, and security waiting inside.

The living room itself radiates these feelings. Over the fireplace there is a large color photograph of the nineteen members of Lars' and Ann's extended family. During the meetings, when talk turns to sons, daughters, and grandchildren, Ann frequently points to the picture, identifying the child or grandchild being discussed. What one member says she noticed first about the room is that everything is warm but not pretentious. Many of the possessions are handmade, "reflecting the concerns of people who have moved beyond materialism," she says. The lighting is warm and indirect. At the three meetings just prior to Christmas, there was also an Advent candle. Ann or Lars would light this and place it on the table around which we sat. In the fall and winter months, there was the friendly glow of a small fire in the fireplace.

As members arrive, they greet each other warmly, shaking hands or hugging. Discussion turns to the preceding Sunday's service. People say good things about the church, so the conversation is almost always positive. There is much smiling. People take their accustomed seats, placing well-read Bibles (most of them leather-bound) on the round table in the center of our circle. The seats are arranged to be "friendly" but not too close. No one is left out. Lars has a big reclining chair, but he always offers it to someone, typifying the sharing within the group. Except for Lars and Ann, all the couples sit together; most hold hands sometime during the meeting.

Lars begins the meeting by suggesting a few moments' silence. Then Lars leads the opening prayer in a direct and warm manner, stressing the presence of Jesus in our midst. This shifts our focus from the concerns of the day to our fellowship.

After Lars' prayer, we briefly cover announcements and then discuss the senior pastor's sermon of the previous Sunday. One or more of us read aloud the passage from the New Testament that is the focus of the sermon. We discuss questions that Lars, sometimes with Ann's assistance, has formulated in advance. As the response to one question fades, Lars asks another. He also uses these questions to steer us back to the sermon, should the conversation start to stray from the applications of the sermon and Scripture in our lives.

With each meeting we have become increasingly likely to relate incidents from our lives to what is being discussed. This relating to the teaching becomes more personal — covering conflicts at work, worries about children, problem areas in individuals' walks with Jesus, and the like.

The most personal sharing, however, takes place during the next portion of the meeting — "praise and prayer." Lars initiates the transition at about ten minutes to nine; we see this coming because of his glances at his watch. Ann gets out her yellow legal pad and asks, "Are there any praises or prayer requests?" One member after another shares things they have thanked God for during the past week. One praises God for help in finding a new car at a favorable price, another for the birth of a grandchild, and another for the healing of a friend. Ann also inquires about the results of prayer requests from previous weeks. Besides offering praise, members ask for prayers for themselves, their family, their friends, and other members of the group.

"Conversational prayer" follows. We place our Bibles on the table, bow our heads, and join hands. Lars reminds us that anybody who wishes should join in with a single-sentence prayer. John typically begins with a full paragraph, followed by one and then another of us with much shorter prayers. When the pauses between prayers become longer, Lars expresses the group's gratitude to Jesus for having been with us that night

283

and for having died so that we might be saved. He ends with the words, "And all the church said . . ." And we reply, "Amen."

The meeting officially ends at about 9:15 p.m. The women serve nonalcoholic beverages, often hot, and pastries that each of us brings on a rotating basis. We cluster into smaller groups and continue our conversations, but we talk more about our everyday lives; we seldom mention Jesus, the church, and our spiritual walks.

Spirituality: Jesus, Self, and Others

Consider the common questions asked by sociologists, pastors, and small-group practitioners: What is the purpose of this group? Why do people join? How does it help them? For Lars' and Ann's group, the answers to all of these questions revolved around what we term "spirituality," but what the members talked about in terms of their relationship with Jesus.[12]

For them, spirituality was intensely personal. Joanie evaluated where she was spiritually by saying she had a "close personal relationship with the Lord." John said, "I really have a love for the Lord, and I know the Lord loves me." He also said he wants "to be closer to God." He distinguished this spirituality, as did others, from "religion," which they defined as dogma, rules, and regulations. Kathryn spoke of spirituality as believing God and the Bible without "having been there and not having seen it, to take it on faith." Frank recalled the intensity he had when he first became a Christian (an intensity he was hoping to regain): "I became a real on-fire Christian — insatiable in my study. I was really enjoying the Lord, the Bible, the teaching, and the fellowship."

On an equally personal level, Renee shared that she was struggling spiritually. She did not have a dramatic conversion experience, which she thought (erroneously) everyone else had had. Rather, she recalled, "The Lord had a special place for me, a long time ago. It was instilled in me as a child. God put it in me, and He is the only one that pulled me out of everything I went through. He was my friend." But at this

12. In speaking about their relationship to God, both in the meetings and during the interviews, group members used highly stylized, condensed, rich formulas such as "walking with the Lord." As with any concepts that one takes for granted, it was difficult for many to unpack the many nuanced meanings of these formulas, but nearly all were able to do so.

point Renee found herself questioning things a lot, and even though others told her it was simply a maturing process, she said that she "pine[d] for that feeling and that closeness, because it was blind faith and blind belief." To her, spirituality "just is the knowledge that there is a Supreme Being that made you, and that He filled you with the need for Him."

Group members referred to their relationship with God in terms of "walking with Him." Most did not relate much to the word *spirituality*. No one used the term *journey* to describe their relationship with God, and only two responded neutrally or favorably to it as a metaphor. As Ann put it, "*Journey* is too vague. If I'm walking, it's a little more right here and now." For group members, "walking" seemed to imply a personal closeness, a commonality of direction. It also required action. Essentially, walking with the Lord was being in a relationship that, like all relationships, required work. They believed that as Christians they had to continue to grow in order to maintain their relationship with Jesus. As Lars expressed it, "If you stop growing, you go backwards." It was never enough to maintain a spiritual status quo, and they all agreed that one had to keep encouraging that growth through actions, feelings, and beliefs. Or, in the language of the group, "The feeding of your spiritual life is an absolute necessity." One had to read the Bible, pray, fellowship with other Christians, and share the faith with others.

This dual notion of being in a relationship with Jesus and working on that relationship was captured in Desert Evangelical's exhortation to them to "walk worthy." Lynn described this as "walking in the image of Christ, being what the Lord wants us to be. Do the right things, be helpful to people — all those things that Christ was and that you should be."

Group members also spoke of their walk with God in terms of his presence. If one was walking with God, then God was present in one's life. They believed that Jesus was personally present at their meetings and was with them throughout the week. Accordingly, working on their relationship with the Lord meant acknowledging his presence. Lynn said that spirituality had to do with God's "influence, his presence." Joanie said, "I feel that Jesus is with me all of the time."

Thus, the way this group saw spirituality fell squarely within the evangelical understanding of spirituality as a very individual, personal relationship with God. Yet they also saw spirituality as involving a complex balance between the individual and others, as does broader evangelicalism. This became evident in the interviews. When members explained why they had been part of a small group or why they were part of Lars' and Ann's group, at some point each one stated that spiritual growth was impossible without the involvement of others. One could not walk with the Lord alone.

Hank and Amanda, both of whom had been Christians for about eight years, saw their recent experience as an example. Hank, in his late thirties, worked as a mid-level manager in a local firm and was enrolled in a program for Christian counselors; Amanda, in her mid-thirties, worked for a local manufacturing firm. Hank often mentioned the rocky years they had endured after being saved. They began to grow only after realizing the necessity of Christian fellowship. "It is not enough to be saved," Hank said. "You also have to get connected with a Christian church and to get involved with Christian groups. And we didn't do that. I think our life went awry because of that. I think that we have learned that it is very, very, very important to get connected."[13]

John, sixty-eight years old, was the son of a railroad engineer and a self-employed businessman. Known in the group for emphasizing individual responsibility, he nevertheless commented, "You need the [Christian] fellowship. You need somebody to gird you up, to lift you up, to support you in your ups and downs in life."

Fellowship is necessary to be accountable to others, and indeed, accountability was clearly an important purpose of the group, as indicated by Desert Evangelical's materials and by the discourse of the group. During a discussion of one of the sermons, for example, the group explained how a small group provided correction and constructive criticism. They all agreed that this ongoing correction was essential "if we are going to grow and be able to do God's work."[14]

---

13. Some members supplemented their "spiritual" reasons for joining with other reasons. Amanda said that she and Hank had joined because "we have a large church, and we wanted to get to know some people." Frank and Renee had moved to town just a few months before and said that they had joined the group to nurture their spiritual growth and to make new friends. Aside from Frank and Renee's move to the area, such events did not appear to play a part in joining. No one accounted for his or her views of spirituality or participation in the group by referring to recent crises or early family problems. This seems consistent with the sociological literature on joining behavior and conversion (Snow and Machalek 1984).

14. Their commitment to being involved with others for their spiritual health was evidenced by the fact that eleven of the twelve had been in small groups before. Moreover, they all were regular attenders of Desert Evangelical.

There was another, more fundamental way in which an individual's spirituality was intertwined with others. If an individual was growing in his or her walk with God, that meant that he or she was growing in relationships with others. Specifically, "to walk worthy" meant to love, serve, and care for others. Thus, it is likely (although this was not something specifically discussed in the meetings) that members did not envision a life of isolation, silence, and singularity as especially spiritual.

Members moved easily from talking about the necessity of their loving and caring to their receiving love and care from others in the group. They showed no false humility and made no attempts to appear sacrificial. Nor was loving and caring viewed as burdensome. They greatly appreciated receiving love and care and accepted it freely, especially when the caring involved spiritual or emotional (rather than physical) support. Although most said they had not expected to experience so much caring when they joined the group, all affirmed that this feeling of mutual caring was one of the main reasons they would participate in the group as long as it continued.

Mutual caring was shown in a variety of concrete ways, some obvious and many subtle. Prayer was a major vehicle. When someone asked the others to pray for something, they expressed support by nodding their heads, exchanging glances, and writing down the need on their weekly prayer lists. Someone would ask for more details, such as the full name of the person being prayed for or the location and time of a meeting or a scheduled surgery. One or more would offer this request during the conversational prayer. In addition, the group inquired about each other's needs and prayer requests in subsequent meetings. My own experience in making prayer requests was that the cumulative effects of the group's responses were very powerful. On the six or seven occasions when I made requests, I felt genuinely cared for.

So the group could be seen as a means to an end in the sense that others cared for the individual and helped him or her grow spiritually. Yet participation in the group was also a part of that personal process because growing spiritually, by the group's definition, meant helping and caring for each other.

The interplay between individual and group was rather complex. If we focus on what the individuals received from the group and on the group as a means to individual ends, it is tempting to conclude that the individuals in the group tended toward self-absorption and self-preoccupation. Yet, given their understanding of spirituality, this would be inaccurate. To say that the group was a means to individual ends is to say that it was a means by which individuals applied their Christianity to their everyday lives; participation in the group helped members to be more loving, patient, and caring with people outside the group. Thus, they probably would have been more self-absorbed if the goal of the group had been simply to care for themselves and each other. But that they were expected to apply what they learned to everyday life qualified and limited both the group and the self as ultimate ends.

It is important to note that there was some explicit discussion of self and self-worth in the group. One night, for example, the sermon being discussed was one in which the pastor had stressed that since we are created in God's image, and since he has a plan for each person, we have worth and are to be happy with ourselves. Yet during the discussion the group quickly moved from God's special plan for each person to how to serve the Lord at work. Moreover, there was little explicit use of the language of self-esteem in the group. In fact, only Hank (who was engaged in a training program for Christian counselors) regularly employed this vocabulary.

That the group was both the means and part of the ends was also reflected in the understanding of God's presence. Members in fact understood God to be present in their meetings in a special way, but the idea was never for individuals to strive after this as a kind of emotional experience, to use the group for this purpose. The emphasis instead was on a communal experience of God's presence. Yet this communal experience was also seen as something that could help members make God more real in their everyday lives.

Individuals came to the group already having experienced spiritual growth, but most of them felt that the group helped them sustain and further that growth, as their assessments of the group indicate. Joanie, for example, said, "I think the biggest thing is the fact that I now have a close, personal relationship with the Lord, whereas before, it was a nodding acquaintance. And I feel that He is with me all of the time." Yet nearly all members reported that the group was not the original source of their spiritual growth. Rather, they had for various reasons experienced that growth earlier — some as many as several years ago, some possibly more recently through their attending Desert Evangelical. For instance, in describing her greater closeness to God, Joanie said, "This has happened in the last couple of years. And I think it is even more so since I have been in the group." The members' decision to join a group was part of their closer walk with the Lord. The group helped them further something they had already begun. In this sense, their being in the group was the result of their spiritual growth as well as one of the reasons for their continued spiritual growth.

This complex interweaving of individual and others illustrates in some ways what Philip Hammond (1992) has referred to as increased personal autonomy. He documents a major trend in U.S. religion by showing how individual religiosity, once identified with the primary groups of family, neighborhood, ethnic group, and community, is now more and more a product of individual choice. Increasingly, individuals go to churches, conservative or liberal, in which they know no one from these primary groupings. Moreover, more people today tend to believe that belonging to a church is optional, that one can be spiritual without being part of a group. Clearly, the people in Lars' and Ann's group, like most of the conservative Christians in Hammond's sample, are exceptions to this latter trend. However, they exemplify the larger trend of individuals joining groups in which there is no one from any of their primary social groups, what Hammond calls "voluntary primary groups." These members show that such groups, at least within an evangelical context, can be associated with intense spirituality.

Truth and Self-Expression: Bounded Subjectivity

Lars' and Ann's group held the Bible to be absolute truth, ultimate authority. Scripture informed the language they used when they defined spirituality as a relationship with God, as "walking worthy with God," and as sensing God's presence, and it shaped the actual content of their spirituality. They spoke often of applying faith to daily life, and this seemed to mean applying Scripture to everyday experience. Both the members of the group and the members of Desert Evangelical Church at large shared a belief in what they perceived to be basic absolute biblical truths, from the Trinity to the deity of Jesus to salvation by faith to the exclusivity of salvation through Christ. But Scripture had more than doctrinal importance to them; they also valued having practical knowledge of Scripture and being able to apply it. For example, Frank explained that, in an effort to recapture his early spiritual intensity, he wanted to develop a "spiritual maturity" based on biblical knowledge "that would allow [him] to lead, to guide, to answer."

289

Group members tended to be suspicious of human authority, because they believed that the absolute authority of Scripture and the inspiration of the Holy Spirit relativized the pronouncements of humans. Yet at the same time they saw the pastors of their church as having authoritative expertise. Many praised the senior pastor for sticking closely to Scripture and for admitting that he might be wrong on certain points. Nevertheless, they referred to the senior pastor to authenticate an interpretation of Scripture. An often-repeated phrase at every meeting was "Yes, and as Pastor Ray said . . ." In fact, "Ray said . . ." became almost a drumbeat of authentication at all of the meetings. Thus, even though they acknowledged human limitation, the expert authority of the senior pastor combined with the ultimate authority of Scripture and an implicitly taken-for-granted set of truths provided them with a stock of verities and principles.

Within the group itself there was great tolerance for diverse opinions. This, we think, had two sources. First, all authority (Scripture) and authoritative expertise (pastors) were located outside the group. This fact, coupled with the general suspicion of human authority, provided a context for diverse opinions.

Second, and more important, the group placed great value on individual expression — including interpretations of Scripture and opinions on issues discussed. We discovered that one of the very significant ways in which group members manifested their caring for one another was by listening to each other's opinions and interpretations. One listened without correcting, for to correct would imply that one had greater authoritative knowledge than the other, or simply that the other's opinion (right or wrong) did not count. Lynn recounted a bad experience with a previous small group (she was the only one who had had a bad experience). She had been in a women's group in which two women had corrected the others and had acted as though they knew the definitive interpretation of Scripture. By contrast, she found Lars' and Ann's group to be much more caring and spiritually satisfying.

Just about all the members of the group felt that one of the greatest values of the group was that they could openly discuss Scripture. Several reported that they got more out of the small-group discussions of Pastor Ray's sermons than they had gotten when they had first heard them sitting in the pews. Frank said, "It's not very productive for me personally to simply go and listen to a sermon on Sunday." He explained that before he joined the group, he would "just drift through the rest of the week."

He continued, "I wanted to be in a group where I could continue study and thought." Joanie, who also contrasted discussion in the group with listening to a sermon, said that "with the group you're a part of it. You're discussing it along with them, so you get all of their thoughts, and then you reiterate your own thoughts." She reported being amazed that she would recall the exchanges in the group throughout the week, which would cause her to reflect on the issues that had been discussed.[15]

What we saw was that every individual was given the agency to interpret Scripture, but no single interpretation within the group was taken as authoritative. This resulted in a wide variety of opinions being expressed and frequent references to Pastor Ray as the external authority. These two results reflected a balance between the group's stock of truth and members' personal expression. One way to understand this is to see that the absolutes, rooted in Scripture and expert authority, established boundaries of unquestioned truths. Within those boundaries, individuals were free to explore diverse avenues and express their own opinions. In fact, expressing one's opinions was central to the group.

As a consequence, the group had a very high tolerance for unanswered questions. Different interpretations of a passage might be presented and different opinions offered. Some would in fact be the opposite of others. Someone likely would present what Pastor Ray had said or note what opinion he would agree with. But all of this would remain unresolved. In the course of discussions, a string of questions — some related to the topic and others tangential to it — would be introduced. Some would be ignored; others would be answered by a few and then dropped. From the comments that several group members made in interviews, the result was not confusion but an enlivening of the issues such that members were engaged with them all week. They were also reaffirmed by being allowed to express their opinions freely, without correction.

---

15. Despite the egalitarian spirit and practice, participation was influenced in part by social status. Men tended to be more dominant in the discussions than women. John emerged as a prominent participant in the group, probably because of his abilities to quote Scripture and tell stories. He was the most frequent talker in the group, and occasionally people would use humor to nudge him to give up the floor. Ray attended much less frequently, but he was afforded a level of influence rivaling John's because, as a senior executive in a large transnational firm, he had the highest occupational status of anyone in the group. Our self-imposed rule for Jardine's interaction with the group was for Jardine to participate slightly more than the person who participated least.

All of this suggests a high degree of relativity within the group. It also suggests that the group treated individual members as powerful and highly valued. The combination seemed effective in engaging people in the issues and getting them to think about spiritual issues throughout the week. Moreover, the internal relativity did not seem to threaten the external boundaries set by the implicit absolute truths.

Generally speaking, all groups will have the same structure, though it will vary tremendously from group to group. They will have some implicit taken-for-granted truths in the context of which individuals are free to disagree. Some groups will draw the boundaries fairly tightly, with a large number of truths possibly articulated into a highly specific truth system. Other groups will have internal authoritative expertise, so that while open discussion is allowed in theory, discourse is cut off when the specific truth is pronounced. (It is this type of group that Lynn complained about.) Other groups will have few if any absolute truths and no mechanism for arriving at authoritative agreements, resulting in a more pervasive relativity.

Lars' and Ann's group combined the strong taken-for-granted truth boundaries with the latitude that allowed all members to present their own opinions. What resulted was not a thoroughgoing relativity but a "bounded subjectivity." While the substance of the discussion was important, the value of the individual was also ceremonially dramatized and affirmed. In this group, the individual was perceived as being of great value and being entitled to self-expression, but also as someone who accepted certain fundamental truths, believed in the authority of Scripture, and was committed to an intimate relationship with Jesus. A thoroughgoing liberal might balk at the taken-for-granted truths; a more conservative evangelical might be concerned about the subjectivity and the tolerance of contradictions. Whatever the evaluation, here were evangelicals committed to certain authoritative truths who had a very high tolerance for ambiguity, complexity, disagreement, and open-endedness. They did not fit the stereotype of the closed-minded evangelical who has a psychological need to simplify all issues to black-and-white answers.

This bounded subjectivity sheds new light on the nature of conservative religion and on what is now known as the Kelley (1972) thesis. For some time now the question has been why conservative churches have grown more than liberal ones over the last twenty years. Kelley claims that conservative religion is strong because it is based on certain absolutes according to which claims on individuals can be made and around which individuals can organize their lives. Conversely, weak liberal forms of religion, which are relativistic because truth is defined by the individual, offer little collective truth to which individuals can be committed. In the context of Desert Evangelical Church in the early nineties, Lars' and Ann's small group was something of a mixture. The group exhibited an implicit commitment to collectively held truths and standards, but at the same time exhibited a tolerance of subjectivity regarding how the individual worked out this truth.

Enthusiasm and Tolerance

To draw together these different points, we can ask what traits distinguished the members of Lars' and Ann's group. Two principal ones come to mind. First of all, being part of the group meant pursuing a relationship with God. A member might not currently be "on fire for the Lord," but that was what he or she desired. Second, group members showed each other love and caring by letting everyone express himself or herself. Members showed each other a tolerant enthusiasm.

What type of person wouldn't have fit into the group very well? One group member answered, "Probably an atheist." Others responded with "a very argumentative person," "someone who was always right," "someone who would try to dominate the group," "those who were uncomfortable sharing," "someone not in touch with their spirituality," and "a negative-type person." In other words, someone who was intolerant or authoritarian, who had all of the answers, or who was unenthusiastic or lukewarm would not fit in.[16]

In this group, the tolerance of differences seemed to be associated with a desire to avoid conflict.[17] This desire was also apparent in the group's explicit avoidance of any discussion of doctrine. Applying Scripture to one's life certainly resulted in different expressions; discussing

16. Frequently they cited precisely these qualities, especially being lukewarm, to characterize those Christians not walking worthy and not involved in fellowships.

17. There were several disagreements within the group, some of them ongoing. There also were a few disagreements with the larger church over what would be considered nonessential issues. Lars, following his leadership training, "steered through conflict," bringing the discussion back to more agreed-upon practical applications of Scripture to everyday life.

doctrine, they believed, would just as certainly lead to arguments and conflict. For Lars' and Ann's group, unresolvable doctrinal debates characterized "religion," not walking with God.

A few thought the avoidance of conflict was related to the group's not discussing things as deeply as it might. One member said that up to that point he agreed with the group on most things. But, he added, "[we] haven't approached a lot of subjects that could cause divisiveness," and "we don't really get into a lot of in-depth discussion." He acknowledged that occasionally "we'll get into something and really hash it over, but it's still a little bit surface." He was holding out for the possibility that they would discuss some tougher issues; in about a year he thought it could be "a really wild group to be in."

Another member became a little more assertive and directive. He wanted the group to confront more directly the differences between members' lives and the teachings of the sermons. It struck us that these sentiments might have been on a collision course with the "tolerant enthusiasm" of the group, but the group disbanded without volatile incident.

The Spiritual in Everyday Life

The central purpose of the group was to have people grow spiritually in their everyday lives. To use the language of the group to express its goal, members were to walk worthy and acknowledge the presence and reality of God throughout the week in all areas of life. The group's definition of spirituality was ultimately taken from Scripture, based on the model of Jesus and others, the Ten Commandments, and various other commands and exhortations — those enjoining love, obedience, honesty, patience, and humility. Thus the focus of the group was on practical scriptural knowledge and application, not on doctrine or theology.

As they saw it, two sets of activities characterized daily spirituality. According to the group, those who practice such things are spiritual Christians; those who do not are lukewarm or nominal Christians. The first set of activities included the everyday practices of praying, reading the Bible, having fellowship with other Christians, and sharing one's faith or witnessing. The second set included working through problem areas in relationships, work, and health, where "working through" meant to "give the problem to the Lord" or to acknowledge one's limitations and trust things to God.

For these individuals, a significant part of the practice of fellowship included participating in the small group. Like the other practices of prayer and Bible reading, this was part of the weekly routine of walking with God. Group members believed that participation in the Tuesday-evening meetings gave the week a very different rhythm than if they had only weekly fellowship on Sunday mornings. Moreover, they felt that these practices reinforced each other. They also believed that participating in the group naturally led to heightened personal prayer, Bible study, and evangelism.

In addition, participating in the group provided an arena in which members could find help to work through problems and turn them over to God. This help took the forms of praying, sharing, and relating stories. Although it at first appeared that group members engaged in a stream-of-consciousness flow of prayer requests, praise offerings, stories, and the like, it subsequently became apparent that by acknowledging God's sovereign presence and their limited ability to accomplish spiritual goals, they were bringing all aspects of their lives into the frame of their relationship with God.

The topics and problem areas about which they prayed and shared had to do with relationships, work, and health — virtually every facet of their personal lives. In each area, "walking worthy" meant to work through the problem by turning it over to the Lord. Relationships dominated members' prayers and concerns. For example, both Lynn and Kathryn said they had asked Jesus to help them curb their tongues when dealing with their children. Lynn reported to the group that she had felt a great peace come over her when she had placed her maternal frustrations in Jesus' hands. Kathryn said that she had prayed for "tolerance and patience with the kids." Both Hank and Renee had turned to their faith to help them deal with contentious individuals they encountered in their work situations. Hank in particular felt that through these on-the-job conflicts he was being taught to turn his problems over to God. Hank believed he understood the process, though he frequently chided himself for not being willing to "let go and let God."[18]

18. Hank's understanding of giving problems to Jesus as "let go and let God" was one extreme found in the group. Invariably, John would say that we must make the effort to solve our problems ourselves. The rest of the group held to a moderate but firm notion of having to trust God.

Group members also shared and prayed about problems related to employment. On several occasions Lars reported that he was asking Jesus to give him guidance about whether or not he should change jobs. For Frank, the question was how he might be of greater service to the Lord in the job he currently held. Several members asked the others to pray for them when they felt they might possibly lose their job or their business.

Health was probably the single most frequent topic of prayer requests. Members asked for prayers regarding major surgeries, cancer, a bad back, the side effects of heart medicine, colds, and sore throats. As with other types of requests, many were for family members, friends, and people several times removed: a brother-in-law dying from leukemia, a nephew on dialysis, an unborn grandchild (that it would be healthy). That members included health problems which amounted to minor inconveniences underscored the fact that they believed that God was intimately interested in them, even in the smallest details of their lives.

The sharing of problems and prayer requests demonstrated a level of intimacy the group had, yet for the most part, group members shared safe things. True, there were certain notable occasions on which someone took a risk and shared something deeply emotional, and that sharing created a very special intimacy. But generally members tended to stick to things that did not require them to expose their very deepest emotions. Even in terms of personal problems, members shared things that would not be considered highly intimate — that they worried a lot, that they weren't sure what their spiritual gift was, that they lacked patience, or that they did not read the Bible or pray as often as they should.

While members used highly stylized formulas for problem-solving such as "give it to the Lord," they tended not to give easy answers to each other. In fact, members rarely gave advice to someone who shared or requested prayer for a problem. Apparently, to do so would have implied that one had greater wisdom, expertise, or authority, or that one was being judgmental. This approach assumed that the individual had a personal relationship with God and was actively working out everyday problems. We were struck by the open-endedness of this approach and the work it required.

Both during the meetings and in personal interviews, members said that they believed that the group had helped them make significant progress toward their spiritual goals (although they had usually begun to experience this growth before joining the group). All ten members interviewed said that it was because of participation in the group that they now spent more time in prayer. Most also attributed the increased time they spent reading Scripture to participating in the group. Just about all of them reported having a closer relationship with God. Most members reported that their relationships had become more loving as a result of being in the group. Two said that they had learned to be more tolerant of their grown children. Another said that in submitting to God's law (a process he said he began before joining the group), he was continuing to learn to express love to his wife. Two others said that by being in the group with their husbands, they had gotten closer to them, and so loved them more. In all of these cases, the members equated being loving in relationships with "walking worthy with the Lord" and, by implication, with a growing spirituality.

The Individual in the World

The group took organized social action only once — when it collected Christian books for incarcerated boys. Otherwise, it did not organize any activity for itself or for social or political action. The assumption seemed to be that individuals were involved in the world through their own lives and that the group would affect the world that way. A number of members were involved in helping activities within the larger church community: a food drive for the poor, meal provision for the homeless, and Sunday school classes for the developmentally challenged.[19]

There was very little political discussion, and only at two of the meetings. In the first instance, Lars had left an anti-abortion petition on the meeting table. Although the assumption was that members would sign it, it was hardly mentioned during the meeting. The second and much more substantial instance of political discussion occurred during a meeting close to the time that the group disbanded. In this instance, Frank presented a detailed summary of the senior pastor's discussion of the biblical teaching on capital punishment. Frank's presentation demonstrated the emphasis placed on Scripture by both the group and the

19. Interestingly, members seemed to spend very little time helping each other outside the group, but this perception might have been due to the limitations of the observer. There was evidence that some people discussed more personal issues with Lars and Ann between meetings.

297

church. He offered detailed biblical arguments both pro and con, leaving the actual decision up to each member (with the ensuing discussion tending toward the pro position).

It was clear from the discussion, especially before and after the formal meeting, that group members viewed the world as rapidly declining morally, that it was "a cesspool out there." But larger moral issues were quickly related to personal experience and particular relationships.[20]

Concluding Remarks

These twelve evangelicals came together each week for over six months. Just about all of them had been in small Christian groups before, and most intended to join a new one shortly after this one disbanded. It can be misleading to ask why certain individuals are "so involved" in groups. The question suggests that a "normal," "baseline" spirituality involves meeting together in a relatively large group roughly once a week. The question also suggests that any greater involvement requires explanation, and usually an explanation that links this involvement to some events or crises that push people to seek special support.

The personal practices, accounts, and stories of the people in Lars' and Ann's group clearly give a different understanding of "baseline" spirituality. They believed that spirituality meant walking actively with God and continually desiring a closer relationship with God. This meant active involvement with others on a regular basis. For them, participation in the small group was a part of their weekly rhythm of walking with God. When asked why other Christians were not more involved, their explanation was that they were lukewarm Christians.

They tended to see the group not as providing the ultimate source of their spiritual growth but rather as nurturing growth in progress. Their involvement in the group was a matter of personal choice, arising out of their desire to have a closer walk with God. In this sense they exemplify the trend toward viewing religion and collective religious involvement as matters of individual choice. But for them involvement

20. The group's treatment of political and moral issues exemplifies the fact that the liberal-conservative cleavage within U.S. Christianity (Wuthnow 1988) tends to coincide with the broader cultural liberal-conservative divide (Hunter 1991).

was not optional; they firmly believed that one could not grow spiritually without it. And they did in fact see the group as nurturing their growth.

Group members combined a commitment to authoritative truth and the necessity of applying it to everyday life with a commitment to self-expression and loving tolerance. Many have pointed to evangelicals' belief in absolute biblical truth, and several have pointed to a tendency for evangelicals to prefer subjective opinions over hard doctrinal positions. Each has been used to explain their numerical growth. Yet an interpretation based on only one of these observations is bound to be misleading because it will depict evangelicals as either intolerant or subjectivist. We think that the bounded subjectivity of Lars' and Ann's group is a significant departure from both of these characterizations. It highlights the fact that any group in practice will temper the demands of a collective stock of knowledge with individual expression.

Finally, it is interesting to note that Lars' and Ann's group was not a corporate entity that mobilized its members to develop programs or undertake social-political activity. Given their understanding of spirituality, group members assumed that each of them was affecting the world through his or her own daily life. And through prayer requests, sharing, and stories, they helped each other deal with their day-to-day joys and challenges within their relationships to God.

The people in Lars' and Ann's group believed that their group was a good example of what a group should be, although they knew it could be better. The group worked for them because they came together as individuals who chose to make Jesus real in their everyday lives.

Finding a Place: The Vision of Havurah

ROBERT C. LIEBMAN

The Amidah, a silent prayer, occurs midway through Havurah Shalom's worship service, as it does in the services of all Jewish congregations. A newcomer would find its ritual placement familiar. But how it is prayed here is distinctively different. Havurah's prayerbook announces the Amidah as the special part of the service where we individually seek God. Unlike prayerbooks that have only the traditional Amidah, this prayerbook offers four:

> The first is the traditional Amidah for those at home with the words of countless generations. The second is a modern Amidah by a Jewish woman seeking to give a new interpretation in today's world. The third is a selection by Rabbi Nachman of Bratslav relating the search for God to beauty in Nature. The fourth Amidah isn't written in the book — it is the Amidah each of us has inside that no one else can utter.

The leader invites all to find a special place for the Amidah. Some stand. Some sit. Some leave the chapel to find a quiet corner or to pray amongst the trees. Silence reigns until the sound of a melody calls them back from their separate places to rejoin in worship.

Observing the Amidah is a window into the soul and spirit of Havurah. Finding a place is in many ways what Havurah is about. It is a community of movers and seekers. Havurah began in 1978 when about fifteen families — nearly all newcomers to Oregon — met in a living

300

room to find a meaningful alternative to services and Sunday School at Portland's large synagogues. What started as "picnic Judaism" in their words became by 1993 a congregation of over two hundred families, couples, and singles. Part of a movement of Jewish renewal with one foot in age-old Jewish tradition and the other in the sixties, Havurah is a process of rediscovering Judaism through learning, prayer, and community. Indeed, for most, Havurah is as much a congregation of Jewish return as of Jewish renewal. Many joined hoping to find a place after years of post– Bar or Bat Mitzvah absence or estrangement from organized Judaism. Others joined to more firmly anchor a Jewish identity that they hoped to pass on to children. Still others joined to enter Judaism for the first time through a door that opened through friendship, marriage, or a call from the heart.

Providing a place for those who arrived from all points with such different baggage — or no baggage at all — kept Havurah true to the first part of its self-description as an "inclusive, participatory congregation." Havurah practiced "non-judgmental Judaism," as one put it. From the start, it opened High Holiday services to all unaffiliated Jews, defying the custom of other synagogues that obliged their members and guests to have tickets. It allowed non-Jewish spouses to be called to the Torah and required the rabbi to perform intermarriages. It held services early Friday evening to accommodate families with small children and provided child care for kids who didn't stay during the service. It offered a place to singles, single parents, gays, and lesbians, who found its youthfulness welcoming.

Finding a place for all to participate was equally important. In Havurah's vision, inclusion and participation were interconnected. Through inclusiveness, Havurah would be an open forum that enabled each member to find a more meaningful Judaism. Collectively, these individual searchings would bring forth an effervescent mix of Jewish learning, spirituality, and song. But that hoped-for mix would happen only if members made it happen by sharing their ideas, energies, and experience. Havurah would be an experiment of reconstructing Judaism through community.

In the vision, Havurah would be a process rather than an institution. It eschewed hierarchy and professionalism to assure broad participation. To lead services, members learned new songs and developed new liturgy. They created a Shabbat (religious) school with parents as teachers. They wrote a job description for a rabbi who would be a teacher and resource-person rather than the congregation's leader. Because Havurah refused to have paid staff other than the rabbi, the business of the congregation fell upon the members. Many hands were required not only to run services and to teach, but also to pay the bills, book rental space, and produce a newsletter. While new members marveled at how often people said yes, finding enough willing hands was not always easy. Longtime members sometimes drifted away after their children reached Bar Mitzvah. Newcomers often lacked the experience that would make participation possible. Meanwhile, the demand for members' services grew in step with Havurah's increased membership.

From June 1991 through June 1993, my wife and I observed, interviewed, and took part in Havurah; for the congregation, this was a time of stocktaking coinciding with two years of heady growth. Growth strained Havurah's program of broad participation, challenged its insistence on volunteers over professionals, and at times overwhelmed the rented space where the group met. Renting or buying a new space became a chief item of concern for the congregation.

Indeed, the "building" became the screen upon which was projected the group's struggle to understand its contradictions and to accommodate its new dimensions. Growth and the exigencies that attended it tested Havurah's core beliefs and the structures that supported them. With growth, how could Havurah stay both inclusive and participatory? Would it still be able to operate without paid staff? Could it seat the number of members who arrived for High Holidays?

For some, there was no possible accommodation. To them, talk of a building was anathema because it threatened to transform a community of movers and seekers into a congregation of movers and shakers or, worse yet, synagogue-*machers* (colloquially, big shots; literally, "builders"). Others urged Havurah to reclaim its roots by creating mini-havurot in an act of returning to the ancestral living room. Still others believed that it was time for Havurah to own up to the fact that it was now a small congregation rather than a small group and to acknowledge its need for permanent space. These competing visions showed how contradictions at Havurah's very core made accommodation seem a threat to the group's existence. How could Havurah grow without becoming like the large and impersonal synagogues that many members had left or refused to join?

However much struggling for answers troubled Havurah, the questions it faced will not surprise sociologists of religion. Havurah's journey resembled the life path described by Ernst Troeltsch in his sect-church typology and identified by Max Weber with the routinization of charisma. But, on reflection, the resemblance is loose, and neither theory offers a good fit with the case. For the first, Havurah never separated itself from the world, wanting instead to find a way that Judaism could embrace and transform it. For the second, there was no charismatic personality in Havurah. Rather, charisma resided within the community itself. Consequently, how to define and to configure the community is very keenly contested in Havurah.

Havurah merits sociological attention for its search for a suitable place between its identity as a small and alternative community and the reality of its growing and diverse membership. Its *mythos* is at odds with its *ethos*. Its mythos is unchanging, emblematized by its founding commitments to broad participation, pluralistic worship, and affirming Jewish identity through learning and community. Its ethos, however, is ever-changing as its membership alters its form and composition. Havurah is a congregation growing in numbers that wishes to remain small in spirit.

Havurah's wish to not grow up flies in the face of the theories of institutionalization offered above. They tell a familiar story: changes in size bring changes in a group's authority structure. As intimacy gives way to anonymity, rule-following replaces individual expression. The more people feel invisible and the less they feel that their personal contribution matters to the group's existence, the more rapidly hierarchy replaces participation. Community yields to bureaucracy. What was once a process becomes an institution.

It is the inevitability of these outcomes that marks these theories of increasing size and complexity. But theory is not fate. Could it be that groups such as Havurah deserve a different story? For Havurah, another perspective — path dependence — provides a surer guide. Path dependence refers to the way that remote events limit and orient possible paths of change (David 1985; Conell 1989).

The theory of path dependence fits intentional communities like Havurah that live in the shadow of their beginnings. Regarding beginnings, we need to make an important distinction. The way Havurah was started oriented its path but did not determine it. Rather, myths about Havurah — both real and imagined — informed its practice and pushed it along. These myths were told to newcomers and retold at congregational meetings. They were etched into Havurah's written language and celebrated at important ceremonies like High Holidays. Refusing hierarchy, professionals, and codified rules, these myths reminded members of who they were and what Havurah was about. Here, culture had to hold the weight for which large religious organizations had erected elaborate structures. In Havurah, talk of a building was submerged in the ongoing process of building community. I follow its custom by using the term *Havurah* to describe both the group itself and its members, whether they were families, couples, or singles.

Havurah's history and the way that it informed these myths and was shaped by them is the material of this essay. Here I will look at how Havurah started, the ways it built a community to match its vision, and how the community enabled individuals to experience Judaism. In the last section I will focus on how growth and change forced Havurah to consider its own history. The central question is "Can small religious groups grow in numbers but stay small in spirit?" Through a study of Havurah, one can assess the different imagery offered by evolutionary and path-dependent theories. What can't be discussed is where Havurah will go in the future.

In the Beginning

Havurah was not planned. It just happened. In June 1978, about fifteen families who knew each other through their mutual unhappiness with services and Sunday School at large synagogues met to discuss what might be done to make Judaism more meaningful for their children. They agreed to try a few summer events, so several families joined together on Saturdays to hold a picnic in the park followed by a ten-minute havdalah service and singing. In the words of one participant, it was "picnic religion." Three of the picnickers decided to organize an afternoon service for Yom Kippur at Portland's Neighborhood House, chosen because it was built as a community center for turn-of-the-century Jewish immigrants. They selected prayers and readings, found music and musicians, and led the service. They were amazed by the turnout — roughly a hundred people — and by the outpouring of energy.

This formative event left a powerful legacy. High Holidays would ever after be a time of coming home to Havurah. The innovation of opening services to the unaffiliated would be maintained. Most important, having members write the liturgy and use beautiful music would become the custom for services.

Soon after, about twenty-five families met to form Havurah. All who attended agreed that no one could voice negative sentiments about local synagogues. The intent was to share positive visions of the Jewish community they might create. They decided to hold occasional services, socialize, assemble a mailing list, and collect enough to cover postage. One participant remembered that most refused to use the "C" word, unwilling to acknowledge that they might be forming a congregation.

Knowing how Havurah began helps to understand its history. It arose independently of the national Havurah movement. *Havurah* is the Hebrew word for "friends." While the idea of a minyan — the group of ten men required for prayer — is as old as Judaism itself, the word *havurah* came into usage to describe the small groups that some rabbis created within large synagogues (Reisman 1977). In the sixties, *havurah* was the term chosen by small Jewish countercultural groups committed to participation, creative worship, and the study of Judaism (Neusner 1972). The first, Havurat Shalom, began in Somerville, Massachusetts, in 1968 (Prell 1989). No one remembered how the name Havurah Shalom was chosen, but all agreed that the group, unlike many East Coast *havurot,* did not follow the example of an existing group.

Havurah arose independently in another way. It was a congregation of newcomers. Most had recently finished degrees and had come to Portland to begin careers and families. Over 80 percent were non-natives. Unlike the Jews of Portland, they did not inherit the legacy of their parents' synagogue. Consequently, Havurah began with a clean slate that offered free space to create the alternative its young members desired. One member recalled the wish to recapture the spirit of Jewish summer camp, a place where singing, spirituality, and camaraderie provided his most meaningful Jewish experience. Among the founders, "just about everyone had had a positive camp experience."

The summer camp connection was one of the few resemblances between Havurah Shalom and East Coast havurot (Weissler 1982, 184). The latter mainly attracted Jews from Conservative or traditional backgrounds and had the traditional Saturday-morning Torah reading as their central service. In Havurah Shalom, most had attended synagogue in their youth, but the group was "not very Jewishly literate." Most did not know Hebrew. Few knew enough prayers for the services they were committed to lead or enough about Judaism for the lessons they were committed to teach.

A wish for more Jewish learning led Havurah to back into the business of being a congregation. When it became known that the assistant rabbi at the Reform synagogue wanted time to write a novel, Havurah uttered the "C word," incorporated as a congregation, and collected enough dues to pay his part-time salary. The bylaws provided for each member unit (family, couple, or single) to have an "equal participatory role in determining the direction and goals of the Congregation." To assure broad participation, the bylaws could be changed only by a majority vote at two successive congregational meetings.

Finally and most important, by deciding initially to do some things differently, Havurah *unintentionally* created the conditions that enabled it to become more different. The new congregation's first High Holiday services are remembered as "the cataclysmic event":

> We went to the Jewish Community Center and . . . said we're not going to charge. . . . We're going to have a community thing. We're going to do something for the community, for ourselves but for the community. . . . A series of decisions were made that basically remained intact up until now, [based on the question] "Why are we doing this?" And the "why we are doing this" is that we are going to perform a *mitzvah* [a good deed]. . . . There's not going to be tickets. You're not going to need reservations. You can walk in . . . which we all thought was a revolution. . . . We thought it was the sixties come to Portland.

The JCC board approved the congregation's request, and they set to work planning alternative High Holiday services.

Having a young rabbi who left another congregation enhanced its image as a breakaway congregation. The decision to welcome non-Jews as members whether or not they were intermarried raised additional concerns. So did women's full participation as leaders, cantors, and Torah readers. To many Jews of Portland, Havurah's refusal to undertake fundraising and to have a building was odd, but the option of reading the Amidah outside — even in the parking lot — was scandalous. Havurah's unwillingness to draw boundaries that limited experimentation or restricted membership created a barrier between it and traditional synagogues.

Thus, partly by intention and partly by circumstance, Havurah came to institutionalize a tradition of being nontraditional. It would borrow little from the example of neighboring synagogues. Drawing mainly liberal Jews, it did not follow tradition for its own sake, as Halakhic Judaism prescribed. Rather, Havurah used tradition deliberately as a resource for building Jewish community. It had the best aspects of sixties groups: "creativity, commitment to egalitarian values, non-rabbi-centered leadership structure, ... [and] the struggle of individuals to confront issues ... arising from diversity." And it had many of their vulnerabilities.

Building Community

Asked to name the event that emblematized Havurah, most balked. Their hesitation spoke reams about the character of Havurah. Finding an answer would be easy for the many havurot that centered on traditional Shabbat observance, but Havurah Shalom was a congregation rather than a minyan. It had come to be its own kind of full-service operation. Over time, the part-time rabbi had become full-time. New curricula and a library had been organized for the Shabbat school. It had acquired a cemetery, but still lacked a building. In a rare entry into the big leagues, its men's basketball team had gone head to head with the teams of other synagogues. The variety of activities, services, and celebrations offered newcomers many points of entry and obliged both old and new members to commit their energies. The appearance of these activities, services, and celebrations reflected the synergy that Havurah achieved between inclusion and participation.

Nothing better demonstrates the breadth of effort and the collective "high" of mutual participation than High Holiday services. When forced to choose, most members selected High Holidays as the emblematic event of Havurah. We can use High Holidays as the focal point for understanding the central processes of building community in Havurah: first, the synergy of inclusion and participation; second, the way in which Havurah institutionalized innovation; and third, the way in which its decentralization of authority shaped the rabbi's role.

The holiest of Jewish holidays, Rosh Hashanah and Yom Kippur, were Havurah's unifying moments. They were a homecoming for members and a door into the congregation for newcomers. The ten Days of Awe bracketed by Rosh Hashanah and Yom Kippur mark the end of the old year and the beginning of the new. At Havurah, their celebration was the culmination of months of preparation. Raising their voices in song, interpreting the Torah with the group, and sharing the co-presence of so many for so long combined to make each member feel deeply touched and a part of a spiritual community. The energies that the celebrations of the High Holidays mobilized inspired the community throughout the year.

Feeling part of and taking part in actualized Havurah's core values as an inclusive and participatory community. Inclusion meant making Judaism accessible. Havurah was started by a small group of people who wanted to make services child-friendly, and the group surprised newcomers, who discovered that kids could sit anywhere. Friday-night services often began with everyone, kids included, introducing themselves. Those who assembled Havurah's prayerbook made the language inclusive and user-friendly. Hebrew portions were transliterated so that the poetry of Hebrew prayer would be available to those who could not read the script. English translations were neutered by changing pronouns like "he" to "you" and "Father" to "Parent." The practice of inclusion extended to what one member called "active egalitarianism." A self-adjusting dues system meant that no one would lack the means to join. Those who could afford more paid a "dues supplement" that was never publicized.

Participation was meant to be the flip side of inclusion. Like other Jewish renewal groups, Havurah had a philosophy that being Jewish was not a fact of birth but an act of committing oneself to Torah (study), T'fillah (prayer), and Tzedakah (acts of kindness). Studying Judaism, leading services, and performing community service were the three pillars of participation in Havurah. Doing one or (better) more was emphatically encouraged, because Havurah's refusal to have a paid staff made participation by members a necessity as much as or maybe more than a virtue. Shabbat school provides a good example. At large synagogues, parents dropped off their kids at Sunday school to be taught by professional teachers. Havurah, however, practiced what I called "Suzuki Judaism" — the parents learned alongside the children. All parents met at the beginning of the school year to decide which lessons they would teach or co-teach. Curricula were available, and most parents owned books they would share. It was common for parents to stay during the two-hour class, which was held every other Saturday. Having kids in different classes increased a parent's obligations. One way to handle them was to partner with other parents and meet during the week to divide up the work. These partnerships became the seed of friendships and created partner combinations for leading services. Nevertheless, the benefits of doing religious education this way were debated. Some said it took too much time; others that parent-teachers had too little learning to really do it right. The only point on which everyone could agree was that Shabbat school was a blessing for sellers of Jewish books. Despite their misgivings, parents kept the tradition. When a parent took the time to prepare a text or a class project, it taught children the importance of Jewish learning. When a parent led the class, it taught children that learning was a family responsibility. To Havurah parents, these lessons mattered most. Many acknowledged how little they had learned or remembered from the Sunday schools they had attended.

It is also important to notice how Havurah institutionalized innovation. Interviews with members revealed the difficulty of identifying an event emblematic of Havurah. Even the choice of High Holidays seemed forced, because each year the familiar service was handled in a new way. As one member put it, "There is no typical service." Innovation became a standard feature of these services — as did member participation, which also helped keep things fresh. As a participatory community, Havurah invited and sometimes nudged people to lead services. In most large synagogues, the rabbi leads services. At Havurah, the rabbi alternated with members. Having members lead affirmed Havurah's commitment to democracy. But more important, it encouraged members to make Judaism meaningful. Leading a service was a personal statement and a creative act. An annual workshop introduced and explained the five major elements of the Jewish service. Creating a service meant putting flesh on the skeleton and breathing a spirit into it. One started with the prayerbook, a ringbinder holding photocopied prayers and songs customary for the service. Most leaders chose a theme that sent them off to the library or the bookstore to find certain readings. Music was part of Havurah worship and finding someone with a guitar and a strong voice was obligatory. Services took place in a small chapel where chairs were arranged in half-circles to enable eye contact. That none of the men wore ties added to the informality. Unlike large synagogues, Havurah had no sermon. At Havurah, someone prepared a *drash* (from the Hebrew for "interpretation"). A *drash* might be poetry or a story that was connected with an upcoming holiday, was inspired by a *simcha* like a birth, or illuminated a moral question. The *drash* was followed and sometimes replaced by an open-ended dialogue about that week's portion of the Torah. (At Rosh Hashanah, this involved the entire congregation having a dialogue.) An individual's selecting prayers, incorporating new music, and writing a *drash* kept the service fresh. Arranging the chairs informally and opening up the service for discussion kept it fluid. Like the group itself, Havurah's service was emergent. Judaism Havurah-style was a little like religion based on the principle of desktop publishing.

That everyone could lead services fit with Havurah's decentralization of religious authority, the third piece of building community. Its rejection of hierarchy defined the position of the rabbi. The ways that members described his role are revealing. One called the rabbi the congregration's ultimate service-provider. Another suggested that Havurah had a peer rabbi.

The desire to bring "Judaism down off the *bema* (pulpit)" guided Havurah's search for a new rabbi in 1987. Havurah's job description explicitly stated that the rabbi was a teacher and resource person, not the congregation's leader. The wording brought an outraged letter from the head of placement at the Union of American Hebrew Congregations (Reform) stating that he would not encourage a rabbi to take a position that so limited his professional autonomy. The search led to the hiring of a rabbi trained at the Conservative seminary. Havurah's ambivalence toward tradition cut both ways when the rabbi arrived. After a year without a rabbi, some members left, believing that having a rabbi diminished members' latitude in performing services. Others welcomed the new rabbi because he offered them a chance to learn more about traditional Judaism. Controversies over the scope of the rabbi's influence will be better understood by exploring how the personalization of Judaism coincided with the construction of community in Havurah.

Coming Out as a Jew

In contemporary America, Jews have blended in so well that it seems right to say that all must be Jews by choice. This is especially true in Oregon, a place where high rates of intraregional migration and intermarriage coincide with low ethnic identification and one of America's lowest rates of church membership. And it is true in Portland, in which the once-distinguishable Jewish neighborhood disappeared and more than half the Jews are unaffiliated. This has been reflected in Havurah's membership. While some members came from observant homes which practiced *Kashruth* and regular worship, most did not. They were "cultural" rather than "religious" Jews. Havurah has helped these self-identified cultural Jews to become practicing Jews. It has been a gathering place for those who are or feel they are outsiders to organized Jewish life because of gender, intermarriage, or their departure from the Judaism of their upbringing. The process of coming out as a Jew is central to the experience of Havurah.

Much of the generation that came of age in the sixties left the synagogue when they entered college. For these Jews, higher education, migration, intermarriage, and a late start to careers and childbearing prolonged or deterred their return. What brought them back was wanting to connect with a Jewish community to feel among friends or to pass their heritage on to their children. Havurah opened its doors to them at High Holidays.

One member explained the draw of Havurah: "They come to Havurah as a place to find some peace and calm and a little bit of Jewishness. Then some of them [come] when they have their children join. Or if they lose a parent or go through some other trauma. And I think that they could never have penetrated the scene in a big synagogue."

Why did they join Havurah? Other possible choices could not meet their desire for inclusion or participation as well as Havurah. Traditional minyans were participatory, but unsuitable for those committed to women's equal participation and for those who lacked Jewish education. Large synagogues used more English and were more inclusive, but they were more hierarchical and less intimate.

Havurah offered a third way that reconstructed aspects of the traditional minyan and the suburban synagogue and added the flavor of Jewish summer camp. From the minyan, Havurah embraced community, the need to participate in prayer with other knowledgeable Jews. From the large synagogue, Havurah took mixed seating and accessible liturgy. From summer camp, it took the power of music. What emerged bore only a faint resemblance to its ancestors, just as the practice of Havurah members bore only a faint resemblance to their parents' Jewish practice. The mix that came from diverse backgrounds and openness to "active ritual expression and experimentation" nurtured the creativity that all members identified as the best of Havurah.

Singing was the fuel of Havurah's effervescent spirituality. One member's "early memories of Havurah are walking home singing. Just walking along by myself singing at the top of my voice. . . . A community that can make me do that. . . ." At Havurah, the music is unlike the music at large synagogues. There, one is a spectator. At Havurah, as this member explained, he tried to do something different:

> [At traditional synagogues] you have this operatic voice coming at you through an amplified sound system. You have no peer relationship with this voice. This is not a relationship of equals. You . . . immediately have to question, . . . where do I fit in with this? If I sing along,

then what does that say about me? That I think I have as wonderful a voice? . . . And if I'm quiet, what does it mean? That I have nothing to say? That my involvement here is filling a seat to help the acoustics balance out? . . . The worst thing that can kill prayer, I think, is the inability to hear prayer around you when you have a sound system. You hear . . . the cantor, and you don't hear anybody [else]. . . . You just can't hear them. When I led the High Holiday services last year, . . . one of the things that I did that I want to pass on to other people . . . , is that when I would start a prayer, I would be close to the microphone, and then I would . . . rapidly pull . . . away from the microphone so that people weren't hearing my voice, but would hear their own voice and they would hear the voices of the people next to them. It really worked, I think. I think that we got more people doing it. . . . I like to sing, but even more important I like to hear people singing around me, and I get that at Havurah.

Singing was the way to begin the journey into prayer that Havurah made accessible to newcomers. You started by listening to the other voices until the time when you felt sure enough of your own voice to lean into the prayers with everyone else. Your voice joined their voices. Their voices guided yours. Like other congregations, Havurah practiced nonunison *davening* (praying). But the blending of voices was the main way that Havurah drew the individual into communal participation. As one member explained,

> Prayer is this mixture of individual and group experience. What I think Havurah does well is provide enough space for the individual and . . . recognize that the individual has individual needs. And yet at the same time [it] provides this really strong group sing-along. That's what works.

Thus, Havurah helps cultural Jews find a spiritual place. It is a place for those who are Jews by choice, whether they are converts or Jews choosing to return or to deepen their Judaism. In America, coming out as a Jew requires a community. Jewish identity is not a tag that one shows to the outside. It is a quality that one develops inside among those who share study, prayer, and acts of kindness.

Building a Building?

Spring 1993. Two families staged a *Purimspiel* (Purim holiday play) that caricatured Havurah past, present, and future. Skits poked fun at how the requirement to vote for changes in the bylaws at two successive meetings doubled the length of debates and how choosing officers that year resembled a game of Duck, Duck, Goose. Two other sketches brought the heartiest laughter. "Havurah Present" had the two-hundredth member coming off an assembly line under a banner reading "Spirituality Is Job One." In "Havurah Future," a father and two children wearing Star Trek tunics stood next to a telling sign: "Havurah: The Next Generation. Space: The Last Frontier."

In 1992-93, Havurah felt that it had reached a turning point. Members arrived for High Holidays to find that the congregation no longer fit into the assembly hall. Services remained open to anyone, but there was overflow seating, and those who could not get into the main hall had to watch services over closed-circuit TV from the lobby. Some said that the spiritual energy of years past had dissipated as members sat far from leaders and singers and amid many unfamiliar faces. Soon after, the congregation approved a three-year extension of its lease with the Jewish Community Center, unsure if the Center would re-extend the lease and uncertain if the space would then be adequate.

Growth and the prospect of further growth made Havurah members think about a building. The need for space was undeniable. The Shabbat school was squeezed into every available room. Turnout at Friday-night services sometimes exceeded the capacity of the small chapel. And no room was large enough to accommodate the entire congregation for High Holidays. While having a building promised to solve Havurah's predicament, getting one raised the spectre of sacrificing what was most valued by the congregation. The building issue forced Havurah to examine its character, a process that divided its members.

In the beginning, the decision to rent space was both practical and principled. The first members, mostly young families, lacked the resources to mortgage a building. But not having a building was important for reasons beyond the financial: members refused the machinery of committees, paid staff, and fundraising because they did not want to maintain the "edifice complex" of suburban synagogues. All of that would pull them away from the tasks of learning and teaching which motivated Havurah. In keeping with its egalitarianism, Havurah had no

named endowments, and it avoided what I called "plaque Judaism" —
the practice of marking everything with the name of a wealthy donor.
To be sure, Havurah's capital investment did not lend itself to tributes.
A book trolley contained the library for the Shabbat school. The congregation's torah lived in a handmade plywood ark fitted with wheels.

The movable ark symbolized Havurah's commitment to making
Judaism accessible. It could go anywhere that folding chairs could be set
up, and it made the rounds of High Holidays, Shabbat, and Bar Mitzvahs.
To those who opposed having a building, Havurah, like the ark, represented the ideal of Jews as wanderers. One said,

> I like the idea of Jews dwelling in a tent in the wilderness. I like the
> idea of our spirituality being separated from materialism. . . . When
> you think of Catholicism and Protestantism . . . the way that those
> cultures want to objectify and the amount of energy that's put into
> creating material things as part of the spiritual process. . . . The build-
> ing of the building. What the heart believes, the mind must see. Like
> a cathedral. . . . The nice thing about Judaism is that you can do it in
> a tent. . . . We're wanderers. . . . There's something assimilationist
> about wanting to deal with a beautiful building.

The opponents warned that a building would make Havurah twice
cursed. When it got a building, Havurah would become the very thing
for which it had long been the alternative — a synagogue. And when it
began funding that building, Havurah's egalitarianism would yield to the
influence of donors. At Havurah, almost no one talked about how they
made a living, and talk of fundraising brought fears that the subgroups
that typically had higher incomes would be favored over others — men
would be favored over women, the old over the young, two-parent over
single-parent families.

In the same spirit, talk of a building generated concerns about the
existence of an "in-group." Was there an inner circle quietly at work on
the blueprints for Havurah's future? The formation of a long-range
planning committee awakened suspicions in a group long accustomed
to an open and participatory style. What was less discussed and possibly
less understood was the way that Havurah itself was quietly changing
in form and composition.

Here, it helps to look at some numbers. At the start of my fieldwork
in June 1991, Havurah had about 130 members. At the end of my study,
it had over 200, a significant jump in two years. The increase was

apparent, but the way it happened was hard to see, and the full force of its impact was slow to be recognized. First, Havurah became more diverse. Second, a large turnover in membership accompanied the increase. Third, it coincided with generational succession within Havurah. Singly and in combination, these processes changed the group.

First, greater diversity tested Havurah's commitment to inclusiveness. Havurah professed to be diverse, but it had in fact always been a homogeneous group. Nearly all of the first forty members were young families, well-educated and professionally successful, who were new to Portland. Early members described Havurah as an extended family in which "we became each other's cousins" and recalled that "the impetus for many people was to create something for their children, not for themselves." Over time, families predominated, but their forms and membership proportions changed. In 1980-81, two-parent families made up 80 percent of the membership; couples, 12 percent; and singles, 7 percent; there was one single-parent family. In 1993, two-parent families made up 63 percent of the membership; singles, 16 percent; and couples, 7 percent; 16 percent were single parents. The increase in single parents reflected divorces and the practice of listing only the participating spouse. Among the couples and singles were seniors, gays, and lesbians. In 1993, Havurah changed its statement of purpose to fit its greater diversity. The original language spoke of creating "an identification with Judaism through the participation of the total family" and fostering "family involvement through the identification of the Congregation as a large family." The new wording identified Havurah as "an inclusive participatory community committed to Jewish values, spirituality, learning, and acts of social responsibility" and listed first the goal of "welcoming all people seeking spirituality within an evolving Jewish tradition."

Affirming the place of gays and lesbians tested Havurah's willingness to match words with deeds. Some felt Havurah practiced tolerance but lacked a commitment to active inclusion. In June 1992, these individuals organized a well-attended Gay Rights service for the congregation and the gay Jewish community. It was Ballot Measure 9, however, that moved the congregation. Had it passed, the measure would have limited civil protections of gays and proscribed teaching about homosexuality in public schools and universities. In the fall of 1992, Havurah broke its vow of keeping politics off the *bema* and built High Holidays services around the theme of exile to send a strong "No on 9" message. While the congregation was nearly unanimous in its rejection of Measure

315

9, some felt uncomfortable with the departure from the traditional service and with a subsequent adult education weekend that included outreach to the gay Jewish community. For many, however, the weekend was a first step in learning to reach from tolerance to inclusion.

Second, high turnover worked against full participation. From August 1991 to August 1993, 92 new members joined and 30 members left. The increase in new members was much greater than it had been in the previous two years, when 34 had joined and 32 had left. High turnover was commonplace at Havurah: in an earlier year, about a quarter of members had been new, and in another, more than a quarter had left. What was different was the number of new members: in 1992 new members represented about one-third of all members. Thirty-six arrived in the fall of 1992 alone. Understandably, members both longtime and recent felt that they were amongst unfamiliar faces at High Holidays. Turnover brought three problems. First, the departure of members diminished the reservoir of skills and experiences that running Havurah required. During my study, for example, the number of participants in the Saturday-morning Torah service shrank by half. Second, membership size pushed volunteering beyond its limit, and certain practices became "institutionalized": after twelve years, Havurah rented office space, got a computer, and hired a part-time secretary. Third and most troubling, the number of inactive members grew. One said, "The self-image of Havurah has always involved the concept of group participation. . . . But because of the size of the group, it's gotten somewhat unwieldy." Another worried that many joined "simply for the sake of wanting to belong somewhere . . . but they're not actively involved" and "aren't adding a lot by way of diversity or individuality." At the same time, many new members complained that they were willing to get involved but didn't know who to ask. Clearly, old strategies for provoking participation — leaning on friends and friendly exhortations — didn't work well given the high number of new members. The steering committee decided to assign responsibility for bringing *oneg* (food) to Friday-night services through an alphabetic rotation. However much that challenged Havurah's spontaneous style, making the *oneg* obligatory seemed necessary to assure that the tradition was maintained.

Last, generational succession quietly transformed Havurah. As Havurah members aged, they pushed the group to face a new stage in its own life cycle. Havurah began around a core of families in their late twenties and thirties. Most stayed through their children's Bar and Bat

Mitzvahs, a point when family involvement in Shabbat school came to an end. Because Havurah lacked the numbers and organization to develop an appealing youth group, however, teenaged children sometimes led their parents to other synagogues. (Ironically, the chief reason that Havurah kept its affiliation with Reform Judaism rather than making a better philosophical match with Reconstructionism was to have access to the Reform network of youth groups.) Second, the children of Havurah's "second" generation, those born in the eighties, were coming of age. Along with growing size, Havurah faced the shock of scheduling twenty-four Bar and Bat Mitzvahs in 1994, more than twice as many as had been held in the previous year. Such a large number might be a great burden on Havurah members, who typically baked sweets, arranged chairs, and did everything else necessary to create a celebration. Finally, there were misgivings about Havurah's leadership structure, as earlier concerns about an "in-group" suggested. Havurah's credo was "If you want to do something, then you can do it." Its open style encouraged innovation and participation, but left things undone. A member complained that Havurah's social-action projects stopped because "nobody made it their job to organize that."

A steering committee of five officers and eight members was in charge of setting policy and shepherding Havurah's resources, both material and moral. When governance by this steering committee began, Havurah had about forty members. In the beginning, roughly a third of the "member units" served on the steering committee in a single year. But what started as almost a direct democracy had become at best a representative body because the size of the committee did not keep pace with Havurah's growth. In addition, some worried that the process of selecting the steering committee through a nominating committee gave an advantage to longtime members. These dissenters were a small but vocal minority. And they voiced a concern shared by many: that Havurah was becoming like a large synagogue, which one member described as a "pyramid" where most members are inactive and at the bottom. Havurah had prided itself on being "an inverted pyramid" with the great majority "actively involved," fewer "inactively involved," and very few "totally inactive."

317

Conclusion

One member called Havurah an "experiment which has become institutionalized." Whether Havurah can be both experimental and institutionalized speaks to the chapter's central question: Can small religious
groups grow in numbers but stay small in spirit? Can small religious
groups break from the life path of bureaucratization and centralization
predicted by theories of institutionalization?

Studying Havurah demonstrates that while these theories point in
the right direction, they often set up a false trail by ignoring the starting
points of small religious groups. Intentional communities like Havurah live
in the shadow of their beginnings. The way Havurah's formation is understood — its myth of origin — is different from the way it actually started.
While it was self-consciously started as an experiment, it is wrong to say
that Havurah was uninstitutionalized. Reflecting the backgrounds of its
founders, Havurah sought to revitalize Judaism from a non-Orthodox
orientation. For many of them, it represented a deliberate exodus from the
familiar model of the suburban synagogue into an unknown Promised
Land. Ideally, they wanted a form of family Judaism that made possible
participation of the full family through a community that served as an
extended family. But because they have made their journey open to
everyone, Havurah has been continuously recreated by its changing membership. Growing size has not stopped the experiment. While Havurah's
growth has made intimacy more difficult, it has also made innovation more
likely. Newcomers have brought new traditions and fresh energies to the
mix. And because this is a well-educated and relatively affluent group,
many have been able to attend national conferences, make trips to Israel,
and visit other congregations; all these activities have resulted in new
knowledge and a greater awareness of what has made Havurah special.

What has made Havurah special is, in large part, how the past — both
real and imagined — has shaped the present. Through its rejection of
hierarchy and its adherence to participation, Havurah has continued to tell
the story of its exodus. In its prayers and everyday practice, Havurah has
embraced a religious form best called Peter Pantheism — acknowledging
that Havurah knows best all the religious organizations that it does *not* want
to be when it grows up. Nothing has brought greater doubt and division
than confrontations with institutional permanence. In the beginning, the
group refused to use the "C word," and a fragment left when it was clear
that Havurah would become a congregation with dues and a rabbi. Having

a building represented another large step toward institutional permanence. Finding new space promised relief to those who grew tired of moving and arranging chairs and a way to accommodate the growth of the Shabbat school. But it reignited old worries that the machinery required to run a building would diminish spirituality and that fundraising to pay for it would sacrifice egalitarianism.

This discussion helps us understand the seeming paradox of growing larger while thinking small that characterizes Havurah. Relative to the congregations that many members have known, Havurah is small, and it works in "small" ways. New members are socialized into thinking small via how they participate in Havurah: much of their involvement takes place in small groups. Even the exceptions prove the rule. The largest event — High Holiday services — is put together by a number of small groups. Thinking small is a sine qua non for access and participation. This is how Havurah has staved off the bureaucracy and the paid staff of synagogues. But there has been a down side to this voluntary participation. Sometimes people haven't committed themselves to making things happen, so certain things haven't gotten done and have faded away. Letting some celebrations and activities disappear has been the price that Havurah has grudgingly paid for standing by its principles.

Havurah's desire to grow without having intimacy give way to anonymity speaks to another dimension of the group: how its decision-making has affirmed its commitments to inclusion and participation. Reaching decisions by deliberation and consensus has been part of Havurah's self-image. Congregational meetings, held three times a year, have offered a forum for all to speak out and vote. Steering-committee meetings have been open. The committee in charge of long-range planning has worked at involving the entire congregation. However, as Havurah has grown larger, each member has become less visible. The more invisible these people have felt, the less they have felt their personal contribution mattered to the group's existence. Thus, Havurah's growth pattern has created an unintended propensity toward oligarchy. The longer someone has been part of Havurah's history, the more visible they have felt, and the more they have felt that their contributions matter. In addition, the more experience someone has, the greater the chance that he or she will be asked to join the steering committee. Like other "sixties" groups, Havurah has found that its preference for experience has valued seniority to the detriment of egalitarianism. The fact that the steering committee has stayed small has reinforced these tendencies. As one member put it, "Our institutions haven't necessarily caught up with our size."

Size is one of the most central concepts in sociology's armory but also one of the least understood. This is so, I think, because sociologists fail to unpack the multiple dimensions of size. For Havurah, growing larger has involved changes in three separate dimensions: diversity in membership, turnover in membership, and the succession of generations. Each has differed in its influence on Havurah's institutionalization.

Havurah's greater diversity has increased its capacity for experimentation. Part of the legacy of its start as an alternative congregation is that Havurah has come to institutionalize a tradition of being nontraditional. While Havurah has drawn mainly liberal Jews, it has appealed to more observant Jews as well because it affirms women's full participation. As newcomers have enriched the mix of traditions, they have continued Havurah's institutionalization of innovation.

Turnover, however, has deinstitutionalized Havurah because it has diminished participation. The arrival of new members and the departure of some longtime members has altered the group's culture of commitment. The more arriving newcomers have lacked the ethos of participation, the more Havurah has retold the myths of its origins. The greater the number of longtimers leaving, the greater Havurah's vulnerability to leaving things undone. Leaning on friends is always a surer strategy than friendly exhortation.

Finally, the succession of generations has pushed hard toward reinstitutionalizing Havurah. As Havurah grows older, it has become more differentiated through the appearance of distinguishable generations. Because Havurah's program of family Judaism has not always anchored families after Bar and Bat Mitzvah, and because most of the newcomers have been younger, the proportion of longtime members has declined. Possessing more experience and having contributed to more of Havurah's history, this generation has been disproportionately represented on the steering committee and willing to rework the vision to fit new circumstances. The presence of different generations, each with a different sense of Havurah's history and possibilities, holds out the strongest chance for transforming it.

But because size is an ambivalent quantity (Liebman, Sutton, and Wuthnow 1988), it has no sure relationship with institutionalization. Studying Havurah suggests how the concept of path dependence can contribute to our understanding of institutionalization. Events in

Havurah's past — notably, its alternative beginnings and its incorporation as a congregation — have "locked in" its myth and limited its range of possibilities. Recent growth has not newly institutionalized Havurah. Rather, Havurah has in some ways been deinstitutionalized and in other ways reinstitutionalized by the coincidence of growth and a particular moment in its generational cycle (Saarinen 1986). History — both what has happened and what is remembered — orients Havurah, but it does not ordain one path as inevitable.

At this writing, Havurah has made no decision about a building. For its 1993 High Holiday services, Havurah has rented a hall that will seat over eight hundred. It will open its doors to the community, just as it had during its first service in 1978. Soon after, the long-range planning committee will present its report. As always, Havurah will remember what it has been and debate what it wants to be.

"I Come Away Stronger":
The Religious Impact of a
Loosely Structured Jewish Feminist Group

LYNN DAVIDMAN

Over the past twenty years, as "New Religious Movements" and sectarian religious communities proliferated, the sociology of religion flourished as scholars conducted studies of these intensive identity-transforming organizations (ITOs). Researchers analyzed the social organization of these groups, their ideologies and their techniques for inculcating them, the characteristics of the members they attracted, and the process of conversion. Most of these groups were found to be tightly knit organizations that demand numerous signs of commitment and a high level of conformity by members. Participants were typically young adults in search of a core to their identities in an alienating world, a sense of meaning in life, clarity about gender, models of family life, and a tightly knit community of like-minded people. The organizations that recruited them created "encapsulating" structures that would minimize newcomers' exposure to competing worldviews and thus make them more likely to find the solution to their quest within the group. Studies of these groups individually as well as reviews of the research literature

I gratefully acknowledge the assistance of Steven Freedman, Larry Greil, and Shelly Tennenbaum, who generously devoted their time to discussing with me the ideas in this paper and who thoughtfully and critically read drafts of the essay in progress. Gaelan Benway provided skilled and insightful research assistance.

found that the higher the intensity of commitment mechanisms and encapsulation, the more likely the group was to be successful, as gauged by its growth in membership (Kelley 1972, 1978), its longevity (Kanter 1972), and its members' commitment (Greil and Rudy 1984). In fact, it was precisely the placing of many demands that generated commitment: by involving many aspects of their lives within the group, people became increasingly committed to it.

One of the established linkages that emerged from this body of research on contemporary religious movements — that between strictness of commitment demands and social strength of the group — has been challenged by Perrin and Mauss in a recent essay in the *Journal for the Scientific Study of Religion* (1993). They question whether a group's ability to "instill in its members an ardor that 'catches up their lives in a surge of significance and purpose'" truly depends on its strictness — the extent of its absolutism, conformity, and fanaticism (126). In order to show that these dimensions are conceptually and empirically separable, Perrin and Mauss provide a counterexample of an evangelical church in which members state that they are able to have strong commitment without fanaticism and "strictness." The authors conclude that contrary to the assumptions in the literature, strength and strictness are two separable aspects of religious organizations.

In this essay I, too, challenge the necessity of linking religious effectiveness with strictness. I further question the presumption that there is a necessary correlation between the effectiveness of a group and the degree of encapsulation of their members. I present a counterexample of a small religious group that is not encapsulating physically, socially, or ideologically, and that is not demanding and strict in terms of its commitment mechanisms, yet nevertheless is strong in terms of its impact on members' lives: the Aytz Hachayim[1] Rosh Hodesh (New Moon) group. It is a small, loosely knit Jewish feminist association that nevertheless deepens members' religious commitments, helps consolidate and solidify their religious identities, and empowers them in ways that carry over into other important areas of their lives.

In its form, organization, and purpose, this Jewish feminist group does not resemble a sect or an ITO, but rather what Robert Wuthnow has referred to as a "special purpose" religious group — it "focuses on limited objectives, attracts participants with special interests," has limited

---

1. This is a pseudonym. "Aytz Hachayim" translates as "Tree of Life."

formal structure, and makes few commitment demands (p. 108). Nevertheless, Wuthnow asserts that such groups can indeed have important religious effects on their members — they are "a valuable way of sustaining religious commitment" (p. 125). By developing a case study of such a group and analyzing whether, in what ways, and under what conditions such a group can be loosely structured and still have a strong impact, I have tried to expand our notions of the various forms and workings of contemporary religious groups.

The Setting

The Aytz Hachayim Rosh Hodesh group is a small, loosely structured group of bright, searching, creative Jewish feminist women who meet monthly — on the Sunday night closest to the New Moon — for an evening of study, discussion, and socializing. The group is an offshoot of the Aytz Hachayim Havurah, an independent community of about seventy members founded in the early 1970s in "Eastern City" by a group of leftist, egalitarian Jews who sought ways to create a form of Jewish worship and ritual that was consonant with their progressive politics. The group does not have its own building or rabbi.[2] Instead, it conducts weekly member-led services at the Hillel house of a local university and runs a variety of social-action programs. The Rosh Hodesh group was started ten years ago by women who attended the Aytz Hachayim Havurah and includes both Aytz Hachayim members and women who do not belong to the larger community; it has almost no formal ties with the larger group except that Aytz Hachayim publicizes the Rosh Hodesh meetings in its newsletter. These meetings, which last for about two-and-a-half hours, are typically attended by about ten women. The group is basically a study/discussion group dealing with issues that arise when women try to balance their feminism with their Judaism. The meetings are held at various members' homes; the evening's hostess provides snacks and beverages.

Rosh Hodesh groups originated in 1972 in New York City when a small group of Jewish feminist women came together to explore the nature of women's spirituality and their role in Jewish ritual. Since the

2. See Robert Liebman's essay in this volume on a similar havurah. It differs from the Aytz Hachayim Havurah in that it is an offshoot of a larger synagogue.

realm of public ritual belongs primarily to men, these women sought ways to expand their religious roles. One of the founders of the first contemporary Rosh Hodesh group said that she and the other women in her group felt that they had three options for increasing women's spiritual expression in Judaism: "to retain the traditional role and attempt to enrich it, to adopt the male rituals and hope to find spiritual satisfaction in them, or to create new or parallel rituals" (Agus 1976, 84). Since none of these options was fully satisfying, the women drew upon their rediscovery of an ancient tradition — that the New Moon had traditionally been a holiday for Jewish women, who refrained from work on that day — to provide a context for developing ritual and exploring feminine spirituality.[3] The women decided to meet monthly to celebrate Rosh Hodesh with a ritual and a feast.

As this group developed, its members described their activities to other women, who initiated Rosh Hodesh groups of their own. In 1976, the first collection of essays on Jewish feminism was published, and it included an essay about this first Rosh Hodesh group (Koltun 1976). In 1986, a volume on Rosh Hodesh rituals entitled *Miriam's Well* was published by Biblio Press, a small Jewish feminist publishing house. As word spread and more literature became available, Rosh Hodesh groups were initiated in areas where Jews live around the world. The National Jewish Women's Committee in New York City maintains a partial list of such groups; it contains more than a hundred groups across the United States and in Israel, Europe, and Latin America. Rosh Hodesh groups take a wide variety of forms. The women in these groups use their meetings to pray, study, and create new ritual, all in various combinations. While some groups are fairly traditional, other groups utilize physical movement, meditation, and New Age rituals, and still others pray to a goddess.

Rosh Hodesh groups are part of a larger movement by feminist women who seek to transform patriarchal religions by increasing women's presence in religious activities and in all levels of religious hierarchies. In order to discover paths to meaningful religious expression within the context of their historically male-dominated religions, and reduce the split between their feminist and religious selves, Christian as

3. "By Talmudic times, it was held that God had given women *Rosh Hodesh* as a reward for the righteousness of their foremothers, those who wandered in the wilderness and went with Moses to Mount Sinai but refused to give the men their jewelry to help make the Golden Calf" (Umansky 1985, 488).

well as Jewish women have organized groups that elaborate gender-sensitive theologies, reinterpret biblical texts, and develop new women-centered rituals (Lummis, Stokes, and Winter 1992; Plaskow 1990; Wuthnow 1988). Prominent students of religion see these groups as having some of the most significant impact on contemporary American religion, both now and in the future (Marty 1988).

Methods and Members

Between September 1991 and July 1992, I attended and participated in nearly all monthly meetings of the Aytz Hachayim Rosh Hodesh group, interviewed its ten most regular members, and spent time with them in social contexts. Due to the very small size of the group and its high turnover rate, I tried to interview only women who had come more than three times during my year of fieldwork. Since there was a core of seven women who came regularly, I interviewed all of them. I also interviewed the founder of the group, a new member who had come once toward the end of my study, and a woman who had previously been an important member of the group whose attendance had only recently been dropping off due to events in her personal life.

The women are quite diverse in many ways. They range in age from twenty-three to sixty-two: several are in their early twenties, a couple are in their late twenties, and most of the others are in their early to late thirties. As their ages indicate, they are in different life-cycle stages: several members live alone or with roommates and have never been married, two are married, and two are divorced (one of whom had raised a college-age daughter on her own). None of the women is a mother of small children. All of the women have college degrees, and a couple have advanced professional degrees. Their employment varies from part-time sales work to artistic endeavors to progressive political work to highly paid professional positions.

The women's religious backgrounds and present level of religious observance also vary quite a bit. One woman, who was brought up Orthodox and trained in the details of traditional Jewish law and practice, still tries to maintain a fairly traditional level of observance by strictly observing the Sabbath and the dietary laws of Kashrut. Another woman, who was brought up Reform, is starting to observe the Sabbath and kosher laws more strictly. The other women, roughly equal numbers of which came from unaffiliated, Conservative, and Reform upbringings, are unconcerned about strict ritual observance, although they generally maintain some Jewish practices in their lives, such as commemorating the Sabbath and other holidays in some fashion. Two members of the group stated that they do not believe in God but nevertheless feel strongly about their membership in the Jewish community.[4] Several members are politically active in a variety of progressive causes ranging from feminism to Latin American politics to tutoring homeless children.

Loose Structure and Low Conformity Demands

When the women in the Aytz Hachayim Rosh Hodesh group gather together to create new rituals and reinterpret classic Jewish texts, they do so within a group that would appear to be "weak" from the perspective of the research findings on new religious movements. The Rosh Hodesh group is a loosely knit, informal social organization with what one member referred to as a "very fluid membership." Since the group is always open to new people dropping in, regular attendance is not required, and meetings occur only once a month, the group is clearly not encapsulating. Nor does it demand other measures of sacrifice or commitment. As one of the most active members described it,

> The group is very much just individuals coming together once a month to discuss things, but there is no pressure, social pressure, because the group isn't a group in any other way or at any other time, so it's not like everybody's trying to win each other's favor or make each other do things. It's very much just a group for those three hours or whatever and then everybody goes and does their own things.

Members place a high value on this loose structure because it allows a variety of women to attend, and they can interact with and learn from women with a range of interesting life experiences. Accordingly, the group does not take a sectarian-exclusivist form, develop highly elaborated worldviews to which all members must subscribe, or impose any strict demands for conformity. Instead, it remains open to a variety of religious perspectives and forms of religious observance.

4. Judaism as a religion is more oriented toward elaborating the details of proper religious observance than theology.

The purpose of this group allows for its loose form of social organization. Unlike sects and ITOs, this group does not aim to give individuals new lives and new identities, but rather seeks to help them support and strengthen their already existing identities. Rosh Hodesh group members basically know what kinds of lives they want to lead; the group allows them to come together to get support for grappling with the challenges of what they already do and want to do better — finding ways to be feminists and Jews.

Purposes of the Group

Contemporary religious groups attempt to offer innovative solutions to important structural tensions in our society (Beckford 1989, 1992; Robbins and Bromley 1992). One central strain that all groups now must address is created by the vast changes in women's educational, occupational, marital, and childbearing patterns that have taken place in the United States over the past thirty years. These fundamental transformations have occasioned passionate debates in our culture about women's true nature and proper social roles. Since religious groups have always offered solutions to the dilemmas of personal life, including gender definitions and roles, and since established religious traditions such as Judaism and Christianity have based their religious worlds upon a distinct conception of gender definitions and relations, contemporary religious groups all must articulate their own solutions to the dilemma of women's place in modern society. While some groups have resisted the liberalizing tendencies of the times and consequently attract a segment of the population eager to embrace ideologies and rules that recreate "traditional" gender and family arrangements, other groups offer solutions to these dilemmas by developing practices and legitimations that support current efforts to broaden women's and men's religious and other roles. The Aytz Hachayim Rosh Hodesh group clearly follows the latter pattern.

Although this Rosh Hodesh group is loosely structured, its members are united by a powerful bond: they are all committed feminists who share a common set of assumptions about the patriarchal nature of their ascribed religious tradition. They, along with other Jewish feminists, complain that traditional Jewish life depends on a hierarchical, gendered social order shaped by several key factors: women are primarily defined as wives and mothers; only men can actively participate in public rituals and receive ritual honors; various laws regulate women's sexuality in order to protect men's ritual purity; the Hebrew Bible tells its stories from the male point of view; and the Law has been interpreted and formulated over time by a rabbinate that was exclusively male. Nevertheless, unlike some other women who conclude that the mainstream religions (including Judaism) are too irredeemably sexist and go on to found their own alternative spiritual communities (Neitz 1991; Plaskow and Christ 1989) or abandon religious observance altogether, the Rosh Hodesh women are not prepared to abandon their Judaism. Indeed, it is as essential an aspect of their identities as is their feminism. According to one active member of the group, they believe that Judaism is fundamentally "a good thing" even though there are a lot of "distortions and problems." Thus the Rosh Hodesh group provides its members with a context in which to mutually engage in activities — ritual and study — that create a new feminist Jewish perspective and understanding.

The women in the Rosh Hodesh group come together with a very clear purpose in mind: to "re-norm Judaism"[5] — that is, to reinterpret the tradition and create a Jewish way of living that is compatible with their strong feminist beliefs. Unlike individuals who join sectarian groups and ITOs, the Rosh Hodesh women are not looking to transform their identities or be taught a total way of life. Rather, they are looking for a way to bring together two elements of their identities that they experience as incompatible. My respondents all stated that they had felt hampered in their ability to fully claim their Judaism because of the sexism in it. As a married (childless) woman told me, "As I start to think of how I want to pass this on to my children and communicate my sense of Jewish identity, I feel I'd like to work through some of the traditions of Judaism that feel sexist with being a feminist in the modern world."[6]

5. One of the women I interviewed described the purpose of the group this way.

6. Another woman in the group, who is single, also said that she wanted to clarify her relationship to Judaism so she could pass on what she learned to her children. In this respect, these women resemble the women in my study of newly Orthodox Jews. During the course of that study, several single women told me that they wanted to increase their Jewish knowledge and strengthen their Jewish identity so that they could pass on what they learned to their children (Davidman 1991). Perhaps for women — especially those ascribing to Judaism, in which the religious identity of the child is traditionally imparted by the mother — making peace with their ascribed religion and defining their role within it is especially important for raising children.

Many of these women seek to strengthen and affirm their Jewish identities, which had not always been strong or well-defined when they were growing up. However, as they have learned more about Jewish tradition and ritual, they have found it difficult to square it with their feminist sensibilities, as one woman explained: "I had been trying to find my way to my Jewish identity and I felt like I had been so far away from being Jewish. But I can't leave my feminism behind. So it's been a struggle for me in Judaism to find the balance between being a feminist and being strongly Jewish, which obviously is the case for a lot of people."

The women are drawn to the Rosh Hodesh group because it offers them a context in which to meet and interact with other women who are similarly struggling and collectively seek solutions to their concerns. According to one member, "The group gives me an opportunity to meet people who are struggling with being Jewish and being a woman, and even though their individual lives are very different, all are grappling on some level with wanting as a woman to have more of a leadership role in the religion, which is a part of their relationship with God."

Not only is the group's feminist approach to Judaism attractive, but so is its feminist style of organization: the group is egalitarian and anti-hierarchical in form, leadership is rotated, and members provide each other with support and affirmation. As one highly articulate member expressed it,

> I was looking for thinking people. I was looking for an egalitarian environment. I was looking for a place where there wasn't one leader, there wasn't one fount of wisdom from where all good things came. I heard about this Rosh Hodesh group, and it seemed like it involved women with a similar orientation — they could be excited by ideas, they questioned things, they were feminists, really.

The bonding that takes place between the members of the group and the intimacy they establish help them work toward their goals. Since the group's structure and purpose encourage the women to connect with each other "as women in a personal way and emotional way and also very much in an intellectual way," it helps them "find a stronger identity for [them]selves as both women and Jews." The group empowers the women by providing them with a context in which to "build community" and "celebrate being women." As one member reflected, "The group is just so amazing [in terms of] how personal people are willing to get.

Obviously, that's easier in a smaller group of women, where you readily establish some sort of bond with people, but it's just really fortifying and meaningful. I come away feeling stronger. It builds caring within the community."

Because of the context Rosh Hodesh provides — an all-women's group — the members feel that they are able to build intimacy and trust. They have established a "women's space" that attracts women who want to relate to and learn from each other. Members offer each other support for the varieties of marginality they experience — as women in a patriarchal religion, as females in a sexist society, and as Jews in a Christian world. One young woman described the group's closeness this way:

> There is the female bonding thing there, definitely. I mean, we've talked about *mikveh*, about rape, and even how women are different from men. The evening we talked about my story about the rape, people talked about their feelings about relationships they've had with men and their feelings of vulnerability as [women]. This level of intimacy would likely not be present in a group with men.

By sharing their experiences with each other, the women are brought closer together than if they limited their discussions to the texts they analyze. One member said that although a central part of the group's activities is engaging in "heady, intellectual discussions about a piece of literature," the group tries to combine personal stories with study, which is what "separates us as an all-women's group from a coed one." Members provide each other (particularly the younger women in the group) with models of how to be "strong, bright, yet gentle women" and are inspired by learning about the various ways they each create feminist ways of living and working in the world.

In addition, the group provides them with a safe space in which to learn about and question Judaism without worrying about revealing their ignorance in front of men, a particular concern because many of the men in the Aytz Hachayim Havurah are very proficient in Jewish prayer and learning. As a woman who grew up in an assimilated Jewish family told me,

> Since I did not have any Jewish scholarly background, I was looking to learn about Jewish things and Jewish texts. And in Rosh Hodesh meetings we've talked about Jewish law, prayer, and the Bible, which is very valuable to me, especially since it is done from a feminist point

of view. It [offers a] more protected environment [in which] to do that kind of learning, because as somebody who can barely follow the Hebrew in the Saturday morning services, I feel too uneducated and unknowledgeable to ask questions or bring things up for discussion in the larger coed group context of Aytz Hachayim.

A few other members also told me how much they valued the safe space in which they could feel comfortable expressing themselves, and they contrasted it with their previous experiences of feeling ignored and intimidated in coed classes or other groups. By developing the confidence to express themselves in this group, the women feel better able to speak up in Aytz Hachayim Havurah services and in other coed settings.

By participating in the Rosh Hodesh group and learning to strengthen their Jewish skills, activities, and commitments, the women develop abilities and a sense of mastery that help them feel empowered in other areas of their lives. The group encourages members to transcend gender barriers not only in the Jewish realm but also in other areas of their lives. By sharing experiences with other strong, activist women, they learn to better trust their feminist critical thinking and their techniques for challenging gendered limits and boundaries. One group member beautifully described this development: "I think the Rosh Hodesh group has become an important part of my life, although I haven't been going to it all that long. I see it as a place that I'm learning to blossom and I'm learning to grow and add things to the group and to my own life."

Activities of the Group

The Rosh Hodesh group's monthly meetings provide members with the opportunity to explore ways of reconciling their feminism and their Judaism. What activities do they engage in toward this end? The primary means by which they attempt to bridge this gap is by creating rituals that are comfortable and meaningful to them as feminists, and by studying texts together, reading a variety of literature from the Bible, Rabbinic writings in the Mishnah and the Talmud, works by contemporary Jewish feminists, even short stories written by one of the members. Overall, the group is more oriented toward study; ritual is somewhat less emphasized, although it, too, clearly plays an important role in the group. The group's dual focus — study and ritual — is congruent with the emphases of the

Jewish religion, except that study has traditionally been seen as a male province. By claiming the male privilege of becoming learned in Jewish texts, the women are empowering themselves with knowledge of their tradition, and developing a basis for constructing and claiming a Jewish identity.

The adoption of traditionally male rituals — an option which had been considered by the founders of the original modern Rosh Hodesh group in New York City — has been an interesting topic for the Rosh Hodesh women; they have explored it in a few of their meetings. One woman described a meeting about tefillin that had been held during the year prior to my research. *Tefillin* are the phylacteries worn by Jewish men who are traditional members of the faith. They are small, square leather boxes containing sacred scrolls that the men strap to their heads and left arms for weekday morning prayers. The woman explained,

> I've liked those evenings that are specifically shedding new light on something to do with women in Judaism and pushing forward new frontiers in women's observance . . . it's just really encouraging to see. Like this one on women laying tefillin. That's only going to come out of something like a women's Rosh Hodesh group. That's not going to emerge anywhere else really.

Although this woman has not begun observing this ritual herself, a few of the Rosh Hodesh women have, within the context of the group, explored their interest in, and developed legitimations for, taking on male ritual observance. During the course of my fieldwork, the woman who was brought up Orthodox developed her own solution to the dilemma of how to be committed to traditional Jewish observance without compromising her feminism by choosing "ritual heroism" — that is, by adapting the more demanding male standards of observance. As she told me in our interview,

> I decided that I should put my money where my mouth is and to actually take on all the responsibilities and just stop kvetching about everything and just do it. Now I put on tefillin every morning. I think it had something to do with the Rosh Hodesh group, too, because it became a focus of my year to decide about these issues and to really think about them.

Another group member, a young woman who had become her close friend, was also beginning to adapt some of the male religious symbols such as laying tefillin and wearing a yarmulke (skullcap) for services.

Most of the group's members, however, have not been particularly interested in adopting male rituals and have preferred to explore those rituals that involve reclaiming and transforming women's traditional rituals by giving them a new feminist meaning. One obvious example of this is the formation of the group itself. Although, according to tradition, the New Moon was a Jewish holiday for women on which they refrained from work, we have no evidence that women actually ever gathered together to celebrate the New Moon. Nevertheless, out of the knowledge that the New Moon has some historical roots as a celebration for Jewish women, contemporary feminists have given the holiday new forms by participating in a wide variety of gatherings to commemorate it.

The first group participation in the *mikveh* in June of 1992 was another attempt by the group to reclaim and redefine Jewish feminist ritual. The *mikveh* is the ritual in which Orthodox women immerse themselves for purposes of purification one week after completing their menstrual cycles. Although many feminists eschew the *mikveh* because of its symbolic implication that women's natural bodily functions render them ritually impure, several Rosh Hodesh group members feel that since it involves one of the few commandments specifically for women, it is too central a ritual for them to ignore. As one woman said, "*Mikveh* was an issue for me. I didn't really want to think about it for a bunch of years. I just didn't want to think about it. And then I wound up saying, 'No, this is too important.' I want a way to reclaim it. We need to reframe it in feminist terms."

During the previous year, the group had held a meeting on *mikveh* that had been very well attended, and a number of women had wanted to explore it. Their interest, combined with the enthusiasm for and love of *mikveh* expressed by a group member who currently administered the ritual (in her own reinterpreted form), generated enough energy for a subgroup of the women to agree to go together. In order to feel comfortable attending the *mikveh*, the women reinterpreted the meaning of ritual immersion. Traditionally the *mikveh* serves to remove women's postmenstrual ritual impurity and thereby render them sexually available to their husbands. But the Rosh Hodesh women chose to use the *mikveh* as a context in which to celebrate their community. Although their first experience with the *mikveh* (which I attended) proved somewhat disappointing for the women because they found it hard to create a proper atmosphere of intentionality and derive meaning from the strange ritual, a small subgroup of the women continues to observe the *mikveh* monthly, precisely on the day of the New Moon. By repeating the ritual regularly, the women are creating a context for constructing and deriving meaning from it.

Like women in other feminist spiritual groups, the Rosh Hodesh women are also experimenting with new forms of God language. The women have used feminine pronouns for God, and have recited prayers, such as the blessing of the Hanukkah candles, using a feminine noun for God that means "spirit of the universe." For many of the women in the group, this has had a very empowering effect. As one woman said, "Now I know God is not a He. And I have some other words to address God. And I have some new prayers with which to address God. So you can see that being in the group has really affected my relationship with God."

Besides making innovations in ritual, the group has used study and discussion to do much of its work of reconciling feminism and Judaism. Members have explored a variety of texts from a feminist perspective with feminist goals in mind. For example, as they have read the Hebrew Bible (most of the women read the English translation), the women have sought to reclaim the experiences of women which were not deemed important enough to be described by the male authors. Group members have created new readings of biblical narratives so that women's experiences become central in the story, a widely used principle in feminist historiography. They have argued over rabbinic writings, such as those concerning women's inability to study the Torah, and have reinterpreted the texts so that they affirm contemporary women's desire to develop skills in textual study and analysis. The women have also spent evenings exploring the writings of other contemporary Jewish feminist women in order to see the solutions they have devised in response to the dilemmas of being a Jewish feminist.

An example from my fieldwork illustrates one form of this feminist rereading of Jewish texts: the retelling of biblical stories so that the women's experiences become central. During an evening devoted to studying biblical texts about the *emahot*, the foremothers, one of the women noticed an anomaly in the passage in Genesis 25 concerning Rebekah's infertility. (Inquiry into textual anomalies in order to discover deeper meaning is a common rabbinic form of biblical interpretation.) Typically, when a woman is infertile, she is the one who prays to the Lord, as can be seen in the story about Hannah in 1 Samuel 1 and 2. But in this passage, Isaac prays about Rebekah (Gen. 25:21). One group member suggested that although the biblical texts typically assume that infertility is a woman's problem, perhaps in this case Isaac prayed because he was the infertile one!

In suggesting this kind of interpretation, the women took for granted their authority to reread the Bible. In place of the patriarchal view that stigmatizes women who are infertile — since bearing children is women's primary role in traditional Judaism — the Rosh Hodesh women created an alternative interpretation that empowered them to see and break out of stereotypes. One group member was so impressed with that analysis that she wrote a short story about a childless couple who had been married for forty years; at this juncture the wife had begun to question whether she had truly been responsible for the couple's infertility. "I played on that whole thing, . . . that they never had children, she and her husband, and they always assumed it was her fault, and then . . . all of a sudden she gets this idea that maybe it wasn't her fault." Through this story, which dramatized the removal of the stigma of infertility from the woman, the group members learned skills for challenging sexism in other arenas of their lives and for going beyond limited views of women's capacities and roles.

Although the women clearly strive to make connections between what they do and the historical tradition of Judaism, by changing ritual and reinterpreting biblical texts from a feminist point of view, the women are actually acting to incorporate modern values, including feminism, into Judaism. While traditional Judaism is hierarchical and undemocratic, the women bring their modern values of egalitarianism, antihierarchalism, individualism, and democracy to bear upon it. This is a common feature of Rosh Hodesh groups, most of which "have neither appointed leaders nor fixed liturgies to which they must adhere. Instead, leadership responsibilities are either alternated or shared" (Umansky 1985, 488).

In contrast with evangelical and fundamentalist religious groups, which are grounded in tradition, which resist modernity to varying degrees, and which invest religious authority in rabbis or ministers, the Rosh Hodesh group members base their activities on the modern notion that religious authority is rooted in the individual and is based on her own experiences. Such assumptions are also often behind Christian feminist attempts to revise tradition (Lummis, Stokes, and Winter 1992). The Rosh Hodesh group members do not question their right to claim religious authority in this fashion; they simply assume it. As one woman explained, "As I learned more about how Judaism discriminates against women, my attitude was, 'Well, this has to be changed, and this is wrong,' rather than the opposite of trying to realize that I have worth, despite the traditional views."

Feminist special-purpose groups hold a creed and values inflected by the modern world, in contrast with fundamentalist and sectarian groups, which base their creed and their values on tradition. These different approaches shape the way they perform rituals and engage in study. In traditionalist religious groups, the emphasis is on learning the details of rituals in order to conduct them in the traditional manner. (This is particularly evident in traditional Jewish groups, in which ritual observance is so important.) Similarly, sectarian groups that engage in biblical study are likely to teach newcomers and members a "correct" reading of the Bible. In contrast, the Rosh Hodesh group members transform rituals so that they are consonant with feminist principles and render a multiplicity of readings and interpretations of biblical and rabbinic texts, all of which place women at the center.

The Strength of the Group

Despite having a loose structure and few commitment demands, the Rosh Hodesh group has a strong impact on its members, on the larger Havurah in which they participate, and indirectly on the American Jewish community and on general trends in contemporary religion. Since the focus of my research was on the microcosm of this group in particular, I will elaborate on the ways that the Rosh Hodesh group is effective in terms of its influence on members' lives and will comment only briefly on its larger impact.

Although attendance is not required, many members show the intensity of their commitment to the group by planning their lives around the meetings. One quotation illustrates the sentiment expressed by several of the women: "I really look forward to the group. I wouldn't think of not coming. I mean, I would plan my month around it. If I were planning a weekend trip, I would plan it so that I would be here for that. I think the group's really important, and I really would miss it if I didn't go one month." Core members make sure to attend, because they feel that they always get something out of the meetings. One woman commented,

I think everyone feels that they've gained something personally. I know that after each meeting I feel very glad that I put forth the effort to get to [the next town over] or wherever it's happening. I come back feeling really glad that I got to know someone better or learned something more about someone's life or learned a new song or a new concept. I mean, there's always something that I come away with that I feel happy about and that I wouldn't have gotten if it weren't for this. Or it wouldn't come across my path in any other way.

Members further demonstrate their commitment to the group by actively helping each other in times of need. Many members of the group told me that when the father of one group member died, she requested that group members perform the required "watch" over his body until he was buried. Although many of the younger women had not encountered death before and found it traumatic to fulfill their friend's request, everyone came through and supported her.

More importantly, the group has a strong impact on the women's religiosity. This can be seen in several ways. First, because the group helps these women to strengthen their identities by bringing together what they have experienced as conflicting components, the group makes it easier for some of its members to claim their identity as Jews. As one member said, "The Rosh Hodesh group gives me an 'in' to experiencing Judaism as a woman, and so it gives me a very personal sense of the Jewish experience, where[as] before I think it was much more removed and alienating. I had problems identifying myself as a Jewish woman." Several women also stated that the group allowed them to feel more a part of the Jewish community and thus helped them reclaim their Jewish identities.

In addition, the group has also deepened members' religious commitments and observances. By encouraging the members to expand their options as women within the tradition and thereby feel less alienated, the group stimulates them to further explore their spirituality and enriches their spiritual growth. One member said that because she learned within the group that she was free to amend the prayers of the faith with feminine pronouns and say "as [she] wishes," she felt closer to the prayers than ever before. Another woman told me that her relationship with God has deepened through studying the Torah with the other women in the group. Another member expressed this sentiment strongly when she said, "I think God has become more a part of my life now."

338

The Rosh Hodesh group has also increased members' participation in Jewish activities, such as engaging in study and broadening their religious observances. Several women told me that as a result of the group, they have become "more interested in Jewish subjects" and desire to "study more." A couple of women, because of encouragement from other group members, learned to chant the Torah reading in the classic melody (a skill typically taught only to men), and then led the Torah service at the Aytz Hachayim Havurah. A highly involved member told me that the group led her to make many decisions that year about her Jewish feminism. In addition to beginning to wear tefillin, she had also started wearing something to cover her head. She explained, "I decided to do it not as a thing like covering up my hair because it's a sexual kind of thing [the standard reason married Orthodox women cover their hair] but more the reason why men wear a yarmulke, like to remind myself that there's something above me and that kind of thing."

Within the context of the group, this member received support for making an important decision regarding her synagogue attendance. Within six months of joining the Rosh Hodesh group, she began to experience a conflict about attending Saturday services with her husband, because they attended an Orthodox synagogue in which the women were separated from the men and were denied access to public ritual participation. When she discussed her feelings with the group members, they were very supportive of her emerging decision to worship instead at the egalitarian Havurah, and thus to pray separately from her husband:

> I decided that it's very important to not daven [to recite the prescribed prayers in a Jewish liturgy] in a place with a *mehitzah* [the barrier in an Orthodox synagogue separating the women from the men], not to daven like that, ever. If someone invites you to come to a Bat Mitzvah or something in a shul [synagogue] that's Orthodox, then fine, but I decided that it's important to support egalitarian groups and to be a part of them.

Besides helping to strengthen its members' religious commitments, the group also serves to bring women's Jewish experiences and perspectives into the larger community of the Havurah. By encouraging members to speak up in the Havurah services, the Rosh Hodesh group ensures that women's points of view are represented in the weekly Torah discussions. As the group members stimulate each other to develop new skills such as learning to chant the Torah and leading services, the active presence in the worship service is increased. (The Havurah does have among its members other women who are skilled and knowledgeable in Jewish traditions, too.) In addition, group members sometimes lead discussions of the Bible in the Havurah, showing how different the text looks when presented from a woman-centered perspective, and even act out dramatizations of their reconstructed biblical narratives. For example, at the Havurah services one Rosh Hashanah, several group members presented a skit with dialogue that explicated the feelings between the foremother Sarah, her husband Abraham, and her maidservant Hagar at the time that Sarah banished Hagar and her son, Ishmael, from her household.

Within contemporary American Judaism, the presence of over a hundred similar Rosh Hodesh groups and the flowering of a wide range of other Jewish feminist activities and rituals have contributed to the increasing presence of women at all levels of Jewish religious and communal life. Women who belong to groups such as the Aytz Hachayim Rosh Hodesh bring their insights and new skills into the other social arenas in which they participate, thus spreading the influence of the group's work. Feminist rituals such as writing new liturgy and holding naming ceremonies for baby girls are becoming more normative within a religion that historically has concerned itself more with men's spiritual life and ritual activities. Feminist activism is also gradually introducing changes into the leadership structure of Jewish communal associations and federations, perhaps leading these organizations to pay more attention to women's concerns. The cumulative impact of these various groups within Judaism and the thousands of similar special-interest groups within Catholic and Protestant denominations are producing profound changes in American religious life and worship.

Accounting for the Impact of the Rosh Hodesh Group

How does the Rosh Hodesh group succeed in having a strong impact on members' religious identities and observances, despite the looseness of its structure and its low commitment demands? There are several possible structural explanations.

First, this group is unlike an ITO, in which members are taught a new way of looking at the world and a new way of living that transforms their lives in restrictive ways. The Rosh Hodesh group offers a context in which women find support for their feminist values and commitments in many other areas of their lives. Several of the women either have participated or are currently participating in feminist groups such as consciousness-raising groups, the National Organization for Women, and various abortion-rights leagues. One woman was in a "goddess consciousness" group for women; another was an active member of a women's group studying the Talmud. Several women have also participated in feminist and peace activities in Israel. Many of the women are accomplished and assertive in their professions, and have close friends who share and support their feminist perspectives.

The Rosh Hodesh group is also different from an ITO in a second significant way. Because an ITO resists the incursion of modernity, seeks to dramatically transform members' identities, and has an ideology that deviates sharply from widely held contemporary values, it requires higher levels of encapsulation and strong commitment demands. Conversely, because the Rosh Hodesh group generally embraces modern attitudes and ideas and attempts to incorporate them into the tradition, the group is not especially "deviant" from the wider society. Because its values are basically consonant with the general values of modern life — democracy, individualism, privatization of religion, self-fulfillment, and egalitarianism — it has no need for strong boundary control that minimizes contact with the wider society. By contrast, groups that incorporate modern values and ideals may succeed in the absence of these demands.

A final factor in the group's strength is that members see themselves as part of a wider network of Jewish women who are working to bring feminism and Judaism closer together. Although as individuals they might not have a widespread influence, as part of a larger network of activist Jewish feminist women, they have an impact on the larger American Jewish community. As Rebecca Alpert, herself a well-known Jewish feminist activist, has written, "Although Jewish women's spiritual expressions are not a unified movement with an ideology, structure, or leadership, they do share a common goal, and common methods to achieve that goal" (1991, 67). These collective efforts are working to change the nature of American Jewish life in profound and lasting ways.

Jewish feminism is a movement for cultural transformation, a process that occurs as women who participate in small, fluid associations such as the Aytz Hachayim Rosh Hodesh group carry the group's ideas and values into all their other activities and relationships. As Mary Jo Neitz explained in her study of contemporary feminist witches, cultural change occurs through an accretion of individual transformations that take place in small groups. The changes in the lives and views of participants also have an impact on the public level as the "nature of public discourse shifts, what had been unthinkable becomes taken for granted, and individuals reflect on the movement and monitor society in new ways" (Neitz 1990, 4).

Conclusions

Since most studies of religious groups over the past two decades have focused upon sectarian communities with high commitment demands, measures of religious success have been defined in terms of institutional factors — membership growth and organizational longevity. This approach, however, leaves out precisely those religious forms that are becoming increasingly important in contemporary U.S. society: those fluid, loosely knit, special-purpose associations such as the Rosh Hodesh group presented in this essay. Feminists have long recognized the powerful impact that small support groups (such as consciousness-raising groups) can have on their members, and through them on the larger society and culture; now sociologists of religion are beginning to turn their attention to this type of religious formation. This is a significant development. By expanding our conceptions of religion to include groups that take a wider variety of forms than ITOs and sectarian groups and that have various structures and purposes, we become open to new ways of studying religion and its interaction with society.

Out of this more inclusive approach, a new understanding of religious groups has been emerging. Instead of focusing largely on the groups' institutional structures, sociologists of religion have been exploring various dimensions of their forms, purposes, and impact. Tom Robbins and David Bromley have suggested that the significance of new religious movements is that they are "laboratories of social experimentation" in which members collectively — through trial and error — work out solutions to common problems of living (1992). Such special-purpose groups develop as like-minded individuals get together to resolve key structural tensions in our society. The Aytz Hachayim Rosh Hodesh group clearly was founded in order to help women deal with a critical set of tensions in American society—those that have developed in response to women's roles in religion and in society at large. Through their activities together, the women have produced critiques, rituals, and biblical interpretations that have both empowered them and helped them shape a new conception of Judaism. The innovations of the Rosh Hodesh women and those in countless other feminist religious groups ultimately will contribute to larger cultural changes by becoming part of a "cultural pool" upon which similar groups might draw.

The transformations that such special-purpose groups produce in their members and their potential cultural and social impact suggest that these types of groups are indeed "strong" and that sociologists of religion need to come up with new ways of assessing the strength and impact of religious communities. That these groups can be strong despite their limited commitment demands and their lack of an encapsulating social organization further implies that a variety of religious forms can be effective. As new forms of organizations are studied and measures of effectiveness that are relevant to these groups are generated, we will expand our understanding of the trends in religion as we approach the twenty-first century.

The Small-Group Movement in the Context
of American Religion

ROBERT WUTHNOW

Small groups are no stranger to American religion. They have deep roots in the Methodist class meetings and Baptist prayer meetings of the nineteenth century. They resemble the Sunday school classes and youth groups that have characterized many other religious traditions as well. Yet, the current popularity of small groups — the extent to which people are turning to them in search of spirituality, and the ways in which religious leaders are championing them — is unprecedented. So it becomes necessary to ask, What are the consequences of small groups for the religious faith of the American people? What are the potential dangers? And how may small groups themselves be encouraged to contribute to the deepening of American spirituality?

Dimensions of Faith in the American Context

Assessing the contribution of small groups requires some sense of what American religion has been like in the past. There are, of course, countless ways in which to describe the contours of American faith. Some, for example, would argue that America has always been a nation of spiritual seekers. In this view, the present interest in small groups is simply an extension of long-familiar patterns. Others, however, would suggest that American culture — especially in the twentieth century — has been

344

characterized by shallow or superficial religious commitments, and that the society has been subject to growing secularity. In this view, small groups are likely to be regarded as a new force, stemming the tide of disbelief and moral relativism.

Both of these views, in fact, have some validity. The extent to which small groups are now engaged in promoting spirituality cannot be understood apart from the earlier quests for the sacred. Throughout American history, a sizable share of the population has been deeply interested in matters of faith. This interest has continued during the twentieth century, as evidenced by the fact that more people are now affiliated with churches and synagogues than were a century ago, and by the fact that large numbers of people attend religious services regularly, pray daily, and acknowledge the importance of religion in their daily lives. The small-group movement has drawn strength from this interest. At the same time, American culture has become very secularized. People are concerned about the lack of "morals" in public schools and on television. Many Americans feel pressured by advertising and by their employers and by a myriad of other cultural influences to live in ways that pay little attention to questions of spirituality. Some are finding the support to resist these pressures in small groups.

Neither view, however, offers much insight into the *quality* of small-group spirituality. The reason is that American religion does not simply wax and wane; it is also characterized by deep internal tensions. As it has developed historically, it has incorporated a variety of theological emphases. It has also been shaped by differing currents in the larger culture. These influences have been incorporated into the debates that animate the work of religious leaders. At the close of the twentieth century, new social developments are also shaping the nature of these debates. The small-group movement is poised within these internal tensions, responding to them but also contributing to the continuing discussion.

Two axes of debate are, in my view, critical to the way in which small groups are now shaping American faith. One of these has to do with the question of individual responsibility. It focuses on the degree to which an individual should take an active role in the shaping of his or her faith. The other has to do with the question of faith and works. It concerns not only the appropriate balance between the two but also what the nature of works should be. The two are, of course, related. But they also provide somewhat different issues for the small-group movement to address.

345

The question of individual responsibility predates even the founding of American religion itself, but has been profoundly debated throughout our nation's history. The Reformation tradition, especially Calvinism (but also to some extent Lutheranism), placed great emphasis on God's sovereignty and grace. God extended mercy, forgiveness, and salvation to the believer. The believer, in turn, was empowered through the Holy Spirit to affirm that grace, but did not bear an entirely separate responsibility, as it were, to choose salvation or to discover God. Nevertheless, individual responsibility took the form of shaping one's will to that of God, especially in matters of corporate worship and personal moral conduct. Other traditions that grew in popularity during the nineteenth century extended the realm of individual responsibility. Believers were held to be more responsible for choosing to know God in the first place and, in some traditions, bore the added responsibility of gaining periodic emotional assurance that they were indeed ministered to by the Holy Spirit.

Twentieth-century discussions of individual responsibility focus less on the relative weight of divine sovereignty and personal freedom in matters of eternal salvation and pay more attention to questions of spiritual growth in the present life. In some perspectives, the role of the individual is chiefly to be quiet, attentive, and accepting of God's leading. More common, it appears, are various perspectives that encourage individuals to take an active role in developing their faith. Greater knowledge of the Bible, for example, is likely to be considered a prerequisite for spiritual maturity. More time spent in prayer is likely to be encouraged as well. Certain experiences, such as speaking in tongues or otherwise sensing the "indwelling" of the Holy Spirit, and certain activities, such as ministering to the needs of the poor and working for social justice, are also likely to be emphasized. Metaphors are often the primary way in which spiritual growth is discussed. For instance, spiritual growth may be likened to muscle building, training for a race, climbing stairs, or going on a journey.

In few instances is it assumed that spiritual growth is actually necessary to enter into the heavenly realm after death. But active, responsible effort on the part of the individual to develop his or her faith is widely encouraged both as a way of pleasing God and as a way of attaining a happier, more effective daily life. The relative weight given to one or the other varies, but there is generally an assumption that life has a spiritual dimension, and therefore that living a full life requires paying attention to this dimension. The individual can find guidance by observing others or by reading the Bible and other religious writings. But the individual also bears a special responsibility for cultivating spirituality in his or her own way. This is the case because each individual is different — because each has been granted a different "plan" for his or her life, because each has different talents or gifts, or simply because each has been placed in different circumstances.

The contemporary small-group movement makes sense only against the backdrop of this emphasis on individual responsibility in matters of faith. It presupposes that members are concerned about developing their spirituality. It also presupposes that spiritual development is not easy, and for this reason requires encouragement and support. Developing one's spirituality is much like learning to play a musical instrument. Hard work is required, and that work will be more effective if certain techniques are followed. To follow them requires personal discipline, and, human nature being what it is, the company of others may be necessary to sustain that discipline. And, like a musical instrument, spirituality can be "played" or "practiced" alone, but its value will be amplified if it is used to perform in harmony with others.

Both the contributions and the limitations of small groups can be understood against this backdrop. Small groups encourage individual members to take greater responsibility for their faith, to support one another, and to extend ideas about faith into new realms of their lives. But because they are of value in these ways, they can also inadvertently emphasize some aspects of spirituality at the expense of others. Individual responsibility may result in faith being focused too much on the needs and interests of the individual. When this happens, it may also encourage each individual to do his or her "own thing" to the extent that faith becomes highly relativistic. Informal norms of support and encouragement may also work against the hard efforts actually required to develop one's spiritual muscles. Small groups, therefore, reinforce the emphasis in American religion on taking responsibility for one's faith, but may alter (or even undermine) this emphasis at the same time.

The conjunction of faith and works has also been transformed in the twentieth century. Whereas at one time the issue focused more on faith as a means of salvation, or works as a way of attaining eternal life, it now focuses more on finding an appropriate balance between attitudes and action, or, in other terms, between an inward orientation and an external lifestyle. Most Americans would probably pay lip service to the

347

view that "faith without works is dead." Yet some would argue that closeness to God, prayer, and biblical knowledge should be emphasized, the assumption being that activities such as witnessing and helping the needy would then automatically follow. Others, by contrast, would argue that these activities — or other ones, such as refraining from sexual immorality, participating faithfully in religious services, teaching one's children biblical principles, and lobbying for certain kinds of social and moral legislation — should take priority, the effort required then motivating individuals to develop their inner spiritual lives as well.

Coupled with norms of individual responsibility, both of these orientations encourage people of faith to *do something*. Translating faith into action can involve working at a soup kitchen, or it can mean spending an hour a day learning how to meditate or praying or studying the Bible. The assumption is that spirituality cannot truly be cultivated (or genuine) without engaging in some special behavior, and presumably something that requires effort. Thus, a spiritual experience associated with viewing a pretty sunset might be deemed legitimate, but not as worthy as one attained after having learned how to quiet one's thoughts and understand more fully the divine meaning of sunsets. Or, a physician attending to the sick might be regarded as someone who is putting her faith into practice, and yet not living a fully developed spiritual life unless she is consciously thinking about faith-work connections.

Small groups, then, come into play in this context as well. They provide ways of putting faith into practice. For the most part, their focus is on practical applications, not on abstract knowledge, or even on ideas for the sake of ideas themselves. A secular book-discussion group, for example, might focus on a novel simply to enjoy the craft of its author. But a religious group would be more likely to have as its goal nurturing the faith of its members in their everyday lives. The positive contribution of religious small groups is that they do, in fact, provide occasions for members to consider how to apply ideas to their lives. Their members can hold each other accountable, checking to see, for example, whether someone who promised to invite his neighbor to church that week actually did so. But the limitations of small groups also revolve around this axis. In focusing on practical applications, they can overlook the importance of basic truth itself. They can emphasize effort to the point that faith for its own sake is devalued. In more subtle ways, they can also provide members with easy ways to put their faith into practice, thereby derailing some of the hard lessons that may need to be learned. In addition, small groups can refocus faith to the point that how well it works for the individual becomes the ultimate test of its validity.

The proponents of small groups are of course correct in arguing that such gatherings have precedents that go back many centuries prior to our own. But in making this claim, they also run the risk of rewriting history in a way that obscures important differences. Small groups today may be likened to the band of disciples who followed Jesus, for example. But few small-group members nowadays follow their leader from town to town, few blend into the multitudes as he preaches and heals the sick, and few are prompted by their group experiences to become missionaries and martyrs. It is for this reason that small groups must be placed in their specific cultural context, and their contributions and limitations evaluated within this setting. Countless books and pamphlets tell us about the formal expectations of their proponents, but we must draw on information about what actually goes on in small groups to see how well they realize these expectations.

The Contributions of Small-Group Spirituality

One of the key reasons why the small-group movement is so vital in contemporary America is that it makes faith available to everyone. It may seem odd to mention this contribution first, especially when there are churches and synagogues everywhere. But the secret of American religion has always been its penchant for disestablishment. In the seventeenth century, Europeans fled to America to escape established religions; in the eighteenth century, religious monopolies were broken and the colonies became religiously pluralistic; and in the nineteenth century, new denominations and sects sprang up that democratized faith in the early republic. Now, at the end of the twentieth century, American religion is undergoing yet another period of disestablishment. The authority of denominational structures is eroding. People no longer need to be members in good standing to receive communion. Fearful of losing congregants to their competitors, churches are throwing their doors open to everyone. Clergy, no longer as willing to present themselves as the mouthpieces of God, have also lost authority. At the same time, enormous resources are still required to run these institutions. Staff salaries, mortgage payments, and utilities compose the lion's share of church budgets. Religious leaders struggle to raise the necessary cash.

By comparison, small groups cost virtually nothing. They meet in church rooms that stand empty during the week. Or, if those are unavailable, they meet in private homes. They are run by lay leaders, so clergy need not be involved at all. And for a few dollars, study guides can be purchased that provide predigested lesson plans and questions to prompt discussion. Time commitments are kept to a minimum as well. People can come for a couple of hours a week and leave it at that. There is no obligation to serve on a church board, help paint the vestibule, run the youth program, or staff the nursery. More importantly, people can usually "put in" those two hours at a time convenient for them. Suppose a young couple with two children has to choose between attending a traditional Sunday-morning service and joining a small group. The Sunday-morning service is scheduled for the convenience of the pastor. Only one or two options are available. The couple may well have conflicts — a soccer game for the kids, an outing to grandma's, a strong desire to sleep in on the only morning they can, or a weekend shift at his job or hers. By contrast, the church may sponsor several dozen small groups, which give the couple a range of meeting times to choose from. If the one on Wednesday night is not convenient, the one on Thursday night may be. And, since a small group involves relatively few people, it may be possible to shift time and location to suit everyone. Now it is true, of course, that most people who attend Bible-study groups do not yet have to choose between a small group and the Sunday-morning service. Yet, people are clearly attracted to participating in something that can be arranged to fit their schedule.

The present orientation, in a sense, goes back to the basics, creating what some scholars refer to as a kind of religious "primitivism." It resembles the mood of early Christianity or that of the Israelites during their sojourn in the wilderness. Home meetings were preferred over public spectacles. Tabernacles were favored over temples. Faith was portable. Throughout much of American history, the course of events has run in the other direction. Bigger was better. Religious leaders tore down small meeting houses and built larger ones. More advanced degrees were required in order to preach. Services required more elaborate planning, larger choirs, more expensive organs, and thicker padding on the pews. All those trends, incidentally, are still at work, especially in the so-called megachurch movement. Congregants are attracted by high ceilings and inspiring choral arrangements. But those amenities exact a cost — not only in terms of dollars, but also in terms of who can participate. The person who feels comfortable talking to a few friends but not addressing an audience of thousands is excluded from taking a leadership role. The trend toward large structures has thus necessitated a counter-trend toward small groups. In these settings, faith moves from the pulpit to an assembly of peers. And, curiously, some of the same forces that make one kind of service possible also contribute to the other. Video equipment that makes it possible to telecast services from megachurches to the general public also makes it possible for small-group leaders to bring in a "guest speaker"— on videotape. Recorded music can also be brought in to set the tone for the meeting. Add a candle and a leather cross, and soon there is a portable worship service available. Small groups can be the settings in which such technologies bring spiritual tutelage within the reach of all.

Even more important is the fact that small groups are diverse and can therefore meet diverse needs and interests. The problem with the traditional weekend service (no doubt a problem more significant than the time it is held) is that it cannot be all things to all people. In a crowd of three hundred people, for example, some will find the sermon beneath their level of intelligence, while others may consider it hard to understand. Some will be offended by the personal stories the minister tells, while others may be put off by high-sounding theological language. More likely still, personal contact with the minister will be minimal. The sermon may seem impersonal. Being used to speaking up at home and at work, congregants may find it strange to sit quietly and only listen. They may want to air their own opinions, but find themselves in a context that doesn't allow such exchange. Small groups alter those dynamics. People can gather with their own kind— their own age group, their neighbors, people with similar addictions, people with comparable levels of education or biblical understanding. They can choose their own topics. They can talk as much as they want, freely offering their personal opinions. They can also focus the discussion on their personal needs. While the minister may pray generally for "the sick," they can ask the group to pray specifically for their bout of indigestion.

Small groups are thus a means of extending the ministries of established congregations into the crevices of society. Clergy may already have full schedules, preparing sermons, counseling, running programs. They could not possibly meet regularly with all their congregants. But, with a little help from lay leaders, they can draw people into small units where sharing and caring are the norm. They may not be able to structure

351

their entire congregations around the needs of young single professionals, but they can draw them in by initiating a prayer fellowship for this group. They can provide other groups for people wanting to learn the basics of faith, or different gatherings to encourage people to probe their faith more deeply.

Another contribution of small groups is that they encourage greater individual responsibility for the nurturing of one's faith. Although people may, in a sense, become dependent on the group, they also feel that the group helps them take responsibility. This is so because the norm of most groups is to encourage individual spirituality. Groups that emphasize personal study and applications are especially likely to do this. The dynamics of journeys and growth, discipline, and working on one's faith are part of this as well. People are encouraged to move beyond sitting and listening. They are prompted to think more actively about what they really believe and why. One of the women in the Methodist group studied provided a vivid example of this process. She felt that prior to the Disciple program, her faith wasn't personal. It wasn't something she could hold on to in a crisis. She felt that for much of her life she had been relying on other people, the church, and the minister to tell her what to believe. They were like go-betweens in her relationship with God. She said she felt like she was only a passenger on the bus, and that she needed to take a more active role in her own faith development and become the driver of the bus.

Part of taking responsibility is adapting a childlike faith to adulthood. Some people realize that the simple answers they learned as children to such questions as "Who is God?" and "What is the purpose of life?" no longer make sense to them. Their groups support them while they are rethinking these questions. Many of the people we talked to said they hadn't found new answers. But, as a result of discussing their questions with fellow group members, they now felt more comfortable with not having firm answers. The group showed them that other people don't know, either. Or, in studying biblical characters again, they saw some that had failings just like they did. Or there were group norms that said it is okay to doubt God or to yell at God.

Another way in which groups encourage greater responsibility in matters of faith is by giving people opportunities to discover what biblical teachings *mean*. Ours is a culture in which meanings are both fundamentally important and perplexingly problematic. They are important because we recognize that truths take on different shadings, or need to be applied differently under various circumstances and by different individuals. For example, we have to decide what it means to "honor thy father and thy mother" when they are putting us through school, or when they are divorced and abusing us, what it means when our parents are forty and when they are eighty. Meanings are problematic for the same reason. Varied circumstances necessitate individual interpretations. We can read what others have written, or talk to people in similar situations, but we must ultimately decide what something means to us. And because our own circumstances — and our selves — are constantly in flux, we must periodically renegotiate these meanings.

An example was given by a member of the Cathedral Nights group in New York. She said that the Lord's Prayer had been like a mantra for her. She said it to be saying it, largely without thinking about the words. But then someone suggested that she come up with a personal interpretation of it. That was a new idea for her. So she began thinking about what the words really meant to her. She realized that the clause about "power and glory" conjured up images of Hitler and Donald Trump, so she tried hard to visualize what power and glory might be in reference to God. The clause about forgiveness also began to have meaning for her. She decided that freedom from her own debts depended on forgiving others. The intimate relationships in her group made it possible for her to put that idea into practice. For more than five years she kept thinking about what the Lord's Prayer meant to her, and in the process its meanings shifted, grew, and deepened.

This example illustrates yet another contribution of small groups — helping individuals put their faith into practice. They do this in a variety of ways. Some groups encourage members to be better mothers or fathers, to have the patience, for example, to read a story to their son or daughter at bedtime, or the courage to set a better example. For others, putting faith into practice means staying sober. In another case, it may mean sending in a petition to support legislation favoring arms reduction. Groups encourage members to think about the meaning of their faith and how they should apply it in their particular callings. One person shares a story about some application that worked, and another goes away thinking about similar possibilities. Groups nurture practical applications by discussing them, by praying about them, by communicating information about needs and opportunities, and by affirming members in their individual ministries.

In the process, groups undergird the plausibility of faith as well. In

353

discussing ways in which their faith worked for them, members reinforce each other's belief that spiritual development does indeed lead to a better life. Daniel Olson writes in his field notes, for example, that "these discussions have a function not unlike testimonies in more conservative churches. When you hear someone say that they went through some struggle and they really felt the presence of God with them, this helps confirm the reality of one's own religious belief. If other people experience God as real and relevant for daily living, then it seems more likely that one can call upon God when one faces similar problems. In Peter Berger's (1967) terms, these discussions function as micro plausibility structures." Many members are themselves aware of this process, recognizing that one of the reasons that they are in the group is to strengthen their faith. When they testify to other members that the group has helped them to be more disciplined ("kept their feet to the fire"), they communicate positive feelings about the group and raise expectations about its positive effects on members' lives.

Perhaps the most important contribution small groups make is simply providing a time for prayer. Were someone from another culture to visit the United States, it would probably seem strange to that person that prayer could not be offered in other contexts. It is, of course. Public opinion polls suggest that most Americans pray by themselves or with their families on a fairly regular basis. But small groups are the main context — possibly the only context — in which most Americans share their prayer concerns with others and pray on one another's behalf. How much time is spent in prayer varies from group to group. Yet devoting at least some time to prayer is nearly universal in small groups.

Part of the reason that group prayer is a significant contribution to spiritual formation is that people learn how to pray by listening to others. Approaching the God of the universe with a request about one's aching back could well seem implausible (if not presumptuous). But hearing others do it normalizes it. Group leaders often use prayer to reinforce some of the lessons they wish to communicate. Consequently, prayer can also be a way of learning spiritual truths — for example, about the nature of God, about sin and forgiveness, about grace, and about trust. These functions of group prayer are often noted in manuals published for group leaders. What we learned from our research in small groups, however, is that prayer actually serves another important function.

In practice, prayer is the primary way in which group members care for each other. Individual members are encouraged to share their personal concerns not to evoke pity from the group or even to secure assistance but simply to serve an organizational convenience — so that members' concerns can be "collected" for the group prayer. This in itself takes away some of the embarrassment that might be present if members were blatantly asking the group for help. Yet, as members share, most groups deviate from the task at hand long enough to offer words of encouragement or even some advice. For example, in one of the groups we studied, the wife of a self-employed businessman requested prayer because the business was experiencing a slowdown in sales. This prompted one of the members to ask her if she was helping out. Several others offered comments about women they knew who worked in their husbands' businesses, detailing some of the pluses and minuses. Their remarks generally affirmed the woman's decision not to get involved. In addition, another member offered to buy something after the meeting. Following a few other comments, the leader pointed out how good it was for group members to encourage each other in this way.

Sharing prayer requests can thus be a way in which small groups fulfill a therapeutic function for their members. Making a personal concern public becomes part of the solution for an individual. Words of encouragement from the group help reduce his or her anxiety. Certainly this practice involves dangers as well as benefits — for example, there may be too much emphasis on encouragement from the group and too little on divine resources. Yet this is also a way in which the group draws a tangible link between caring and spirituality. Group prayer occurs in sanctified space. God is felt to be especially close. The discussion takes on seriousness and reverence. In this context, small expressions of encouragement become more than that. They indicate the group's willingness to take each member's concerns before the most sacred authority in their lives.

In groups that pray together over extended periods of time, the sharing of personal concerns is an effective way of bonding people together, and this in turn allows prayer to connect with spirituality at an even deeper level. At first, norms of self-sufficiency prevent people from praying about anything that might be taken as a sign of vulnerability or weakness. For example, people in some of the groups prayed for friends rather than for themselves, or prayed about medical problems, for which they were not at fault, rather than mistakes or sins of commission. In groups that had cultivated closer bonds, however, members gradually disclosed their fears, their anger, their doubts, and their shame. In these ways, then, their spirituality touched deeper parts of their lives.

355

The Limitations of Small-Group Spirituality

Small groups cultivate spirituality, but it is a *particular kind* of spirituality. They cannot be expected to nurture faith in the same way that years of theological study, meditation, and reflection might, or for that matter, in the same way that certain challenges could — serving on the mission field, working with the poorest of the poor in the streets of Calcutta, enduring a long illness. Accordingly, although small groups encourage many Americans to think about their faith, they also have limitations.

One of their clearest limitations can be seen in their promotion of what might be called "me-first religion." They do this as a by-product of focusing faith on personal needs. Group members are encouraged to think about the ways in which spirituality can help them, to apply faith concepts to their personal problems, and to share these problems with the group. In the process, it is easy for these practical, personal applications of faith to take precedence over everything else.

In the groups we studied, me-first religion was most evident during times of prayer. The prayer requests that members made generally focused on personal needs, such as illness, depression, and trouble in families. They seldom dealt with larger social or moral issues, such as war, international conflicts, hunger, poverty, and social justice. It is, of course, understandable that people would bring their personal needs to God in these ways. Group leaders encouraged them to do so, and some of their needs were indeed quite serious. Yet, in many cases, members also emphasized prayer items that seemed to have as their chief function the communication of tidbits of personal experience to the group. For example, one member might offer a prayer for Andy's liver condition, only to have another member point out that he had just talked to Andy's neighbor and that Andy actually had a kidney problem. Or, in giving praise, one person might offer thanks that her houseplants are blooming, another that his neighbor is looking forward to going to a ballgame on Saturday, and still another that her mother phoned the day before with some interesting piece of news.

What sometimes prevents group members from seemingly becoming obsessed with first-person issues is that they are then asked to pray for each other. One will thank God for another's blooming houseplants; that person, in turn, will pray that the individual who has mentioned Andy will "have peace" about his condition. There is sharing. But the group functions as a kind of mutual-aid society. Each person affirms what another has said, knowing that the deed will be reciprocated. The result is that each person is the focus of the group's attention at least twice — once in offering a prayer item, and once in having that item mentioned in prayer.

Studies of the Bible and of other religious books often turn out to be me-first sessions as well. The topic can be almost anything — God's wisdom, creation, grace, justice, the needy — but the group discussion emphasizes personal needs, personal experience, and personal insight. An example of all three comes from a discussion that one of the groups had about God's attributes. Immutability was the topic of the week. The leader quickly focused the discussion on the needs, experiences, and insights of individual group members: "God's immutability means that he watches over you and me, and he can talk to me, and he can talk to you at the same time." The point, the leader noted, was to just fall in love with God because he is so wonderful, just as one falls in love with and marries a wonderful person. To get the idea, the leader said, each member of the group should just pause and think for a moment about his or her marriage. The leader did read several statements from theologians and other religious figures about immutability, but these were offered quickly and without comment. Then the discussion opened up. One member was able to draw an insight from her reading of children's literature. Another pointed out that growth as a Christian is the important issue; still another, that each of us is on a spiritual journey. Several members then gave examples of how they had grown; another concluded by affirming the value of life experiences.

I emphasize this example because it provides a subtle, moderate example of me-first religion. The discussion that elicited it was richer than most in theological content. It was not a blatant example of trying to justify self-interest, or of finding Bible verses to justify wealth and the pursuit of happiness. Yet the thrust of the conversation was that God exists mainly to encourage the spiritual growth of individual believers. The main reason offered for believing in the immutability of God was that one's own life would be better as a result. The discussion also personified this attribute of God, encouraging members to understand it through the lens of their private lives — their marriages, their devotions, their personal struggles — rather than attempting to draw connections with nature or with social institutions. Operationally, it also affirmed the assumption that each individual has some special insight into the matter of God's immutability. No comment was rejected or criticized. Every personal experience was regarded as equally valid.

Another limitation of small groups is that they often promote an anything-goes form of spirituality. In small, intimate settings it is particularly difficult for people to tell others that they are wrong. Even small criticisms of other members take more fortitude than most people seem to have. It is much easier to accept all views — or at least to find some way of affirming what a fellow participant has said. Indeed, the groups we studied all developed norms of tolerance and acceptance. Some of the groups positively valued diverse perspectives on theological questions. Members might disagree, but they were reluctant to say that one view was any closer to the truth than another. In other groups, there was a deliberate effort to impart orthodox teachings to group members. Yet the ways in which members interpreted these teachings also displayed a wide range of opinion.

In addition to the fact that group members are reluctant to hurt one another's feelings, we discovered at least three other reasons why anything-goes spirituality becomes the norm in many groups. One is the emphasis that small groups place on personal experience. Rather than consulting the Bible itself, or a study guide or some scholarly interpretation, members judged the validity of ideas by assessing them against their own experiences. This tendency sometimes gave leaders or older members an advantage. But generally it gave each member an unassailable position from which to express opinions. For example, a person could claim to have been miraculously healed of a grave illness, or to have heard God tell him to quit his job, or to have found that wives being submissive to their husbands makes for marital harmony, and nobody in the group could legitimately challenge those claims. Second, group discussions often take on the appearance of the blind leading the blind. The point here is not that leaders and other members lacked knowledge about theology, the Bible, or other religious teachings (although this was, indeed, often the case). The point is that in general these groups, besides valuing personal experience, distrusted heavy reliance on the opinions of leaders or the ideas in study guides. Members openly expressed doubts about what they read, registered concern that some concept was too abstract or did not apply to them, and often sidetracked discussions by telling personal anecdotes or making jokes. As a result, stories were told that members found interesting and sometimes applicable to their own lives, but seldom was there a searching attempt to arrive at deeper understandings of spiritual truth. Third, a norm emphasizing good feelings also prevailed in most of the groups. This norm added to the pressure not to offend anyone. Members were supposed to come away from meetings having their self-esteem bolstered and feeling good about themselves.

In small groups that meet over long periods of time, the subtle pressures to conform to such norms are especially strong. Some members certainly felt challenged to lead better lives. But it was more likely that they felt reassured by their groups that they were basically on the right track in the way they were living now — certainly compared with the way in which many people in the outside world lived, or even compared with the way they themselves may have lived in the past. Group discussions often provided small insights about how to solve some personal problem. But it was equally likely that the insight would carry an implicit message suggesting that there might be many solutions or no solutions. These notions were especially reassuring. In deciding that it was okay not to have answers, for example, some people had their own spiritual doubts legitimated. In this way they got the message that it was okay to live pretty much as they would choose to anyway, and yet they could say that they felt more "at peace" or comfortable, or had a better sense of who they were. Also, many members emphasized just accepting yourself, going with the flow, rolling with the punches, not being anxious, and taking things one step at a time. Consequently, the idea of discipline was transmuted into one that said, in effect, that the real challenge in life is just to accept things as they are. As one group member observed following a study of the life of Paul, a study that on paper at least appeared to emphasize the discipline, rigor, and sacrifice associated with Paul's life, "He was a man who just rolled with the punches!"

In most groups, tolerance of diversity does not lead to radically unorthodox ideas being promulgated. The norm of personal comfort militates against this. Someone who presents an opinion that deviates too widely from others' beliefs and experiences is likely to experience subtle pressure to conform (or perhaps leave). The greater danger of anything-goes spirituality is that a bland attitude toward spirituality is reinforced, one that says, in effect, "Hold a few basic beliefs, try to live a good life, and all will be well." As a result, it becomes easier for the group to stay at a relatively superficial level, treading familiar ground, than to move into more challenging territory. As one of the researchers recorded in his field notes, some members in the group he was observing had been participants for more than twenty years, and yet their level of biblical knowledge remained well below that of a first-year seminary student.

However, an anything-goes attitude can also be promoted in groups that attempt to delve deeply into religious traditions. One of the groups we studied tried hard to keep people from following rigid rules and from seeking simplistic answers in their spiritual journeys. It recognized the dangers of a prepackaged faith. Yet its solution was to expose members to a wide variety of books, ethical writings, theological traditions, and inspirational literature; basically what this amounted to was the group's reading certain books and articles and listening to certain guest speakers that individual members happened to know about. Most of the members found these experiences enriching. They were stimulated to think more deeply about spirituality. But for some, spirituality also came to be a kind of toy, almost like Silly Putty. They could mold it, push it around, squeeze it, manipulate it, often just for fun. And the group legitimated this attitude by asserting that spirituality was indeed malleable, impossible to pin down. Always a mystery, it was thus something to be poked at and explored, and members were encouraged to be curious seekers capable of being delighted by whatever radical insight might turn up next.

Yet another limitation of small groups is that they can cultivate cheap-grace spirituality. That is, members may be challenged to lead better lives, to put their faith into practice, and yet fail to do this in any significant measure. As twelve-step language puts it, they talk the talk, but don't walk the walk. Or, they may in fact do a few things to transform belief into action — for example (as our survey showed), helping needy individuals or taking a more active part in their church — but still do nothing that constitutes a serious sacrifice of time or money, or that even begins to make full use of their talents and resources. For instance, several of the groups we studied occasionally spent time discussing ways that they could be more generous, and yet these discussions resulted mainly in comments about what the church was doing to help alcoholics or needy people in the community. The discussions seldom challenged members to do anything differently in their personal lives. Or, to take a more extreme example, in one of the groups a discussion of world hunger turned into a condemnation of the undeserving poor who do not work hard and do not take care of their own children.

The problem, of course, should not be laid wholly at the door of small groups. It has more to do with prejudice and the frailties of human nature. But the norms of small groups can also encourage cheap-grace spirituality. They are in business fundamentally to encourage talk. Their meetings consist of talking to God, talking about God, talking about themselves, and even include talking about *how to talk* about all these subjects. They are not fundamentally task-oriented groups. Many of them seek to foster an experience of closeness to God, a kind of emotional high point, rather than focusing on behavior. And closeness to God, in turn, consists mainly of talking. It means talking to God more often, telling God one's personal secrets, and feeling that God is an invisible friend. God, in turn, may be silent. But the silence may be readily filled by the words of fellow group members. And their words can, in effect, become the words of God. For example, a group told one of its members that she looked tired and worn out from trying to diet, and the next week she offered praise that God had given her permission to go off her diet. Another problem is that many groups cultivate a "rosier-than-thou" orientation toward spirituality. That is, they emphasize blessings, happiness, good feelings, and positive attitudes to such an extent that admitting to genuine struggles becomes unacceptable. In group discussions, talk of living a "victorious Christian life" and "claiming God's promises" takes precedence over admitting one's fears, even though facing up to pain may be necessary to experience genuine growth. Still another problem is that small groups are specifically designed to provide temporary retreats from life. They take *only* a couple of hours a week. People are attracted to these groups because they know their commitment can be limited. They will not be asked to change jobs, give away half their income, or become involved in long-term projects.

Nurturing Small-Group Spirituality

Small groups, then, have positive contributions to make, but they also have limitations. Recognizing the potential limitations is itself a step toward elevating the quality of spirituality in small groups. In addition, our research points to several ways of nurturing small-group faith that may have fairly wide applicability.

Most groups go through cycles, gingerly exploring new ground at first, moving into deeper issues along the way, and eventually dying or, in effect, being reborn by an infusion of new members. Some groups need to remain open, giving prospective members a chance to test the waters and, if the group is not to their liking, retreat to a different setting. Many of the pastors we talked to in the course of our research mentioned special groups, such as fellowships for newcomers or adult Sunday school classes, as settings in which such casual experimentation could take place. But deeper faith development is likely to require longer-term commitments. Churches and synagogues can advertise such requirements in advance so that prospective members know what they are getting into.

The real issue, however, is not length of involvement itself. Our research shows that most people stay in their groups for fairly long periods of time, anyway. But they can do this and still not progress to the point where they deal with harder issues. What is required is a commitment to attend regularly and to work on tough issues from week to week, not only in group meetings but also in between them. It may also be helpful to designate some groups as requiring greater commitment than others. One example from our research is the Methodist Disciple II program, which requires completion of the Disciple I program as a prerequisite and attempts to build on that base. Other churches also have one or two groups that specifically require greater commitment than other groups, perhaps including preparing lessons prior to meetings, memorizing certain Scripture passages, or taking on leadership roles. Twelve-step programs sometimes sort themselves out in these ways as well. The ACOA group included in our study was an example of a group that was basically at beginners' level, whereas a "Step 11" group in the same community provided its members with time to reflect more deeply on their spirituality.

One pitfall to be avoided in planning such groups is that of aiming to achieve goals that may be inherently contradictory. Most groups, for example, aim to include both "support" and "study." Yet the balance between these two purposes may not be easy to maintain. The women's Bible study we examined, for example, would not have functioned as well without a topic for study and discussion each week, and yet the studies clearly took second place to the women's needs for support. Thus, a pressing need in the group could cause the study to be canceled entirely, and affirmations and anecdotes often derailed the discussion and kept members from probing more deeply into theological issues. By contrast, the Methodist group was so dedicated to study that its members were sometimes unable to provide emotional support when such support was sorely needed.

Three ways of resolving this dilemma seem to be common. One is to offer a range of groups and encourage potential members to join one or more, depending on their particular needs and interests. Part of the reason why the Methodist group was able to get along without providing more emotional support, for example, was that members saw each other in different settings. Another strategy is one used by twelve-step groups: what permits many of them to function mainly as support groups is that they encourage members to read "program" literature on the side, but not to let such literature derail them from dealing with their own "issues" in group meetings. A third strategy is to differentiate parts of particular group meetings for different purposes. Groups that set aside an allotted time for study and then encourage support at other times, such as during prayer or over dessert, provide perhaps the clearest examples.

This strategy can also be used effectively to prevent group discussions from turning entirely into pragmatic, "it worked for me" kinds of sessions. The way that the Methodist group divided its standard meeting into two separate study times, one focusing on biblical knowledge and the other on applications of biblical principles, provides an example. By setting aside part of the time to deal with "what's in it for me?" issues, the group could devote the rest of its time to considerations of truth for its own sake. In this way, me-first religion can perhaps be turned into me-second applications.

Another way of combatting me-first religion is to draw explicit connections between group discussions and larger institutional concerns. The Pax Christi group provides an extreme example of making such connections. Its members' concerns about national and international issues associated with peace, disarmament, and social justice obviated virtually any discussion of personal needs, other than that which occurred informally before and after meetings. The Methodist group sought to include such concerns in its "Word and world" discussions. The women's Bible study also did this to some extent, at least by mentioning needs of the larger congregation. However, because it was virtually a freestanding group, it focused to a much greater extent on the personal needs of its own members. And even the groups that tried to bring in institutional issues sometimes faltered because these issues clearly were not of interest to members. What is probably needed, therefore, is explicit guidance, perhaps from leaders who bring in examples from current headlines or who provide ways for members to work on community projects or to mail in petitions about legislative matters.

There is a danger, of course, in treating small groups as cells whose aim is to serve some larger institutional cause. Especially if members attend a group because they need emotional support and have personal issues they need to have addressed, their enthusiasm will diminish if the group's attention shifts decidedly to denominational, national, or political issues. Nevertheless, one of the advantages that church-sponsored groups have is their connection to larger bodies. These bodies can funnel ideas and information to the group, and it, in turn, can mobilize its members, thus feeding energy back into the programs of larger agencies. One example: discussions in Catholic groups of statements issued by the U.S. Conference of Bishops on peace, social justice, and other social teachings. A different kind of example is provided by prayer fellowships in fundamentalist churches that become staging grounds for pro-life or anti-gay demonstrations.

Short of engaging in direct action of these kinds, small groups can at least focus periodically on their relationships — and those of their members — to the larger institutions on which any good society depends. Many small groups do this with some effectiveness when they discuss family issues. Although these discussions can easily become preoccupied with *my* spouse and *my* children, they can also raise questions about legislation that may impinge on families, resources that need to be made available to poor families, and the ways in which churches and synagogues may minister to families. Some small groups have also been able to do an effective job of discussing the connections between faith and economic institutions, raising issues, for example, about ethics in the workplace or about the meanings and uses of money. The important point is that small groups themselves depend on institutional arrangements, and so does a vibrant spirituality. Neither exists simply because a few individuals happen to have needs in their personal lives. Both require freedom, commitments, and other resources, and both depend on individuals giving back in full measure to the wider community.

Implicit in all these suggestions is the assumption that small groups are *led* — that is, that they are planned, guided, and have someone behind the scenes trying to manipulate them to accomplish higher aims. That assumption needs to be addressed squarely. Our research shows that virtually all groups do, in fact, have leaders and that a majority of groups have other structures as well, ranging from connections with clergy and church-growth plans to elected officers, business meetings, formal names, fixed agendas, stated goals, and in some cases terms, contracts, and membership fees. These structures help keep things running smoothly. They may even be necessary in order to prod group members to take on new projects or to focus on deeper spiritual issues. What group members themselves say they like about their groups, however, has much less to do with formal structure. It is the sense that they can say what they want to, share their problems, and still be appreciated. They like feeling that they can trust each other, be honest with each other, and receive emotional support.

Group leaders interested in spiritual formation must, therefore, walk a fine line between imposing structure on groups and simply letting groups "do their own thing." Too much structure can kill the spirit. Group members need to feel a sense of ownership toward their groups. If they don't, they will simply blame the clergy or their leaders when things go wrong rather than taking an active role in keeping the group functioning effectively. Part of what it means to take responsibility for one's faith must include taking responsibility for the group that nurtures this faith. On the other hand, groups that function without structure and without guidance often take the path of least resistance, talking about safe topics and affirming each other rather than challenging their members to grow spiritually.

Part of the solution again is that different groups can be devised to meet different tastes. In several of the groups we studied, a few members wanted more structure than their groups provided, so they simply left and joined other groups. Another part of the solution is to have structure but to keep it in the background. Several of the groups, for example, were closely supervised by pastors, and yet these pastors did not personally attend the groups because their presence alone would have stifled the spontaneity and curbed the openness of group members. Still another part of the solution is to have groups confront from time to time their own implicit norms. The ACOA group, for example, used business meetings for this purpose. On such occasions the usual discussion of personal needs was set aside, and comments were focused on the nature of the meetings themselves. Members who felt there was too much "crosstalk," for example, could say so, or the group could gently nudge members who talked too much to talk less. Confronting implicit norms is, of course, not something to be done casually. It may be painful to admit that the group is really nurturing callous attitudes toward the poor, engaged in fundamentalist-bashing, or affirming an anything-goes religion. But that pain may be essential to growth.

Still another point that leaders and members alike need to bear in mind is that some groups can legitimately fail, or can succeed, accomplishing their aims for a time, and then legitimately be allowed to die.

The Cathedral Nights group we studied provides an example. It failed, largely through no fault of its own, and its failure was painful to some of its members. Yet, only by dying could it be transformed into something new, or could a space develop in which former members could move in new directions. Some of the groups also had definite terms, or at least checkpoints at which members could decide to keep the group going or terminate it. Such occasions also permit groups to celebrate their accomplishments and, if need be, say farewell to the group itself. What is more difficult, as we learned from talking with former members of some groups, is finding a way to celebrate with individual members who may decide to terminate their participation. Those who move away are often given parties, whereas those who choose simply to drop out do so without fanfare, incurring guilt or resentment in the process. It is generally the responsibility of the group leader to seek them out and find a suitable way to commemorate their departure.

Finally, a point that cannot be emphasized too much is that small groups must not be used as substitutes for the other ways in which spirituality is developed and enacted. Small groups provide brief times for members to come together and share some of their personal concerns, pray about them, and gain insights from discussing matters of common interest. But spiritual development also requires time spent alone, performing the daily office of prayer and meditation, or reading the wisdom of scholars and saints. Group discussions themselves will be richer as a result (as the Chicago group illustrates). And serious groups will generally encourage the members to engage in such activities as well. Spiritual formation also requires putting faith into action, perhaps in ways that small groups can encourage but in themselves cannot completely fulfill (e.g., through careers, political action, or religious institutions).

Small groups are perhaps most effective when they are part of a balanced program of activities within congregations. They can provide occasions for fellowship. But other occasions — for worship, learning, and service — must also be provided. Balanced programs must also encourage a balanced understanding of faith development itself. Group members should cultivate a more complex interior life that spills over into their exterior life. But they should also be wary of becoming overly introspective and so interested in personal piety that it removes them from service in everyday life and from sensing the work of God being accomplished in ordinary activities. Small groups can, in these ways, add significantly to their members' understanding that all of life is sacred.

Appendix:
Small Groups — A National Profile

ROBERT WUTHNOW

T his essay provides a brief overview of the small-group movement in the United States. The information was obtained in a national survey of the adult U.S. population conducted in November 1991 as part of the Lilly Endowment research project on small groups and spiritual formation. Respondents were selected randomly and contacted in person by trained interviewers from the Gallup Organization. All respondents were asked a few questions about their communities and whether they were currently involved in a small group. Those who said they belonged to a small group were then asked approximately 45 minutes of questions about the nature of their group and its relationship to their faith. Those who were not involved in small groups were asked a short series of questions about their backgrounds and current interests. In all, 1,021 persons who were members of small groups and 962 persons who were not members were interviewed.[1]

Other aspects of Americans' faith have been studied in this way many times since the inception of public opinion polling a half century ago. Surveys are inevitably limited. They cannot, for example, probe the nuances of a person's theological understandings or determine whether someone truly lives out his or her faith. Such research has been valuable, however, in mapping out the broad contours of religion in America. It

1. Details of the study are presented in Wuthnow (1994).

reveals, for instance, that approximately two adults out of three are currently members of some religious organization and that about two individuals in five attend religious services in any given week. This research has also made it possible to answer such questions as whether women are more likely to attend church than men (they are) and whether churchgoing makes much of a difference to the ways in which people spend their money (it does not). Because surveys have been done over a number of years, it has been possible to keep track of trends as well.

Although previous surveys have occasionally included questions about participation in Bible studies or prayer groups, our survey is the first to examine the phenomenon of small-group participation in detail. Thus, with these data it is not possible to say for sure whether participation in small groups is currently increasing or decreasing. What we can say is that this participation is quite extensive. Most of the leaders within the small-group movement to whom we spoke *believe* that participation is rising. And the survey results are at least consistent with this view, showing, for instance, that more people report current than past involvement.

The main contribution of the survey, however, is to provide descriptive evidence on the kinds of people who are involved in small groups, the kinds of groups in which they are involved, and the nature of their involvement. Clearly, this is the sort of information one must have in order to put any specific group in context. To some, for example, it might appear that most Americans who are involved in small groups are in twelve-step groups, such as Alcoholics Anonymous. Others, however, might be involved in a Wednesday-evening Bible study group, and might suppose that that kind of group is the norm. Indeed, reading the anecdotal literature can lead to these varying impressions as well.

In addition, the survey permits some generalizations to be made about the relationships between small-group participation and spiritual formation. It becomes possible, for example, to answer questions about the ways in which members perceive their faith to have been influenced by their participation. How we view small groups will be considerably affected by whether these groups do, as many of their proponents claim, foster closeness to God, biblical knowledge, and other attributes of faith, or whether most members are there simply to have a good time.

I turn first to an overall portrait of Americans' involvement in small groups, focusing on the extent and intensity of participation, and on the characteristics of members and their motives for being involved. Because church-sponsored groups differ considerably from nonchurch groups, I then consider each of these separately, discussing the main varieties of each, and their activities. Finally, I explore how members of small groups describe the changes that have taken place in their faith as a result of being in these groups.

The Scope of the Movement

The best estimate of how widespread the small-group movement has become in American society is that about four adults in ten appear to be involved in some kind of group. If there are about 200 million adults altogether, this means that about 80 million people are currently participating in small groups. This estimate is based on a question in the survey that asked, "Are you currently involved in any small group that meets regularly and provides support or caring for those who participate in it?" Exactly 40 percent said "yes." This question had been pretested in a small national survey and in in-depth interviews. The pretests showed that people were sometimes unsure about what type of group might be relevant, and on occasion realized only later that they were indeed involved in something that they should have mentioned. For these reasons, respondents who hesitated were shown a list of groups that contained phrases such as "Bible study group," "discussion group," "support group," "Sunday school class," "couples group," and comparable terms. Had respondents not been shown this list, the percentage responding affirmatively would likely have been lower. However, judging from other questions, the 40 percent seems to be a reliable figure. This conclusion is supported by the fact that, when asked then to say how many such groups they belonged to, all but 2 percent were able to answer, and when asked how meaningful their group was to them, only 2 percent said it was not very meaningful.

What does this finding mean? It certainly suggests that the small-group movement has become a major feature of American life. The proportion of the population that participates in small groups, for example, is equal to that which attends religious services in any given week. It is larger than the "market share" that even the most popular television programs (except for the Super Bowl) attract. It is much larger than the proportions of the population that have been involved in some other aspects of American religion which have received attention in recent decades. For example, the much-discussed Moral Majority of the 1980s never enlisted more than about 5 percent of the population, and even the wider "fundamentalist" movement was restricted to no more than about 10 percent of the population (at least if moderate evangelicals were excluded). And the so-called new religions of the 1970s, such as Zen, Transcendental Meditation, and Krishna consciousness, probably did not attract more than 3 or 4 percent of the population collectively. So, by these indications, the small-group movement is indeed a significant phenomenon.

The question about how many groups people belonged to also elicited some important information. If every participant belonged to only one group, the total number of groups in the United States would probably be around three million (given what the survey found about the average size of groups). Many people, however, belong to more than one such group. In fact, 19 percent of the people who belong to at least one group (8 percent of the total population) say they participate in two groups, and another 19 percent belong to three or more groups. This is another indication, then, of how extensive the small-group movement has become. It also raises questions, of course, about *which* group respondents had in mind when they answered other questions. To reduce ambiguity, we instructed respondents who participated in more than one group to base their answers on the group that was most important to them at the time.

Another indication of the scope of small groups comes from examining the proportion of Americans who have *ever* belonged to a small group. This figure is 55 percent. In other words, in addition to the 40 percent who are currently involved, another 15 percent of the public has been in a group in the past.

Comparing previous involvement with present involvement is also the best indication from the survey that the small-group movement is probably growing. Approximately one American in six (16 percent) is a first-time member of a small group; that is, they are currently involved in a small group but were never involved in any such groups previously. This figure, compared with the 15 percent who have been involved in a small group at some point in their lives but are no longer involved, would suggest that the movement is not growing very much. However, that comparison includes even people who participated in small groups as children or who may have participated briefly as long as twenty or thirty years ago. A better baseline is the number who have dropped out of small groups in recent years. For example, only 5 percent of the public has dropped out within the past three years.[2] In other words, new membership appears to be substantial, while the attrition rate is fairly small. Still another indication that small-group participation may be growing is the fact that a quarter (24 percent) of those not currently involved in a small group say they would like to join one. Approximately half of these (53 percent) say it is very likely or fairly likely that they will do so within the next year.

In addition to the sheer numbers of Americans who are involved, the most important gauge of the small-group movement comes from questions about participation itself, and what this participation means to those involved in small groups. Fifty percent of all small-group members attend meetings of their group at least once a week. Another 40 percent attend at least once a month, participating either biweekly (13 percent) or monthly (27 percent). Only 10 percent participate less often than this. These figures correspond closely with information obtained in the survey about how often the groups actually held meetings, too. In other words, the vast majority of small-group members attend their groups faithfully. This impression was also shared, incidentally, by members themselves, two-thirds of whom said almost everyone in their group attends every time a meeting is held.

Some meetings, of course, last longer than others. Some are brief meetings — say, over the lunch hour — that people can participate in rather easily. But this is not the norm. Forty percent of all members say their groups meet at least two hours at a time. Twenty-five percent say their groups usually meet for an hour and a half. Only a third (33 percent) meet for about an hour. In short, the typical member is likely to spend most of an evening, or, in some cases, much of a morning, whenever his or her group meets.

Judging from the frequency and duration of the meetings, it would seem likely that members of small groups are quite committed to them. That this is the case emerges from various other kinds of information collected in the survey. For example, 71 percent of all members say their group is very important or extremely important to them. Another 26 percent say the group is fairly important, while only 3 percent say it is not important. Satisfaction among group members also runs quite high.

2. These figures do not allow more precise estimates of the growth of small-group participation because a complete history of involvement was not obtained.

Specifically, 84 percent say they are very satisfied or extremely satisfied with their group, 15 percent say they are somewhat satisfied, and only 1 percent say they are dissatisfied.

Why is commitment to small groups so strong? Apparently the main reason is that members feel they benefit from their groups in a number of important ways. The desire for community and companionship, for example, has often been noted as a feature of contemporary life, and small groups play a role in meeting this need. Eighty-two percent of small-group members, for instance, say their group has "made them feel like they weren't alone." Almost as many (72 percent) said the group "gave them encouragement when they were feeling down." Although the percentages are smaller, a substantial minority of group members have also benefitted in more specific ways from participating. Forty-three percent said the group had helpled them through an emotional crisis. Thirty-eight percent said it had helped them make a difficult decision. The same proportion said the group had helped them when someone was sick. And about one member in five (21 percent) said the group had given them physical care or support. Thus, there seems to be some validity in using the phrase "support groups" to characterize the small-group movement. Most members do indeed feel cared for and supported.

The other reason that commitment to small groups runs deep is that most members feel their groups function well. Five people out of six (84 percent) rate their group as "excellent" or "good" in terms of "drawing everyone into the discussion." Even more (89 percent) give equally favorable marks to their group for "respecting all different points of view." Nearly as many (82 percent) express confidence that their group is "addressing important issues." About the same number (84 percent) say the group does an excellent or a good job of "making me feel appreciated." A high proportion (87 percent) say their leaders are "well prepared." Four members out of five (81 percent) give excellent or good ratings to their group for "having everything working smoothly and efficiently."

Problems do exist, apparently. But they bother a small minority of group members. And they do not dampen the enthusiasm that most members express for their groups. One problem, for example, is welcoming newcomers. Only 6 percent of group members, however, say their group does a "poor" or only a "fair" job of doing this. Another problem is conflict among group members. This, however, is experienced as a problem by only 11 percent, at least according to what was reported in the survey. Incidentally, considerably more (53 percent) admit that they have had disagreements with other members. But most groups seem able to withstand such disagreements. In addition, relatively few members admit to other sorts of unease. For example, only 12 percent say they have felt "like you couldn't really be open and honest with the group." About the same number (11 percent) have felt "like the group didn't understand you." And even fewer had felt that "people in the group were criticizing you" (8 percent), that "[you were] not appreciated by the group" (7 percent), or that "the group was invading your privacy" (3 percent).

In sum, the small-group movement has been successful in attracting a relatively large segment of the American public into its ranks. Its members attend meetings frequently and over long periods of time. Most who have ever been involved are still involved. Current members express high levels of satisfaction with their groups. They feel cared for and supported. And they believe their groups function well.

Church-based Groups

The small-group movement is also quite diverse. Some are for men; others are for women. Some are quite formal; others are informal. Some are quite large; others, quite small. Some meet in churches; others meet in homes. They also vary in their goals and in the main activities they include. One of the most crucial distinctions is between groups that are sponsored by churches (or synagogues) and groups that have no connections with religious organizations.

Slightly more than half (57 percent) of all group members say their group is "part of the regular activities of a church or synagogue." This figure reveals how deeply indebted to religious organizations the small-group movement is. People who attend these church-based groups use a variety of labels to describe them. And, because several labels can apply to the same group, it is impossible to sort them out completely. Yet, even the labels themselves indicate the vast range of groups that have been initiated by churches. Seventy percent of members, for example, say their group can be described as a "Bible study." Almost this many (67 percent) say the term "prayer fellowship" fits their group. And nearly half (49 percent) say their group is a "Sunday school class." Other labels suggest some additional dimensions of variation. For example, 33 percent say their group is a "women's group." Nearly a quarter (24 percent) say the label "youth group" applies. Almost this many (21 percent) define their group as a "couples group." One person in six (17 percent) describes his group as a "men's group." And one person in eight (12 percent) belongs to a "singles group."

The survey reveals clearly how church-based groups are connected to their sponsoring organizations. More than half (56 percent) are "something one of the clergy helped to start." Nearly two-thirds (65 percent) are "under the supervision of one of the clergy." Four in five (79 percent) are "using plans, lessons, or other materials provided by a church or synagogue." And an equally large number (82 percent) are "part of the church's or synagogue's plan to grow."

Several other characteristics of the connections between these groups and churches are worth noting. One is that most members are attending groups sponsored by *their own* church, rather than some other church. Virtually all (95 percent), for example, say their group is "connected to the church or synagogue that you personally belong to," and virtually all (94 percent) say their group is "composed mostly of members of this church or synagogue." This means that church-based groups are probably strengthening the local congregation, rather than causing it to break down. That is, people are joining groups where they attend worship services, instead of being drawn away from the life of their congregation by seeking out groups in other churches. It also suggests, however, that church-based groups are not drawing in large numbers of people from the wider community who are not members of a local church already. Another question in the survey, for example, revealed that 96 percent of those who attend church-based groups are currently members of a church or synagogue. It could be, of course, that small groups attracted people who *then* joined the church. What the exact sequence of events may have been is difficult to sort out. We do know, at least, that 6 percent of those who belong to church-based groups have been attending their present church for less than a year. And another 7 percent have been attending for less than two years.

What is clearer from the survey is that church-based groups are an effective means of keeping church members active, and perhaps even of activating nominal members. For example, 61 percent say they have "taken a more active part in other programs sponsored by your church or synagogue." Moreover, half (50 percent) say they have "increased the amount of money you give to your church or synagogue." Other questions verify that small-group members are, in fact, quite actively involved in their churches. For example, an astonishing 85 percent say they attend religious services at least once a week (compared with about 30 percent of the public at large). Nearly this many (81 percent) say they are involved in at least one "special activity, program or committee" at their church, and nearly a third (31 percent) say they are involved in *three* or more such activities. The extent to which group members are drawn into their congregations is also evident in friendship patterns. Five group members out of six (86 percent) say that at least one of their closest friends attends their congregation. Perhaps more impressively, a majority (52 percent) say that *more than five* of their closest friends attend the same congregation.

We can also gauge how common church-based groups are within different kinds of congregations and religious traditions. Some writers have speculated that small groups may be more common in large congregations (where fellowship is harder to provide in other ways) than in smaller congregations. The survey, however, suggests that church-based groups are distributed fairly evenly across all sizes of congregations. Specifically, 14 percent of the members of these groups say they belong to churches of fewer than 100 members, 18 percent belong to churches of between 100 and 200 members, another 14 percent are members of churches with 200 to 300 people, 17 percent belong to churches with 300 to 500 members, 18 percent are in churches of 500 to 1,000 members, and 16 percent are in churches with more than 1,000 members.

There are some differences among denominations, but these are quite small. Remembering that virtually all members of church-based groups attend groups sponsored by their own churches, we can assess the relative involvement of various denominations by comparing the religious composition of group members with the religious composition of the U.S. population at large. The biggest difference, of course, is that all of the members of church-based groups have a religious preference, whereas about one person in ten, 9 percent of the general public, claims to have no religious preference. If we factor out those differences, we can then make the following comparisons: the proportion of group members who are Southern Baptists and the proportion of the general public who have a religious preference and who claim to be Southern Baptists are 15 percent and 11 percent, respectively; other Baptists, 11 percent and 11 percent, respectively; United Methodists, 7 percent and 10 percent, respectively; Lutherans, 4 percent and 4 percent, respectively; Presbyterians, 4 percent and 2 percent, respectively; United Church of Christ,

4 percent and 2 percent, respectively; Episcopalians, 1 percent and 2 percent, respectively; other Protestants, 23 percent and 21 percent, respectively; Roman Catholic, 21 percent and 30 percent, respectively; and Jewish, 2 percent and 2 percent, respectively.

Some of these figures are based on small numbers and, for this reason, may be inaccurate. Nevertheless, several conclusions appear warranted. First, Catholics are somewhat underrepresented among the members of church-based groups. Second, Southern Baptists and members of some of the more conservative denominations included in the "other Protestant" category (such as Assemblies of God, Pentecostal churches, and The Church of the Nazarene) are somewhat overrepresented in small groups. And third, mainline Protestants show a divided pattern, with Presbyterians and Lutherans overrepresented, and Methodists and Episcopalians underrepresented.

The conclusion that members of more conservative churches — either in conservative denominations or in other denominations — are more likely to be involved in church-based small groups is substantiated by several other findings from the survey. When asked about their own "religious views," 41 percent of the members of church-based small groups described themselves as conservatives (on a six-point scale), 39 percent put themselves in the middle, and only 16 percent described themselves as liberals. (In surveys of the general public, the ratio of religious conservatives to liberals is about even.) Moreover, when asked about the religious composition of their *group*, 39 percent said it was composed mostly of religious conservatives, 30 percent said it was a mixture of conservatives and liberals, 18 percent said it was mostly "middle-of-the-road," and only 5 percent said it was mainly liberals. Substantial numbers of those in church-based groups also gave answers to specific belief questions that in other studies have been taken as indications of religious orthodoxy or conservatism. For example, 57 percent said they had experienced a powerful religious awakening, 91 percent had made a personal commitment to Jesus Christ, and 49 percent said that "everything in the Bible should be taken literally, word for word."

Several other characteristics of the members of church-based groups also help to clarify the overall picture of these groups. About two-thirds (63 percent) of their members are women. They vary widely in age, and are only slightly older on average than women in the public at large. For example, 32 percent are younger than age 35, while 41 percent are older than age 50 (compared with 35 percent of the public). They do not differ significantly from the rest of the population in the percentage who have graduated from college (about 20 percent) or who are white, Hispanic, or black. They are, however, somewhat more likely to be located in the South than are members of the general population, and are underrepresented in the Northeast. They are also underrepresented in large cities and are overrepresented in small towns and rural areas.

On balance, then, the members of church-based small groups are not markedly different from the rest of the public — except for the fact that they display some of the characteristics which distinguish other religiously involved people. Women, for example, are generally more active in religious organizations than men. The South and rural areas also remain more religiously involved than other areas. In most other ways, church-based small groups register the same racial, ethnic, and religious diversity that characterizes the society as a whole.

What do people actually do in these groups? This, of course, is the crucial question. In fact, these groups feature a wide range of activities. But these activities are also oriented clearly toward nurturing spirituality. Virtually all of their members (94 percent) say their group prays together. More than nine in ten (92 percent) discuss religious topics. Nearly this many (86 percent) study or discuss the Bible in their groups. Other activities that help to forge relationships among group members are also fairly common. For example, 75 percent say their groups eat together, 75 percent also sing together on occasion, and more than half (62 percent) have parties. A substantial minority (39 percent) also say they sometimes get together for sports activities or to pursue hobbies, and a few (18 percent) even engage in physical exercise together.

Most church-based groups also depend on formal structures of some kind to keep things going smoothly. Almost all members (94 percent) say their group has a leader. Nearly this many (85 percent) say their group has a stated goal or purpose. About three-quarters (74 percent) have an agenda or schedule. About half have elected officers (51 percent), and about half hold business meetings (49 percent).

Other structures, however, are much less common. For example, only 12 percent say their groups have a membership fee. Approximately one in seven (15 percent) says the group has a contract that people have to agree to, and an equally small number (14 percent) have a term after which the group disbands.

What means the most to group members, of course, is not the formal structure, but the fact that caring and support takes place within the group. When asked what things had helped them most, for example, 62 percent responded that "seeing love and caring acted out in the group" had been very important to them. Other kinds of support had also been helpful to many. For instance, a slight majority (52 percent) said that "hearing other members share their views" had been very important to them; nearly as many (49 percent) said that "people in the group giving you encouragement" had been very helpful. And, not surprisingly, 52 percent said that "studying particular lessons from the Bible" had also been very important.

These findings should be encouraging to clergy and lay leaders who have found small groups beneficial in their own churches. The survey suggests that church-based groups are an important part of the larger small-group movement and that these groups are in fact providing people with opportunities to pray and learn more about the Bible. Their members are also apparently receiving support and finding inspiration in the caring they see enacted in their groups. The survey also provides evidence about the ways in which members believe their groups are nurturing their faith. Before considering that evidence, however, it will be helpful to focus briefly on the 43 percent of group members whose groups are not part of the activities of churches or synagogues.

Nonchurch Groups

These groups are perhaps best described as special interest groups or as support groups. In fact, of the people surveyed who were in nonchurch groups, a majority (62 percent) said the term "special interest group" applied to their group, and almost as many (52 percent) said the term "support group" was appropriate. The term "self-help group" was also used by 30 percent of these respondents. These terms can, of course, overlap.

Other questions in the survey indicate some of the variety that exists among small groups in nonchurch settings. For example, 22 percent of the members of these groups said the term "women's group" was an appropriate label for describing their group. About the same proportion (20 percent) said theirs was a "men's group." In comparison, only 12 percent were in a "couples group." Nearly one person in six (15 percent) described his or her group as a "therapy group." And the same proportion (15 percent) said it was an "anonymous group."

The activities sponsored by these groups also help fill out the profile of what they are like. For example, a majority (61 percent) do things for the community, work together on projects (69 percent), or discuss social and political issues (58 percent). So, it appears, a number of these groups are oriented toward civic activities. This conclusion is also suggested by the fact that many of the members of these groups say they have become more involved in such issues as a result of their group. For instance, 47 percent say they have become more interested in social or political issues. Almost this many (44 percent) have become involved in volunteer work in their community. And one in six (16 percent) has participated in a political rally or worked for a political campaign.

Other nonchurch small groups are more deeply concerned with emotional crises, addictions, and other personal issues. About one person in six (17 percent) who belongs to a nonchurch small group says that his or her group focuses on addictions, for example. Almost the same number (16 percent) say their group follows a "twelve step" program (Alcoholics Anonymous would be an example). Another indication of this emphasis is the fact that 12 percent of the members of nonchurch small groups say the group helped them overcome an addiction. In addition, 37 percent say their group helped them through an emotional crisis.

As with church-based groups, other activities point to a wider range of interests being included in nonchurch small groups. Book discussion clubs are probably one popular type of group, judging from the fact that 40 percent of the members of nonchurch groups say they discuss books. About the same proportion (43 percent) say they engage in sports or pursue hobbies together. And about a quarter (26 percent) engage in physical exercise together.

Nonchurch groups are seldom oriented primarily toward spiritual issues. There are groups, however, that have some connection with churches or synagogues. For example, 12 percent of them use a church or synagogue as a place to meet. Some of them also include religious activities. For instance, 35 percent of their members say they pray together. A quarter (24 percent) discuss religious topics. And 15 percent study or discuss the Bible. Indeed, 9 percent of their members describe their groups as Bible studies, and 13 percent say the term "prayer fellowship" applies to their groups.

The kinds of people who participate in nonchurch groups are somewhat different from those involved in church-based groups. Whereas women are overrepresented in church-based groups by a ratio of two to one, women and men are involved in nonchurch groups in virtually equal numbers.[3] Education levels are somewhat higher in non-church groups than in church-based groups.[4] People who live in the Northeast and on the West Coast are more likely to join nonchurch groups than church-based groups, whereas the opposite is true of those who live in the South and the Midwest.[5] Nonchurch groups are some-what more likely to draw members who do not have children, whereas church-based groups attract more people with children (although the average age of members in the two kinds of groups is similar).[6] Dwellers in large cities are disproportionately drawn to nonchurch groups rather than to church-based groups.[7] Those who seldom attend church and who hold liberal religious views are, of course, more inclined to join non-church groups than church-based groups.[8] Catholics are also more in-clined to join nonchurch groups rather than church-based groups.[9]

Nevertheless, the two kinds of groups attract people for some of

3. In nonchurch groups, 48 percent of members are men and 52 percent are women (compared with 63 percent and 37 percent, respectively, in church-based groups).

4. For example, 25 percent of nonchurch group members have graduated from college and 31 percent have some college education (compared with 20 percent and 27 percent, respectively, in church-based groups).

5. In the Northeast, 56 percent of group members belong to nonchurch groups, and 43 percent belong to church-based groups; in the West, 52 percent and 47 percent, respectively; in the South, 29 percent and 71 percent, respectively; and in the Midwest, 38 percent and 61 percent, respectively.

6. Thirty-eight percent of nonchurch group members have children, com-pared with 47 percent of church-based group members.

7. In large cities, 53 percent of group members belong to nonchurch groups, and 46 percent belong to church-based groups; in medium or small cities, 40 percent and 59 percent, respectively; and in small towns or rural areas, 38 percent and 62 percent, respectively.

8. Of all group members who attend church once a year or never, 95 percent are in nonchurch groups, compared with 65 percent of those who attend church monthly, and 23 percent of those who attend weekly; of group members who define their religious views as liberal, 59 percent are in nonchurch groups, compared with 48 percent of moderates, and 22 percent of conservatives.

9. Of all group members who are Catholics, 57 percent are in nonchurch groups, compared with 31 percent of Protestants.

the same reasons. For example, a majority of nonchurch and of church-based group members alike (63 percent and 59 percent, respectively) say they started attending because someone they knew invited them. About a quarter of those in each kind of group (26 and 29 percent, respectively) started attending because they needed emotional support. And about one in six (17 percent and 16 percent, respectively) became involved because of a personal crisis. Other data also indicate that the personal needs of members in the two kinds of groups are often similar. For example, about the same proportions of each say they are trying to figure out what is important in life, are worried about money or their health, are having problems with their family or work, or are suffering from anxiety, depression, or loneliness.[10]

Not surprisingly, therefore, people in the two kinds of groups expressed appreciation for receiving similar kinds of support. For example, a large majority of the members of church-based groups (88 percent) and of nonchurch groups (74 percent) said their group had "made you feel like you weren't alone." Nearly as many (79 and 63 percent, respectively) said the group "gave you encouragement when you were feeling down." Large minorities of each (47 and 37 percent, respectively) had been "helped through an emotional crisis." And more than a third (38 percent in each case) said the group "helped you make a difficult decision."

What distinguishes the two kinds of groups most clearly is that *spirituality* itself is one of the primary factors of participation in church-based groups. Two-thirds of the members of church-based groups (68 percent) say that "wanting to become more disciplined in your spiritual life" was a reason why they became involved in their group. In contrast, only 15 percent of the members of nonchurch groups listed this among their reasons. Thus, we need to consider what the nature of this spirituality is and how members feel their groups have nurtured it.

10. Among church-based and nonchurch group members, respectively, the following percentages said they were bothered "a lot" by each of the following: "trying to figure out what is important in life," 15 percent and 20 percent; "worrying about money," 16 percent and 18 percent; "worrying about your health," 16 percent and 17 percent; "problems with your spouse or family," 11 percent and 15 percent; "problems with your work," 7 percent and 9 percent; "anxiety," 5 percent and 9 percent; "feeling depressed or sad," 4 percent and 7 percent; and "feeling lonely," 4 percent and 5 percent.

The Contribution to Spiritual Formation

Members of church-based groups join in hopes of deepening their spirituality—and most believe that their faith is, in fact, deepened as a result. When asked about their personal needs, 97 percent say they have experienced a need to be "part of a group that helps you grow spiritually." And 64 percent say this need has been fully met.

When asked about changes that have occurred in their lives over the past five years, most of the members of church-based groups indicate that their faith has, in various ways, become more important to them. For example, 56 percent say that "spiritual matters" have become much more important to them, and another 23 percent say spiritual matters have become somewhat more important, while only 20 percent say spiritual matters have stayed the same, and a mere 1 percent say they have become less important. Much the same patterns are evident in their responses to other questions. A slight majority (53 percent) say their "church or synagogue" has become much more important to them. Even more (60 percent) say that "prayer" has become much more important. And almost half (48 percent) say this about "studying the Bible." Of course, some of these changes may be the result of experiences other than participating in their group.

Most members of church-based groups, however, also attribute changes in their spirituality directly to their small groups. When asked, "From being involved in this group, has your faith or spirituality been influenced?" 84 percent said yes. And of this 84 percent, 58 percent said their faith has been "deepened a lot," 40 percent said it had been "deepened a little," and 2 percent said it had "changed in some other way" (none said it had become less important). In addition, 59 percent said they had "sensed God's presence in the group" many times, and 27 percent had experienced this a few times.

Members of church-based groups also attribute *specific changes* to involvement in their groups. Ninety percent say they feel "closer to God" as a result of participating in their group, 87 percent say they have "a deeper love toward other people," 85 percent say they have "a better ability to forgive others," 84 percent say they have experienced "the Bible becoming more meaningful to you," 82 percent have "a better ability to forgive yourself," 75 percent have experienced "answers to prayers," and 75 percent have been helped in "sharing your faith with others outside the group."

The by-products of spiritual development are also much in evidence. Fifty-three percent say they have experienced "healings of relationships." Eighty percent say they have "worked with the group to help someone inside the group who was in need." Almost as many (72 percent) say they have "worked with the group to help other people in need outside of the group." A majority (61 percent) say they have "become more interested in peace or social justice." And a sizable minority (42 percent) have "become involved in volunteer work in your community."

As we saw earlier, a majority say they have become more actively involved in the programs of their church. Their financial giving, it appears, is also encouraged. Specifically, 47 percent say they have "increased the amount of money you give to your church or synagogue." About the same number (46 percent) say they have "donated money to a charitable organization other than your church or synagogue" as a result of being in their group.

Members of church-based groups also feel they have grown in self-understanding and acceptance. Five out of six (87 percent) say they have experienced "feeling better about yourself." Almost this many (84 percent) say they are "more open and honest with yourself." And about the same number (83 percent) say they have experienced "more open and honest communication with other people."

The members of nonchurch groups are much less likely to say their faith has been nurtured by participating in a small group. They are less likely to have joined for this reason. And, as we have seen, their groups are less likely to include activities such as prayer, Bible study, and the discussion of religious topics. Nevertheless, it is important to recognize the extent to which these groups nourish spirituality for at least a minority of their members.

Eighty percent of the members of nonchurch groups say they have experienced a need to be part of a group that helps them grow spiritually. Nearly half of this number (38 percent) say this need has been fully met for them. Of course, this could have occurred in the past or in some other setting. Nevertheless, 37 percent describe themselves as being "on a spiritual journey." And nearly half (48 percent) say that spiritual matters have become more important to them in the past five years. In short, many of the members of these groups are spiritual seekers.

A sizable minority also feel that their group has contributed positively to their faith. About a third (31 percent) say their faith has been influenced from being involved in their group. And most of this number say their faith has been influenced positively: 55 percent say it has been deepened a lot, 38 percent say it has been deepened a little, 5 percent say it has been changed in some other way, and none say it has been made less important (0 percent).

About a third also attribute specific changes in their spirituality to their group. For instance, 33 percent say they feel closer to God, 29 percent have received help in sharing their faith with others, 25 percent have experienced answers to prayers, and 21 percent say the Bible has become more meaningful.

It is worth noting that much higher percentages also experience changes that people in religious settings would associate with "fruits of the spirit." Seventy percent say they are more honest with themselves, 57 percent have served people outside their group, 55 percent claim to have a deeper love toward other people, 53 percent feel more capable of forgiving others, 52 percent have been able to forgive themselves, and 32 percent have experienced healings of relationships.

In addition, 65 percent have worked with the group to help a member of the group who was in need, and 49 percent have worked with the group to help needy people outside the group. Fifty-one percent have become more interested in peace or social justice. And 44 percent say they have become involved in volunteer work in their communities.

There is even evidence that participation in nonchurch small groups is encouraging some members to take a more active part in their churches. Twelve percent say they have taken a more active part in other programs sponsored by their church or synagogue. And 13 percent say they have increased the amount of money they give to their church or synagogue.

Questions for Further Consideration

On the whole, these results are consistent with the assertions of writers and religious leaders who suggest that small groups can be enormously important in nurturing the spirituality of individuals and revitalizing the work of religious organizations. Churches, synagogues, and other religious organizations have been highly successful in promoting small groups. They provide leadership, study guides, and places to meet, and they sponsor small-group programs as ways of expanding their congregations. People from all parts of the society — from different age groups, racial and ethnic backgrounds, regions, and faiths — are becoming involved. They like their groups, attend faithfully, stay involved over long periods of time, and feel cared for and supported.

They also experience spiritual growth as a result. Many, at least, claim to be more interested in spirituality and believe their faith has been deepened. They feel that their groups have helped them develop a closer relationship with God, to gain a better understanding of the Bible, and to experience answers to prayer. Many are thereby encouraged to love their neighbors, care for the needy, forgive others and themselves, and become more actively involved in their churches and synagogues. By their own accounts, at least, they give more generously of their time and money, and become more responsible members of their communities as well.

More than half of the members of small groups belong to groups that are formally sponsored by churches +or synagogues. Virtually all of these groups include prayer, Bible study, and the discussion of religious topics among their activities. It would be surprising, therefore, if their members did not experience some deepening of their faith. Other groups are more varied, focusing on civic activities, involvement in sports and hobbies, recovery from addictions, and other special interests. Yet, a number of these groups also contribute to the spiritual formation of their members. Some do so explicitly. They are neighborhood Bible studies or home fellowships, for example, that have no formal connection to religious organizations and yet have members who have come to the group with specific interests in spirituality. Other groups deal at least tangentially with issues of faith, for example, by discussing the role of a "higher power" in dealing with addictions, or in providing religiously motivated people with ways of helping the needy in their communities.

Other evidence points to the possibility that the small-group movement may be having an even broader impact than its current membership would indicate. For example, of those who are not currently involved in a small group but who were involved in one in the past, 63 percent say they were in a group that focused on religious or spiritual matters. Moreover, of those who have never been involved in a small group but who say they would like to join one, 40 percent say they are very interested in developing their faith or spirituality, and another 36 percent say they are fairly interested in doing this.

The survey, then, provides answers to some of the questions that observers of the small-group movement have raised. It demonstrates that small groups are indeed very widespread in American society. It reveals the great extent to which the small-group movement is connected with religious organizations. It shows, for example, that many Americans find caring and support in Bible study groups and Sunday school classes, whereas twelve-step and other self-help groups (while they play a vital role in dealing with addictions) are a much smaller part of the overall movement. It also demonstrates that the members of small groups take their groups seriously and devote considerable time and energy to them. In addition, it documents clearly that there is a connection between small groups and spiritual concerns. Many people turn to small groups because they are lonely, in need of support, and want stronger ties to their communities. Yet the desire for community appears to be less significant as a factor driving the small-group movement than the desire for spiritual growth. To be sure, there is enormous variation in the types of groups. Among the majority that are concerned with spiritual issues, however, the survey shows clearly that they do include prayer and Bible study, and that most members feel their faith has been deepened in a number of important ways.

What the survey cannot ascertain is the *quality* of the spirituality being cultivated in small groups. It can, of course, be used to check up on some of the answers people gave to see if their claims are at least consistent with other answers given in the survey. Elsewhere, for example, I have shown that people who attended their groups more often were more likely to say their faith had deepened than people who seldom attended, that people who were actually in groups gave different answers than people who were just interested in being in a group, and that people who said their faith had deepened were also more likely to say they had experienced answers to prayer and other specific changes in their lives. But the survey also hints at some worrisome dimensions of faith in small groups. Group members, for example, are no more likely than nonmembers to answer some factual questions about the Bible (e.g., where Jesus was born) correctly (Wuthnow 1994, chaps. 8-9). Some of the questions also suggest that group members may be more concerned about themselves than about God. For example, the proportion who said they joined because of a "desire to grow as a person" (73 percent) was much higher than the proportion who joined seeking spiritual discipline (46 percent).[11] The percentage who came away feeling better about themselves was, as we have seen, higher than the number who actually increased their charitable giving or involve-

---

11. Among members of church-based groups, 84 percent said the desire to grow as a person was a reason why they became involved, compared with 68 percent who said they wanted more spiritual discipline.

ment. Despite the fact that people talk about their faith in their groups, there is also some evidence that faith remains private, focused on individual needs, and deeply influenced by individualistic norms. For example, 49 percent of the members of church-based groups agree that "my religious beliefs are very personal and private." Almost this many (47 percent) agree that "my spirituality does not depend on being involved in a religious organization." And 40 percent agree that "it doesn't matter what you believe, as long as you are a good person."

The other question that the survey cannot adequately address is *how* small groups effect changes in spirituality. That is, it is necessary to understand the mechanisms, activities, processes, and group dynamics in order to know what exactly it is about groups that contributes to spiritual formation. Still, it is possible to shed some light on these questions with the survey. Elsewhere, for example, I have shown that many of the formal structures that have been discussed in the literature on small groups — such as contracts, terms, able leadership, and fixed agendas — contribute less to the successful functioning of groups than do informal norms and activities, such as encouraging all members to share, respecting their views, and making them feel appreciated (Wuthnow 1994, chap. 5).

Statistical analysis of the survey also permits some conclusions to be drawn about activities that are particularly conducive to spiritual development. For example, Bible study itself is particularly important, but prayer that involves collective sharing and participation is even more important. The telling of stories makes a substantial contribution. Most groups, in fact, encourage members to tell stories about themselves, to compare their experiences with the stories of others and with biblical narratives, and as a result see more clearly how their faith can grow. In church-based groups, for instance, 77 percent of members said they had "told stories about some experience in your life," 73 percent had "compared your own experiences with stories told by other members of the group about themselves," 74 percent had "discussed the story of the Good Samaritan in the group," and 70 percent had "discussed the story of the Prodigal Son in the group."[12] Statistical analysis also reveals that

---

12. In nonchurch groups, 67 percent had told their own stories, 66 percent had compared their stories with those told by other members, 49 percent had compared their stories with ones they had read about and discussed in the group, 27 percent had discussed Bible stories, 19 percent had discussed the story of the Good Samaritan, and 13 percent had discussed the story of the Prodigal Son.

having a leader to look up to, admire, and gain answers from can be especially valuable for members who may lack the confidence or training to seek answers in other ways. And yet, the survey also reveals that looking up to someone in the group is less likely to nurture spirituality than having a close friend in the group who functions more as a peer and a confidant (Wuthnow 1994, chaps. 9-10).

The enormous diversity of small groups also suggests that an understanding of the quality and processes of spiritual formation must take these differences into account. Statistical analysis reveals that there are, to be sure, generalizations that can be made about small groups. For example, Sunday school classes generally include more structure than Bible study groups, but in other respects the two function quite similarly. Larger groups, it appears, do not differ very much from smaller groups, nor do groups that have been in existence over longer periods differ much from groups that have been in existence for shorter periods. Nevertheless, each group is unique. And the ways in which the various components come together must be understood with this uniqueness in mind.

It is for this reason that the survey results must be supplemented with observations about particular groups. Readers who participate in small groups can benefit from the survey by knowing that they are, for example, part of a large national movement and that the satisfaction they experience in their group is common to most group members. They can compare their group with the national norms, even asking fellow members some of the same questions from the survey to see how closely their answers correspond to the survey responses. But these comparisons can also be sharpened by focusing in depth on a particular group, hearing how its members describe their participation, and seeing how its meetings are organized. On that basis, we will also be in a better position to say what the quality of small-group spirituality is, and what the mechanisms are by which various kinds of spiritual formation are encouraged.

References

Adelman, Penina V. 1986. *Miriam's Well: Rituals for Jewish Women around the Year.* New York: Biblio Press.

Agus, Arlene. 1976. "This Month Is for You: Observing Rosh Hodesh as a Women's Holiday." Pp. 84-93 in *The Jewish Woman: New Perspectives,* ed. Elizabeth Koltun. New York: Schocken Books.

Alpert, Rebecca T. 1991. "Our Lives *Are* the Text: Exploring Jewish Women's Rituals." *Bridges* 2 (Spring): 66-80.

Ammerman, Nancy T. 1987. *Bible Believers: Fundamentalists in the Modern World.* New Brunswick, N.J.: Rutgers University Press.

———. 1990. *Baptist Battles.* New Brunswick, N.J.: Rutgers University Press.

Andersen, Margaret L. 1993. *Thinking about Women: Sociological Perspectives on Sex and Gender.* New York: Macmillan.

Arnold, Jeffrey. 1992. *The Big Book on Small Groups.* Downers Grove, Ill.: InterVarsity Press.

Attneave, Carolyn L., and Speck, Ross V. 1974. "Social Network Intervention in Time and Space." In *The Group as Agent of Change,* ed. Alfred Jacobs and Wilford Spradlin. New York: Behavioral Publications.

Barry, William A., S.J. 1991. *Finding God in All Things.* Notre Dame, Ind.: Ave Maria Press.

Beckford, Jim. 1989. *Religion and Advanced Industrial Society.* London: Unwin Hyman.

————. 1992. "Religion, Modernity and Post-modernity." Pp. 11-23 in *Religion: Contemporary Issues,* ed. B. R. Wilson. London: Bellew.

Bellah, Robert. 1970. *Beyond Belief: Essays on Religion in a Post-Traditional World.* New York: Harper & Row.

Bellah, Robert, et al. 1985. *Habits of the Heart: Individualism and Commitment in American Life.* Berkeley and Los Angeles: University of California Press.

Bender, Courtney J. 1991. "A Radical Reformulation: Mennonites in the Age of the Spirit." B.A. thesis, Swarthmore College.

————. 1992. "Mennonites and the Worship Center: Community Change and a Charismatic Context in Lancaster County, Pennsylvania, 1968-1990." *Pennsylvania Mennonite Heritage* 15 (October): 17-29.

Berger, Peter L. 1967. *The Sacred Canopy: Elements of a Sociological Theory of Religion.* Garden City, N.Y.: Doubleday.

Blumhofer, Edith. 1989. *The Assemblies of God, Volume Two — Since 1941: A Chapter in the Story of American Pentecostalism.* Springfield, Ms.: Gospel Publishing House.

Briggs, Kenneth A. 1992. *Holy Siege: The Year that Shook Catholic America.* San Francisco: Harper San Francisco.

Bright, Bill. 1985. *Come Help Change the World.* Rev. ed. San Bernardino, Calif.: Here's Life Publishers.

Calvin, John. 1960. *Institutes of the Christian Religion,* ed. John T. McNeill, trans. Ford Lewis Battles. Philadelphia: Westminster Press.

Coleman, Lyman. 1988. *Philippians/Ephesians: Becoming a Caring Community.* Littleton, Colo.: Serendipity House.

Conell, Carol. 1989. "Inserting History into Sociology." Unpublished paper, Department of Sociology, Stanford University.

Crabb, Larry. 1988. *Inside Out.* Colorado Springs, Colo.: NavPress.

Davidman, Lynn. 1991. *Tradition in a Rootless World: Women Turn to Orthodox Judaism.* Berkeley and Los Angeles: University of California Press.

Day, Thomas. 1991. *Why Catholics Can't Sing: The Culture of Catholicism and the Triumph of Bad Taste.* New York: Crossroad.

Dolan, Jay P. 1985. *The American Catholic Experience.* New York: Image Books.

Douglas, Mary. 1982. *Natural Symbols: Explorations in Cosmology.* New York: Pantheon Books.

Dulles, Avery. 1988. *The Reshaping of Catholicism.* San Francisco: Harper & Row.

Durkheim, Emile. 1915. *The Elementary Forms of the Religious Life: A Study in Religious Sociology.* New York: Macmillan.

Eisenstadt, S. N., ed. 1968. *Max Weber on Charisma and Institution Building: Selected Papers.* Chicago: University of Chicago Press.

Ellingsen, Mark. 1988. *The Evangelical Movement: Growth, Impact, Controversy, Dialog.* Minneapolis: Augsburg Publishing House.

Falk, Nancy. 1985. "Introduction." In *Women, Religion and Social Change,* ed. Yvonne Yazbeck Haddad and Ellison Banks Findly. Albany: State University of New York Press.

Farley, Edward. 1987. "Interpreting Situations: An Inquiry into the Nature of Practical Theology." Pp. 1-26 in *Formation and Reflection: The Promise of Practical Theology,* ed. James Martin. Philadelphia: Westminster Press.

Fisher, James Terrence. 1989. *The Catholic Counterculture in America.* Chapel Hill, N.C.: University of North Carolina Press.

Galloway, Dale E. 1986. *20/20 Vision: How to Create a Successful Church with Lay Pastors and Cell Groups.* Portland, Ore.: Scott Publishing Co.

Gallup, George, Jr., and Jim Castelli. 1987. *The American Catholic People.* Garden City, N.Y.: Doubleday.

Ginsburg, Faye. 1989. *Contested Lives: The Abortion Debate in an American Community.* Berkeley and Los Angeles: University of California Press.

Gouldner, Helen, and Mary Symons Strong. 1987. *Speaking of Friendship: Middle-Class Women and Their Friendships.* New York: Greenwood Press.

Greeley, Andrew M. 1990. *The Catholic Myth: The Behavior and Beliefs of American Catholics.* New York: Charles Scribner's Sons.

Greil, Arthur L., and David R. Rudy. 1984. "Social Cocoons: Encapsulation and Identity Transforming Organizations." *Sociological Inquiry* 54 (Summer): 260-78.

Hadden, Jeffrey K. 1969. *The Gathering Storm in the Churches.* Garden City, N.Y.: Doubleday.

———. 1969. "The House Divided." In *The Church, the University, and Social Policy,* vol. 2, ed. Kenneth Underwood. Middletown, Conn.: Wesleyan University Press.

Hamman, Adalbert. 1993. *How to Read the Church Fathers.* New York: Crossroad.

Hammond, Phillip E. 1966. *The Campus Clergyman.* New York: Basic Books.

———. 1969. "The Radical Ministry." In *The Church, the University, and Social Policy,* vol. 2, ed. Kenneth Underwood. Middletown, Conn.: Wesleyan University Press.

———. 1992. *Religion and Personal Autonomy: The Third Disestablishment in America.* Columbia, S.C.: University of South Carolina Press.

Hammond, Phillip E., and James Davison Hunter. 1984. "On Maintaining Plausibility: The Worldview of Evangelical College Students." *Journal for the Scientific Study of Religion,* vol. 23, no. 3, pp. 221-38.

Hargrove, Barbara. 1976. "Church Student Ministries and the New Consciousness." In *The New Religious Consciousness*, ed. Charles Y. Glock and Robert N. Bellah. Berkeley and Los Angeles: University of California Press.

Harris, Maria. 1989. *Fashion Me a People: Curriculum in the Church*. Louisville, Ky.: Westminster/John Knox Press.

Harris, W. Russell, III. 1973. "Urban Place Fellowship: An Example of a Communitarian Social Structure." Ph.D. diss., Michigan State University.

Hestenes, Roberta. 1983. *Using the Bible in Groups*. Philadelphia: Westminster Press.

Hostetler, Beulah. 1986. "Midcentury Change in the Mennonite Church." *Mennonite Quarterly Review* 60 (January): 58-82.

Hostetler, John A. 1987. *American Mennonites and Protestant Movements: A Community Paradigm*. Scottdale, Penn.: Herald Press.

Hoyt, Robert G. 1992. "The Catholic Conscience: Moving to the Next Parish." *Commonweal*, February 14, pp. 4-5.

Hunt, Gladys M. 1971. *It's Alive: The Dynamics of Small Group Bible Study*. Wheaton, Ill.: Harold Shaw Publishers.

Hunt, Keith, and Gladys Hunt. 1991. *For Christ and the University: The Story of InterVarsity Christian Fellowship of the U.S.A., 1940-1990*. Downers Grove, Ill.: InterVarsity Press.

Hunter, James Davison. 1983. *American Evangelicalism: Conservative Religion and the Quandary of Modernity*. New Brunswick, N.J.: Rutgers University Press.

————. 1987. *Evangelicalism: The Coming Generation*. Chicago: University of Chicago Press.

————. 1991. *Culture Wars: The Struggle to Define America*. New York: Basic Books.

Iannaccone, Laurence R. 1989. "Why Strict Churches Are Strong." Paper presented at the meetings of the Society for the Scientific Study of Religion, Salt Lake City, Utah.

————. 1992. "Sacrifice and Stigma: Reducing Free Riding in Cults, Communes, and Other Collectives." *Journal of Political Economy* 100 (April): 271-91.

Jackson, Dave, and Neta Jackson. 1974. *Living Together in a World Falling Apart: A Handbook of Christian Community*. Carol Stream, Ill.: Creation House.

Jacobs, Alfred, and Wilford W. Spradlin, eds. 1974. *The Group as Agent of Change*. New York: Behavioral Publications.

Job, John B., ed. 1972. *Studying God's Word*. London: Inter-Varsity Press.

Johnston, William, ed. 1973. *The Cloud of Unknowing and the Book of Privy Counseling.* Garden City, N.Y.: Doubleday.

Kanter, Rosabeth Moss. 1972. *Commitment and Community: Communes and Utopias in Sociological Perspective.* Cambridge: Harvard University Press.

Kelley, Dean M. 1972. *Why Conservative Churches Are Growing: A Study in the Sociology of Religion.* New York: Harper & Row.

————. 1978. "Why Conservative Churches Are Still Growing." *Journal for the Scientific Study of Religion* 17 (June): 165-72.

Kennedy, Eugene. 1988. *Tomorrow's Catholics, Yesterday's Church: The Two Cultures of American Catholicism.* San Francisco: Harper & Row.

Knechtle, Cliff. 1986. *Give Me an Answer that Satisfies My Heart and My Mind.* Downers Grove, Ill.: InterVarsity Press.

Kniss, Fred. 1991. "Religious Organizational Conflict in Global Context, Mennonites in Eastern Pennsylvania, 1870-1985." *Pennsylvania Mennonite Heritage* 14 (January): 13-20.

Koltun, Elizabeth, ed. 1976. *The Jewish Woman: New Perspectives.* New York: Schocken Books.

Kraft, Vickie. 1992. *Women Mentoring Women: Ways to Start, Maintain, and Expand a Biblical Women's Ministry.* Chicago: Moody Press.

Kraybill, Donald. 1979. "Mennonite Women's Veiling: The Rise and Fall of a Sacred Symbol." *Mennonite Quarterly Review,* vol. 53, pp. 298-320.

Kurtz, E. 1979. *Not-God: A History of Alcoholics Anonymous.* Center City, Minn.: Hazelden.

Lancaster Mennonite Conference Board of Bishops. 1971. "Statement Concerning the Holy Spirit." Reprinted in *The Gospel Herald* 64 (November): 904.

Lawson, Matthew. 1992. "Freedom to Choose: Submission in the Lives of Catholic Charismatics." Paper prepared for the annual meeting of the Association for the Sociology of Religion held in Pittsburgh, Pennsylvania.

Leith, John H. 1990. *From Generation to Generation: The Renewal of the Church according to Its Own Theology and Practice.* Louisville, Ky.: Westminster/John Knox Press.

Liebman, Robert, John Sutton, and Robert Wuthnow. 1988. "Exploring the Social Sources of Sectarianism: Schisms in American Protestant Denominations, 1890-1980." *American Sociological Review,* vol. 53, pp. 343-52.

Lopata, Helena Znaniecki. 1971. *Occupation: Housewife.* New York: Oxford University Press.

Lummis, Adair T. 1992. "Feminist Spirituality Groups: Types and Impact."

Paper presented at the annual meeting of the Society for the Sociological Study of Religion in November in Washington, DC.

Lummis, Adair, Allison Stokes, and Miriam Therese Winter. 1992. "The Nature and Influence of Feminist Spirituality Groups in Roman Catholic and Major Protestant Denominations." First draft of a preliminary report to the Lilly Foundation.

MacEoin, Gary. 1992. "Lay Movements in the United States before Vatican II." *America,* August 10, pp. 61-65.

McBride, Neal F. 1990. *How to Lead Small Groups.* Colorado Springs, Colo.: NavPress.

McDowell, Josh. 1980. *Answers to Tough Questions Skeptics Ask about the Christian Faith.* San Bernardino, Calif.: Here's Life Publishers.

McGee, Robert S. 1985. *The Search for Significance.* Houston: Rapha Publishing.

McGuire, Meredith. 1982. *Pentecostal Catholics: Power, Charisma, and Order in a Religious Movement.* Philadelphia: Temple University Press.

Marty, Martin. 1988. "Front Page Religion." *New York Times Book Review,* April 3, p. 17.

Miles, Margaret R. 1992. *Desire and Delight: A New Reading of Augustine's Confessions.* New York: Crossroad.

Miller, J. Keith. 1991. *A Hunger for Healing: The Twelve Steps as a Classic Model for Christian Growth.* San Francisco: Harper San Francisco.

Moltmann, Jürgen. 1977. *The Church in the Power of the Spirit: A Contribution to Messianic Ecclesiology.* New York: Harper & Row.

———. 1990. *The Way of Jesus Christ: Christology in Messianic Dimensions.* San Francisco: Harper San Francisco.

Nace, Edgar P. 1992. "Alcoholics Anonymous." Pp. 486-95 in *A Comprehensive Textbook of Substance Abuse,* 2nd ed., ed. Joyce Lowinson et al. New York: Williams & Wilkins.

Neighbour, Ralph W., Jr. 1988. *The Shepherd's Guidebook.* Houston: Touch Outreach Ministries.

Neitz, Mary Jo. 1987. *Charisma and Community: A Study of Religious Commitment within the Charismatic Renewal.* New Brunswick, N.J.: Transaction Publications.

———. 1990. "Movements for Cultural Transformation: Fieldwork Approaches." Paper presented at the Qualitative Research Conference in Toronto, Canada, May 1990.

———. 1991. "In Goddess We Trust." Pp. 353-72 in *In Gods We Trust: New Patterns of Religious Pluralism in America,* ed. Thomas Robbins and Dick Anthony. New Brunswick, N.J.: Transaction Publications.

Neusner, Jacob, ed. 1972. *Contemporary Judaic Fellowship in Theory and In Practice.* New York: Ktav.

Nolt, Steven M. 1992. "Church Discipline in the Lancaster Mennonite Conference: The Printed Rules and Discipline, 1881-1968." *Pennsylvania Mennonite Heritage* 15 (October): 2-16.

Olson, Daniel V. A. 1993. "Fellowship Ties and the Transmission of Religious Identity." Pp. 32-53 in *Beyond Establishment: Protestant Identity in a Post-Protestant Age,* ed. Jackson W. Carroll and Wade Clark Roof. Louisville, Ky.: Westminster/John Knox Press.

Olson, Daniel V. A., and Jackson W. Carroll. 1992. "Religiously Based Politics: Religious Elites and the Public." *Social Forces* 70 (March): 765-86.

Parks, Sharon. 1986. *The Critical Years.* San Francisco: Harper & Row.

Peace, Richard. 1985. *Small Group Evangelism.* Downers Grove, Ill.: InterVarsity Press.

Peachy, Paul. 1968. "Identity Crisis among American Mennonites." *Mennonite Quarterly Review,* vol. 42, no. 4, pp. 243-59.

Perrin, Robin D., and Armaund L. Mauss. 1993. "Strictly Speaking . . .: Kelley's Quandary and the Vineyard Christian Fellowship." *Journal for the Scientific Study of Religion* 32 (June): 125-35.

Perrin, Thomas W. 1991. *I Am an Adult Who Grew Up in an Alcoholic Family.* New York: Continuum Publishing Company.

Piehl, Mel. 1982. *Breaking Bread: The Catholic Worker and the Origin of Catholic Radicalism in America.* Philadelphia: Temple University Press.

Pizzorno, Alessandro. 1986. "Some Other Kinds of Otherness: A Critique of 'Rational Choice' Theories." Pp. 355-73 in *Development, Democracy, and the Art of Trespassing: Essays in Honor of Albert O. Hirschman,* ed. Alejandro Foxley et al. Notre Dame, Ind.: Notre Dame University Press.

Plaskow, Judith. 1990. *Standing Again at Sinai: Judaism from a Feminist Perspective.* San Francisco: Harper San Francisco.

Plaskow, Judith, and Carol P. Christ. 1989. *Weaving the Visions: New Patterns in Feminist Spirituality.* San Francisco: Harper San Francisco.

Poloma, Margaret. 1989. *The Assemblies of God at the Crossroads: Charisma and Institutional Dilemmas.* Knoxville, Tenn.: University of Tennessee Press.

Prell, Riv-Ellen. 1989. *Prayer and Community: The Havurah in American Judaism.* Detroit: Wayne State University Press.

Redekop, Calvin. 1989. *Mennonite Society.* Baltimore, Md.: Johns Hopkins University Press.

Redekop, Calvin, and Samuel Steiner. 1988. *Mennonite Identity: Historical and Contemporary Perspectives.* Lanham, Md.: University Press of America.

Redmont, Jane. 1992. *Generous Lives: American Catholic Women Today.* New York: William Morrow.

Reisman, Bernard. 1977. *The Chavurah: A Contemporary Jewish Experience.* New York: Union of American Hebrew Congregations.

Richards, Lawrence O. 1987. *99 Ways to Start a Study Group and Keep It Growing.* Grand Rapids, Mich.: Zondervan Publishing House.

Richardson, Alan. 1956. *Preface to Bible-Study.* London: Student Christian Movement Press, Ltd.

Robbins, Thomas, and David Bromley. 1992. "Social Experimentation and the Significance of American New Religions: A Focused Review Essay." *Research in the Social Scientific Study of Religion,* vol. 4, pp. 1-28.

Robertson, Nan. 1988. *Getting Better: Inside Alcoholics Anonymous.* New York: William Morrow.

Rogers, David. 1986. *Care Group Manual for Fellowship and Outreach.* Rockwall, Tex.: Church on the Rock.

Roof, Wade Clark. 1993. *A Generation of Seekers: Baby Boomers and the Quest for Spiritual Style.* San Francisco: Harper San Francisco.

Roof, Wade Clark, and William McKinney. 1987. *American Mainline Religion: Its Changing Shape and Future.* New Brunswick, N.J.: Rutgers University Press.

Rose, Susan. 1991. "Women Warriors: The Negotiation of Gender in a Charismatic Community." *Sociological Analysis,* vol. 48, no. 3, pp. 245-58.

Rubin, Nancy. 1982. *The New Suburban Woman: Beyond Myth and Motherhood.* New York: Coward, McCann & Geoghegan.

Ruether, Rosemary Radford, and Eleanor McLaughlin, eds. 1979. *Women of Spirit.* New York: Simon & Schuster.

Ruether, Rosemary Radford, and Rosemary Skinner Keller, eds. 1986. *Women and Religion in America,* vol. 3: *1900-1968.* New York: Harper & Row.

Ryan, Mary P. 1975. *Womanhood in America: From Colonial Times to the Present.* New York: New Viewpoints.

Saarinen, Martin F. 1986. *The Life Cycle of a Congregation.* Washington, D.C.: Alban Institute.

Santora, Alexander M. 1992. "Anna Quindlen: From the '60s to the '90s." *Commonweal,* February 14, pp. 9-13.

Schlabach, Theron. 1980. *Gospel versus Gospel.* Scottdale, Penn.: Herald Press.

Seidler, John, and Katherine Meyer. 1989. *Conflict and Change in the Catholic Church.* New Brunswick, N.J.: Rutgers University Press.

Shedd, Clarence P. 1934. *Two Centuries of Student Christian Movements.* New York: Associated Press.

Snow, David A., and Richard Machalek. 1984. "The Sociology of Conversion." *Annual Review of Sociology,* vol. 10, pp. 167-90.

Stafford, Tim. 1991. "The Hidden Gospel of the 12 Steps." *Christianity Today,* July, pp. 14-19.

Stark, Rodney, and William Sims Bainbridge. 1985. *The Future of Religion: Secularization, Revival, and Cult Formation.* Berkeley and Los Angeles: University of California Press.

Stark, Rodney, and Charles Y. Glock. 1968. *American Piety: The Nature of Religious Commitment.* Berkeley and Los Angeles: University of California Press.

Taylor, Brian C. 1989. *Spirituality for Everyday Living: An Adaptation of the Rule of St. Benedict.* Collegeville, Minn.: Liturgical Press.

Tracy, David. 1981. *The Analogical Imagination: Christian Theology and the Culture of Pluralism.* New York: Crossroad.

Umansky, Ellen. 1985. "Feminism and the Reevaluation of Women's Roles within American Jewish Life." Pp. 477-94 in *Women, Religion and Social Change,* ed. Yvonne Yazbek Haddad and Ellison Banks Findly. Albany, N.Y.: State University of New York Press.

Underwood, Kenneth, ed. 1969. *The Church, the University, and Social Policy,* vol. 1. Middletown, Conn.: Wesleyan University Press.

Vanderhaar, Gerard, and Patricia McNeal. 1992. "A History Worth Celebrating." *Pax Christi USA* 17 (Spring/Summer).

Van Maanen, John. 1988. *Tales of the Field: On Writing Ethnography.* Chicago: University of Chicago Press.

Wagner, C. Peter. 1979. *Your Church Can Be Healthy.* Nashville, Tenn.: Abingdon Press.

Wallace, Ruth A. 1992. *They Call Her Pastor: A New Role for Catholic Women.* Albany, N.Y.: State University of New York Press.

Walsh, Michael, ed. 1985. *Butler's Lives of the Saints.* San Francisco: Harper & Row.

Ward, Benedicta. 1980. "Introduction." Pp. 3-45 in *The Lives of the Desert Fathers,* trans. Norman Russell. Kalamazoo, Mich.: Cistercian Publications.

Warner, R. Stephen. 1988. *New Wine in Old Wineskins: Evangelicals and Liberals in a Small-Town Church.* Berkeley and Los Angeles: University of California Press.

————. 1993. "Work in Progress toward a New Paradigm for the Sociological Study of Religion in the United States." *American Journal of Sociology* 98 (March): 1044-93.

————. Forthcoming. "The Place of the Congregation in the American

Religious Configuration," in *The Congregation in American Life*, ed. James Lewis and James Wind. Chicago: University of Chicago Press.

Weaver, Mary Jo. 1985. *New Catholic Women: A Contemporary Challenge to Traditional Religious Authority.* San Francisco: Harper & Row.

Wedam, Elfriede. 1993. "Moral Cultures and the Movement against Abortion." Ph.D. diss., University of Illinois at Chicago.

Weissler, Lenore. 1982. "Making Judaism Meaningful: Ambivalence and Tradition in a Havurah Community." Ph.D. diss., University of Pennsylvania.

Welter, Barbara. 1966. "The Cult of True Womanhood, 1820-1860." *American Quarterly,* vol. 18, pp. 151-74.

Westley, Dick. 1992. *Good Things Happen: Experiencing Community in Small Groups.* Mystic, Conn.: Twenty-Third Publications.

Whitfield, Charles. 1987. *Healing the Child Within: Discovery and Recovery for Adult Children of Dysfunctional Families.* Deerfield Beach, Fla.: Health Communications.

———. 1992. "Co-Dependence, Addictions, and Related Disorders." Pp. 816-31 in *A Comprehensive Textbook of Substance Abuse,* 2nd ed., ed. Joyce Lowinson et al. New York: Williams & Wilkins.

Williams, Dan. 1991. *Seven Myths about Small Groups.* Downers Grove, Ill.: InterVarsity Press.

Wilson, Bill. 1984. *Alcoholics Anonymous* (The Big Book). New York: Alcoholics Anonymous World Services.

Wuthnow, Robert. 1988. *The Restructuring of American Religion: Society and Faith since World War II.* Princeton, N.J.: Princeton University Press.

———. 1989. *The Struggle for America's Soul: Evangelicals, Liberals, and Secularism.* Grand Rapids, Mich.: William B. Eerdmans.

———. 1991. *Acts of Compassion: Caring for Others and Helping Ourselves.* Princeton, N.J.: Princeton University Press.

———. 1994. *Sharing the Journey: Support Groups and America's New Quest for Community.* New York: Free Press.

Young-Eisendrath, Polly, and Wiedemann, Florence. 1987. *Female Authority.* New York: Guilford Press.

Contributors

Antony Alumkal is a graduate of the University of California at Berkeley, where he studied with Robert Bellah. He is currently a doctoral student in sociology at Princeton University and is writing a dissertation on Asian-American churches.

Courtney J. Bender is an advanced graduate student in sociology at Princeton University. She is specializing in the sociology of religion and is writing a dissertation on the role of religion in everyday life.

Lynn Davidman teaches sociology and Judaic studies at Brown University. She is the author of the award-winning *Tradition in a Rootless World*, an ethnographic study of Jewish women who return to Orthodoxy. She has also taught sociology, including courses in qualitative research methods, at Brandeis University, Princeton University, and the University of Pittsburgh.

Elaine Friedman, who assisted with the field work for the chapter by Robert Liebman, is an independent researcher and a freelance writer who worked as a field researcher for the *Acts of Compassion* project under the supervision of Robert Wuthnow. More recently, she has authored a book on Portland, Oregon, entitled *The Facts of Life in Portland*.

Douglas S. Jardine, who assisted George Thomas with his research, has worked in the nonprofit sector for a number of years and is a doctoral student in sociology at Arizona State University, where he is working under the supervision of George Thomas.

Kathleen M. Joyce, who teaches religion at Duke University, is a graduate of Princeton Theological Seminary and a doctoral candidate in the religion department at Princeton University. Under the supervision of Albert Raboteau and John F. Wilson, she is writing a dissertation on Roman Catholicism in the United States from 1870 to 1930, paying special attention to beliefs about health, illness, and death.

Matthew P. Lawson is a doctoral candidate in sociology at Princeton University who is writing his dissertation on the Catholic charismatic movement under the supervision of Robert Wuthnow. He has also received graduate training in anthropology at the University of Chicago and served as program officer at the Spencer Foundation.

Robert C. Liebman teaches sociology and international studies at Portland State University. With Robert Wuthnow, he is the co-editor of *The New Christian Right: Mobilization and Legitimation.* With John Sutton, he is currently writing a book about schisms and mergers in U.S. denominations since 1890, a project funded by the Lilly Endowment.

Daniel V. A. Olson teaches sociology at Indiana University at South Bend and has been a postdoctoral fellow at the Center for the Study of American Religion at Princeton University. He has also been a research fellow at Hartford Seminary, where, with William McKinney, he has written a forthcoming book on leaders in six Protestant denominations. He is currently writing a book on friendship networks in Baptist congregations.

Natalie Searl is a freelance writer and the president of Legacy, Inc., in Philadelphia. She has worked as an editor at Random House and is currently working with Robert Wuthnow on a study of values among Protestant and Catholic clergy.

George M. Thomas teaches sociology at Arizona State University. He is the author of *Revivalism and Cultural Change* (winner of the distinguished book award given by the Culture Section of the American Sociological Association).

R. Stephen Warner teaches sociology at the University of Illinois at Chicago, where he directs the New Ethnic and Immigrant Congregations Project, a training and support program for ethnographic research funded by the Lilly Endowment and the Pew Charitable Trusts. He is the author of the award-winning book *New Wine in Old Wineskins,* an ethnographic study of change in a Protestant congregation in California between the 1960s and the 1980s. He is currently writing a book interpreting change and continuity in U.S. religion since the 1960s.

Elfriede Wedam received her Ph.D. in sociology from the University of Illinois at Chicago in 1993. She also received her master's degree from UIC in 1990; she earned her bachelor's degree in 1970 from Loyola University of Chicago. She is currently a research associate with the Religion in Urban America Program at the University of Illinois at Chicago.

J. Bradley Wigger is an independent researcher, writer, and consultant living in Oshkosh, Wisconsin. A graduate of Louisville Presbyterian Theological Seminary, he has recently received his Ph.D. from Princeton Theological Seminary. In his dissertation he examines the character of educational materials, curricula, and teaching strategies in Protestant Sunday School programs.

Diane Winston is a doctoral candidate in the religion department at Princeton University who is specializing in nineteenth- and twentieth-century American religion and writing a dissertation on the Salvation Army under the supervision of John F. Wilson. She has also worked for several years as an award-winning journalist for the *Baltimore Sun,* and holds graduate degrees from the Columbia University School of Journalism and the Harvard Divinity School.

Robert Wuthnow teaches sociology at Princeton University and directs the Center for the Study of American Religion. His books include *The Restructuring of American Religion* and *Acts of Compassion.*

Sara Wuthnow is chair of the Department of Nursing and Allied Health at Eastern College in Philadelphia. She has published articles on holistic health, new class theory, and the history of the professions. The director of the Philadelphia Oral History of Nursing Project, she also teaches courses in research methods.

Wendy Young received her D.Phil. in sociology from Oxford University and has taught at Bryn Mawr College. For the past five years she has conducted ethnographic research on new religious and human potential movements in Great Britain. She has also served as project coordinator for the small groups and spirituality project.